The Collected Works
of
J. Krishnamurti

Volume III

1936–1944

The Mirror of Relationship

KENDALL/HUNT PUBLISHING COMPANY

2460 Kerper Boulevard   P.O. Box 539   Dubuque, Iowa 52004-0539

Photo: J. Krishnamurti, ca 1935 by Ralph T. Gardner

Copyright © 1991 by The Krishnamurti Foundation of America
P.O. Box 1560, Ojai, CA 93024

Library of Congress Catalog Card Number: 90–62735

ISBN 0–8403–6236–6

Printed in the United States of America
10   9   8   7   6   5   4   3   2   1

Contents

Preface

Jiddu Krishnamurti was born in 1895 of Brahmin parents in south India. At the age of fourteen he was proclaimed the coming World Teacher by Annie Besant, then president of the Theosophical Society, an international organization that emphasized the unity of world religions. Mrs. Besant adopted the boy and took him to England, where he was educated and prepared for his coming role. In 1911 a new worldwide organization was formed with Krishnamurti as its head, solely to prepare its members for his advent as World Teacher. In 1929, after many years of questioning himself and the destiny imposed upon him, Krishnamurti disbanded this organization, saying:

Truth is a pathless land, and you cannot approach it by any path whatsoever, by any religion, by any sect. Truth, being limitless, unconditioned, unapproachable by any path whatsoever, cannot be organized; nor should any organization be formed to lead or to coerce people along any particular path. My only concern is to set men absolutely, unconditionally free.

Until the end of his life at the age of ninety, Krishnamurti traveled the world speaking as a private person. The rejection of all spiritual and psychological authority, including his own, is a fundamental theme. A major concern is the social structure and how it conditions the individual. The emphasis in his talks and writings is on the psychological barriers that prevent clarity of perception. In the mirror of relationship, each of us can come to understand the content of his own consciousness, which is common to all humanity. We can do this, not analytically, but directly in a manner Krishnamurti describes at length. In observing this content we discover within ourselves the division of the observer and what is observed. He points out that this division, which prevents direct perception, is the root of human conflict.

His central vision did not waver after 1929, but Krishnamurti strove for the rest of his life to make his language even more simple and clear. There is a development in his exposition. From year to year he used new terms and new approaches to his subject, with different nuances.

Because his subject is all-embracing, the *Collected Works* are of compelling interest. Within his talks in any one year, Krishnamurti was not able to cover the whole range of his vision, but broad amplifications of particular themes are found throughout these volumes. In them he lays the foundations of many of the concepts he used in later years.

The *Collected Works* contain Krishnamurti's previously published talks, discussions, answers to specific questions, and writings for the years 1933 through 1967. They are an authentic record of his teachings, taken from transcripts of verbatim shorthand reports and tape recordings.

The Krishnamurti Foundation of America, a California charitable trust, has among its purposes the publication and distribution of Krishnamurti books, videocassettes, films and tape recordings. The production of the *Collected Works* is one of these activities.

Ojai, California, 1936

First Talk in The Oak Grove

People come to these talks with many expectations and hopes and with many peculiar ideas; and for the sake of clarification, let us examine these and see their true worth. Perhaps there are a few of us here whose minds are not burdened with jargons, which are but wearisome verbal repetitions. There may also be others who, having freed themselves from beliefs and superstitions, are eager to understand the significance of what I say. Seeing the illusory nature of imitativeness, they can no longer seek patterns and molds for their conduct. They come in the hope of awakening their innate creativeness, so that they may live profoundly in the movement of life. They are not seeking a new jargon or mode of conduct, smartness of ideas or emotional assertiveness.

Now, I am talking to those who desire to awaken to the reality of life and create for themselves the true way of thinking and living. By this I do not mean that my words are restricted to the few or to some imaginary clique of self-chosen intellectuals.

What I say may not seem vital to those who are merely curious, for I have no empty phrases or bold assertions with which to excite them. The curious, who merely desire emotional stimulation, will not find satisfaction in my words.

Then there are those who come here to compare what I have to say with the many schools of thoughtlessness. (Laughter) No, please, this is not a smart remark. From letters I have received and from people who have talked to me, I know there are many who think that by belonging to special schools of thought they will advance and be of service to the world. But what they call schools of thought are nothing but imitative jargons which merely create divisions and encourage exclusiveness and vanity of mind. These systems of thought have really no validity, being founded on illusion. Though their followers may become very erudite and defend themselves with their learning, they are in reality thoughtless.

Again, there are many whose minds have become complicated by the search for systems of human salvation. They seek, now through economics, now through religion, now through science, to bring about order and true harmony in human life. Fanaticism becomes the impulse for many who try, through dogmatic assertions, to impose on others their own imaginings and illusions, which they choose to call truth or God.

So you have to find out for yourself why you are here, and under what impulse you came to listen to this talk. I hope we are here to discover together whether we can live sanely, intelligently, and in the fullness of understanding. I feel that this should be the labor of both the speaker and the audience. We are going to start on a journey of deep inquiry and individual experiment, not on a journey of dogmatic assertions, creating new sets of beliefs and ideals. To discover the reality of what I say, you must experiment with it.

Most of us are held by the idea that by discovering some single cause for man's suffering, conflict, and confusion, we shall be able to solve the many problems of life. It has become the fashion to say "Cure the economic evils, then man's happiness and fulfillment are assured." Or "Accept some religious or philosophical idea, then peace and happiness can be made universal." In search of single causes we not only encourage specialists but also develop experts who are ever ready to create and expound logical systems in which the thoughtless man is entrapped. You see exclusive systems or ideas for the salvation of man taking form everywhere throughout the world. We are so easily entrapped in them, thinking that this seemingly logical simplicity of single causes will help us to remove misery and confusion.

A man who gives himself over to these specialists and to the single cause finds only greater confusion and misery. He becomes a tool in the hands of experts or a willing slave of those who can readily expound the logical simplicity of a single cause.

If you deeply examine man's suffering and confusion, you will see without any doubt whatsoever that there are many causes, some complex, some simple, which we must understand thoroughly before we can free ourselves from conflict and suffering. If we desire to understand the many causes and their disturbances, we must treat life as a whole, not split it up into the mental and emotional, the economic and religious, or into heredity and environment. For this reason we cannot hand ourselves over to

specialists, who naturally are trained to be exclusive and to be concentrated in their narrow divisions. It is essential not to do this; nevertheless, unconsciously we give ourselves over to another to be guided, to be told what to do, thinking that the religious or economic expert, because of his special knowledge and achievements, can direct our individual lives. Most specialists are so trained that they cannot take a comprehensive view of life; and because we adjust our lives, our actions, to the dictates of experts, we merely create greater confusion and sorrow. So, realizing that we cannot be slaves to experts, to teachers, to philosophers, to those people who say they have found God and who seemingly make life very simple, we should beware of them. We should seek simplicity, but in that very search we should be aware of the many illusions and delusions.

Being conscious of all this, what should we, as individuals, do? We have to realize profoundly, not casually or superficially, that no one particular person or system is wholly going to solve for us our agonizing problems and clarify our complex and subtle reactions. If we can realize that there is no one outside of ourselves who is going to clear up the chaos and confusion that exist within and without us, then we shall not be imitative, we shall not crave for identification. We shall then begin to release the creative power within us. This signifies that we are beginning to be conscious of individual uniqueness. Each individual is unique, different, not similar to another; but by this I do not mean the expression of egotistic desires.

We must begin to be self-conscious, which most of us are not; in bringing the hidden into the open, into the light, we discover the various causes of disharmony, of suffering. This alone will help to bring about a life of fulfillment and intelligent happiness. Without this liberation from the hidden, the concealed, our efforts must lead us to delusions.

Until we discover, through experiment, our subtle and deep limitations, with their reactions, and so free ourselves from them, we shall lead a life of confusion and strife. For these limitations prevent the pliability of mind-emotion, making it incapable of true adjustment to the movement of life. This lack of pliability is the source of our egotistic competition, fear and the pursuit of security, leading to many comforting illusions.

Though we may think we have found truth, bliss, and objectify the abstract idea of God, yet, while we remain unconscious of the hidden springs of our whole being, there cannot be the realization of truth. The mouthing of such words as *truth, God, perfection,* can have no deep significance and import.

True search can begin only when we do not separate mind from emotion. As we have been trained to regard life, not as a complete whole, but as broken up into body, mind, and spirit, we shall find it very difficult to orient ourselves to this new conception and reaction towards life. To educate ourselves to this way of regarding life, and not to slip back into the old habit of separative thought, requires persistence, constant alertness. When we begin to free ourselves, through experiment, from these false divisions with their special significances, pursuits, and ideals, which have caused so much harm and falsely complicated our lives, then we shall release creative energy and discover the endless movement of life.

Can the mind-heart know and profoundly appreciate this state of endlessness, this ceaseless becoming? Infinity has a profound significance only when there is liberation from the limitations which we have created through our false conceptions and divisions—as body, mind, and spirit, each with its own distinctive ideals and pursuits. When the mind-heart detaches itself from harmful and limiting reactions and begins to live intensely, with deep awareness, then

only is there the possibility of knowing profoundly this ceaseless becoming. Mind-emotion must be wholly free from identification and imitation to know this blessedness. The awakening of this creative intelligence will alone bring about man's humanity, his balance and deep fulfillment.

Until you become conscious both of your environment and of your past and understand their significance—not as two contrasted elements, which would only produce false reactions but as a coordinated whole—and until you are able to react to this whole, profoundly, there cannot be the perception of the endless movement of life.

True search begins only when there is a release from those reactions which are the result of division. Without the understanding of life's wholeness, the search for truth or happiness must lead to illusion. In pursuit of an illusion, one often feels an exhilaration, an emotionalism; but when one examines this emotional structure, it is nothing but a limitation, the building up of walls of refuge. It is a prison, though one may live in it and even enjoy it. It is an escape from the conflict of life into limitation; and there are many who will help and encourage you in this flight.

If these talks are to have any significance for you, you must begin to experiment with what I am saying and live anew by becoming conscious of all your reactions. Be conscious of them, but do not at once discard some as being bad and accept others as being good; for the mind, being limited, is unable to discern truly. What is important is to be aware of them. Then through that constant awareness, in which there is no sense of opposites, no division as mind and emotion, there comes the harmony of action which alone will bring about fulfillment.

Question: Are there not many expounders of truth besides yourself? Must one leave them all and listen only to you?

KRISHNAMURTI: There can never be expounders of truth. Truth cannot be explained, any more than you can explain love to a man who has never been in love. Such a phrase as "expounders of truth" has no meaning.

What are we trying to do here? I am not asking you to believe what I say, nor am I subtly making you follow me in order that you may be exploited. Independently of me, you can experiment with what I say. I am trying to show you how one can live sanely and deeply, with creative richness, so that one's life is a fulfillment and not a continual frustration. This can be done when the mind-heart liberates itself from those false reactions, conceptions, and ideas which it has inherited and acquired—the reactions born of egotistic fears and limitations, the reactions born of division and the conflict of the opposites. Those limitations and narrow reactions prevent the mind-heart from adjusting itself to the movement of life. From this lack of pliability arise confusion, delusion, and sorrow. Only through your own awareness and endeavor, and not through authority or imitation, can these limitations be swept away.

Question: What is your idea of infinity?

KRISHNAMURTI: There is a movement, a process of life, without end, which may be called infinity. Through authority, imitation, born of fear, mind creates for itself many false reactions and thereby limits itself. Identifying itself with this limitation, it is incapable of following the swift movement of life. Because the mind, prompted by fear and in its desire for security and comfort, seeks an end, an absolute with which it can identify itself, it becomes incapable of following the never-ending movement of life. Until the mind-heart can free itself from these limitations, in full consciousness, there cannot be the comprehension of this endless process of becoming. So do not ask what is infinity, but discover for yourself the limitations which hold the mind-heart in bondage, preventing it from living in this movement of life.

April 5, 1936

Second Talk in The Oak Grove

Most thoughtful people have the desire to help the world. They think of themselves as apart from the mass. They see so much exploitation, so much misery; they see scientific and technical achievements far in advance of human conduct, comprehension, and intelligence. Seeing all this about them and desiring to change the conditions, they consider that the mass must first be awakened.

Often this question is put to me: "Why do you emphasize the individual and not consider the mass?" From my point of view, there can be no such division as the mass and the individual. Though there is mass psychology, mass intention, action or purpose, there is no such entity as the mass apart from the individual. When you analyze the term, *the mass,* what is it? You will see that it is composed of many separate units, that is, ourselves, with extraordinary beliefs, ideals, illusions, superstitions, hatreds, prejudices, ambitions, and pursuits. These perversions and pursuits compose that nebulous and uncertain phenomenon which we call the mass.

So the mass is ourselves. You are the mass and I am the mass, and in each one of us there is the one and the many—the one being the conscious and the many, the unconscious. The conscious can be said to be the individual. So in each one of us we have the one and the many.

The many, the unconscious, is composed of unquestioned values—values that are false to facts, values which through time and usage have become pleasant and acceptable—it is composed of ideals which give us security and comfort, without deep significance; of standards of conformity, which are preventing clear perception and action; of thoughts and emotions which have their origin in fear and primitive reactions. This I call the unconscious, the mass, of which each one of us is a part, whether we know it or not, whether we acknowledge it or not.

If there is to be a clear reflection, the mirror must not be distorted; its surface must be even and clean. So must the mind-heart—which is an integrated whole, not two distinct and separate parts—be free from its self-created perversions before there can be discernment, comprehension, balance, or intelligence. To live completely, experience must continually be brought into the conscious.

Most of us are unconscious of the background, of the perversions, the twists that prevent discernment, making us incapable of adjusting ourselves to the movement of life. Some of you may say "All this is quite obvious; we know this, and there is nothing new in it." I fear that if you merely dismiss what I say without deep thought, you will not awaken your creative intelligence.

If we are to understand life wholly, completely, we must bring the unconscious, through experience, through experiment, into the conscious. Then there will be balance and deep intelligence. Only then can there be true search. So long as the mind-heart is bound by beliefs, ideals, or vain and illusory pursuits, what we call the search for truth or reality will inevitably lead to escapes. No psychologist or teacher can free the mind; its freedom can come only through its own inherent necessity.

The search for truth or God—the very naming of it helps to create a barrier—can truly begin only when there is this harmonious intelligence. As the mind-heart is perverted, limited by the reactions of ignorance, it is incapable of discerning that which is. How can one understand what is

true if one's mind-heart is prejudiced? These prejudices are so deep-rooted and stretch so far into the past that one cannot discover their beginning. With a mind so prejudiced, how can we truly discern, how can there be happiness or intelligence? The mind-heart must become aware of its own process of creating illusions and limitations. No teacher can free it from this process. Until the mind-heart is deeply, profoundly conscious of its own process, its own power to create illusions, there cannot be discernment. To bring about this harmonious intelligence, there must be a fundamental change in our habits of thought-emotion, and this requires patient perseverance, persistent thoughtfulness.

Until now it has been said that there is God, that there is truth, that there is something absolute, final, eternal, and on that assertion we have built our thought and emotion, our life, our morality. It has been said: "Act in this manner, follow that, do not do this." Most people consider such teachings to be positive. If you examine these teachings, which are called positive instructions, you will discover that they are destructive of intelligence; for they become the frame within which the mind limits itself, to imitate and copy, thus making itself incapable of adjustment to the movement of life, twisting life to the pattern of an ideal, which only creates further sorrow and confusion.

To understand and awaken this harmonious intelligence, one must begin, not with assumptions and authoritative assertions, but negatively. When the mind is free of these ignorant responses, there is then the deep harmony born of intelligence. Then begins the joy of penetration into reality. No one can tell you of reality, and any description of it must ever be false.

To understand truth, there must be silent observation, and description of it but confuses and limits it. To comprehend the infinite process of life, we must begin negatively, without assertions and assumptions, and from that build the structure of our thought-emotion, our action and conduct. If this is not deeply understood, what I say will merely become mechanical beliefs and ideals and create new absurdities based on faith and authority. We shall unconsciously revert to primitive attitudes and reactions born of fear, with its many delusions, though these may be clothed in new words.

When you are really able to think without any craving, without any desire to choose— for choice implies opposites—there is discernment.

What makes up this background? It is the result of a process without a beginning. It is composed of many layers, and a few words cannot describe them. You can take one or two layers and examine them—not objectively, for the mind itself is their creator and is part of them—and in analyzing and experimenting with them, the mind itself begins to perceive its own make-up and the process of creating its own prison. This deep understanding not only brings into consciousness the many layers, but also brings about the cessation of creating further limitations and barriers.

One of the layers or sections of this background is ignorance. Ignorance is not to be confounded with the mere lack of information. Ignorance is the lack of comprehension of oneself. The 'oneself' is not of a given period, and no words can cover the whole process of individuality. Ignorance will exist so long as the mind does not uncover the process of creating its own limitations, and also the process of self-induced action. To do this, there must be great perseverance, experimentation, and comprehension.

The deep understanding of 'oneself', the 'oneself' without a beginning, is prevented through accumulative processes. I call accumulative processes the craving for identification with truth, the imitation of an ideal, the desire for conformity, all of which create authority and engender fear, leading to many delusions. The accumulative process continues while thought is caught up in and pursues the opposites—good and bad, positive and negative, love and hate, virtue and sin. The accumulative process gives to the mind-heart comfort and shelter against the movement of life. If the mind-heart perceives itself in action, then it will observe that it is creating those accumulative illusions for its own limited continuance and security. This process brings about pain, misery, and conflict.

How can the mind disentangle itself from its own fears, ignorant reactions, and the many delusions? All influences which force the mind to free itself from these limitations will only create further escapes and illusions. When the mind relies on outer circumstances to bring about these fundamental changes, it is not acting as a whole, it is separating and dividing itself as the past and the present, the outer and the inner. If such a division exists, the mind-heart must create for itself further illusions and sorrow.

Please try to understand all this carefully. If the mind tries to free itself from these limitations because of compulsion, reward, or punishment, or because it is sorrow-laden and so seeks happiness, or for any superficial reason, its attempt must inevitably lead to frustration and confusion.

It is important to understand this, for there is freedom from these limitations only when the mind itself comprehends the utter necessity for it. This necessity cannot be self-induced or self-imposed.

Question: How may we help the hopelessly insane?

KRISHNAMURTI: Now, insanity is a problem of subtle varieties, for one may think that one is sane and yet appear completely insane to others. There is the insanity which is brought about through organic, physical defect, and there is the lack of balance induced through the mind-heart being incapable of adjustment to life. Of course there is no such clear division and distinction between the purely physical and the purely mental causes leading to the many disturbances and maladjustments in life. I should think in most cases this lack of cohesion and balance begins when the individual, brought up and trained in ignorant, narrow, and egotistic responses, is incapable of adjusting himself to the ever-changing movement of life.

Most of us are not balanced, as most of us are unconscious of the many layers of limited values which bind the mind-heart. These limited values cripple thought and prevent us from understanding the infinite values which alone can bring about sanity and intelligence. We accept certain attitudes and actions as being in accord with human values. Take, for example, competition and war. If we examine competition, with its many implications, we see that it springs from the ignorant reaction of strife against another; whereas in fulfillment there cannot be this competitive spirit. We have accepted this competitive spirit as being a part of human nature, from which arises not only individual combativeness but also racial and national strife, thus contributing one of the many causes of war. A mind caught up in this primitive reaction must be considered incapable of deep adjustment to the realities of life.

A man whose thought-emotion is based on faith, and so on belief, must of necessity be unbalanced, for his belief is merely a wish fulfillment. When people say that they believe in reincarnation, in immortality, in God—these are but emotional cravings which to them become objectified concepts and facts. They can discover actuality only when they have understood and dissolved the process of ignorance. When one says, ''I believe,'' one limits thought and turns belief into a pattern according to which one guides and conducts one's life, thus allowing the mind-heart to become narrow, crystallized, and incapable of adjustment to life and reality. With most people, belief becomes merely an escape from the conflict and confusion of life.

Belief must not be confused with intuition, and intuition is not wish fulfillment. Belief, as I have tried to point out, is based on escape, on frustration, on limitation, and this very belief prevents the mind-heart from dissolving its own self-created ignorance.

So each one has the capacity, the power, to be either sane, balanced, or otherwise. To discover whether one is balanced, one must start negatively, not with assertions, dogmas, and beliefs. If one can think profoundly, then one will become aware of the extraordinary beauty of intelligent completeness.

Question: You said last Sunday that most people are not self-conscious. It seems to me that quite the contrary is true, and that most people are very self-conscious. What do you mean by self-conscious?

KRISHNAMURTI: This is a difficult and subtle question to answer in a few words, but I will try to explain it as well as I can, and please remember that words do not convey all the subtle implications involved in the answer.

Every living thing is force, energy, unique to itself. This force or energy creates its own materials which can be called the body, sensation, thought, or consciousness. This force or energy in its self-acting development becomes consciousness. From this there arises the 'I' process, the 'I' movement. Then begins the round of creating its own ignorance. The 'I' process begins and continues in identification with its own self-created limitations. The 'I' is not a separate entity, as most of us think; it is both the form of energy and energy itself. But that force, in its development, creates its own material, and consciousness is a part of it; and through the senses, consciousness becomes known as the individual. This 'I' process is not of the moment, it is without a beginning. But through constant awareness and comprehension, this 'I' process can be ended.

April 12, 1936

Third Talk in The Oak Grove

To have united thought, and so action, there must be agreement, accord, and to have agreement seems to be very difficult. Agreement does not mean thoughtless acceptance or tolerance, for tolerance is superficial. Agreement demands deep intelligence and requires a mind that is very pliable. In this world, apparently, one is more easily convinced by foolishness than by thought that is integral and intelligent. There is an emotional agreement which is not agreement at all. It is merely an excitement which carries one on to certain activities, attitudes, and assertions but does not lead to the full, intelligent awakening of individual fulfillment.

Now, if you agree—as apparently most people agree—with foolishness, there must be confusion. You may feel for the moment that you are supremely happy, contented, and thus think that you have understood life; but if you allow your mind to consider your assumed happiness, you will see that what you have is really a superficial emotional excitement induced by the repeated assertions of another. Any action born of this superficiality must inevitably lead to confusion, whereas agreement with intelligent thought leads to true happiness and complete well-being.

I am emphasizing this point because I feel it is very important and necessary that one should not have within oneself any barriers which create division, disagreement. These barriers create confusion and struggle in the individual and also prevent united and intelligent action in the world. Intelligent agreement is essential for concerted action; but it is not agreement when there is any kind of compulsion or authority, whether subtle or gross. Please see why such deep understanding is necessary, and also please find out whether you are profoundly in agreement with what I say. By agreement, I do not mean a superficial and tolerant acceptance of certain ideas which I express. You should consider the whole implication of what I say and discover whether you are deeply in agreement with it. This needs thought and careful analysis, and then only can you accept or reject. As the majority of us seem to yield to emphatically repeated assertions, I feel it would be a waste of time if you merely allowed yourself to be convinced by certain statements which I often repeat. Such surrender on your part would be utterly useless and even harmful.

In this world there are so many contradictory opinions, theories, grotesque assertions, and emotional claims that it is difficult to discern what is true, what is really helpful for individual comprehension and fulfillment. These affirmations—some fantastic, some true, some violent, some absurdly confusing—are thrown and shouted at us. Through books, magazines, lecturers, we become their victims. They promise rewards and at the same time subtly threaten and compel. Gradually we allow ourselves to take sides, to attack and defend. So we accept this or that theory, insist on this or that dogma, and unconsciously the repeated assertions of others become our beliefs, on which we try to mold our whole lives. This is not an exaggeration; it is happening in us and about us. We are constantly being bombarded with claims and oft repeated ideas, and unfortunately we tend to take sides because our own unconscious desire is for comfort and security, emotional or intellectual, which leads us to accept these affirmations. Under such conditions, though we may think that we examine these assertions and intuitively know them to be true, our minds are incapable of examination or of any intuition. Hardly anyone escapes this constant attack through propaganda; and unfortunately, through one's own craving for security and for permanence, one helps to create and encourage fantastic declarations.

When the mind-heart is burdened with many barriers, prejudices, national and class distinctions, it is impossible to come to an intelligent agreement. What is happening is not intelligent and sane agreement among people, but it is a war of belief against belief, doctrine against doctrine, group against group, vested interest against vested interest. In this battle, intelligence, comprehension, is denied.

It would really be a calamity if out of these meetings you developed dogmas, beliefs, and instruments of compulsion. My talks are not intended to engender beliefs or ideals, which can only offer you an escape. To understand what I say, mind must be free from beliefs and from the prejudice of "I know." When you say, "I know," you are already dead. This is not a harsh statement.

It is a very serious undertaking to try to discover what is true, why we are here, and where we are going. This discovery cannot be made by the superficial solution of our immediate problems. The mind-heart must free itself from those dogmas, beliefs, and ideals of which most of us are unconscious. We are here to discover intelligently what is true; and if you understand this, you will discern something which is real, not something which is self-imposed or invented by another. Please believe that I am really not concerned with particular views, but with individual understanding, happiness, and fulfillment.

There are many teachers who maintain various systems, meditations, disciplines, which they claim will lead to the ultimate reality; there are many intermediaries who insist on obedience in the name of the Masters; and individuals who assert that there is God, that there is truth—unfortunately I myself have made these assertions in the past. Knowing all this, I have realized that the moment there is an assertion, its very significance is lost. How then shall we comprehend this world of contradictions, confusions, beliefs, dogmas, and claims? From where shall we start? If we attempt to understand these from any other point of view than through the comprehension of ourselves, we shall but increase dissension, struggle, and hatred. There are many causes, many processes at work in this world of becoming and decaying, and when we try to investigate each process, each cause, we inevitably come up against a blank wall, against something which has no explanation, for each process is unique in itself.

Now, when you face the inexplicable, faith comes to your aid and asserts that there is a God, that He has created us and we are His instruments, that we are transcendent beings, with a permanent identity. Or if you are not religiously inclined, you try to solve this problem through science. There again you try to follow cause after cause, reaction after reaction; and though there are scientists who maintain that there is a deep intelligence at work, or who employ different symbols to convey to us the inexplicable, yet there comes a point beyond which even science cannot go, for it deals only with the perception and reaction of the senses.

I think there is a way of understanding the whole process of birth and death, becoming and decaying, sorrow and happiness. When I say "I think," I am being purposely suggestive, rather than dogmatic. This process can be truly understood and fundamentally grasped only through ourselves, for it is focused in each individual. We see around us this continual becoming and decaying, this agony and transient pleasure, but we cannot possibly understand this process outside of ourselves. We can comprehend this only in our own consciousness, through our own 'I' process; and if we do this, then there is a possibility of perceiving the significance of all existence.

Please see the importance of this; otherwise we shall be entangled in the intricate question of environment and heredity. We shall understand this question when we do not divide our life into the past and the present, the subjective and the objective, the center and the circumference—when we realize the working of the 'I' process, the 'I' consciousness. As I have often said, if we merely accept the 'I' as a living principle, a divine entity in isolation, created by God, we shall but create and encourage authority, with its fears and exploitations; and this cannot lead to man's fulfillment.

Please do not translate what I say about the 'I' process into your particular phraseology of belief. That would be of no help to you at all; on the contrary, it would be confusing; but please listen with an unprejudiced mind and heart.

The 'I' process is the result of ignorance, and that ignorance, like the flame that is fed by oil, sustains itself through its own activities. That is, the 'I' process, the 'I' energy, the 'I' consciousness, is the outcome of ignorance, and ignorance maintains itself through its own self-created activities; it is encouraged and sustained through its own actions of craving and want. This ignorance has no beginning, and the energy that created it is unique to each individual. This uniqueness becomes individuality to consciousness. The 'I' process is the result of that force, unique to each individual, which creates, in its self-development, its own materials as body, dis-

cernment, consciousness, which become identified as the 'I'.

This is really very simple, but it appears complicated when put into words. If, for example, one is brought up in the tradition of nationalism, that attitude must inevitably create barriers in action. A mind-heart narrowed and limited in action by prejudices must create increasing limitations. This is obvious. If you have beliefs, you are translating and molding your experiences according to them, and so you are continuously forcing and limiting thought-emotion, and these limitations become the 'I' process. Action, instead of liberating, freeing the mind-heart from its own self-imposed bondages, is creating further and deeper limitations, and these accumulated limitations can be called ignorance. This ignorance is encouraged, fed by its own activities, born of its own self-created desires. Unless you realize that ignorance is the result of its own self-created, self-sustained activities, the mind-heart must ever dwell in this vicious circle. When you deeply comprehend this, you will discern that life is no longer a series of conflicts and conquests, struggles and attainments, all leading to frustration. When you truly have an insight into this process of ignorance, living is no longer an accumulation of pain, but becomes the ecstasy of deep bliss and harmony.

Most of us have an idea that the 'I' is a separate being, divine, something that is enduring, becoming more and more perfect. I do not hold with any of this. Consciousness itself is the 'I'. You cannot separate the 'I' process from consciousness. There is no 'I' that is accumulating experience which is apart from experience itself. There is only this process, this energy which is creating its own limitations through its own self-sustained wants. When you discern that there is no 'I' apart from action, that the actor is action itself, then gradually there comes a completeness, an unfathomable bliss.

When you grasp this, there can be no method to free you from your own limitations, from the prison in which you are held. The 'I' process must dissolve itself. It must wean itself away from itself. No savior nor the worship of another can liberate you; your self-imposed disciplines and self-created authorities are of no avail. They but lead to further ignorance and sorrow. If you can understand this, you will not make of life a terrible, ugly struggle of exploitation and cruelty.

Question: Last Sunday you seemed very uncertain in what you said, and some of us could make nothing of it. Several of my friends say they are not coming any more to hear you because you are becoming vague and undecided about your own ideas. Is this impression due to lack of understanding in us, or are you not as sure of yourself as you used to be?

KRISHNAMURTI: You know, certain things cannot be put into words definitely, precisely. I try to express my comprehension of life as clearly as possible, and it is difficult. Sometimes I may succeed, but often I seem not to be able to convey what I think and feel. If one thinks deeply about what I have been saying, it will become clear and simple; but it will remain merely an intellectual conception if there is no comprehension in action. Some of you come repeatedly to these meetings, and I wonder what happens to you in the intervals between these talks. It is during these intervals that you can discover whether action is liberating, or creating further prisons and limitations. It is in your hands to fashion your own life, either to comprehend or to increase ignorance.

Question: How can one be free of the primitive reactions of which you speak?

KRISHNAMURTI: The very desire to be free creates its own limitation. These primitive or ignorant reactions create conflicts, disturbances and sorrow in your life, and by getting rid of them you hope to acquire something else—happiness, bliss, peace, and so on. So you put to me the question: "How am I to get rid of these reactions?" That is, you want me to give you a method, lay down a system, a discipline, a mode of conduct.

If you understand that there is no separate consciousness apart from the 'I' process, that the 'I' is consciousness itself, that ignorance creates its own limitations, and that the 'I' is but the result of its own action, then you will not think in terms of denudation and acquisition.

Take, for example, the reaction towards nationalism. If you think about it, you will see that this reaction is ignorant and very harmful, not only to yourself but to the world. Then you will ask me, "How is one to get rid of it?" Now, why do you want to get rid of it? When you perceive why you want to get rid of it, you will then discern how it has come into being, artificially, with its many cruel implications; and when you deeply comprehend it, then there is not a conscious effort to get rid of this ignorant reaction; it disappears of itself.

In the same way, if mind-heart is bound by fears, beliefs, which are so dominant, potent, overwhelming that they pervert clear perception, it is no good making great efforts to get rid of them. First you have to be conscious of them; and instead of wanting to get rid of them, find out why they exist. If you try to free yourself from them, you will unconsciously create or accept other and perhaps more subtle fears and beliefs. But when you perceive how they have come into being—through the desire for security, comfort—then that very perception will dissolve them. This requires great alertness of mind-heart.

The struggle exists between those established values and the ever-changing, indefinite values, between the fixed and the free movement of life, between standards, conventionalities, accumulated memories, and that which has no fixed abode. Instead of trying to pursue the unknown, examine what you have—the known, the established prejudices, limitations. Comprehend their significance; then they disappear like the mists of a morning. When you perceive that what you thought was a snake in the grass is only a rope, you are no longer afraid, there is no longer a struggle, an overcoming. And when, through deep discernment, we perceive that these limitations are self-created, then our attitude towards life is no longer one of conquering, of wanting to be freed through some method or miracle, of seeking comprehension through another. Then we will realize for ourselves that though this process of ignorance appears to have no beginning, it has an end.

April 19, 1936

Fourth Talk in The Oak Grove

Many of you come to these meetings with the hope that by some miracle I am going to solve your difficulties, whether economic, religious, or social. And if I cannot solve them, or if you are incapable of solving them for yourselves, you hope that some miraculous event or circumstance will dissolve them; or else you lose yourselves in some philosophic system, or hope that by joining a particular church or society your difficulties will of themselves disappear.

As I have often tried to point out, these problems, whether social, religious, or economic, are not going to be solved by depending on any particular system. They must be solved as a whole, and one must deeply comprehend one's own process of creating ig-

norance and being caught up in it. If one can understand this process of accumulating ignorance, with its self-sustaining action, and discern consciousness as the combination of these two—ignorance and action—one will then profoundly comprehend this conflicting and sorrowful existence. But unfortunately most of us are indifferent. We wait for outward circumstances to force us to think, and this compulsion can only bring about greater suffering and confusion. You can test this out for yourself.

Then there are those who depend on faith for their understanding and comfort. They think that there is a supreme being who has made them, who will guide them, who will protect and save them. They fervently believe that by following a certain creed or a certain system of thought, and by forcing themselves into a certain mold of conduct and discipline, they will attain to the highest.

As I tried to explain last Sunday, faith or acceptance is a hindrance to the deep comprehension of life. Most of us, unfortunately, are incapable of experimenting for ourselves, or we are disinclined to make the effort; we are unwilling to think deeply and go through the real agony of being uncertain. So we depend on faith for our understanding and comfort. We often think that we are changing radically, and that our attitude is being fundamentally altered; but unfortunately we are merely changing the outward forms of our expression, and we still cling to the inner demands and cravings for support and comfort.

Most of us belong to the category of those who depend on faith for the explanation of their being. I include in that word *faith* the many subtle demands, prayers, and supplications to an external being, whether he be a Master or saint; or the appeal to the authority of beliefs, ideals, and self-imposed disciplines. Having such a faith, with all its implications, we are bound to create duality in our life—that is, there is the actor ever trying to approximate himself and his actions to a concept, to a standard, to a belief, to an ideal. So there is a constant duality. If you examine your own attitude and action in life, you will see that there seems to be a separate entity who is looking at action, who is trying to mold, to shape the process of life according to a certain pattern, with the result that there is an ever-increasing conflict and sorrow. If you observe, you will perceive that this duality in action is the cause of friction, conflict, and misery, for one's effort is spent in making one's life conform to a particular pattern or concept. And we think that a man is happy and intelligent who is able to live in complete union with his ideal, with his preconceived beliefs. A person who can completely shape his actions to a principle, to an ideal, is considered sincere, wise, and noble. It is but a form of rigidity, a lack of deep pliability, and hence a decay.

So in one's life there is the abstract and the actual; the actual being the conflict, and the abstract, the unconscious, made up of those beliefs and ideals, those concepts and memories that one has so sedulously built up as a means of self-protection. There is taking place in each one a conflict between the abstract and the actual, the unconscious and the conscious. Each one is trying to bridge over the gap that exists between the unconscious and the conscious, and this attempt must lead to rigidity of mind-heart and hence to a gradual withering, a contraction, which prevents the complete understanding of oneself and so of the world. One often thinks this attempt to unify the actual with the abstract will bring about deep fulfillment; but if one discerns, it is but a subtle form of escape from the conflict of life, a self-protection against the movement of life.

Before we can attempt to bring about this unity, we must know what is our unconscious, who has created it, and what is its significance. If we can deeply comprehend this, that is, if we can become aware of our own subtle motives, concepts, conceits, actions and reactions, we will then discern that there is only consciousness, the 'I' process, which becomes perceptible to sense as individuality. This process must ever create a duality in action and bring about the artificial division of the conscious and the unconscious. From this process there arises the conception of a supreme deity, an ideal, an objective towards which there is a constant striving. Until we comprehend this process, there must be ignorance and hence sorrow.

The lack of comprehension of oneself is ignorance. That is, one must discern how one has come into being, what one is, all the tendencies, the reactions, the hidden motives, the self-imposed beliefs and pursuits. Until each one deeply understands this, there can be no cessation of sorrow, and the confusion of divided action, as economic and religious, public and private, will continue. The human problems that now disturb us will disappear only when each one is able to discern the self-sustaining process of ignorance. To discern needs patience and constant awareness.

As I have explained, there is no beginning to ignorance; it is sustained by its own cravings, through its own acquisitive demands and pursuits, and action merely becomes the means of maintaining it. This interacting process of ignorance and action brings about consciousness and the identity of the 'I'. As long as you do not know what you are and do not discern the various causes that result in the continued 'I' process, there must be illusion and sorrow.

Each one of us is unique in the sense that each one is continually creating his own ignorance, which is without a beginning and is self-sustained through its own actions. This ignorance, though it has no beginning, can come to an end when there is a deep discernment of this vicious circle. Then there is no longer the 'I' attempting to get outside of the circle to a greater reality, but the 'I' itself perceives its own illusory nature and so weans itself away from itself. This demands alertness and constant awareness.

We are now making an effort to acquire virtues, pleasures, possessions, and are developing many tendencies towards greater accumulation and security; or, if we are not doing this, we go about it negatively by denying these things and trying to develop another series of subtle self-protections. If you examine this process carefully, you will perceive that consciousness, the mind, is ever isolating itself through acquisitive and self-protective desires. In this separative process duality is created, which brings conflict, suffering, and confusion. The 'I' process itself creates its own illusions, sorrows, through its self-created ignorance. To understand this process, there must be awareness without the desire to choose between opposites. Choice in action creates duality, and this affirms the process of consciousness as individuality. If the mind-heart, not cognizant of its own secret demands, pursuits, of its hopes and fears, chooses, there must be the further creation of limitation and frustration. Thus, through the lack of understanding of ourselves, there is choice, which creates circumstances necessitating a further series of choices, and so mind-heart is caught over and over again in its own self-created circle of limitation.

Those of you who want to experiment with what I am saying will soon discover that there is no such thing as an external entity or environment guiding you, and that you are entirely responsible for yourself, for your own limitations and sorrows. If you see this, then environment does not become a separate force in itself, controlling, dominating, twisting the fulfillment of the individual. Then you begin to realize that there is only consciousness, perceived as individuality, and that it does not conceal or cover any reality.

The 'I' process is not proceeding to reality, to greater happiness, intelligence, but it is itself creating its own sorrow and confusion.

Take a very simple example and you can test this out for yourself. Many of you have very strong beliefs, which you make out to be the result of intuition; but they are not. These beliefs are the outcome of secret fears, longings, and hopes. Such beliefs are unconsciously guiding you, forcing you into certain activities, and all experience is translated according to your ideals and beliefs. Hence there is no comprehension of life, but only the storing up of self-protective memories which increase in their intensity and limitation through further experience. If you are aware, you will observe that this process is taking place in you, and that your activities are being approximated to a standard, to an ideal. The complete approximation to an ideal is called success, fulfillment, happiness; but what one has really achieved is a rigidity, a complete isolation, a self-protection through escape into security, and so there is no comprehension of life, nor is there the cessation of ignorance with its sorrow and confusion.

Question: What is the purpose of suffering? Is it to teach us not to repeat the same mistake?

KRISHNAMURTI: There is no purpose in suffering. Suffering exists because of the lack of comprehension. Most of us suffer economically, spiritually, or in our relationships with each other. Why is there this suffering? Economically, we have a system based on acquisitiveness, exploitation, fear; this system is being encouraged and maintained by our cravings and pursuits, and so it is self-sustaining. Acquisitiveness and a system of exploitation must go together, and they are ever present where there is ignorance of oneself. It is again a vicious circle; our craving has produced a system, and that system maintains itself by exploiting us.

There is suffering in our relationships with others. It is created by an inner craving for comfort, security, possession. Then there is that suffering caused by profound uncertainty, which prompts us to find peace, security, reality, God. Craving certainty, we invent many theories, create many beliefs, and the mind becomes limited and enmeshed in them, overheated with them, and so it is incapable of adjusting itself to the movement of life.

There are many kinds of suffering, and if you begin to discern their cause, you will perceive that suffering must coexist with the demand on the part of each individual to be secure, whether financially, spiritually, or in human relationship. Where there is a search for security, gross or subtle, there must be fear, exploitation, and sorrow.

Instead of comprehending the cause of sorrow, you ask what is its purpose. You want to utilize sorrow to gain something further. So you begin to invent the purpose; you say that sorrow is the result of a past life, it is the result of environment, and so on. These explanations satisfy you, so you continue in your ignorance, with the constant recurrence of sorrow.

Suffering exists where there is ignorance of oneself. It is but an indication of limitation, of incompleteness. There is no remedy for suffering itself. In the discernment of the process of ignorance, suffering disappears.

Question: Is it not true that good deeds are rewarded, and that by leading a kind and an upright life, we will attain to happiness?

KRISHNAMURTI: Who rewards you? Reward in this world is called making a success of life, getting on the top, by exploiting people, being decorated by the government or by your party, and so on. And if you are denied this kind of reward, you want another

kind, a spiritual reward—either discipleship from a Master, initiation, or a recognition for having done good in your past life.

Do you seriously think that such a thing exists, except as a childish encouragement and impetus, that it has any validity? Are you kind and do you love because you are going to get a reward now or in a future life? You may laugh at this, but if you deeply examine and understand your motives and actions, you will perceive that they are tinged with this idea of reward and punishment. So our actions are never integral, complete, and full. From this arise sorrow and conflict, and our lives become small, petty, and without any deep significance.

If there is no reward or punishment, and so the utter freedom from fear, then what is the purpose of living? This would be the natural question you would ask because you have been trained to think in terms of reward and punishment, achievement, competition, and all those qualities that make up what you consider to be human nature. When we understand profoundly the significance of our existence, of the process of ignorance and action, we will see that what we call purpose has no significance. The mere search for the purpose of life covers up, detracts from the comprehension of oneself.

Reward has no significance; it is merely a compensation for the effort you have put forth. All effort put forth in order to gain a reward, here or in the hereafter, leads to frustration, and reward becomes so much dust in your mouth.

Question: Do you not consider philanthropy an important element in creating a new environment leading to human welfare?

KRISHNAMURTI: If we understand philanthropy to be the love of man and the effort to promote his happiness, then it will have value only in so far as we consider him as a unique individual and help him to realize that in his own hands lie his happiness and the welfare of the whole. But, I fear, this would not be considered as philanthropy; for most of us do not realize that we are unique, that the process of creating ignorance and sorrow lies within our own power, and that only through the comprehension of ourselves can there be freedom from them. If this is fully and deeply comprehended, then philanthropy will have significance.

Charity merely becomes a compensation, and with it go all the subtle and gross exploitations to which man has become so accustomed.

April 26, 1936

Fifth Talk in The Oak Grove

I wish to explain this morning one idea, and if we can grasp it, not so much as a fact, but deeply and significantly, I think then it will have a profound value in our lives. So please help me by thinking with me.

Most of us have created a concept of reality, of immortality, of a constant, eternal something. We have a vague inclination to seek what we call God, truth, perfection, and we are constantly striving to realize these ideals, these conceptions. To help us to attain these objectives, we have systems, modes of conduct, disciplines, meditations, and various aids. These include the paraphernalia of churches, ceremonies, and other forms of worship, and all these are supposed to help us to realize those conceptions of reality that we have created for ourselves. So we have set in motion the process of want.

Now, there is in us a perpetual want, a continual striving after satisfaction which we call reality. We try to mold ourselves after a pattern, according to a particular system of conduct, of behavior, which promises to give us the satisfying understanding of what we call reality, happiness.

This want is quite different from search. Wanting indicates an emptiness, a trying to become something, whereas true search leads to deep comprehension. Before we can understand what is truth, reality, or know if there be such a thing, we must discern what it is that is constantly seeking. What is it that is ever in the movement of want? What is it that is ever craving, pursuing attainment? Until we have understood this, want is an endless process which prevents true discernment; it is a constant striving without understanding, a blind following, a ceaseless fear with its many illusions.

So the question is not what is reality, God, immortality, and whether one should believe in it or not, but what is the thing that is striving, wanting, fearing, and longing? What is it and why does it want? What is the center in which this want has its being? What is the consciousness, the conception from which we start and in which we have our being? From this we must begin our inquiry. I am going to try to explain this process of want, which creates its own prison of ignorance; and please cross over the bridge of words, for the mere repetition of my phrases can have no lasting significance.

This thing that is continually wanting is the consciousness which has become perceptible as the individual. That is, there is an 'I' that is wanting. What is the 'I'? There is a self-sustaining energy, a force which, through its development, becomes consciousness. This energy or force is unique to each living being. This consciousness becomes perceptible to the individual through the senses. It is at once both self-maintaining and self-energizing, if I may use those words. That is, it is not only maintaining, supporting itself through its own ignorance, tendencies, reactions, wants, but also by this process it is storing up its own potential energies; and this process can be fully comprehended by the individual only in his awakened discernment.

You see something that is attractive, you want it, and you possess it. Thus there is set up this process of perception, want, and acquisition. This process is ever self-sustaining. There is a voluntary perception, an attraction or repulsion, a clinging or a rejecting. The 'I' process is thus self-active. That is, it is not only expanding itself by its own voluntary desires and actions, but it is maintaining itself through its own ignorance, tendencies, wants, and cravings. The flame maintains itself through its own heat, and the heat itself is the flame. Now, exactly in the same way, the 'I' maintains itself through want, tendencies, and ignorance. And yet the 'I' itself is want. The material for the flame may be a candle or a piece of wood, and the material for the 'I' process is sensation, consciousness. This process is without a beginning and is unique to each individual. Experiment with this and you will discern for yourself how real, how actual it is. There is no other thing but the 'I'; that 'I' does not conceal anything, any reality. It is itself and maintains itself continually through its own voluntary demands and activities.

So this process, this continual process of want, creates its own confusion, sorrows, and ignorance. Where there is a want there cannot be discernment. That is very simple if one thinks it out. You crave for happiness. You look to the means of getting it. Someone offers you the means. Now, your mind-heart is so blinded by the intense desire for happiness that it is incapable of discernment. Though you may think that you are examining and analyzing the means that is offered to you, yet this deep craving for satisfaction, happiness, security, prevents clarity of comprehension. So where there is a want there cannot be true discernment.

Through want we create confusion, ignorance, and suffering, and then we set in

movement the process of escape. This escape we call the search for reality. You say, "I want to find God, I want to attain truth, liberation, I seek immortality." You never ask yourself what is the 'I' that is seeking. You have taken for granted that the 'I' is something enduring, a something in itself, and that it is created by some supreme entity. If you examine profoundly you will discern that the 'I' is nothing but self-accumulated ignorance, tendencies, wants, and that it does not conceal anything in itself.

Once you deeply grasp this, you will never ask, "Must I get rid of all my wants? Must I have no beliefs? Must I have no ideals? Must I be without desires? Is it wrong to have any craving?" To understand this whole process of the 'I', requires on your part real thinking and deep penetration through discernment. If you comprehend the arising, the coming into being of consciousness through sensation, through want, and see that from consciousness there is born the unit called the 'I' which in itself does not conceal any reality, then you will awaken to the nature of this vicious circle. When there is an understanding of its significance, then there is a new comprehension, a new something that is untrammeled by want, by craving, by ignorance. Then you can live in this world intelligently, sanely, in deep fulfillment, and yet not be of the world. Confusion arises only when you are made incapable of adjustment by your fantastic and harmful conceptions, ideals, and beliefs.

If you can deeply comprehend this self-sustaining process of ignorance which gives a solidity to the 'I' from which arises all confusion, and suffering, then life can be lived fully, without the various subtle escapes and pursuits that, unknowingly, you have created for yourself. Then there comes into being that extraordinary something, a fullness, a bliss. But before this can take place, there must be a profound understanding of the 'I' process; unless there is this comprehension, the 'I' process is ever creating a duality in itself through want. When there is discernment, then the pursuit of virtue, the attempt to unify yourself with a reality, with God, loses its significance. To discern this process, there cannot be the acceptance of any belief, there cannot be the pursuit of any ideal or the molding of yourself after a pattern of conduct. You must discern for yourself, deeply and significantly, the cause of this misery, confusion, and ignorance, through the arising of the 'I' process. Then there comes into being a bliss that has no words for its measure.

Question: In ties of relationship, one may be compelled to do something which one does not care to do, by the very nature of the relationship. Do you think one can live completely in such ties?

KRISHNAMURTI: Before we can understand what it is to live fully, let us discover what we mean by relationship. Relationship is morality. Relationship implies a living contact, whether it be with the one or with the many. This relationship, this morality, becomes impossible when we, as individuals, are incapable of pliability. That is, if one is limited, limited through ignorance, tendencies, various forms of acquisition and want, there is a barrier, a hindrance which prevents living contact with another. As the other also has the same limitations, true relationship becomes almost impossible. Since there is not this living contact, we create a mode of conduct which we call morality, and try to force our behavior to that morality, to that standard. If we understand relationship to be the true, profound comprehension of oneself, then we give to morality, to relationship, quite a different meaning.

Most of us think there should be codes, systems, disciplines for morality. They may

be necessary for those who are incapable of deep thought; but no one can judge who is incapable. Do not say such and such a one needs a code of discipline; one has to discover for oneself this active morality, this living relationship, and that demands deep, creative pliability, which can be experienced only when individual limitations are deeply discerned and their causes understood. When your life is one of acquisitiveness and of want, then there must be a continual tension with the other, who is also acquisitive, and this prevents true relationship, whether it be between individuals or nations. And this tension leads to conflicts, wars, and the many gross and subtle forms of exploitation.

If you are aware of your own particular demands, the many forms of acquisitiveness, and so comprehend the process of self-active ignorance, then there is no longer a choosing, a withholding, a rejecting, but these very cravings and wants wear themselves out, they drop off as leaves in the autumn. Then there can be true relationship, in which there is no longer the constant struggle to adjust oneself to another.

Question: By meditating on the Master, one may realize the bliss of conscious union with him. In that state, all sense of self disappears. Is this not of great value in breaking down the limitations of the ego?

KRISHNAMURTI: Certainly not. It can never be. The question is wrongly put. Let us go into it.

First, let us understand what you mean by a Master. Unfortunately, a great many books have been written about Masters, initiations, and discipleship, and many supposed spiritual societies have been formed around all this. There exist many swamis and yogis, who encourage and cultivate all these conceptions. You who are seeking satisfaction, which you call happiness, truth, become their tools and are exploited by these teachers, leaders, and their societies.

A Master can be either a concept or an actuality. If it is a concept, a theory, it can never become dogmatic. Then it is open to speculation, to be discussed from the point of view of what is called evolution. So it must remain abstract and can never be used as an actuality for furthering certain activities, action, modes of conduct. Being an abstraction, it has not the stimulation of fear as reward and punishment. But this is not so with those who talk about the Masters and their work. They confuse the two, the abstract and the actual. One moment they talk about the abstract idea of Masters, and the next they make of them an actuality by telling you, the followers, what the Masters desire you to think and to do. So you are caught up in confusion, and curiously enough, it is your own wants that create this confusion. This process of making the Masters into actual entities comes slowly, through hints and messages, until you believe that your leaders have actually met the Masters, and that these beings have told them how to save humanity; and you, through so-called devotion, which is really fear, follow the leaders and are exploited. So there is a constant mingling of the conceptual and the concrete.

Who is to judge what a Master is? To some, a Master is a person who possesses extraordinary powers, and to others he may be one who reveals some special knowledge. But wisdom is not realized through another, either though a Master or through a scientist. You are judging someone to be a Master according to your own particular idiosyncrasies, prejudices, and tendencies. This must be so, even with those who are supposed to represent the Masters. People are always judging others, whether called Masters or neighbors, according to their own peculiar background. You never question the background of the person who says that he represents the

Masters, that he is their messenger, because you are seeking happiness, and you merely want to be guided, to be told exactly what to do. So you obey through fear, which you call love, intuition, voluntary choice, or loyalty. You think that you have examined, analyzed, understood, and that you intuitively agree with what your particular leaders say. But you cannot truly discern, for you are being carried away by your own intense wants. So, unfortunately, people in this country, and elsewhere, fall into this trap of exploitation.

I do not want you to agree with me; but if, without any want, you examine this whole idea of a Master leading you to truth, then you will see how foolish it is. If you have somewhat grasped what I have explained about the process of the 'I', then you will not meditate on a Master, either in the form of what you call a high ideal or a higher self, or as an image, graven in your mind through pictures and propaganda. Such forms of meditation become merely subtle escapes. Though you may have some kind of sensation out of it and marvel at it and be thrilled by it, you will find that it has no validity, but only leads to a rigidity of mind-heart.

Meditation is constant awareness and pliability, not an adjustment to any standard or mode of conduct. Try to be aware of your own idiosyncrasies, fancies, reactions, and wants in your daily life, and understand them; out of that comes the reality of fulfillment. For this deep comprehension there cannot be any system. No Master can ever give it to you or lead you to it. If one claims he can, he is not a Master. The process of self-active ignorance and its discernment is unique to yourself. Another cannot free you from it. Beware of him who offers to destroy for you the walls of your limitation. If you really comprehend this, you will see what a significant change takes place in your life. Being free of fear, of want, which is so often called love, devotion, you are no longer exploited by churches, by societies supposed to be religious and spiritual, by priests, by the so-called messengers of the Masters, and by the swamis and yogis. True meditation is the discernment of one's own unique process of creating and being caught in ignorance, and being aware of this process.

Question: The economic system cannot change until human nature changes, and human nature will not change so long as the system exists and encourages human nature to remain as it is. How, then, will the break come?

KRISHNAMURTI: Do you think that this system has come into being spontaneously, of its own accord? It is created by human nature, as it is called. Human nature must first change and not the system. A system may help or hinder, but fundamentally the individual must begin to transform himself.

Surely, if all of you really thought profoundly about the whole question of war, for example, this murder on a grand scale, this murder in uniform, with decorations, shouts of joy and praise, with trumpets and banners, with blessings from priests; if you thought and felt deeply about this and perceived its cruelty and infantile absurdities, its appalling maltreatment of man, forcing him to become a military machine through the many exploiting means of nationalism and so on—if you, as individuals, really perceived this horror, surely you would refuse to be used for furthering war and exploitation. You, as individuals, would not be used, exploited through propaganda. You, as individuals, would lose all sense of nationality.

How are we going to change any exploiting system, economic, religious, or social, unless we begin with ourselves, unless we see profoundly the necessity for such a change—not just for a moment, during this meeting, but continually in our daily lives?

But when you feel the pressure of a system being exerted by your neighbor, by your bosses, by your employees, then it becomes very difficult for you to maintain this profound comprehension. So the mind-heart must perceive the utter necessity of freeing itself from its own apparently ceaseless wants. As this needs individual effort, which we dislike, we look to a system to help us out of this misery; we hope that a system will force us to behave decently and intelligently. That way leads to regimentation and greater misery, not to deep fulfillment.

Unless you profoundly feel all this, and are making an effort to be free from your self-imposed limitations, the system will imprison you, the system will become a self-sustaining process. Though it is lifeless, it will be maintained by your unique individual energies. Here again there is a vicious circle. Want creates the system of exploitation, and the system maintains that want. So the individual is caught up in this machine, and he says, "How am I to get out of it?" He looks to others to lead him out of it, but he will be led only to another prison, to another system of exploitation. He himself, through his ignorance and its self-active process, has created the machine that holds him, and it is only through himself, through his own discernment of the process of the 'I', that there can ever be true freedom and fulfillment.

Question: In rare moments one is not conscious of oneself as a separate, thinking entity. However, most of the time one is conscious of oneself, and of presenting a resistance toward life. Please explain why there is this resistance.

KRISHNAMURTI: Isn't prejudice a resistance? Prejudice is so deep-rooted—the prejudice of class, nationality, religious and other forms of belief. Such tendencies are forms of the 'I' process. Until we discern this process of creating beliefs, prejudices, tend-encies, there must ever be resistance to life. For example, if you are a religious person and have a strong belief that there is immortality, this belief acts as a resistance to life and hinders the very understanding of immortality. This belief is continually strengthening the barrier, the resistance, because it has its foundation in want. You think that for you, the individual, there is a continuity, an abode where you will be safe forever. This belief may be subtle or gross, but in essence it is a craving for personal continuity. As the vast majority of people have this belief, when reality begins to show itself, they are bound to reject it and therefore resist it, and such resistance creates conflict, misery, and confusion. But you will not relinquish this idea of immortality because it gives you hope, encouragement, the deep satisfaction of security.

We have many prejudices, subtle and gross, and each individual, being unique, sustains his own ignorance through his volitional activities. If you do not comprehend fully, in all its entirety, this self-active ignorance, you are constantly creating barriers, resistances, and so increasing misery. So you must become aware of this process, and with that discernment there comes, not the development of an opposite, but the comprehension of reality.

May 3, 1936

Sixth Talk in The Oak Grove

Some of you may think that I am repetitive, and I may be so, for the questions that have been sent in, the interviews and general conversations I have had with people, have given me the impression that there is little understanding of what I have been saying; and so I have to repeat the same thing in different words. I hope those of you who have more or less grasped the fundamental ideas will have the patience to listen again to what I have to say.

There is so much suffering, in such a variety of ways, that one agonizes over it. This is not an empty phrase. One perceives so much exploitation and cruelty around one, that one is constantly asking oneself what is the cause of sorrow and by what means can it be dissipated.

There are some who firmly believe that the misery of the world is the result of some evil misfortune beyond the control of man, and that happiness and freedom from sorrow can exist only in another world, when man returns to God. This attitude towards life is completely erroneous, from my point of view, for this chaos is of man's own making.

To discern the process of suffering, each one must comprehend himself. To understand oneself is one of the most difficult tasks and demands the most strenuous effort and constant alertness, and very few have the inclination or the desire to comprehend deeply this process of suffering and sorrow. We have more opportunities to dissipate our energies through absurd amusements, futile conversations, and vain pursuits, than to search out, to penetrate deeply into our own psychological demands, needs, beliefs, and ideals. But this involves strenuous effort on our part, and as we do not wish to exert ourselves, we would rather escape into all manner of easy satisfactions.

If we do not escape through diversions, we escape through beliefs, through the activities of organizations with their loyalties and commitments. These beliefs become a shield, preventing us from comprehending ourselves. Religious societies promise to help us to understand ourselves, but unfortunately we are exploited and we merely repeat their phrases and succumb to the authority of their leaders. So these organizations, with their increasing restrictions and secret promises, lead us away into further complications which make us incapable of understanding ourselves. Once we have committed ourselves to a particular society, to its leaders and their friends, we begin to develop those loyalties and responsibilities which prevent us from being wholly honest with ourselves. There are, of course, other forms of escape, through various superficial activities.

To understand oneself profoundly, one needs balance. That is, one cannot abandon the world, hoping to understand oneself, or be so entangled in the world that there is no occasion to comprehend oneself. There must be balance, neither renunciation nor acquiescence. This demands alertness and deep awareness. We must learn to observe our actions, thoughts, ideals, beliefs, silently and without judgment, without interpreting them, so as to be able to discern their true significance. We must first be cognizant of our own ideals, pursuits, wants, without accepting or condemning them as being right or wrong. At present we cannot discern what is true and what is false, what is lasting and what is transient, because the mind is so crippled with its own self-created wants, ideals, and escapes that it is incapable of true perceptions. So we must first learn to be silent and balanced observers of our limitations and frictions which cause sorrow.

If you begin to observe, you will see that you are seeking new explanations, definitions, satisfactions, ideals, graphic images, and pictures as substitutes for the old. You accepted the old beliefs, explanations, and pictures because they satisfied you; and now, through friction with life, you are finding out that they no longer give you what you crave. So you seek new explanations, new hopes, new ideals, and escapes, but with the same background of want and satisfaction. Then you begin to compare the old explanations with the new, and choose those which give you the greatest security and contentment. You think that by accepting these new ex-

planations and ideals, you will find happiness and peace. As your demand is for contentment and satisfaction, you help to create and accept beliefs and explanations that fulfill your want, and then you begin to shape your thought and conduct according to these new molds. If you observe, you will perceive that this is so. As there is so much suffering, both within and without, you desire to know the cause, but you are easily satisfied with explanations and you continue to suffer. Explanations are as so much dust to a discerning mind.

Some of you believe in the idea of reincarnation. You come and ask me what I believe, whether reincarnation is a fact or not, whether I remember my past lives, and so on. Now, why do you ask me? Why do you want to know what I think about it? You want a further confirmation of your own belief, which you call a fact, a law, because it gives you a hope, a purpose in life. Thus belief becomes to you a fact, a law, and you go about seeking confirmation of your hope. Even though I may confirm it, it cannot be of vital importance to you. Whatever it may be to me, real or false, what is important for you is that you should discern for yourself these conceptions, through action, through living, and not accept any assertions.

There are three conditions of mind: "I know," "I believe," and "I do not know." When you say, "I know," you mean you know through experience, and through that experience you become certain and convinced of an idea, a belief. But that certainty, that conviction may be based on imagination, on a wish fulfillment, which to you gradually becomes a fact, and so you say, "I know." Some say reincarnation is a fact, and to them perhaps it is so, as they say they can see their past lives; but to you who crave for continuity, reincarnation gives hope and purpose, and so you cling to the idea, saying that it is your intuition that prompts you to accept it as a fact, as a law. You accept the idea of rebirth on the assertion of another, without ever questioning his knowledge, which may be imagination, hallucination, or the projection of a wish. Craving self-perpetuation, immortality, you become incapable of true discernment. If you do not say, "I know," you then say, "I believe in reincarnation because it explains the inequalities of life." Again, this belief, which you say is prompted by intuition, is the outcome of a hidden hope and craving for continuity.

Thus both the "I know" and "I believe" are insecure, uncertain and not to be relied on. But if you can say, "I do not know," fully comprehending its significance, then there is a possibility of perceiving that which is. To be in a state of not knowing demands great denudation and strenuous effort, but it is not a negative state; it is a most vital and earnest state for the mind-heart that does not grasp at explanations and assertions.

One can casually and easily say that one does not know, and most people say it. One hears and reads so much about the cause of suffering, that unconsciously one begins to accept this explanation and reject that, according to the dictates of satisfaction and hope. As most people have minds cluttered up with beliefs, prejudices, hidden hopes, and demands, it is almost impossible for them to say, "I do not know." They are so bound to certain beliefs by their inner longings, that they are never in a state of complete bankruptcy. They are never in that state of utter denudation when all the supports, explanations, hopes, influences have completely ceased.

We begin to discern what is true only when all want has ceased, for want creates beliefs, ideals, hopes, which are mere escapes. When the mind is no longer seeking security in any form, or demanding explanations, or relying on subtle influences, then, in that state of nakedness, there is the real, the

permanent. If the mind is able to discern that it is creating its own ignorance through craving and perpetuating itself through its own action of want, then consciousness changes to reality. Then there is permanency; then there is the ending of the transiency of consciousness. Consciousness is the action or friction between ignorance and the external provocations of life, of the world, and this consciousness, this strife and sorrow, is self-perpetuating through want, through craving, which creates its own ignorance.

Question: Please explain more clearly what you mean by pliability of mind.

KRISHNAMURTI: Is it not necessary to have a supple, alert mind? Must not one have a mind that is supremely pliable? Must not the mind be like a tree that has its roots deep in the earth, yet yields to passing winds? It is itself, and so it can be pliable. Now, with what are we occupied? We are trying to become something, and we glory in that becoming. That becoming is not fulfillment but imitation, the copying of a pattern of what is called perfection; it is a following, obeying, in order to achieve, to succeed. That is not fulfillment. A rose or a violet that is lovely is a perfect flower, and that in itself is fulfillment; it would be vain to wish that a violet could be as the rose. We are making constant effort to be something, and so the mind-heart becomes more and more rigid, limited, narrow, and incapable of deep pliability. So it creates further resistances for self-protection against the movement of life. Those self-created resistances prevent the mind-heart from comprehending its own activities which engender and increase ignorance. Pliability of mind is not in becoming something, in worshipping success, but it is known when the mind denudes itself of those resistances which it has brought into being through craving. This is true fulfillment. In that fulfillment there is the eternal, the permanent, the ever pliable.

Question: I know all my limitations, but they stay with me still. So what do you mean by bringing the subconscious into the conscious?

KRISHNAMURTI: Sir, merely to know one's limitations is surely not enough, is it? Haven't you to discern their significance? I have said for many years that certain things are limitations, and you may perhaps be repeating my words without deeply understanding them, and then you say, "I know all my limitations." The strenuous awareness of your own limitations brings about their dissipation.

Ceremonies, as other perversions of thought, are to me limitations. Suppose you agree, and you want to discover if your mind is held in these limitations. Begin to be aware of them, not by judging, but by silently observing and discerning whether certain reactions are harmful, limited. That very discernment, that awareness itself, without creating an opposite quality, dislodges from the mind those resistances and harmful restrictions. When you ask, "How am I to get rid of my limitations?" it indicates that you are not aware of them, that there is not a strenuous effort to discern. There is a joy in this strenuous awareness, in the struggle itself. Awareness has no reward.

Question: I have listened to your talks for several years, but to be frank, I have not yet grasped what you are trying to convey. Your words have always seemed vague to me, whereas the writings of H. P. Blavatsky, Rudolf Steiner, Annie Besant, and a few others, have greatly helped me. Is it not that there are different ways of presenting truth,
and that your way is the way of the mystic as distinct from that of the occultist?

KRISHNAMURTI: I have answered this question I do not know how often, but if you wish I shall answer it again. Any explanation, any measure of truth must be erroneous. Truth is to be comprehended, to be discerned, not to be explained. It is, but is not to be sought after. So there cannot be one way or many ways of presenting truth. That which is presented as truth is not truth.

But then you can ask me, "What are you trying to do? If you are not giving us a graphic picture of truth, measuring for us the immeasurable, then what are you doing?" All that I am trying to do is to help you to discern for yourself that there is no salvation outside of yourself; that no Master, no society, can save you; that no church, no ceremony, no prayer can break down your self-created limitations and restrictions; that only through your own strenuous awareness is there the comprehension of the real, the permanent; and that your mind is so cluttered up, so overheated with beliefs, ideals, wants, and hopes that it is incapable of perception. Surely this is simple, clear, and definite; it is not vague.

Each one, through his own want, is creating ignorance, and that ignorance, through its volitional activities, is perpetuating itself as individuality, as the 'I' process. I say that the 'I' is ignorance, it has no reality, nor does it conceal anything permanent. I have said this often and explained it in many ways, but some of you do not want to think clearly, and so you cling to your hopes and satisfactions. You want to avoid deep strenuousness; you hope that through the effort of another your conflicts, miseries, and sorrows will be dissipated, and you wish that the exploiting organizations, whether religious or social, would be miraculously changed. If you make an effort you want a result, which excludes comprehension. Then you say, "What is the point of making an effort if I don't get something out of it?" Your effort, through want, creates further limitations which destroy comprehension. The mind is caught up in this vicious circle, effort through want, which maintains ignorance; and so the 'I' process becomes self-sustaining. The people who have gathered money, properties, qualities, are rigid in their acquisition and are incapable of deep comprehension. They are slaves to their own want, which creates a system of exploitation. If you give thought to it, it is not difficult to understand this, but to comprehend it through action demands strenuous effort.

To some of you, what I say is empty and meaningless; to others, coming to these meetings is a habit; and a few are vitally concerned. Some of you take one or two statements of mine, separate them from their contexts, and try to work them into your own particular system. In this there is no comprehension, and it will only lead to further confusion.

Question: Since the Masters founded the Theosophical Society, how can you say that spiritual societies are a hindrance to man's understanding? Or does this not apply to the Theosophical Society?

KRISHNAMURTI: That is what every society, sect, or religious body declares. Roman Catholics have maintained for centuries that they are the direct representatives of the Christ. And other religious sects have similar assertions, only they use different names. Either their teaching is inherently true in itself, and so does not need the support of any authority, however great it is; or it can stand only because of authority. If it stands on any authority, whether of the Buddha, the Christ, or the Masters, then it has no significance. Then it merely becomes the means

of exploiting people through their fears. This is constantly happening the world over: the use of authority to coerce people through their fear—which is called love or respect for a particular form of activity—or to found a religious organization. And you who want happiness, security, follow without thought and are exploited. You do not question the whole conception of authority. You submit yourself to authority, to exploitation, thinking that it will lead you to reality; but only greater confusion and misery await you. This question of authority is so subtle that the individual deceives himself by saying that it is his own voluntary choice to submit himself to a particular form of belief or action. Where there is want, there must be fear and the creation of authority with its cruelties and exploitation.

I have repeated this in different words very often. Some have come and told me that they have resigned from this or that organization. Surely that is not the most important thing, though resignation must necessarily follow if there is comprehension. What is important is why did they join at all? If they can discover the impulse that drives them to join these religious sects, groups, and discern the deep significance of that impulse, then they will themselves abstain from joining any religious organization. If you analyze that urge, you will perceive fundamentally that where there is a promise of security and happiness, the desire for these is so great that it blinds comprehension, discernment; and authority is worshipped as a means to the satisfaction of the many cravings.

Question: Are you, or are you not, a member of the Great White Lodge of Adepts and Initiates?

KRISHNAMURTI: Sir, what does it matter? I am afraid this country, and especially this coast, is inundated with this kind of mystery, which is used to exploit people through their credulity and fear. There are so many swamis, both white and brown, who tell you about these things. What does it seriously matter whether there is a White Lodge or not? And who talks or writes about these mysteries except those who, consciously or unconsciously, wish to exploit man in the name of brotherhood, love, and truth? Beware of such people. They have set going incredible and harmful superstitions. Often I have heard people say that they are guided by Masters who send out forces, and so on. Don't you know, cannot you perceive for yourself that you are your own master, that you create your own ignorance, your own sorrow, that no other can by any means free you from suffering, now or ever? If you discern this fundamental fact, truth, law, that you create your own limitation and sorrow, that you yourself help to bring about a system which exploits man ruthlessly, and that out of your own inner demands, fears and wants are created religious and other organizations for cunning exploitation, then you will no longer encourage or help to create these systems. Then authority ceases to have any significant position in life; then only can man come to his own true fulfillment.

This demands a tremendous self-reliance. But you say, "We are weak and must be led; we must have nurses." Thus you continue the whole process of superstition and exploitation. If you will discern deeply that ignorance is perpetuating itself through its own action, then there will be a profound change in your relationship to life. But I assure you, this demands a deep comprehension of yourself.

May 10, 1936

Seventh Talk in The Oak Grove

One must have often asked oneself if there is a something within us that has con-

tinuance, a living principle that has a permanency, a quality that is enduring, a reality that persists through all this transiency. In my talk this morning I shall try to explain what lies behind this desire for continuance, and consider whether there is really anything that has a permanency. I would suggest that you kindly listen to what I say with critical thought and discernment.

Life is every moment in a state of being born, arising, coming into being. In this arising, coming into being, in this itself there is no continuity, nothing that can be identified as permanent. Life is in constant movement, action; each moment of this action has never been before, and will never be again. But each new moment forms a continuity of movement.

Now, consciousness forms its own continuity as an individuality through the action of ignorance and clings, with desperate craving, to this identification. What is that something to which each one clings, hoping that it may be immortal, or that it may conceal the permanent, or that beyond it may lie the eternal?

This something that each one clings to is the consciousness of individuality. This consciousness is composed of many layers of memories, which come into being, or remain present, where there is ignorance, craving, want. Craving, want, tendency in any form, must create conflict between itself and that which provokes it, that is, the object of want. This conflict between craving and the object craved appears in consciousness as individuality. So it is this friction, really, that seeks to perpetuate itself. What we intensely desire to have continue is nothing but this friction, this tension between the various forms of craving and their provoking agents. This friction, this tension, is that consciousness which sustains individuality.

The movement of life has no continuity. It is at every moment arising, coming into being, and so is in a state of perpetual action, flow. When one craves for one's own immortality, one must discern what is the deep significance of this craving and what it is that one desires to continue. Continuity is the self-maintaining process of consciousness, from which arises individuality, through ignorance, which is the outcome of want, craving; from this there is friction and conflict in relationship, morality, and action.

The 'I' process that seeks to perpetuate itself is nothing but accumulated craving. This accumulation and its memories make up individuality, to which we cling and which we crave to immortalize. The many layers of accumulated memories, tendencies, and wants make up the 'I' process; and we demand to know whether that 'I' can live forever, whether it can be made immortal. Can these self-protective memories become or be made permanent? Or, running through them like a solid cord, is there the permanent? Or, beyond this 'I' process of friction, limitation, is there the eternal? We desire to make the accumulated limitations permanent, or we think that through these layers of memories, of consciousness, there exists a something that is everlasting. Or else we imagine that beyond these limitations of individuality there must be the eternal.

Again, can the memories of accumulated ignorance, wants, tendencies, from which arise friction and sorrow, be made to last? That is the question. We cannot deeply accept that there is running through individuality something which is eternal, or that beyond this limitation there is something permanent, for this conception can only be based on belief, faith, or on what is called intuition, which is almost always a wish fulfillment. From our inclinations, hopes, and cravings for self-perpetuation, we accept theories, dogmas, beliefs, which give us the assurance of self-continuity. Nevertheless, deep uncertainty continues, and from this we try to escape by searching for certainty, by piling belief upon belief, by going from one system to another, by following one teacher after another, thereby merely increasing confusion and conflict.

Now, I do not want to create further beliefs or systems: I want to help you to discern for yourself whether there is continuity and understand its significance.

So, the important question is: Can the 'I' process be made permanent? Can the consciousness of tendencies, wants, and accumulated memories, from which arises individuality, be made permanent? In other words, can these limitations become the eternal? Life, energy, is in a perpetual state of action, movement, in which there can be no individual continuity. But, as individuals, we crave to perpetuate ourselves; and when you deeply discern what is individuality, you will perceive that it is nothing but the result of ignorance, maintaining itself through the many layers of memories, tendencies, and wants. These limitations must inevitably cause sorrow and confusion.

Can these limitations, which we can call individuality, be made permanent? This is really what most people are seeking when they desire immortality, reality, God. They are deeply concerned with the perpetuation of their own individuality. Can limitation be made eternal? The answer is obvious. If one deeply discerns its obvious transiency, then there is a possibility of realizing the permanent, and in this alone there is true relationship, morality.

Now, if one can deeply discern the arising of the 'I' process and become strenuously aware of the building up of limitations and their transiency, then that very awareness brings about their dissolution; and in that there is the permanent. The quality of this permanency cannot be described, nor can one search it out. It comes into being with the discernment of the transient process of the

'I'. The reality of the permanent can only happen, take place, and is not to be cultivated. One is either seeking the permanent, something that is enduring, beyond oneself, or one is trying to make oneself into the permanent. Both these conceptions are erroneous. If you are seeking the eternal beyond yourself, then you are bound to create and be caught up in illusions, which will only offer you means of escape from actuality, and in this there cannot be the comprehension of *what is*. The individual must be cognizant of himself, and in knowing himself, he will then be able to discern whether there is permanency or not. Our search for the eternal must lead us to illusion; but if, through strenuous effort and experiment, we can comprehend ourselves deeply and discern what we are, then only can there be the arising of the permanent—not the permanency of something outside of ourselves, but that reality which comes into being when the transient process of the 'I' no longer perpetuates itself.

To many, what I say will remain a theory, it will be vague and uncertain; but if you will discern its validity or accept it as an hypothesis, not as a law or as a dogma, then you can comprehend its active significance in daily life. Our morality, conduct, concepts, and longings are based fundamentally on the desire for self-perpetuation. The self is but the result of accumulated memories, which causes friction between itself and the movement of life, between the definite and the indefinite values. This friction itself is the 'I' process, and it cannot be made into the eternal. If we can grasp this fundamentally, fully, then our whole attitude and effort will have a different significance and purpose.

There are two kinds of will—the will that is born out of desire, want, craving, and the will that is of discernment, comprehension. The will that is the outcome of desire is based on the conscious effort of acquisition, whether the acquisition of want or the acquisition of nonwant. This conscious or unconscious effort of wanting, craving, creates the whole process of the 'I', and from that arise friction, sorrow, and the consideration of the hereafter. From this process arises also the conflict between the opposites, and so the constant battle between the essential and the inessential, choice and choicelessness. And from this process there arise the various self-protective walls of limitation, which prevent the real comprehension of indefinite values. Now if we are aware of this process, aware that we have developed a will through the desire to acquire, to possess, and that that will is creating a continual conflict, suffering, pain, then there takes place, without conscious effort, the comprehension of reality which may be called the permanent.

To discern that want is present where there is ignorance and so brings about suffering, and yet not to let the mind train itself not to want, is a most strenuous and difficult task. We can discern that to possess, to acquire, creates suffering and perpetuates ignorance, that the movement of craving prevents clear discernment. If you think about it, you will perceive that this is so. When there is neither want nor nonwant, there is then the comprehension of what is the permanent. This is a most difficult and subtle state to comprehend; it requires strenuous and right effort not to be caught between the opposites, renouncing and accepting. If we are able to discern that opposites are erroneous, that they must lead to conflict, then that very discernment, that very awareness, brings about enlightenment. To talk about this is very difficult, as whatever symbol one may use must awaken in the mind a concept, which has in it the opposite. But if we can discern fully that we, through our own ignorance, create sorrow, then there is not the setting up of the process of the opposite.

To discern demands right effort, and only in this right effort is there the comprehension of the permanent.

Question: All intelligent people are against war, but are you against defensive war, as when a nation is attacked?

KRISHNAMURTI: To consider war as defensive and offensive will lead us only to further confusion and misery. What we should question is killing, whether in war or through exploitation. What is, after all, a defensive war? Why does one nation attack another? Probably the nation that is attacked has provoked that attack through economic exploitation and greed. If we deal with the question of war as defensive or offensive, we shall never come to any satisfactory and true solution. We shall be dealing only with acquisitive prejudices. There is such a thing as voluntarily dying for a cause; but that a group of people should send out other human beings to be trained to kill and be killed is most barbarous and inhuman. You will never ask this question about war—in which there is the regimentation of hatred, mechanizing man through military discipline—and whether it is right to kill in defense or in aggression, if you can discern for yourself the true nature of man.

From my point of view, to kill is fundamentally evil, as it is evil to exploit another. Most of you are horrified at the idea of killing; but when there is the provocation, you are up in arms. This provocation comes through propaganda, through the appeal to your false emotions of nationalism, family, honor and prestige, which are words without deep significance. They are but absurdities to which you have become accustomed, and through which you exploit and are exploited. If you think about this deeply and truly, then you will help to break down all these causes that create hatred, exploitation, and ultimate-

ly lead to war, whether called offensive or defensive.

You seem to feel no vital response to all this. Some of you, being trained in religion, probably often repeat the phrase that one must love one's neighbor. But against others you have such deep-rooted prejudices of nationalism and of racial distinctions that you have lost the human and affectionate response. One is so proud of being an American or belonging to some particular race; the class and racial distinction is so falsely and ruthlessly stimulated in each one of us that one despises foreigners, Jews, Negroes, or Asiatics. Until we are free of these absurd and childish prejudices, wars of various kinds will exist. If you who listen with discernment to these talks feel and act with comprehension and so free yourselves from those limiting, harmful, and mischievous ideas, then there is a possibility of having a peaceful and happy world. That is not mere sentiment; but as this question of exploitation and killing concerns each one of you, you have to make strenuous efforts to free your mind from these self-imposed ideas of security and individual perpetuation, which create confusion and misery.

Question: Must we not have some idea of what is pure action? Merely becoming aware, even profoundly aware, seems to be a negative state of consciousness. Is not positive consciousness essential for pure action?

KRISHNAMURTI: You want me to describe to you what is pure action; such a description you would call a positive teaching. Pure action is to be discerned by each one, individually, and there cannot be a substitution of the true in place of the false. Discernment of the false brings about true action. Mere substitution or having a notion of pure action must inevitably lead to imitation, frustration, and to the many practices that destroy true intelligence. But if you discern your own limitations, then out of that comprehension will come positive action.

If you experiment with this, you will see that it is not a negative attitude towards life; on the contrary, the only positive way of living, fulfilling, is to discern the process of ignorance, which must be present where there is craving, and from which arises sorrow and confusion. The mind seeks a definition with which to make a mold for itself in order to escape from those reactions which cause friction and pain. In this there is no comprehension. I have said this very often. Inwardly the 'I' process, with its demands, cravings, vanities, and cruelties, persists and continues. Through the comprehension of this process—not that it may bring you reward, happiness, but for itself—lies true and clear action.

Question: You have said that so-called spiritual organizations are obstacles to one's attainment of spirituality. But, after all, do not all obstacles that prevent the attainment of spiritual life lie within oneself, and not in outward circumstances?

KRISHNAMURTI: Most of us turn to so-called spiritual organizations because they promise rewards; and as most of us are seeking spiritual, emotional or mental security and comfort, in one form or another, we succumb to their promises and become instruments of exploitation and are exploited. To discover for yourself whether you are caught in this self-created prison, and to be free of its subtle influences, demands great discernment and right effort. These organizations come into being and exist because of our craving for our own egotistic spiritual well-being, and our continuity and comfort. Such organizations have nothing spiritual about them, nor can they free man from his own ignorance, confusion, and sorrow.

Question: If we are not to have ideals, if we must be rid of the desire to improve ourselves, to serve God and our less fortunate fellow-beings, what then is the purpose of living? Why not just die and be done with it?

KRISHNAMURTI: What I have said concerning ideals is this: that they become a convenient means of escape from the conflict of life, and thus they prevent the comprehension of oneself. I have never said that you must not help your less fortunate fellow beings.

Now, ideals act merely as standards of measure; and as life defies measurement, mind must free itself from ideals so that it may comprehend the movement of life. Ideals are impediments, hindrances. Instead of merely accepting what I say and therefore saying to yourself that you must not have ideals, discern for yourself whether they do not cloud your comprehension. When the mind frees itself from preconceptions, explanations, and definitions, then it is able to confront the cause of its own suffering, its own ignorance, and its own limited existence. So the mind must be concerned with suffering itself, and not with what it can get out of life. The mere pursuit of ideals, the craving for happiness, the search for truth, God, is an indication of escape from the movement of life. Do not concern yourself with what is the object of living, but become aware and discern the cause of suffering; and in the dissolution of that cause there is comprehension of *what is.*

Question: Will you please explain what you mean by the statement that even keeping accounts can be creative? Most of us think that only constructive work is creative.

KRISHNAMURTI: Isn't it a matter of how you regard work, whether it is bookkeeping, tilling the ground, writing books, or painting pictures? To a man who is lazy and uninterested, all work becomes uncreative. Why ask what is and what is not creative work, whether painting a picture is more creative than typewriting? To fulfill is to be intelligent; and to awaken intelligence, there must be right effort. This strenuousness cannot be artificial; living must not be divided into work and inward realization. Working and inward life must be united. The very joy of right effort opens the door to intelligence. The discernment of the 'I' process is the beginning of fulfillment.

May 17, 1936

Eighth Talk in The Oak Grove

Question: Can we stop war by praying for peace?

KRISHNAMURTI: I do not think that war can be stopped by prayer. Isn't praying for peace merely a particular form of emotional release? We think that we are incapable of preventing war and so we find in prayer a release from this horror. Do you think that by merely praying for peace you are going to stop violence in the world? Prayer only becomes an escape from actuality. That emotional state which results in prayer can also be worked upon by propagandists for the purposes of war, hatred. As one eagerly prays for peace, so, equally enthusiastically, one is persuaded about the beauties of nationalism and the necessity of war. Prayer for peace is utterly useless. The causes of war are manufactured by man, and it is of no value to appeal to some outside force for peace. War exists because of psychological and economic reasons. Until those causes are fundamentally altered, war will exist, and praying for peace is of no value.

Question: How can I live simply and fully if I have to analyze myself and make conscious effort to think deeply?

KRISHNAMURTI: To live simply is the greatest of arts. It is most difficult, as it demands deep intelligence and not the superficial comprehension of life. To live intelligently and simply, one must be free of all those restrictions, resistances, limitations, which each individual has developed for his own self-protection and which have hindered his true relationship with society. Because he is enclosed within these restrictions, these walls of ignorance, for him there can be no true simplicity. To bring about a life of intelligence, and so of simplicity, there must be the tearing down of those resistances and limitations. The process of dissolution implies great thought, activity, and effort. A man who is prejudiced, nationalistic, bound by the authority of traditions and concepts, and in whose heart there is fear, surely cannot live simply. A man who is ambitious, narrow, worshiping success, cannot live intelligently. In such a person there is no possibility of deep spontaneity. Spontaneity is not mere superficial reaction; it is deep fulfillment, which is intelligent simplicity of action.

Now, most of us have walls of self-protective resistance against the movement of life; of some we are conscious, of others we are not. We think that we can live simply by merely avoiding or neglecting the undiscovered ones; or we think that we can live fully by training our minds to certain standards of life. It is not simplicity to live by oneself, apart from society, or to possess little, or to adjust oneself to particular principles. This is merely an escape from life. True simplicity of intelligence, that is, the deep adjustment to the movement of life, comes only when, through comprehensive awareness and right effort, we begin to wear down the many layers of self-protective resistance. Then only is there a possibility of living spontaneously and intelligently.

Question: What is your idea of ambition? Is it ego-inflation? Is not ambition essential for action and achievement?

KRISHNAMURTI: Ambition is not fulfillment. Ambition is ego-inflation. In ambition there is the idea of personal achievement ever in opposition to the achievement of another; there is the worship of success, ruthless competition, the exploitation of another. In the wake of ambition there is constant dissatisfaction, destruction, and emptiness; for in the very moment of success there is a withering, and so a renewed urge for further achievements. When you deeply discern that ambition has within it this constant struggle and strife, then you comprehend what is fulfillment. Fulfillment is the fundamental expression of what is true. But often a superficial reaction is mistaken for fulfillment. Fulfillment is not for the few alone, but it demands deep intelligence. In ambition there is an objective and the drive towards its achievement, but fulfillment is the intelligent process of completeness. The comprehension of fulfillment involves continual adjustment and the reeducation of our whole social being. Where there is ambition, there is also the search after rewards from governments, churches, or society, or there is the desire for the rewards of virtue with its consolations. In fulfillment the idea of reward and punishment has utterly disappeared, for all fear has wholly ceased.

Experiment with what I am saying and discern for yourself. Your present life is involved with ambition, not with fulfillment. You are trying to become something instead of being aware of those limitations which prevent true fulfillment. Ambition holds within it deep frustration, but in fulfillment there is bliss.

Question: I belong to one of the religious societies and I want to withdraw from it, but I have been warned by one of its leaders that if I left it, the Master would no longer help me. Do you think that the Master would really do this to me?

KRISHNAMURTI: You know, this is the whip of fear which all religious societies use to control man. They first promise a reward, here or in heaven, and when the individual begins to comprehend the foolishness of the idea of reward and punishment, he is grossly or subtly threatened. Because you crave for happiness, security, and for what is called truth—and this is really an escape from actuality—you create and play into the hands of exploiters. The churches and other religious bodies have throughout the ages threatened man for this independent thought and fulfillment. It is not principally the fault of the exploiters. The organizers and their leaders are created by their followers, and so long as you want those mysterious aids and depend on authority for your own righteous effort, conduct, and inward richness, these and other forms of threats will be used, and you will be exploited.

Some people, I see, laugh easily at this question, but I am afraid they too are involved in this process of reward and punishment. They may not belong to any religious society, but they perhaps seek their rewards from governments, from their neighbors, or from the immediate circle of their friends and relatives. Thus, through their craving, subtly or unconsciously, they are engendering fear and illusions which create an easy path to exploitation.

You know, this idea of following a Master is utterly erroneous and wholly unintelligent. I have recently and very often explained the folly of this idea of being guided, of worshipping authority, but apparently the questioner and others do not understand its deep significance. If they would try to discern, without prejudice, they would perceive the great harm that lies in this conception. Discernment alone can free them from the bondage of their habitual thought. Romanticism and escapes are offered by churches and religious bodies, and you get caught up in them. But when you discover their utter valuelessness, you find that you have involved and committed yourself financially and psychologically, and instead of giving up these absurdities, you try to find excuses for your beliefs and commitments. Thus you encourage and maintain a whole system of exploitation, with its cruel stupidities. Unless you discern fundamentally that no one can truly free you from your own ignorance and its self-sustaining activities, you become trammeled in these organizations, and fear, with its many illusions and sorrows, continues. Where there is fear, there must be subtle and gross forms of exploitation and suffering.

Question: You have many interpreters and associates of your youth who are creating confusion in our minds by saying that you have a purpose—well known to them but not disclosed by you to the public. These individuals claim to know special facts about you, your ideas, and work. I sometimes have a feeling from their words that they are really antagonistic to you and to your ideas, but they profess a warm friendship towards you. Am I mistaken in this, or are they exploiting you to justify their own actions and the organizations to which they belong?

KRISHNAMURTI: Why do these interpreters exist? What is it that is so difficult in what I am saying that you cannot understand it for yourself? You turn to interpreters and commentators because you do not want to think fully, deeply. As you look to others to lead you out of your trouble, out of your confusion, you are bound to create authorities, interpreters, who only further confuse your own thought. Then after being confounded, you put this question to me. You yourself are creating these interpreters and allowing yourself to become confused.

Now, with regard to past associates, I am afraid they and I have parted company long ago. There are some immediate friends who are working with me and helping me, but the associates of my youth, as they call themselves, are of the past. Deep friendship and cooperation can exist only where there is true comprehension. How can there be true cooperation and the action of friendship between a man who thinks authority is necessary and a man who considers authority to be pernicious? How can there be companionship between a man who thinks that exploitation is a part of human nature and another who maintains that it is ugly and wicked; between a man who is bound by beliefs, theories, and dogmas and a man who discerns their fallacy? How can there be any work common to a man who is creating and encouraging neuroticism and a man who is attempting to destroy its cause?

I have no private teaching; I have no private classes. What I say here to the public, I repeat in my conversations and interviews with individuals. But these self-styled associates and interpreters have their own axes to grind, and you like to be ground. You may laugh, but this is just what is happening. You listen to me, and then you go back to your leaders to interpret for you what I have said. You don't consider what I say and think it out fully by yourself. Surely, to think about what I am saying, for yourself, would be more direct and clear. But when you begin to think for yourself clearly, directly, action must follow; and to avoid drastic action, you turn to your leaders, who help you not to act. And so, through your own desire, by not acting clearly, you maintain these interpreters with their positions, authorities, and their systems of exploitation.

What profoundly matters is that you free yourself from beliefs and dogmas and limitations, so that you can live without conflict with another individual, with society. True relationship, morality, is possible only when barriers and resistances are entirely dissolved.

Question: If the whole process of life is self-acting energy, as I understand from your previous talk, that energy, judging from its creations, must be super-intelligent, far beyond human comprehension. What part, then, does the human intellect play in life's process? Would it not be better to let that creative energy work in us and through us, and not interfere with it by means of our human intellect? In other words, "Let go and let God," as Father Divine says.

KRISHNAMURTI: I am afraid the questioner has not understood what I have been saying. I have said that there is energy, force, unique to each individual. I have not qualified it; I have not said that it is super-intelligent or divine. I have said that through its own self-acting development, it creates its own substance. Through its own ignorance it is creating for itself limitation and sorrow. There is no question of letting something super-intelligent act through its creation, the individual. There is only consciousness as the individual, and consciousness is created through that friction between ignorance, craving, and the object of its want. When you consider this, you will discern that you are wholly responsible for your thoughts and actions, and that there is not something else acting through you. If you regard yourself and other human beings as merely instruments in the hands of other energies and forces un-

known to you, then I fear you will be a plaything of illusions and deceptions, confusion and sorrow. How can a superior force or intelligence act through a man whose mind-heart is limited, crooked?

You know, this is a most fallacious idea that we have developed in order not to delve into ourselves and discover our own being. To know ourselves needs constant thought and effort, but few of us are eager to discern, so we vainly try to make ourselves into convenient instruments for some super-intelligence, God. This conception in various forms exists throughout the world. If you really think about it fundamentally, you will see that, if it were true, the world would not be in this unintelligent, chaotic condition of hatred and misery. We have created this confusion and sorrow through ignorance of ourselves, through craving, and through the resistances of self-protection, and we alone can break down these limitations and barriers which cause misery, hatred, and the lack of adjustment to the action of life.

As this is my last talk here, I should like to make a brief résumé of what I have been saying during the past few weeks. Those of you who are really interested can think about it and experiment with it and prove its truth for yourselves, so that you do not follow anyone, any dogma, any explanation, any theory. Out of discernment will come comprehension and bliss.

There is contradiction of ideas, of theories, there is confusion created through constant assertions by leaders, of *what is* and what is not. Some say there is God, some say there is not; some maintain that the individual lives after death; the spiritists claim to have proved for themselves that there is a continuance of the individual mind; others say that there is only annihilation. Some believe in reincarnation, and others deny it. There is the piling up of theory upon theory, uncertainty upon uncertainty, assertion upon assertion. The result of all this is that one is wholly uncertain; or else one is so hedged about, bound by particular concepts and forms of belief, that one refuses to consider what is really true.

Either you are uncertain, confused, or you are certain in your own belief, in your own particular form of thought. Now, for a man who is truly uncertain, there is hope; but for a man who is entrenched in belief, in what he calls intuition, there is very little hope, for he has closed the door upon uncertainty, doubt, and takes rest and consolation in security.

Most of you who come here are, I think, uncertain, confused, and so deeply desire to comprehend what is actuality, what is truth. Uncertainty engenders fear, which gives rise to depression and anxiety. Then, consciously or unconsciously, one sets about escaping from these fears and their consequences. Observe your own thoughts, and you will perceive this process at work. As you crave to be certain of the purpose of life, of the hereafter, of God, you begin to be aware of your desires, and through this inquiry there comes doubt, uncertainty. Then that very uncertainty, doubt, creates fear, loneliness, emptiness about you and in you. This is a necessary state for the mind to be in, for then it is willing to face and comprehend actuality. But the suffering involved in this process is so great that the mind seeks shelter and creates for itself what it calls intuitions, concepts, beliefs, and clings to them desperately, hoping for certainty. This process of escape from actuality, from uncertainty, must lead to illusion, abnormality, neurosis, and unbalance. Even though you accept these intuitions, beliefs, and take shelter in them, yet if you examine yourself deeply you will see that there is still fear, for uncertainty continues.

This vital state of uncertainty, without the desire to escape from it, is the beginning of all true search for reality. What is it that you are really seeking? There can be only a state of comprehension, a direct perception of *what is,* of actuality; for comprehension is not an end, an objective to be gained. Discernment of the actual process of the 'I', of its coming into being and its true dissolution, is the beginning and the end of search.

To understand *what is,* comprehension must begin with oneself. The world is a series of indefinite, varied processes which cannot be fully comprehended, for each force is unique to itself, and cannot be truly perceptible, in its completeness. The whole process of life, of existence in the world, is entirely dependent on unique forces, and you can understand it only through that process which is focused in the individual as consciousness. You may superficially gather the significance of other processes, but to comprehend life fully, you must understand this process working in you as consciousness. If each one deeply and significantly understands this process as consciousness, then each one will not fight for himself, exist for himself, be concerned about himself. Now, each one is concerned about himself, fighting for himself, acting antisocially because he does not understand himself fully; and it is only through the comprehension of his own unique force as consciousness that there is the possibility of understanding the whole. In completely discerning the 'I' process, you cease to be a victim who struggles alone in an emptiness.

Now, this force is unique and in its self-development becomes consciousness, from which arises individuality. Please do not learn the phrase by heart, but think about it, and you will see that this force is unique to each one, and through its self-acting development becomes consciousness. What is this consciousness? It cannot have any location, nor can it divide itself as high and low. Consciousness is composed of many layers of memories, ignorance, limitations, tendencies, cravings. It is discernment and has the power of comprehending ultimate values. It is what we call individuality. Don't ask, "Is there nothing else beyond this?" That will be discernible when this 'I' process comes to an end. What is important is to know oneself, and not what is beyond oneself. You are only seeking reward for your efforts, a something to which you can cling in your present despair, uncertainty, and fear when you ask, "Is there something else beyond this 'I'?"

Now, action is that friction, tension, between ignorance, craving, and the object of its want. This action is self-maintaining, which gives a continuity to the 'I' process. So ignorance, through its self-sustaining activities, perpetuates itself as consciousness, the 'I' process. These self-created limitations prevent true relationship with other individuals, with society. These limitations isolate one, and hence there is constant arising of fear. This ignorance with regard to oneself ever creates fear, with its many illusions, and hence the search for unity with the higher, with some superhuman intelligence, God, and so on. From this isolation comes the pursuit of systems, methods of conduct and disciplines.

In the dissolution of these limitations you begin to discern that ignorance is without a beginning, that it is self-maintaining through its own activities, and that this process can come to an end through right effort and comprehension. You can test this out by experimenting and discern for yourself the beginningless process of ignorance and its end. If the mind-heart is bound by any particular prejudice, its own action must create further limitations and so bring about greater sorrow and confusion. Thus it perpetuates its own ignorance, its own sorrows.

If you become fully cognizant of this actuality, through experiment, then there is the comprehension of what the 'I' is, and through right effort it can be brought to an end. This effort is awareness in which there is not the choice or conflict of opposites—one part of consciousness conquering the other part, one prejudice overcoming another. This needs strenuous thought, which will free the mind of fears and limitations. Then only is there the permanent, the real.

May 24, 1936

New York City, New York, 1936

---　✳　---

First Talk in New York

In the world today, there are those who maintain that the individual is nothing but a social entity, that he is merely the product of conflicting environment. There are others who assert that man is divine, and this idea is expressed and interpreted in various forms to be found in religions.

The implications in the idea that man is a social entity are many and seemingly logical. If you deeply accept the idea that man is essentially a social entity, then you will favor the regimentation of thought and expression in every department of life. If you maintain that man is merely the result of environment, then system naturally becomes supremely important, and on that all emphasis should be laid; then molds by which man must be shaped acquire great value. You have then discipline, coercion, and ultimately the final authority of society calling itself government, or the authority of groups or of ideal concepts. Then social morality is merely for convenience; and our existence, a matter of brief span, is followed by annihilation.

I need not go into the many implications in the idea that man is merely a social entity. If you are interested you can see for yourself its significance, and if you accept the idea that individuality is merely the product of environment, then your moral, social, and religious conceptions must necessarily undergo a complete change.

If, however, you accept the religious idea that there is some unseen, divine power which controls your destiny and so compels obedience, reverence, and worship, then you must also recognize the implications in this conception. From the deep acceptance of this divine power, there must follow a complete social and moral reorganization. This acceptance is based on faith, which must give birth to fear, though you cover up this fear by asserting that it is love. You accept this religious idea because in it there is the promise of personal immortality. Its morality is subtly based on self-perpetuation, on reward and punishment. In this conception there is also the idea of achievement, of egotistic pursuit and success. And, if you accept it, then you must seek guides, Masters, paths, disciplines, and perpetuate the many subtle forms of authority.

There are these two categories of thought, and they must inevitably come into acute conflict. Each one of us has to discover for himself if either of these seemingly contradictory conceptions of man is true; whether the individual is merely the result of environmental influences and of heredity, which develop certain peculiarities and characteristics, or whether there is some hidden power which is guiding, controlling, forcing man's destiny and fulfillment. Either you accept simultaneously both these conceptions though they are diametrically opposed to each other, or you make a choice between them, that is, a choice between regimentation of thought and expression of the individual, and the religious conception that some unseen intelligence is creating, guiding, and shaping man's future and his happiness—an idea based on faith, on craving for self-perpetuation which prevents true discernment. Now if you are indifferent to this idea, again your very indifference is but an indication of thoughtlessness, therefore a prejudice, preventing true comprehension.

Choice is based on like and dislike, on prejudice and tendencies, and so it loses all validity. Instead of belonging to either of these two groups, or being forced to make a choice, I say that there is a different approach to the comprehension of individuality, of man. This approach lies through direct discernment, through the proof of action, without violation of sanity and intelligence.

How are you, as individuals, going to discover whether man is divine in limitation or merely a plaything of social events? This problem loses its mere intellectual significance and becomes tremendously vital when you test it in action. Then, how is one to act? How is one to live?

If you accept the idea that you are merely a social entity, then action becomes seemingly simple; you are then trained through education, through subtle compulsion, and through the constant instilling of certain ideas to conform to a certain pattern of conduct, relationship. On the other hand, if you truly accepted the religious conception of some unseen power controlling and guiding your life, then your action would have a totally different significance from what it has now. Then you would have a different relationship, which is morality, with other individuals, with society;

and it would imply the cessation of wars, class distinction, exploitation.

But as this true relationship does not exist in the world, it is obvious that you are wholly uncertain about the real significance of individuality and of action. For, if you truly accepted the religious idea that you are guided by some supreme entity, then, perhaps, your moral and social action would be sane, balanced and intelligent; but as it is not, you obviously do not accept this idea, although you profess to accept it. Hence the many churches, with their various forms of exploitation. If you maintain that you are nothing but a social entity, then likewise there must be a complete change in your attitude and in your action. And this change has not taken place. All this indicates that you are in a state of lethargy and are only pursuing your own idiosyncrasies.

To be completely and vitally uncertain is essential in order to understand the process of individuality, to find out what is permanent, to discover that which is true. You have to find out for yourself whether you are in this state of complete uncertainty, neither accepting the individual as a social entity, with all its implications, nor accepting the individual as something supreme, as being divinely guided, with all the implications in this idea. Then alone there is a possibility of true discernment and comprehension.

If you are in this state, as most thoughtful people must be, not following any dogma, belief, or ideal, then you will perceive that to understand *what is*, you must know what you are. You cannot understand any other process—the world as society is a series of processes which are in a state of being born, of becoming—except the one which is focused in the individual as consciousness. If you can understand the process of consciousness, of individuality, then there is a possibility of comprehending the world and its events. Reality is to be discerned only in knowing and in understanding the transient process of the 'I'. If I can comprehend myself, what I am, how I have come into being, whether the 'I' is an identity in itself and what is the nature of its existence, then there is a possibility of comprehending the real, the true.

I will explain this process of the 'I', of individuality. There is energy which is unique to each individual, and which is without a beginning. This energy—please do not attribute to it any divinity or give to it a particular quality—in its process of self-acting development, creates its own substance or material, which is sensation, discernment, and consciousness. This is the abstract as consciousness. The actual is action. Of course, there is no such absolute division. Action proceeds from ignorance, which exists where there are prejudices, tendencies, cravings, that must result in sorrow. So existence becomes a conflict, a friction. That is, consciousness is both discernment and action. Through the constant interaction between those cravings, prejudices, tendencies, and the limitations which this action is creating, there arises friction, the 'I' process.

If you examine deeply, you will perceive that individuality is only a series of limitations, a series of accumulative actions, of hindrances, which give to consciousness the identity called the 'I'. The 'I' is only a series of memories, tendencies, which are born of craving, and action is that friction between craving and its object. If action is the result of a prejudice, a fear, of some belief, then that action produces further limitation. If you have been raised in a particular religious belief or if you have developed a particular tendency, it must create a resistance against the movement of life. These resistances, these self-protective, egotistic walls of security, give birth to the 'I' process, which is maintaining itself through its own activities.

To understand yourself, you must become conscious of this process of the building up of the 'I'. You will then discern that this process has no beginning, and yet by constant awareness and by right effort it can be brought to an end. The art of living is to bring this 'I' process to an end. It is an art that needs great discernment and right effort. We cannot understand any other process except that process which is consciousness, upon which depends individuality. By right effort, there is the discernment of the coming into being of the 'I' process, and by right effort there is the ending of that process. From this arises the bliss of reality, the beauty of life as eternal movement.

This you can prove to yourself, it does not demand any faith, nor does it depend upon any system of thought or of belief. Only, it demands an integrated awareness and right effort, which will dissolve the self-created illusions and limitations and thus bring about the bliss of reality.

Question: A genuine desire to spread happiness around and help to make of this world a nobler place for all to live in is guiding me in life and dictating my actions. This attitude makes me use the wealth and prestige I possess, not as a means of self-gratification, but merely as a sacred trust, and supplies an urge to life. What, fundamentally, is wrong in such an attitude, and am I guilty of exploiting my friends and fellow beings?

KRISHNAMURTI: Whether you are exploiting or not depends on what you mean by helping and spreading happiness. You can help another and so enslave him, or you can help another to comprehend himself and so to fulfill deeply. You can spread happiness by encouraging illusion, giving superficial comfort and security which appear to be lasting. Or you can help another to discern the many illusions in which he is caught; if you are capable of doing this, then you are not exploiting. But, in order not to exploit fundamentally, you must be free yourself from those illusions and comforts in which you or another is held. You must discern your own limitations before you can truly help another. Many people throughout the world earnestly desire to aid others, but this help generally consists in converting others to their own particular belief, system, or religion. It is but the substitution of one kind of prison for another. This exchange does not bring about comprehension but only creates greater confusion. In deeply comprehending oneself lies the bliss for which each individual is struggling and groping.

Question: Don't you think that it is necessary to go through the experience of exploitation in order to learn not to exploit, to acquire in order not to be acquisitive, and so on?

KRISHNAMURTI: It is a very comforting idea that you must first possess, and then learn not to acquire! Acquisition is a form of pleasure, and during its process, that is, while acquiring, gathering, there comes suffering, and in order to avoid it you begin to say to yourself, "I must not acquire." Not to be acquisitive becomes a new virtue, a new pleasure. But if you examine the desire that prompts you not to acquire, you will see that it is based on a deeper desire to protect yourself from pain. So you are really seeking pleasure, both in acquisitiveness and in nonacquisitiveness. Fundamentally, acquisitiveness and nonacquisitiveness are the same, as they both spring from the desire not to be involved in pain. Developing a particular quality merely creates a wall of self-protection, of resistance against the movement of life. In

this resistance, within these prison walls of self-protection, lies sorrow, confusion.

Now there is a different way of looking at this problem of opposites. It is to discern directly, to perceive integrally, that all tendencies and virtues hold within themselves their own opposites, and that to develop an opposite is to escape from actuality.

Would it be true to say that you must hate in order to love? This never happens in actuality. You love, and then because in your love there is possessiveness, there arise frustration, jealousy, and fear. This process awakens hatred. Then begins the conflict of opposites. If acquisitiveness in itself is ugly and evil, then why develop its opposite? Because you do not discern that it is ugly and evil, but you want to avoid the pain involved in it, you develop its opposite. All opposites must create conflict because they are essentially unintelligent. A man who is afraid develops bravery. This process of developing bravery is really an escape from fear, but if he discerns the cause of fear, fear will naturally cease. Why is he not capable of direct discernment? Because, if there is direct perception, there must be action, and in order to avoid action one develops the opposite and so establishes a series of subtle escapes.

Questions: As social entities we have various responsibilities, as workers, voters, and executive heads. At present the basis of most of these activities is class division, which has fostered a class consciousness. If we are to break down these barriers which are responsible for so much social and economic chaos, we at once become antisocial. What contribution have you to make toward the solution of this modern worldwide problem?

KRISHNAMURTI: Do you really think that it is antisocial to break away from this system of exploitation, of class consciousness, of competition? Surely not. One is afraid of creating chaos—as though there were not confusion now—in breaking away from this system of division and exploitation; but if there is discernment that exploitation is inherently wrong, then there is the awakening of true intelligence which alone can create order and the well-being of man. Now the existing system is based on individual security, the security and comfort that are implied in immortality and economic wellbeing. Surely it is this acquisitive existence that is antisocial and not the breaking away from a conception and a system that are essentially false and stupid. This system is creating great chaos, confusion, and is bringing about wars. Now we are antisocial through our acquisitive pursuits, whether it is the acquisitive pursuit of God or of wealth. Since we are caught up in this process of acquisition, whether it is of virtue or of power in society, since we are caught up in this machine which we have created, we must intelligently break away from it. Such an act of intelligence is not antisocial, it is an act of sanity and balance.

Question: Have you no use for public opinion? Is not mass psychology important for leaders of men?

KRISHNAMURTI: Public opinion is generally molded by the bias of leaders, and to allow oneself to be molded by that opinion is surely not intelligent. It is not spiritual, if you like to use that word. Take, for example, war. It is one thing to die for a cause, voluntarily, and it is quite another thing that a group of people or a set of leaders should send you to kill or be killed. Mob psychology is developed and is deliberately used for various purposes. In that there is no intelligence.

Question: All I gather from your writings and utterances is an insistence on self-denudation, the necessity of removing every emotional comfort and solace. As this leaves me no happier, in fact less happy than before, to me your teaching only carries a destructive note. What is its constructive side, if it has one?

KRISHNAMURTI: What do you mean by constructive help? To be told what to do? To be given a system? To have someone direct and guide you? To be told how to meditate, or what kind of discipline you should follow? Is this really constructive, or is it destructive of intelligence?

What is the motive which prompted this question? If you examine it, you will see that it is based on fear—fear of not realizing what is called happiness, truth, fear and distrust of one's own effort and of uncertainty. What you would call positive teaching is utterly destructive of intelligence, making you thoughtless and automatic. You want to be told what to think and how to act; but a teaching that insists that through your own ignorant action—ignorance being the lack of comprehension of oneself—you are increasing and perpetuating limitation and sorrow; such a teaching you call destructive. If you truly understand what I am saying, you will discern that it is not negative. On the contrary, you will see that it brings about tremendous self-reliance, and so gives you the strength of direct perception.

Question: What relation has memory to living?

KRISHNAMURTI: Memory acts as a resistance against the movement of life. Memory is but the many layers of self-protective responses against life. Thus action or experience, instead of liberating, creates further limitation and sorrow. These memories with their tendencies and cravings form consciousness, on which individuality is based. From this there arise division, conflict, and sorrow.

The present chaos, conflict, and misery can be understood and solved only when each individual discerns the process of ignorance which he is engendering through his own action. To bring about order and the well-being of man, each one, through his own right endeavor, has to discern this process and bring about its end. This demands an alertness of mind and right effort, not the following of a particular system of thought, nor the disciplining of the mind and heart, in order to gain that reality which cannot be described or conceived. Only when the cause of sorrow is dissolved is there the bliss of reality.

June 1, 1936

Second Talk in New York

In the midst of great confusion and strain, we are caught up in the struggle for success and security, and so have lost the deep feeling for life, the true sensibility which is the essence of understanding. We admit intellectually that there is exploitation, cruelty, but somehow there is not that comprehension which leads to drastic action and change. True and vital action can spring only from a comprehensive and intelligent view of life.

There is every conceivable form of exploitation in man's social, religious, and creative activities. We see man living on man, making others work for his own personal gain and advantage, buying and selling for his own benefit and ruthlessly seeking and establishing his own personal security. There are class distinctions with their antagonisms and hatreds. There are distinctions in work. One kind is regarded as superior and another inferior, one type is despised and another is praised. It is a system of competition and

ruthless elimination of those who are, perhaps, less cunning, less aggressive, and who have not had the fortunate opportunities of life.

We have racial pride and national prejudices which often lead us to war, with all its horrors and cruelties. And even the animals do not escape from the cruelties of man.

Then we have the exploitation by religions, with their cruelties, the competition between faiths, with their churches, gods, and temples. Each system of belief and faith is maintaining its own divine right, its own certainty to lead man to the highest, and the individual loses that true religious experience which is not encumbered with beliefs and dogmas of organized religion. There is systematized superstition in the name of reality, the instilling and maintaining of fear with its assertions and doctrines. Thus there is confusion of beliefs, ideals, and doctrines.

And, in the field of creative work, there is an immense gap between creative expression and the art of living. In that creative work there is personal ambition, self-conceit, and competition producing a superficial reaction which is often mistaken for creative expression and fulfillment.

In this civilization we are forced, whether we like it or not, by a system which each individual has helped to create, to live without deep fulfillment, and few escape from its cruelties. In every avenue of life there is confusion, misery, and everyone as a social and religious entity is caught up in this machine of exploitation and cruelty. Some are conscious of this process, with its sorrow, and although they recognize its ugliness, they continue in the old habits of thought and action, saying to themselves that they must perforce live in this world. There are others who are wholly unconscious of this system of misery.

When you begin to examine the various ideas that are put forth for the solution of man's misery, you will perceive that they divide themselves into two groups: one which maintains that there must be complete social reorganization of man, so that exploitation, acquisitiveness, and wars may cease; the other which asserts and lays emphasis on the volitional activities of man.

To lay emphasis on either is erroneous. Social reorganization is obviously necessary. But if you critically examine this idea of organizing man and his expression, you will perceive, if you are not carried away by its superficial assurances of immediate results of security and comfort, that in it there are many grave dangers. The mere creation of a new system can again become a prison in which man will be held, only by different dogmas, ideas, and creeds.

There are those who maintain that we must put bread first, and other things vital to man will then rightly follow. That is, they maintain that there must be control of environment and through this man will come to his true fulfillment. This exclusive emphasis on bread frustrates its own purpose, for man does not live by bread alone.

So then, which shall we emphasize, the inner or the outer? Shall we begin first from the outer, by controlling, directing, and dominating; or shall we lay the emphasis on the inner process of man? To emphasize the one or the other destroys its own end. To divide man into the outer and the inner is to prevent the true comprehension of man. To understand the problem of class distinction, wars, exploitation, cruelties, hatreds, acquisitiveness, we must discern man as a whole, and from that point of view consider his activities, desires, and fulfillment.

To regard man as merely the result of environment or of heredity, to lay emphasis only on bread and discard the inner process, or to concern oneself entirely with the inner and discard the outer, is wholly erroneous, and this must ever lead to confusion and misery. We have to comprehend man as an integral whole, not as an entity with separative functions—as those of a worker, a citizen or a spiritual being—but as an interdependent and interacting, complete being. We must have the insight to know that ignorance of our own being is the previous condition of all sorrow and conflict. As long as we do not comprehend ourselves—the hidden and the conscious—then whatever we may do, in whatever field of activity, we must inevitably create sorrow.

This comprehension of oneself—that is, of the process of the building up of the 'I', with its ignorance, tendencies, and cravings—must become actual and not remain theoretical. It can only become actual, real to you, if you discern and comprehend through experimentation that the process of ignorance can be brought to an end. With the cessation of ignorance—ignorance ever being the lack of comprehension of oneself and the 'I' process—there is reality and the bliss of enlightenment.

There are two kinds of experience, that of wish and that of actuality. But to experience the actual, the real, the experiences of wish must cease. The experience of wish is the mere continuance of separative self-consciousness and this prevents the comprehension of actuality. Although you may think that you are experiencing the actual, you are really experiencing your own wishes, and these wishes become so real, so concrete, so definite, that you take them for actuality. The experience of wish continues to create division and conflict.

What are the results of the experiences of wish? They are the coverings or masks that we have developed through our own volitional activities, based on fear and the search for security—the security of the here with its acquisitiveness or of the hereafter with its hopes and longings, the security of opinion, beliefs, and ideals. These masks and coverings, the product of the volitional activity of craving, continue the beginningless process of the 'I', that consciousness which we call individuality. As long as these masks exist there cannot be the comprehension of the real, the actual.

You will ask, "How can I live, exist, without any craving or wish?" You ask this question because for you this conception is only theoretical, and as you have not experimented, you have not proved to yourself its validity, its actuality. If you experiment, you will perceive that you can live without craving, integrally, completely, actually, and so comprehend reality, the beauty and the fullness of life. Whether you can live, work, and create without craving, wishing, can be discovered not by another for you but only by yourself.

So long as the process of re-forming the 'I' continues through the experiences of wish, there must be confusion, sorrow, and friction from which the mind tries to escape into the search after immortality or other comfort and security, thus engendering the process of exploitation. With the cessation of all experiences of wishing, which sustains separative individuality, there is the nameless, immeasurable reality, bliss. To be able to experience reality, you must be free of all the masks which you have developed in the struggle for acquisition, born of craving.

These masks do not conceal reality. We are apt to think that by getting rid of these masks we will find reality, or that by uncovering the many layers of want we will discover that which is hidden. Thus we are assuming that behind this ignorance, or in the depths of consciousness, or beyond this friction of will, of craving, lies reality. This consciousness of many masks, of many layers, does not conceal within itself reality. But as we begin to comprehend the process of development of these masks, these layers of consciousness, and as consciousness frees itself from its volitional growth, there is

reality. Our conception that man is divine but limited, that beauty is concealed by ugliness, wisdom buried under ignorance, supreme intelligence hiding in darkness, is utterly erroneous. In discerning how through this beginningless ignorance and its activities there has arisen the 'I' process and in bringing that process to an end, there is enlightenment. It is an experience of that which is immeasurable, which cannot be described, but *is*.

How is one to discern this beginningless ignorance with its volitional activities? How is one to bring about its end? How can one become deeply thoughtful, integrally aware of the process of consciousness with its many layers of tendencies, cravings, hatreds, and desires? Can any discipline or system help one to recognize and end this process of ignorance and sorrow?

By experiment you will perceive that no system, no guide, and no discipline can ever help you to discern this process or bring ignorance to an end. You need an eager, pliable mind, capable of direct discernment in which there is no choice. But as your mind is prejudiced, divided in itself, it is incapable of true discernment. As you are prejudiced you have to become aware of that fact before you can begin to discern what is actual and what is illusory. To discern, there must be awareness. You must become aware of the movement of your thought and its activity. Whatever you do, do it with the fullness of mind and you will perceive that in this awakening process, many hidden and subtle thoughts and cravings are revealed. When the mind is no longer bound by choice, there is the experience of actuality. For choice is based on wish, and where there is wish there cannot be discernment. By right effort of awakening interest, the beginningless process of ignorance, with its self-sustaining activities, is brought to an end. It is by right endeavor that the mind, freeing itself from its own self-created fears, tendencies, and cravings, is able to discern the real, the immeasurable.

Question: I have lost all the enthusiasm and zest in life that I once had. I have sufficient for my material needs, yet life is now to me a purposeless and empty shell, an aching existence which drags on and on. Would you put forward some thoughts which might possibly aid me in breaking through this sphere of apparently hopeless void?

KRISHNAMURTI: One loses enthusiasm or the zest for life when there is no fulfillment. As long as one is merely a slave to a system, or trained merely to fit into a particular social mold or to adjust oneself thoughtlessly to an established mode of conduct, there cannot be fulfillment. In merely responding to a reaction and thinking that it is the full expression of one's being, there must be frustration; and where there is frustration, there must be emptiness and suffering.

If one is deeply conscious of frustration, then there is some hope, for it creates such misery and discontent that one is forced to strip oneself of the many tendencies which one has developed through craving, and free oneself from the illusions and impositions of opinion. This demands right effort, for it is necessary to break away from the old, established custom of thought and action. Where there is frustration, there must be emptiness, an aching void and suffering; but to fulfill is arduous—it needs deep comprehension and an alert mind-heart.

Question: Is not desire for security rather a natural instinct, like that of self-protection in the presence of danger? How then can we get over it, and why should we try to?

KRISHNAMURTI: The search after security indicates frustration and the gnawing of constant fear. Intelligence, which has no concern with the conception of security, arranges the well-being of the whole and not merely of the particular. Now, each one is individually seeking his own security and is thus creating confusion and misery. Each one is concerned about himself, seeking his own individual security here and in the hereafter, and is thus ever coming into conflict with another who is also pursuing his own end. So there is constant friction, antagonism, hatred, and strife. Intelligence alone can arrange humanely the necessities of life for all.

This is actuality, and to experience it you must discern the true significance of security. If you consider it deeply, you will perceive that this idea of seeking security has no lasting value, here or in the hereafter. This has been proved over and over again during upheavals. But in spite of it, each one pursues his own security and so continues to live in constant fear and confusion. Where there is no search for security, there alone can be the bliss of the real.

Question: Example is said to be better than precept. Cannot the value of personal example to another be considerable, like your own?

KRISHNAMURTI: What is the motive that lies behind this question? Is it not that the questioner desires to follow an example, thinking that it may lead him to fulfillment? The following of another never leads to fulfillment. A violet can never become a rose, but the violet in itself can be a perfect flower. Being uncertain, one seeks certainty in the imitation of another. This produces fear, from which arise the delusion of shelter and comfort in another and the many false ideas of discipline, meditation, and the subjugation of oneself to an ideal. All this merely indicates the lack of comprehension of oneself, the perpetuating of ignorance. It is the root of sorrow, and instead of discerning the cause, you think that you can comprehend yourself through another. This looking to the example of another only leads to illusion and suffering.

As long as there is not the comprehension of oneself, there can be no fulfillment. Fulfillment is not a process of rationalization, nor the mere gathering of information, nor does it lie through another, however great. It is the fruition of deep comprehension of your own existence and actions.

Question: If reincarnation is a fact in nature—and also the idea that the ego reincarnates until it attains perfection—then doesn't the attainment of perfection or truth involve time?

KRISHNAMURTI: We often ask if reincarnation is a reality because we can find no intelligent happiness, no fulfillment of the individual in the present. If we are in conflict and misery and have no opportunity and hope in this life, we crave for a future life or fulfillment free from struggle and pain. This future state of bliss we like to call perfection.

To understand this question we must discover what the ego is. The ego is not something real in itself which, like the worm that goes from leaf to leaf, wanders from one existence to another, gathering experience and learning wisdom until it reaches the highest, which we imagine to be perfection. That conception is erroneous, it is merely an opinion and not an actuality. The actual process of the 'I', the ego, can be discerned in perceiving how through ignorance, tendencies, cravings, it is re-formed and its continuity reestablished at each moment. The will of craving is perpetuating itself through its own volitional activities. Through this action of ignorance and its self-sustaining process,

limitation as consciousness creates its own further limitation and sorrow. In this vicious circle all existence is caught.

Can this limitation, friction, this resistance against the movement of life known as the ego, ever be made perfect? Can craving become perfect? Surely selfishness cannot become nobler, purer selfishness; it must ever remain that which it is. This idea that through time the ego will become perfect is utterly false and erroneous.

Time is the result of those volitional activities of craving which bind and give a sense of continuity to life which is in reality ever in a state of being born, a state that has never been nor ever will be, but one that is ever becoming anew, ever in movement.

The point of vital importance is for each one to discover whether, through ignorance with its volitional activities, the process of the 'I' is perpetuating itself or not. If this self-sustained process continues, there cannot be that which is real, true. Only with the cessation of the will of craving with its experiences of wish, is there reality. This beginningless process of the 'I' with its self-active limitations cannot be proved. It must be discerned. It is not a faith but of deep comprehension, of integral awareness, of right effort to discern how craving creates its own limitation, and how any action born of craving must further engender friction, resistance, and sorrow.

Question: How does the psychoanalytic technique of dealing with fixations, inhibitions, and complexes strike you, and how would you deal with such cases?

KRISHNAMURTI: Can another free you from these limitations, or is it merely a process of substitution? The pursuit of the psychoanalyst has become a hobby of the well-to-do. (Laughter) Don't laugh, please. You may not go to a psychoanalyst but you go through the same process in a different way when you look to a religious organization, to a leader, or to some discipline to free you from fixations, inhibitions, and complexes. These methods may succeed in creating superficial effects, but they must inevitably develop new resistances against the movement of life. No person and no technique can really free one from these limitations. To experience that freedom one must comprehend life deeply and discern for oneself the process of creating and maintaining ignorance and illusion. This demands alertness and keen perception, not the mere acceptance of a technique. But as one is slothful, one depends on another for comprehension and thereby increases sorrow and confusion. The comprehension of this process of ignorance and its self-sustaining activities, of this consciousness focused in and perceptible only to the individual, can alone bring about deep, abiding bliss to man.

June 4, 1936

Eddington, Pennsylvania, 1936

✳

First Talk in Eddington

It is important to ask yourself why you come to these meetings, and what it is that you are seeking. Unless you know that for yourself, you are apt to be greatly confused in trying to solve the many problems and issues which confront us all.

To comprehend the motive and the object of your search, if you are seeking anything at all, you must know whether you regard life from the mechanistic point of view, or from the point of view of belief in the other world, which is called religious. Most people will tell you that they are working for a world in which exploitation of man by man, with its cruelties, wars, and appalling miseries, will cease. While they will all agree as to this ultimate object, some will accept the mechanistic, and others the religious view of life.

The mechanistic view of life is that as man is merely the product of environment and of various reactions, perceptible only to the senses, the environment and reactions should be controlled by a rationalized system which will allow the individual to function only within its frame. Please comprehend the full significance of this mechanistic point of view of life. It conceives no supreme, transcendental entity, nothing that has a continuity; this view of life admits no survival of any kind after death; life is but a brief span leading to annihilation. As man is noth-ing but the result of environmental reactions, concerned with the pursuit of his own egotistic security, he has helped to create a system of exploitation, cruelty, and war. So his activities must be shaped and guided by changing and controlling the environment.

The mechanistic view of life deprives man of the true experience of reality. This is not some fantastic, imaginative experience, but that which comes into being when the mind is free of all the encumbrances of fear, dogma, belief, and those psychological diseases resulting from restrictions and limitations, which we accept in our search for self-protection, security, and comfort.

Then there are those who accept the view that man is essentially divine, that his destiny is controlled and guided by some supreme intelligence. These assert that they are seeking God, perfection, liberation, happiness, a state of being in which all subjective conflict has ceased. Their belief in a supreme entity, who is guiding man's destiny, is based on faith. They will say this transcendental entity or supreme intelligence has created the world and that the 'I', the ego, the individual, is something permanent in itself and has an eternal quality.

If you think critically about this, you will perceive that this conception, based on faith, has led man away from this world into a world of conjectures, hopes, and idealism, thus aiding him to escape from conflict and confusion. This attitude of otherworldliness, based on faith and so on fear, has developed beliefs, dogmas, ceremonies, and has encouraged a morality of individual security, resulting in a system of escapes from this world of pain and conflict; it has brought about a division between the actual and the ideal, the here and the hereafter, earth and heaven, the inner and the outer. And out of this conception there has developed a morality based on fear, on acquisitiveness, on individual security and comfort here and in the hereafter, and on a series of immoral, hypocritical, and unhealthy values that are utterly at variance with life. This conception of life with its escapes, based on faith, also deprives man of the true experience of reality.

So, either one is bound to faith, with its fears, organized beliefs, and disciplines; or, rejecting faith, one accepts the mechanistic view of life, with its doctrines, its rationalized beliefs, and conformity to a pattern of thought and conduct.

Most people belong to one of these two groups, to one of these opposites. Opposites can never be true; and if neither of them is true, how is one to understand life, its values, its morality, and the deep significance which one feels it has?

There is a different way of looking at life—not from the point of view of the opposites, of faith and of science, of fear and of the mechanical—and that is to comprehend life, not as manifested in the universe, but as a process focused in each individual. That is, each one has to discern the process of becoming and the process of apparently ceasing, of being born and of dying. This process alone is wholly perceptible to the individual as consciousness. Please see this point clearly. The process that is at work in the universe or in another individual cannot be discerned except as it is focused in you, the individual.

The inclination to accept the mechanistic view of life, or to embrace the security and comfort that faith offers, does not lead to true discernment of *what is*. Reality is to be comprehended only through the 'I' process, as consciousness, from which arises individuality. That is, one has to understand the process of one's own becoming, which involves intelligence, an acute discernment, a constant awareness. In understanding oneself integrally there comes the possibility of having true life values, of true relationship with other individuals, with society.

To belong to either of the two opposing groups of thought I have mentioned will only lead ultimately to greater confusion and misery. All opposites impede discernment. To discern *what is*, one must comprehend oneself, and to do this, one must pierce through all those encumbrances and limitations produced by the mechanistic view of life or by faith; then only is it possible to discern sanely, without violence, the 'I' process as consciousness from which arises individuality.

All things come into being through the process of energy, which is unique to each individual. You and I are the results of that energy which in the course of its development creates those prejudices, tendencies, and cravings that make each individual unique. Now, this process which is without a beginning, in its movement, in its action, becomes consciousness through sensation, perception, and discernment. This consciousness is perceptible to the senses as individuality. Its action is born of ignorance which is friction. The energy which is unique to each individual is not to be glorified.

Of this process of perpetuating ignorance as consciousness, perceptible to sense as individuality, you must become aware, so that to you it becomes an actuality and no longer a theory. Then only will there be a fundamental change of values which alone will bring about true relationship of the individual to his environment, to society. If you are able to discern this process of ignorance, which is without a beginning, and comprehend also that it can be brought to an end through the cessation of its own volitional activity, then you will perceive that you are entirely master of your destiny, utterly self-reliant and not dependent on circumstances or on faith for conduct and relationship.

To bring about this profound change of values and to establish the right relationship of the individual with society, you, the individual, must consciously free yourself from the mechanistic view of life, with its many implications and its structures of superficial adjustment. You must also be free from the encumbrances of faith with its fears, beliefs, and creeds.

Sometimes you think life is mechanical, and at other times when there is sorrow and confusion, you revert to faith, looking to a supreme being for guidance and help. You vacillate between the opposites, whereas only through comprehension of the illusion of the opposites can you free yourself from their limitations and encumbrances. You often imagine that you are free from them, but you can be radically free only when you fully comprehend the process of the building up of these limitations and of bringing them to an end. You cannot possibly have the comprehension of the real, of *what is*, as long as this beginningless process of ignorance is perpetuated. When this process, sustaining itself through its own volitional activities of craving, ceases, there is that which may be called reality, truth, bliss.

To understand life and to have true values, you must perceive how you are held by the opposites, and before rejecting them, you must discern their deep significance. And in the very process of freeing yourself from

them, there is born the comprehension of beginningless ignorance, which creates false values and so establishes false relationship between the individual and his environment, bringing about confusion, fear, and sorrow.

To comprehend confusion and sorrow, you, the individual, must discern your own process of becoming, through intensity of thought and integral awareness. This does not mean that you must withdraw from the world: on the contrary, it involves the comprehension of the numerous false values of the world, and being free from them. You yourself have created these values, and only through constant alertness and discernment can this process of ignorance be brought to an end.

Question: Is there not the possibility that awareness, which demands constant occupation with one's own thoughts and feelings, might produce an indifferent attitude towards others? Will it teach one sympathy, which is a sensibility to the suffering of others?

KRISHNAMURTI: Awareness is not occupation with one's own thoughts and feelings. Such occupation, which is introspection, objectifies action and calculates the results of an act. In that there can be no sympathy, nor the fullness of being. Each one is so occupied with himself, with his own psychological needs, his own security, that he becomes incapable of sympathy.

Now awareness is not this. Awareness is discernment, without judgment, of the process of creating self-protecting walls and limitations behind which the mind takes shelter and comfort. Take, for example, the question of faith, with its fear and hope. Faith gives you comfort, a solace in misfortune or sorrow. On faith you have built up a system of compulsion, discipline, a set of false values. Behind the protective wall of faith you take shelter, and that wall has prevented love, sympathy, and kindliness because your occupation has been with yourselves, with your own salvation, with your own well-being here and in the hereafter.

If you begin to be aware, to discern how you have created this process through fear, how you are constantly taking shelter, whenever there is any reaction, behind these ideals, concepts, and values, then you will perceive that awareness is not occupation with your own thoughts and feelings, but the deep comprehension of the folly of creating these values behind which the mind takes shelter.

Most of us are unconscious that we are following a pattern, an ideal, and that it is guiding us through life. We accept and follow an ideal because we think that it will help us to wade through the confusion of existence. With that we are occupied rather than in comprehending the whole process of life itself. We are therefore unconscious of this constant adjustment to an ideal and never question why it exists; but if we were to examine critically, we should see that an ideal is but a means of escape from actuality, and that in conforming ourselves to an ideal, we are allowing ourselves to become more and more restricted, confused, and sorrow laden. In comprehending the actual, with its sufferings, acquisitiveness, cruelties, and in eliminating them, there is true sympathy, affection. This awareness is not occupation with one's own thoughts and feelings, but a constant discernment, freed from choice, of what is true. All choice is based on tendency, craving, and ignorance, which prevents true discernment. If choice exists, there cannot be awareness.

Question: By intelligent observation of the lives of other people, one can often draw valuable conclusions for oneself. What value do you think such vicarious experience has?

KRISHNAMURTI: Fundamentally, vicarious experience cannot have integral value. There is only that process of perpetuating ignorance as focused in each one, and it is only through the comprehension of this process that one can understand life, not through a bypath—the experience of another. Through the bypath, that is, the following of another or accepting the wisdom of another, there cannot be fulfillment.

Question: Assuming that we usually act in response to some mental bias or some emotional stress, is there any technique by which we may become conscious of such bias or stress at the moment of action, before we have actually performed the action?

KRISHNAMURTI: In other words, you are seeking a method, a system, which will enable you to keep awake at the moment of action. System and action cannot exist together, they kill each other. You are asking me, "Can I take a sedative and yet be awake at the moment of action?" How can a system keep you awake, or anything else except your own intensity of interest, the necessity of keeping awake? Please see the significance of this question. If you are aware that your mind is biased, then you do not want any discipline or system or mode of conduct. Your very discernment of a prejudice burns away that prejudice, and you are able to act sanely and clearly. But because you do not perceive a bias, which causes suffering, you hope to rid yourself of sorrow by following a system, which is but the development of another bias, and this new bias you call the process of keeping awake, becoming conscious. The search for a system merely indicates a sluggish mind, and the following of a system encourages you to act automatically, destroying intelligence. The so-called religious teachers have given you systems. You think that by following a new system, you will train the mind to discern and accept new values. When you succeed in doing this, what you have really done is to deaden the mind, put it to sleep, and this you mistake for happiness, peace.

One listens to all this, and yet there remains a gap between everyday life and the pursuit of the real. This gap exists because change involves not only physical discomfort but mental uncertainty, and we dislike to be uncertain. Because this uncertainty creates disturbance, we postpone change, thus exaggerating the gap. So we go on creating conflict and misery, from which we desire to escape. We then accept either the mechanistic view of life or that of faith, and so escape from actuality. The gap between ourselves and the real is bridged only when we see the absolute necessity for cessation from all escapes and hence the necessity for integral action, out of which is born true human relationship with individuals, with society.

June 12, 1936

Second Talk in Eddington

Question: What is wrong with one's relationship to another when that which is free living to oneself seems to be false living to another, and causes the other deep suffering while one is oneself serene? Is this a lack of true understanding on one's own part, and therefore a lack of sympathy?

KRISHNAMURTI: It all depends on what you call free living. If you are obsessed by an ideal and follow it ruthlessly without deeply considering its integral significance, you are not fulfilling, and you are therefore creating suffering for another and for yourself. Through your own lack of balance, you create disharmony. But if you are truly fulfilling, that is, living in true values, then although that fulfillment may bring about antagonism and conflict, you will truly help the world. But one has to be aware, extremely alert, to see whether one is merely living according to an ideal, principle, or standard, which indicates the lack of real understanding of the present and an escape from actuality. This escape, this imitation leading to frustration, is the true cause of conflict and suffering.

Question: How can I prevent interference with what I think is right action without causing unhappiness to others?

KRISHNAMURTI: If you merely consider not causing unhappiness to others and try to mold your life according to that idea, then you are not acting truly. But if you are freeing yourself from the many subtle layers of egotism, then your action, though it may cause unhappiness, is that of fulfillment.

Question: Morality and ethics, though variable factors, have throughout the ages supplied the motives for conduct, as for instance, the ideal of Christian charity, or Hindu renunciation. Devoid of this basis, how can we live useful and happy lives?

KRISHNAMURTI: There is the morality of the ideal and that of the actual. The ideal is to love one another, not to kill, not to exploit, and so on. But in actuality, our conduct is based on a different conception. The ethic of our everyday existence, the morality of our social contacts, is based fundamentally on egotism, on acquisitiveness, on fear, on self-protectiveness.

As long as these exist, how can there be true morality, true relationship of the individual with his environment, with society? As long as each one is isolating himself through fear, acquisitiveness, egotistic cravings, beliefs, and ideals, how can there be true relationship with another?

The everyday morality is really immorality, and the world is caught up in this immorality. Various forms of acquisitiveness, exploitation, and killing are honored by governments and by religious organizations, and are the basis of accepted morality. In all this there is no love but only fear, which is covered over by the constant repetition of idealistic words that hinder discernment. To be truly moral, that is, to have true relationship with another, with society, the immorality of the world must cease. This immorality has been created through the self-protective cravings and efforts of each individual.

Now, you will ask how one can live without craving, without acquisitiveness. If you deeply think out the significance of freedom from acquisitiveness, if you experiment with it, then you will see for yourself that you can live in the world without being of the world.

Question: In the book entitled The Initiate in the Dark Cycle *it is stated that what you are teaching is Advaitism, which is a philosophy only for yogis and* chelas, *and dangerous for the average individual. What have you to say about this?*

KRISHNAMURTI: Surely, if I considered that what I am saying is dangerous for the average person, I wouldn't talk. So, it is for you to consider if what I say is dangerous.

People who write books of this kind are consciously or unconsciously exploiting others. They have axes of their own to grind, and having committed themselves to a certain system, they bring in the authority of a Master, of tradition, of superstition, of churches, which generally controls the activities of an individual.

What is there in what I am saying that is so difficult or dangerous for the average man? I say that to know love, kindliness, considerateness, there cannot be egotism. There must not be subtle escapes from the actual, through idealism. I say that authority is pernicious, not only the authority imposed by another, but also that which is unconsciously developed through the accumulation of self-protective memories, the authority of the ego. I say that you cannot follow another to comprehend reality. Surely, all this is not dangerous to the individual, but it is dangerous to the man who is committed to an organization and desires to maintain it, to the man who desires adulation, popularity, and power. What I say about nationalism and class distinction is dangerous to the man who benefits by their cruelties and degradation. Comprehension, enlightenment, is dangerous to the man who subtly or grossly enjoys the benefits of exploitation, authority, fear.

Question: Do you discard every system of philosophy, even the Vedanta which teaches renunciation?

KRISHNAMURTI: You must ask yourself why you need a system, not why I discard it. You think that systems help the individual to unfold, to fulfill, to comprehend. How can a system or a technique ever give you enlightenment? Enlightenment comes about through one's own right effort, through one's own discernment of the process of ignorance. To discern, the mind must be unprejudiced; but now, as the mind is prejudiced and cannot discern, surely no system can free it from prejudice. All that a system can tell you is to have no prejudices, or it can indicate various kinds of prejudices, but it is you who have to make the effort to be free from them.

There is no such thing as renunciation. When you comprehend right values of life, the idea of renunciation has no meaning.

When you do not comprehend right values there is fear, and then there is the hope of freeing yourself from it through renunciation. Enlightenment does not come through renunciation.

You think that by going away from actuality, from everyday existence, you are going to find truth. On the contrary, you will find reality only through everyday life, through human contacts, through social relationships, and through the way of thought and love.

Question: What is your idea of meditation?

KRISHNAMURTI: What is called meditation, as practiced by most people, is concentration on an idea and self-control. This concentration helps to develop a strong memory of some principle that guides and controls everyday thought and conduct. This conformity to a principle, to an ideal, is but an escape from actuality, the lack of discernment of the adequate cause of suffering. The man who seeks reality through renunciation, through meditation, through any system, is caught in the process of acquisition, and that which can be acquired is not true.

Meditation is not a withdrawal from life. It is not concentration. Meditation is the constant discernment of what is true in the actions, reactions, and provocations of life. To discern the true cause of struggle, cruelty, and misery is true meditation. This needs alertness, deep awareness. In this awareness, in the course of deep discernment of right values, there comes the comprehension of reality, bliss.

June 14, 1936

Third Talk in Eddington

I am going to sum up what I have been saying during the talks and discussions that we have had here. I need not go into details,

or point out the many implications, but these ideas, when thought over deeply, will reveal to you their detailed significance.

We are all seeking to live without confusion and sorrow and to free ourselves from the struggle, not only with our neighbors, family, and friends, but especially with ourselves, with the conceptions of right and wrong, false and true, good and evil. There is not only the conflict of our relationship with environment, but also the conflict within us which inevitably reflects itself in social morality.

Of course, there are those brutal and stupid exceptions who are wholly at ease; or, fearful of their own personal safety, live without thought and consideration. Their minds are so padded, so invulnerable, that they refuse to be shaken by doubt or inquiry. They do not allow themselves to think; or if they do, their thoughts run along traditional lines. They have their own reward.

We are concerned, however, with those who are seriously attempting to comprehend life, with its miseries and apparently ceaseless conflict. We are concerned with those who, deeply realizing their environment, seek its true significance, and the cause of their suffering, of their transient joys. In their search they have become entangled, either in the mechanistic explanation of life, or in the explanations of faith, of belief. In these opposite explanations, mind has become involved and entrammeled.

The mechanistic view of life, rejecting everything that is not perceptible to the senses, maintains that man is a mere creature of reactions; that the mechanism of his being is kept going, as it were, by a series of reactions, not by force or energy capable in itself of bringing about action; that his development, his ideas and conceptions and his emotions are merely the result of outward impacts; that the adequate cause of each happening is simply a series of antecedent happenings. And from this it is argued that by controlling the happenings and man's reactions to these through the regimentation of his thought and action and through propaganda, he will be enabled to establish right relationship with his environment. That is, the regimentation and control of his various reactions will bring about events that will give man happiness.

Opposed to this stands faith. This view maintains that the adequate cause of man's existence is universal force, a force in itself divine, imperceptible to the senses. This transcendental force, this superintelligence, is ever guiding, watching, and it decrees that nothing shall ever take place without its being cognizant of the happening. From this, naturally, there arises the idea of predestination. If there is superintelligence watching over you and guiding your actions, then you, the individual, have no great responsibility in life. Your destiny is predetermined, and so there can be no free will. If there is no free will, the idea of the soul and its immortality has no meaning. If that is so, then there is no reality or God or universal force. Faith destroys its own end.

Between these two opposites, the mechanistic view of life and that of faith, one vacillates, according to the personal inclination of the moment. Dependence on faith at one moment and at another on its opposite has added to our confusion and sorrow.

Now, I say that there is another way of regarding our existence and of truly comprehending it. Actuality is that which one experiences oneself. It has nothing to do with opposites, either with faith or with the rejection of that which is imperceptible to the senses. All existence is a process of energy which is both conditioned and conditioning. This energy, in its self-acting, self-sustaining development, creates its own substancematerial, sensation, perception, choice, and consciousness, from which arises individuality. This energy is unique to each in-

dividual, to each process which is beginningless.

Individuality or consciousness is the result of the process of this unique energy. With consciousness are compounded ignorance and craving. This consciousness maintains itself by its own volitional activities born of ignorance, tendencies , craving. This self-sustaining process of individuality, which is unique, which has no beginning, is not, as it were, given an impetus, pushed forward, by another force or energy. It is a process which, at all times, is self-active through its own volitional demands, cravings, activities.

If you think this out very carefully and deeply, you will see that this has a totally different significance from the mechanistic view of life or that of faith. Those are theories based on the opposites, whereas that which I have explained is not of the opposites. You, as an individual, have to discover for yourself what is the true cause of existence, of suffering and its apparent continuance. As I said, actuality is that which one experiences oneself; one cannot experience a theory, an explanation. By allowing the mind to accept a theory and to be trained according to that conception, one may have a series of experiences, but they will not be experiences of actuality. Belief or faith has given a certain training to the mind, and experiences based on it are not of actuality, being the product of presuppositions and convictions. Such experiences are merely the result of wish-fulfillment.

To comprehend actuality, or to experience reality, there must be discernment. Discernment is that state of integrated thoughtemotion in which all craving, choice has ceased; it is not a state induced through mere denial and suppression. All want, craving, perverts discernment, even the craving for reality. Want conditions thought-emotion and so makes it incapable of direct discernment. Hence, if the mind is prejudiced by any theory or explanation, or if it is caught in any belief, such as that of any religion or philosophy, it is utterly incapable of discernment.

So, one has to consider first, what are those tendencies and cravings which continue and perpetuate the 'I' process. This deep consideration of the process of want and its results, this constant awareness in action, liberates the mind-heart from want, from those self-protective resistances that it has created for itself as security and comfort. For all want acts as an impediment to discernment; all craving distorts perception.

All craving, and any experience born from it, makes up the self-sustaining process of the 'I'. This 'I' process with its wants and tendencies creates fear, and from this there arises the acceptance of comfort and security which authority offers. There are various kinds of authority. There is the authority of the outer, the authority of an ideal, and the authority of experience or memory.

The authority of the outer is born of fear which makes the mind-heart accept the compulsion of opinion, whether of the neighbor or of the leader, and the assertions of organized belief, called religion, with its systems and dogmas. These assertions and beliefs become part of one's being, and consciously or otherwise one's thoughts and actions are adjusting themselves to the pattern established by authority.

Then there is the authority of an ideal, which prevents true self-reliance, born of comprehension of actuality. As you cannot understand this struggle and misery, you look to an ideal, to a concept, to guide you across this sea of confusion and suffering. If you carefully examine this want you will see that it is only an escape from actuality, from the conflict of the present. To escape from reality, from the now, you have the authority of an ideal, which becomes sacred through time and tradition. The authority of an ideal prevents the comprehension of the actual.

Then there is the authority of experience and memory. We are but the result of the process of time. Each one draws inspiration, guidance, and comprehension from the past; the past acts as a background, the past is the storehouse of experience, and the mind has become merely a record of the various lessons of experience. These experiences, with their lessons, have become memories, and these memories have become self-protective warnings. If you deeply examine the so-called lessons gained from experiences, you will see that they are merely the cunning desire for self-protection which guides you in the present. This cunning self-protective guidance prevents the comprehension of the living present. Thus experience adds to the storehouse more lessons, more memories, cunning knowledge by which to guide yourself in times of tribulation. But if you examine this so-called knowledge, you will see that it is nothing but self-protective memories stored up for the future and which become the authority that guides and directs action.

So, through craving, through want, there is engendered fear, and from this there arises the search for comfort and security found in the authority of the outer, the authority of the ideal, and the authority of experience. This authority, in its various forms, maintains the 'I' process, which is based on fear. Consider your thoughts and activities and the way of your morality, and you will see that they are based on self-protective fear, with its subtle, comforting authorities. Thus, action born of fear is ever limiting itself, and so the 'I' process is self-sustaining, through its own volitional activities.

To put it differently, there is the will of want, which is effort, and the will of comprehension, which is discernment. The will of want is ever in search of reward, of gain, and so it creates its own fears. On this is based social morality, and spiritual aspiration is but the attempt to establish protective relationship with the highest. The individual is the expression of the will of want and in the process of its activity, want is creating its own conflict and sorrow. From this the individual tries to escape into idealism, into illusions, into explanations, and so still maintains the process of the 'I'. The will of comprehension comes into being when there is the cessation of want with its ever-recurring experiences.

If there is right comprehension of the fact that there cannot be true discernment as long as the will of want continues, this very comprehension brings the 'I' process to an end. There is not another or higher 'I' to bring this 'I' process to an end; no environment and no divinity can bring this 'I' process to an end. But the very perception of the 'I' process itself, the very discernment of its folly, of its transient nature, brings it to an end.

The 'I' process is self-sustaining, self-active through its own ignorance, tendencies, cravings. It has to bring itself to an end through the cessation of its own volitional wants. If you deeply understand the significance of this whole conception of the 'I', then you will see that you are not the mere environment, opinion, or chance, but the creator, the originator of action. You create your own prison of sorrow and conflict. Through the cessation of your own volitional activities, there is reality, bliss.

Question: You have said that to comprehend the process of the 'I', strenuous effort is required. How are we to understand your repeated statement to the effect that effort defeats awareness?

KRISHNAMURTI: Where there is the effort of want, there is choice, which must be based on prejudice, on bias. Awareness is not born of choice, it comes into being when there is the perception of the transiency of the will of choice or the will of want.

By constant thoughtfulness and eager interest, the will of want is comprehended and there comes into being the will of comprehension. Where there is the will of want, there must be wrong effort, that effort which must ever produce confusion, limitation, and increase sorrow. Awareness is constant discernment of what is true. Sorrow, and the inquiry into its true cause, not the theoretical but the actual inquiry through experimentation and action, will bring about this awakened pliability of mind-heart. There is no one who does not suffer. He who suffers makes an effort to escape from actuality, and that escape only increases sorrow. But if through silent observation and patience, he discerns the true cause of suffering, that perception itself dissolves the very cause of suffering.

Question: Are you still as uncompromising as ever in your attitude towards ceremonies and the Theosophical Society?

KRISHNAMURTI: Once you see an act to be wholly foolish, you do not revert to it. If you perceive deeply, as I did, the utter folly of ceremonies, then it can never again have any sway over you. No opinion, though it be of the many, no authority, though it be of tradition or of circumstances, can persuade differently one who has discerned its valuelessness. But as long as one does not see its significance completely, there is a going back to it. It is the same with regard to the Theosophical Society. The idea of organized belief, with its authorities, with its propaganda, with its conversion and exploitation, is to me fundamentally evil.

It is not important what I think about the Theosophical Society. What is important is that you shall find out for yourself what is true, what is the actual, not what you want the actual to be; and to comprehend the actual, the real, the true, without any doubt, you must come to it completely denuded of all want, of all desire for security or comfort. Then only is there a possibility of discerning that which is. But as most people are conditioned by want, by craving for security, for comfort, here and in the hereafter, they are utterly incapable of true perception.

Before you can understand what is true, either in the teachings of the Theosophical Society or of any other organization, you must first consider whether you are free from want. If you are not, these organizations, with their beliefs, will become the means of exploiting you. If you merely consider their teachings, then you will be lost in opinions, in explanations. So first begin to discern for yourself the process of craving which distorts perception and maintains the 'I' process, and nourishes fear. Then these systems, these organizations, with their beliefs, threats, and ceremonies, will have no significance at all.

Unfortunately we do not begin fundamentally. We think that systems and organizations are going to aid us in getting rid of our prejudices, sorrows, and conflicts. We think that they will free us from our limitations, and so, through them, we hope to understand reality. This has never happened, nor ever will. No belief or organization can ever set man free from want, with its fears and agonies.

Question: What do you think will become of your soul after the body dies?

KRISHNAMURTI: If the questioner examines the motive which prompted his question, he will see that it is fear. There is no fulfillment, no happiness, in the present, so he demands a future life of happiness and opportunity. In other words, the 'I' is asking itself whether it will continue. To understand the significance of its desire for continuance, you must understand what the 'I' is.

As I have tried to explain, faith destroys its own idea of soul. Faith maintains that there is a universal force, a supreme entity outside of man, directing, guiding man's existence and determining his future. This conception, if you think it out fully, banishes the idea of the soul. If there is no soul, then you turn to the mechanistic view of life and thereby you are merely caught up in the opposites. Truth does not exist in the opposites. If you fully comprehended the significance of the opposites, with their implications, you would then discern the true process of the 'I'. Then you would see that it is a process of want, conceiving itself in fear, thus sustaining itself through itself. This fear prompts the 'I' to ask itself if it has a continuance, if it shall live after the death of the body. The real question then is whether this limitation, the 'I', the ego, passing through many experiences and gathering their lessons, finally becomes perfect. Can selfishness ever become perfect through time, through experience? The 'I' can become bigger, more expanded, more rich in selfishness, in limitation, taking to itself other units of limitation and selfishness. But surely this process must ever remain the 'I' process, however expanded and glorified.

Whether this process continues or comes to an end depends on the comprehension of each individual. When you deeply discern that the 'I' process is maintaining itself through its own limitations, its own volitional activities of craving, then your action, your morality, your whole attitude towards life undergoes a fundamental change. In that there is reality, bliss.

I can give explanations of the cause of existence and of sorrow. But a man who seeks an explanation will not discern reality. Definitions and explanations act merely as a cloud that darkens perception. This 'I' process, about which I have spoken, can be to you but a theory. To discern its actuality you must experience it. To experience this, you must consider it critically, analyze it and experiment with it. The intelligent comprehension of it will alone bring about right action.

June 16, 1936

Ommen, Holland, 1936

✳

First Talk at Ommen

Friends,

I am very glad to see you all here after many years, and I hope this camp will be of some definite help to each one of you. I hope too that you will make every possible effort to understand what I shall try to explain, and carry that comprehension into action.

I should like you to consider what I say without prejudice, without those instinctive reactions that hinder clear and true thinking.

We are not as yet a select body of people who are outside this conflicting world. We are part of it, with its confusion, misery, uncertainty, with its opposing political groups, with its racial and national hatreds, with its wars and cruelties. We are not, as yet, a separate group, nor are we definitely active individuals who, with deep comprehension, are against this present civilization. We are here to understand for ourselves that process of consciousness focused in each individual, and, in so doing, we shall inevitably put away the false values that have become guiding principles throughout the world.

Though you as an individual belonging to a certain class or nation and holding certain beliefs may not be involved in these hatreds and conflicts—you may have by some misfortune protected yourself with different forms of security—yet you must have a definite attitude towards this civilization with its political, social, aesthetic, and religious activities. This attitude leading to action must be the comprehension of the process of individual consciousness.

The emphasis on the comprehension of individual consciousness is not to be taken as a further encouragement of self-centeredness and the narrowing down of comprehensive action. It is only through understanding the process of individual consciousness that there can be spontaneous and true action, without creating or further increasing sorrow and conflict. Please try to understand this point fully. When I talk about individual consciousness, I do not mean that process of introspection and self-analysis which gradually limits all activity. To bring about the plenitude of action there must be the comprehension of the process of individuality. I am not concerned with individual or collective progress or with mass activity, but only with right comprehension which will bring about right attitude and action towards work, towards the neighbor, towards the whole of society. So we must deeply comprehend the process of individuality with its consciousness. We must be able to discern in ourselves comprehensively the influence of the mass through traditions, racial prejudices, ideals, and beliefs to which we have surrendered ourselves, consciously or unconsciously. As long as these dominate us, we, as individuals, are not capable of clear, direct, simple, and comprehensive action. So my emphasis on individuality is not to be mistaken as an encouragement to selfish self-expression, nor is it to be understood as a collective acquiescence in an idea or a principle. It is not to be used as an excuse for subjugating oneself to a group of people or to a set of leaders. It is to bring about the right comprehension of the process of individual consciousness, which alone can give rise to spontaneous and true action.

To understand this process of individuality there must be the urge to know, not to speculate, not to dream.

This comprehension of the process of individuality is not to be confounded with the acceptance of beliefs or of faith, or the giving of oneself over to logical conclusions and definitions. To know really, there must be no inclination to be satisfied by the immediate superficial solution of problems. Many people think that by mere economic rearrangement, most human problems will be solved. Or again, many are easily satisfied with the explanations concerning the hereafter, or with the belief in reincarnation, and so on. But this is not knowledge, this is not comprehension, this is merely a dope that satisfies and dulls the sorrowing mind-heart. To know, to comprehend, there must be will, there must be persistence, there must be a continual and essential curiosity.

So, then, what is individuality? Please understand that I am not laying emphasis on egotism or on your getting rid of it. But when you understand for yourself the process of the 'I', then there is a possibility of bringing it to an end. To comprehend this process you must begin fundamentally. Is the so-called soul real or an illusion, is it unique? Does it exist apart and exert its influence over the physiological or psychological being? Shall we, by studying the tissues and organic fluids, know what is thought, what is

mind, what is that consciousness which is hidden in living matter? By studying his sociological behavior shall we know what man is? Economists and physicists have left all this aside, and we, as individuals, we who are suffering, must go into this question deeply and sincerely. As we are dealing with ourselves we need great persistence, right effort, and patience to comprehend ourselves. Physicists, economists, sociologists may give us theories, systems, and techniques, but we ourselves have to make the right efforts to understand the process of our consciousness, to penetrate through the many illusions to reality.

Philosophers have given out certain theories and concepts regarding consciousness and individuality. There are many conflicting views, beliefs, and assertions concerning reality. Each one of us through introspection and observation realizes that there is a living reality concealed in matter, but it plays very little part in our daily life. It is denied in our activities, in our everyday conduct. Because we have built up a series of walls of self-protective memories, it has become almost impossible to know what is the real. As I said, there are many beliefs, many theories, many assertions about individuality—its processes, its consciousness and its continuity—and the choice of what is true among these varied opinions and beliefs is left to you. Choice is left to those who are not utterly in subjugation to the authority of tradition, belief, or ideal, and to those who have not committed themselves intellectually or emotionally to faith.

How can you choose what is true among these contradictions? Is the comprehension of truth a question of choice involving the study of various theories, arguments, and logical conclusions which demand only intellectual effort? Will this way lead us anywhere? Perhaps to intellectual argumentation—but a man who is suffering desires to know, and to him concepts and theories are utterly useless. Or is there another way, a choiceless perception? It is absolutely essential for our well-being, for our action and fulfillment, to understand what is individuality. You go to religious leaders, psychologists, and perhaps to scientists, and study and experiment with their theories and conclusions. You may go from one specialist to another, trying, according to your pleasure, their methods, but suffering still continues. What is one to do?

Action is vital, but not opinions and logical conclusions. You as individuals have to comprehend the process of consciousness through direct, choiceless discernment. The authority of ideal and of desire prevents and perverts true discernment. When there is want, when the mind is caught up in opposites, there cannot be discernment. Psychological reactions prevent true discernment. If we depend on choice, on the conflict of opposites, we shall ever create a duality in our actions, thus engendering sorrow.

So we have to discern for ourselves truth, through choiceless life or action. Discernment alone can end this self-poisoning process of suffering that is going on through the action of limitation.

Now to discern truth, thought must be unbiased, mind must be without want, choiceless. If you observe yourself in action you will see that your want, through the background of tradition, false values, and self-protective memories, renews each moment the 'I' process which impedes true discernment.

So there must be deep, choiceless perception to comprehend the process of consciousness. Such a necessity arises only when there is suffering. To discover the cause of suffering, mind must be acute, pliable, choiceless, not dulled by want nor subdued by theories. If there is no discernment of the process of individual consciousness, then action will ever create confusion, limitation, and so bring about suffering and conflict. As long as we are in this process, our inquiry should be concerned with the cause. But unfortunately most of us are seeking remedies. The comprehension of the cause of suffering brings about a choiceless change of will in the plenitude of our being. Then experience without its accumulative memories which impede comprehension and action has deep significance.

So true experience leads to the discernment of the process of consciousness which is individuality, and cannot intensify the individual consciousness. To discern deeply the cause of suffering, you cannot separate yourself from the world, from life, and contemplate consciousness apart, for only in the very process of living can you comprehend consciousness.

This deep discernment of choiceless life implies great alertness and right effort. I am going to explain what to me is consciousness from which arises individuality, but please bear this in mind—that it is not an actuality to you, it can only be a theory. To know its actuality your mind must be capable of discernment, of choiceless perception, free from the craving for comfort and security. It is not enough to be merely logical. You will know whether what I say is true only through your own experience, and to experience, the mind must be free of self-created barriers. It is most difficult to be vulnerable, so that the movement of life can be comprehended with a sensitive mind, able to discern that which is enduring and true. To understand the process of individuality you require great intelligence and not the intervention of intellect. To awaken that intelligence there must be the deep urge to know but not to speculate.

Please bear in mind that what to me is a certainty, a fact, must be to you a theory, and the mere repetition of my words does not constitute your knowledge and actuality; it can be but a hypothesis, nothing more. Only through experimentation and action can you discern for yourself its reality. Then it is of no person, neither yours nor mine.

Now, all life is energy; it is conditioning and conditioned, and this energy in its self-acting development creates its own material—the body with its cells and sensations, perception, discrimination, and consciousness. Both energy and forms of energy are ever intermingling, and this makes consciousness appear conceptual as well as actual. Individual consciousness is the result of ignorance, tendency, want, craving. This ignorance is without a beginning and is compounded with energy, which in its self-acting development is unique, and this is what gives uniqueness to individuality.

Ignorance has no beginning but it can be brought to an end. The very comprehension that ignorance is self-sustaining brings that process to an end. That is, you observe how through your own activities you are sustaining ignorance, how through craving, which engenders fear, ignorance is maintained, and how this gives continuity to the 'I' process, to consciousness. This ignorance, this 'I' process, is maintaining itself through its own volitional activities born of want, craving. With the cessation of self-nourishment the 'I' process comes to an end. You will ask me, "Can I live at all without want?" In the lives of most people, want, craving, plays a tremendous part; their whole existence is the vigorous process of want, and so they cannot imagine life, its richness and beauty, its relationship and conduct, without want. When you begin to discern, through experimentation, how action born of want creates its own limitation, then there is a change *of* will. Until then there is only a change *in* will. It is the self-sustaining activity of ignorance that gives to consciousness continuity, ever re-forming itself. The fundamental change *of* will is intelligence.

July 25, 1936

Second Talk at Ommen

All of us are in some measure caught up in suffering, whether economic, physical, psychological, or spiritual. To understand the cause of suffering and to be free from that cause is our constant problem.

To understand the fundamental cause of suffering, we cannot divide man into different parts. Man is indivisible, though he expresses himself through many aspects, and assumes many forms of expression which give him great complexity. There are specialists who study these various divisions and aspects of man and try to discover along their special lines the cause of suffering, but we cannot leave the comprehension of ourselves to another. We must understand ourselves as a whole and examine our own desires and activities. We must discern the 'I' process, which seeks ever to perpetuate and maintain itself separately through its own activities. When we fully comprehend this process, there will be the awakening of that intelligence which alone can free us from sorrow.

This 'I' process is consciousness which is individuality, and the cause of suffering is the ignorance of this self-active process. If we do not comprehend this process, which engenders sorrow, there cannot be intelligence. Intelligence is not a gift but can be cultivated, awakened, through alertness of mind and choiceless life. So action can either create sorrow, or destroy ignorance with its tendencies and cravings and thus end sorrow.

You can see for yourself in your life how this process, with its fears, illusions, and escapes, diminishes creative intelligence, which alone can bring about the well-being of man. The comprehension of reality, truth, comes with the cessation of sorrow. Our consideration of the hereafter, of immortality, is vain pursuit for there can be the bliss of reality only with the cessation of sorrow.

To understand suffering we must begin with ourselves, not with the idea of suffering, which is only the arid emptiness of the intellect. We must begin with ourselves, with the agonies, miseries, and conflicts which seem to have no end. Happiness is not to be sought after, but with the cessation of sorrow there is intelligence, the bliss of reality.

From what source do our daily activities spring? What is the basis of our moral and religious thought? If we examine ourselves deeply, comprehensively, we will see that many of our activities and relationships have their origin in fear and illusion. They are the outcome of craving, of a ceaseless search for both outward and inward security and comfort. This search has produced a civilization in which each individual, subtly or grossly, is fighting for himself, thus engendering hatred, cruelty, and oppression. This process has fostered a civilization of exploitation, wars, and organized religious superstition, the results of a false conception of individuality and fulfillment. The external conflict of races and religions, the division of peoples, the economic struggles, have their roots in false ideas of culture. Our lives are in continual conflict because of fear, belief, choice, and subjugation. Our environment stimulates the process of ignorance, and our memories and wants renew and give continuity and individuality to consciousness.

When you examine this process you will discern that the 'I' is re-forming itself each moment by its own volitional activities based on ignorance, want, and fear. When you begin to realize that the 'I' therefore has no permanency, there will be a vital change in your conduct and morality. Then there can be no subservience, acquiescence, but only the action of awakened intelligence which creates ever-new conditions, without being enslaved by them. This intelligence alone can bring about true cooperation without frustration.

Each one of you must become aware of the process of ignorance. This awareness is not that directive power of a higher comprehension over a lower, which is but a trick of the mind, but that choiceless comprehension which is the outcome of persistent action without fear and want. From this choiceless perception there arise right morality, relationship, and action. Conduct is not then the mere imitation of a pattern or ideal, or a discipline, but it is the outcome of true comprehension of the 'I' process. This discernment is awakened intelligence which, not being hierarchical or personal, helps to create a new culture of fulfillment and cooperation.

Question: Is effort consistent with awareness?

KRISHNAMURTI: Please understand what I mean by awareness. Awareness is not the result of choice. Choice implies opposites, a discrimination between the essential and the unessential, between right and wrong. Choice must create conflict for it is based on self-protective prompting, calculation, and prejudice. Choice is ever based on memories. Discernment is direct perception, without choice, of *what is,* and to perceive directly is to be free from the background of want. This can take place only when effort which is now being exerted between opposites ceases. Opposites are the result of want, of craving, and so of fear. With the cessation of fear there is direct perception of *what is.* We are at present making effort to achieve, to succeed, to conquer one habit by another, to subjugate one fear by another, one longing by another, one ideal by another. So there is constant effort to substitute, to overcome. Such effort is utterly futile, vain; it leads to confusion and not to the awakening of intelligence.

If you begin to be aware of this process of choice, of conflict between the opposites, then there is a change of will, and this will is the result of choicelessness.

When I talk about right effort, I mean that one should become conscious of the false effort one is making now. Become aware of the background, perceive how each moment thought is modifying itself in limitation through its own volitional activities born of ignorance and fear, which give a continuity to the 'I' process, to consciousness.

We suffer and we want to escape from that suffering, so we make an effort to seek a remedy, a substitution, but thereby we do not eradicate the cause of suffering. As mind is burdened with many substitutions, many escapes which prevent the birth of choiceless discernment, so effort merely creates further sorrow and frustration. This is false effort. Right effort is the spontaneous discernment of false effort which seeks substitution or escape through the many forms of security.

Question: How can one come to an agreement with people who have objectives in life radically different from one's own?

KRISHNAMURTI: There cannot be agreement between a false objective and a true objective. There may be agreement between two false objectives. In trying to bring about agreement between the false and the true, we attempt to develop what is called tolerance, with its many false pretenses. There can be real agreement only when the objectives are intelligent and true. When two individuals perceive the fundamental illusion of security, there is agreement, cooperation. But if one comprehends the cruelty of acquisitive security and another does not, then there is conflict, and to overcome this friction the false virtue of tolerance is developed, but this does not mean that he who understands is intolerant.

Instead of trying to agree, instead of trying to find out the common factor between

two absurdities, let us see if we can be intelligent. A man who has fear cannot be intelligent—for fear impedes choiceless discernment. So long as there is acquisitiveness, there cannot be intelligence, for it indicates that the mind is entangled in the process of ignorance and want. The cultivation of virtue is not intelligence. As long as there is the volitional activity of ignorance, there must be fear, delusion, and conflict.

Instead of cultivating tolerance which is but a trick of the mind, there must be the awakening of intelligence which has no self-protective memories and fears.

Question: Those who possess—whether land or machinery or labor—do not willingly share with those who are less fortunate. Have not the latter, therefore, the right and, in the last resort, the duty, to take away from those who possess, for the common benefit of all? Are you not rather inclined to waste your teachings on the more fortunate who are the least likely to want to alter the existing economic and social structure?

KRISHNAMURTI: I know this is a vital problem for many people. I am not evading it when I say that I want to deal with all the problems of life comprehensively, integrally, not separately. Where intelligence is functioning freely, these separative problems will not exist. Where there is no intelligence, though you may take over the machinery, the land, the labor, you will again create division with its cruel acquisitiveness and wars. So, from my point of view, what is important is the cultivation of true intelligence which alone can bring about order. There must be that inward revolution, which to me is much more important than the outward upheaval. This inward revolution is not to be postponed. It is much more vital, much more immediate than the outward one. This complete change of will is in your own power.

The inward, vital revolution is the result of comprehension and not of compulsion. Intelligence does not recognize riches or poverty. I am not talking either to the rich or to the poor, to the fortunate or to the less fortunate. I am talking to individuals to whom I say that it is necessary for them to comprehend the process of life because they, as individuals, are caught up in suffering. They as individuals are the creators of social environment, morality, relationships. So we must deal with man comprehensively and not merely with one of his aspects. As long as there is not that deep comprehension of the process of individuality, mere change will not awaken intelligence. If we discern this truly, we shall not as individuals seek happiness through the various cruelties and absurdities which we call modern civilization.

If you comprehend the utter necessity for this inward revolution, this change of will, then you will help naturally, spontaneously, to bring about right order, right action and conduct.

Question: Is not the Theosophical conception of the Masters of Wisdom and evolution of the soul as sound as the scientific conception of biological growth of life in organic matter?

KRISHNAMURTI: That which is capable of growth is not eternal. The theosophic or the religious conception is one of individual growth—the process of the 'I' becoming greater and greater by acquiring more and more virtue and comprehension. That is, the 'I' is capable of indefinite growth, reaching greater and greater heights of perfection, and to help it onwards, Masters, disciplines, and religious organizations are necessary.

So long as one does not understand what the 'I' is, then Masters of some kind or other become an illusory necessity. It may not be a Master in the theosophical sense; it may be a saint of a church or a spiritual authority of an organization. What we have to understand is not whether the Masters exist or not, whether they are necessary or not, but whether the 'I' in its growth, in its expansion, can become eternal or lead to the comprehension of truth. The problem is not whether Masterhood is a perfectly natural process, but whether discernment of truth can come to a mind which is held in the 'I' process. If you consider the 'I' to be eternal, then it cannot grow, it must be timeless, spaceless. So the idea that the 'I' becomes a Master through growth, experience, is an illusion. Or, the 'I' process is transient. To bring this process to an end, no outside agency however great can ever be of help, for the 'I' process is self-active, sustaining itself through its volitional activities. You have to consider whether the 'I' is eternal or transient. But it is not a question of choice, for all choice is based on ignorance, prejudice, want.

Some of you may not be concerned with the belief in the Masters of the Theosophists, yet when sorrow comes to you, you may seek some other spiritual authority or guidance, and it is this dependence on another that perpetuates the 'I' process, with its subtle exploitation and sorrow.

Question: Many persons find it very hard to be fully concentrated in their actions. In order to train the capacity for concentration, cannot certain exercises be of great help or do you regard them as hindrances?

KRISHNAMURTI: When you are deeply interested there is no necessity for exercises which help you to develop concentration. When you are enjoying beautiful scenery, there is a spontaneity of delight and interest which is beyond all the artificial aids to concentration. It is only when you are not interested that there is a division in consciousness. Instead of trying to find exercises for developing the capacity for concentration, find out if you have deep interest in the things of life. To understand life, you need comprehensive interest, not only in bread and butter, but in the processes of thought, of love, in experiences, in relationship. Where there is deep interest there is concentration. Is not the questioner trying to stimulate concentration artificially? Such artificial stimulation becomes a barrier to the rich comprehension of life. Disciplined meditations are artificial stimulations and become barriers which create a division between living actuality and illusory longings and desires. Do not seek the bliss of reality, for the mere search for reality only leads to illusion, but comprehend that process of thought, consciousness, focused in yourself. This demands not mere concentration but pliability of mind and self-sustained interest.

Question: The idea of leadership is, to many, a great inspiration. Also it leads to the cultivation of respect and a spirit of self-sacrifice. In you, we recognize a great spiritual leader and feel profound reverence towards you. Should we not therefore encourage, in others as well as in ourselves, these great qualities of respect and self-sacrifice?

KRISHNAMURTI: The show of respect is personally distasteful to me. (Laughter) Please do not laugh. If there were true respect you would not only show it to me but to all. Your show of respect to me only indicates a mentality of barter. You think I am going to give you something or help you in some way, and so you show respect. What you are really doing is showing respect to an idea that you should display consideration to a person who may help you, but out of this false respect there is born contempt for others. There is no consideration of the ideas in themselves, but unfortunately only of the person who gives forth these ideas. In this lies grave danger, leading to reciprocal exploitation. The mere respect of authority indicates fear which breeds many illusions. From this false respect, there arises the artificial distinction between leaders and followers, with its many obvious and subtle forms of exploitation. Where there is no intelligence there is respect for the few and disdain for the rest.

July 27, 1936

Third Talk at Ommen

How is one to awaken that intelligence, that creative intuition which comprehends the significance of reality, without the process of analysis and logic? By intuition I do not mean wish fulfillment, which it is for most people. If morality, which is relationship, is based upon intelligence and intuition, then there is richness, fullness, and an abiding beauty in life. But if we base our conduct and relationship on industrial and biological necessities, then action must inevitably make our life shallow, uncertain, and sorrowful. We have the possibility of this intelligence or intuition, but how can it be awakened? What is it that we must do or not do to awaken this intelligence?

All craving with its fears must cease before there can be this creative intuition. The cessation of want is not the result of denial, nor through careful analysis can want be rationalized away. The freedom from want, from its fears and illusions, comes through persistent and silent perception, without the deliberate choice of volition. By this deep observation you will perceive how want engenders fear and illusion, and breaks up consciousness into the past, present, and future , into the higher and the lower, into accumulated memories and those to be acquired. So ignorance, with its wants, prejudices, and fear, is creating duality in consciousness, and from this duality arise the many problems of control and conflict. From this duality there arises the process of self-discipline through the authority of ideal and memory, which controls and limits action and thus brings about frustration. This limitation of action creates, naturally, further limitations and so brings about friction and suffering. Thus the wheel of ignorance, fear, prejudice is set going and prevents complete adjustment to life. Where there is want, there must also be accumulative memories, self-protective calculations, which give to consciousness continuity and identification.

This consciousness with its division and conflict creates for itself limitation through its own volitional activities and so maintains its own individuality. It is imprisoned in its own creation, in its own environment, of dark confusion, incessant struggle, and frustration. If you silently observe without the interference of choice, you will discern this process of ignorance and fear. When the mind perceives that it is engendering its own ignorance and so its own fear, then there is the beginning of choiceless awareness. Through silent observation and deep discernment in which there is no choice and so no conflict, there comes the cessation of ignorance. It cannot be brought about through denial or through mere rationalization. This is the true process of awakening intelligence and intuition.

Limited consciousness is the conflict of innumerable wants. Become aware of this conflict, this ceaseless battle of division, but do not try to dominate one part of consciousness with its wants, by the other. When the mind identifies itself with want or with opposites, there is conflict; then the mind tries to escape through illusion and false values and thus merely intensifies the whole process of want. With deep discernment there comes the cessation of want, the awakening of intelligence, of creative intuition. That intelligence is reality itself.

Question: I have lost all enthusiasm, all urge in life, which at one time I remember I had. Now, life to me is colorless, a hopeless void, a burden that somehow I must bear. Could you indicate the possible causes which might have brought about this condition and explain how I might break through this hard shell in which I seem to be?

KRISHNAMURTI: Through false values we force ourselves into certain grooves of action and adjust our thoughts and feelings to certain conditions. So, through our own conditioning we lose our enthusiasm, and consequently life becomes dull and burdensome. To break through this shell of hopelessness, we must be conscious of our limited thought and action. When we have become aware of this state, and instead of battling against this hopeless void, we deeply consider the causes of frustration, then, without any conflict of antithesis there takes place that vital change which is fulfillment, the rich comprehension of life. If one has merely disciplined the mind without understanding the process of consciousness, or subjugated mental activities and conduct to the authority of an ideal without discerning the stupidity of authority, then life becomes arid, shallow, and vain.

Unless one fully comprehends the process of consciousness, illusion may momentarily give the necessary impetus to action, but such action must inevitably lead to misery and frustration. The conflict between illusions, though seemingly purposeful and satisfying, must inevitably lead to confusion and sorrow. We have to become aware of the many fears and illusions, and when mind frees itself from them, there is the rich plenitude of life.

When you begin to realize the utter futility of want itself, there will be the awakening of that intelligence which brings about right relationship with environment. Then only can there be richness and beauty of life.

Question: It may sound impertinent to say it, but it is easy for you to advise others to experiment with intelligent action; you will never lack bread. Of what use is your advice to the vast numbers of men and women in the world for whom intelligent action will only mean more hunger?

KRISHNAMURTI: Why do you lay so much emphasis on bread? Bread is essential, but by merely laying emphasis on bread you are going to deprive man of it. By laying emphasis on any one need of man, who is indivisible, you are going to deprive him of that very thing which you emphasize. It is fear that leads to unintelligent action and consequently to suffering, and as individuals are held in this fear, I am trying to awaken in them the perception of their self-created barrier of ignorance and prejudice. Because each individual is seeking self-security in many forms, there can be no intelligent cooperation with his environment, and there ensue many problems which cannot be superficially solved. If each one of us were fearless, not craving security in any form whatsoever, whether here or in the hereafter, then in this fearless state intelligence could function and bring about order and happiness. By merely considering one part, an artificial division of man who is indivisible, we cannot comprehend the whole of him, and it is only through the comprehension of the whole that the part can be understood. There has always been this problem, whether emphasis should be laid on bread, environment, or on mind and heart. In the past, too, this division has existed, this dualism in man of the soul and the body, each division insisting on its own set of values and thus creating much con-

fusion and misery. And we continue to perpetuate, perhaps in new forms, this artificial and false division of man. One group considers only the importance of bread, and another lays emphasis on the soul. This division of man is utterly false, and it must ever lead to unintelligent action. Intelligent action is the outcome of understanding man as a complete being.

Question: My sorrows have brought it home to me that I must no longer seek comfort of any kind. I feel convinced that another cannot heal the ache which is in me. And yet, since my sorrow continues, is there something wrong in the way I have taken my suffering?

KRISHNAMURTI: You say you no longer seek comfort, but surely has not that search been brought to an end deliberately, through decision, resolve? It is not the spontaneous result of comprehension. It is merely the outcome of a decision not to seek comfort because the search for comfort has brought you disappointment. So you say to yourself, "I must no longer seek comfort." When a man who has been deeply hurt through attachment begins to cultivate detachment, praising it as a noble quality, what he is really doing is protecting himself from further hurt—and this process he calls detachment. So in the same way, fear of suffering has made you see that comfort, dependence, involves further suffering, and so you say to yourself, "I must not seek comfort, I must be self-reliant." Yet want, with its many subtle forms of fear, continues.

Want creates duality in thought, and when one want creates suffering, the mind seeks the opposite of that want. Whether it is a craving for comfort or the denial of comfort, it is the same, it is still want. So the mind maintains the conflict of opposites. When you begin to suffer, do not say, "I must get rid of this or that want or cause," but silently observe, without denial or acceptance, and out of this choiceless awareness, want with its fears and illusions begins to yield place to intelligence. This intelligence is life itself and is not conditioned by the compulsion of want.

Question: It is said that occult initiations, such as those described by Theosophy and other ancient rites and mysteries, form the various stages of life's spiritual journey. Is this so? Do you remember any sudden change in consciousness in yourself?

KRISHNAMURTI: Consciousness is undergoing constant change within its own restrictions and limitations. Within its own circle it is fluctuating, expanding and contracting, and this expanding is called by some, spiritual advancement. But it is still within the confines of its own limitation, and this expanding is not a change of consciousness but only a change in consciousness. This change of consciousness is not the outcome of mysterious rites, or initiations. He who discerns the futility of the change in consciousness, alone can bring about the change of consciousness. To discern and to change fundamentally needs persistent awareness. What is important is whether we can individually bring about this vital change. Let us concern ourselves not with the immediacy of change but only with the fundamental change of consciousness, and for this the 'I' process with its ignorance, tendencies, wants, fears must of itself come to an end.

July 28, 1936

Fourth Talk at Ommen

Action which springs from the self-preserving process of consciousness with its many layers of ignorance, tendencies, wants, fears cannot liberate the mind from its own self-created limitation, but merely intensifies sorrow and frustration. As long as this process continues, as long as there is no comprehension of this 'I' process, not only in its obvious form and expression, but also in its prodigious subtleties, there must be suffering and confusion. Yet this very suffering, from which we are ever trying to escape, can lead us to the comprehension of the 'I' process, to the profound knowledge of oneself, but all escapes into illusion must cease. The greater the suffering, the stronger is the indication of limitation. But if you do not suffer, it does not necessarily mean that you are free of limitations. On the contrary, it may be that your mind is stagnant within self-protective walls so that no provocations of life, no experiences, can stir it into activity and so awaken it to sorrow. Such a mind is incapable of discerning reality. Suffering can bring about the comprehension of oneself if you do not try to avoid it or to escape from it.

How can we bring to an end the 'I' process, so that our action does not create further limitations and sorrow? To bring this 'I' process to an end, there must be the consciousness of suffering, not the mere conception of suffering. Unless there is the vital provocation of life, most of us are apt to comfort ourselves to sleep and so allow unconsciously the 'I' process to continue. The essential requirement for the discernment of the 'I' process is to be fully conscious of suffering. Then there must be the utter certainty that there are no escapes whatsoever from suffering. All search for comfort and superficial remedies then wholly ceases. All ritualistic palliatives cease to have any significance. We then begin to perceive that no external agency can help us to bring this self-sustaining process of ignorance to an end. When the mind is in this state of openness, when it is wholly able to confront itself, then it becomes its own mirror, then there is undivided consciousness; it does not judge its actions by standards, nor is it controlled by the authority of ideal. It is then its own creator and destroyer. Environment with its conditioning influences, and heredity with its limiting characteristics, yield to the comprehension of the 'I' process. When the mind discerns this process integrally, it sees itself as the process, utilizing all action, all relationship to sustain itself. In the renewal of itself from moment to moment, through its own volitional activities, the 'I' process is perpetuating itself and merely engendering sorrow.

The majority of us try to escape from suffering through illusions, logical definitions, and conclusions, and so gradually the mind becomes dull, incapable of perceiving itself. Only when the mind perceives itself as it is—as the will of itself, with its many layers of ignorance, fear, want, illusion—when it discerns how through its own volitional activities the 'I' process is perpetuating itself, only then is there the possibility of this process bringing itself to an end. When the mind discerns that it is itself creating sorrow, perpetuating the 'I' process, and that it is the 'I' process itself, then there is a change of will, change of consciousness. The ending of the 'I' process is the beginning of wisdom, bliss.

We have sedulously developed the idea of a superior and an inferior will in consciousness. This division merely creates conflict, which we seek to end by discipline. Where there is want or fear, its action is as the fuel to a flame it merely sustains the 'I' process. The comprehension of this process demands great awareness and not the effort of choice or of discipline.

Question: Is fear a fundamental part of life, so that the understanding of it merely enables us the better to accept it; or is it something that can be transmuted into something else; or again, something that can be wholly eliminated? One often seems able to trace the cause of a particular fear, and yet in other forms fear continues. Why should it be so?

KRISHNAMURTI: Fear will exist in different forms, grossly or subtly, as long as there is the self-active process of ignorance engendered by the activities of want. One can wholly eliminate fear, it is not a fundamental part of life. If there is fear there cannot be intelligence, and to awaken intelligence one must fully comprehend the process of the 'I' in action. Fear cannot be transmuted into love. It must ever remain as fear even though we try to reason it away, even though we try to cover it up by calling it love. Nor can fear be understood as a fundamental part of life in order to enable us to put up with it. You will not discover the deep cause of fear by merely analyzing each fear as it arises. There is only one fundamental cause of fear, though it may express itself in different forms. By mere dissection of the various forms of fear, thought cannot free itself from the root cause of fear. When the mind neither accepts nor rejects fear, neither escapes from it nor tries to transmute it, then only can there be a possibility of its cessation. When the mind is not caught in the conflict of opposites, then it is able to discern, without choice, the whole of the 'I' process. As long as this process continues there must be fear, and the attempt to escape from it only increases and strengthens the process. If you would be free of fear, you must fully comprehend action born of want.

Question: I am beginning to think that material possessions tend to foster vanity and in addition are a burden; and now I have decided to limit my own material requirements. However, I find it difficult to come to a decision as regards leaving inheritance to my children. Must I, as their parent, take a decision in the matter? I know that I would not consciously pass on a contagious disease if I could possibly avoid it. Would I be right in taking a similar view regarding inheritance and so depriving my children of it?

KRISHNAMURTI: The questioner himself says he would not willingly pass on a contagious disease. Now, is inheritance such a disease? To possess or acquire money without working for it breeds a form of mental illness. If you agree with this statement and act by it, then you must be willing to face the consequences of your action. You will help to upset the present social system with its exploitation, its cruel and stupid power through the accumulation of money and the privileges of vested interest. Whether possessing or acquiring money without working for it is a disease or not, you must discover for yourself.

When you as individuals begin to free yourselves from the disease of fear, you will not ask another whether you should leave your wealth to your children or not. Your action then will have a profound and different significance. Then your attitude with regard to family, class, work, wealth, or poverty will undergo a deep change. If there is not this significant change, which is brought about through comprehension and not through compulsion, then artificial problems can only be answered superficially, without any consequence or value.

Question: You have talked about the vital urge, the ceaseless awakened state, which, if I understand rightly, would be possible only after one had been through utter loneliness. Do you think it is possible for one to have that great urge and yet be married? To me it seems that however free the husband and wife may be, there will always be invisible threads between the two which must inevitably prevent each from being wholly responsible to himself or herself. Will not the awakened state, therefore, lead to utter and complete detachment from each and all?

KRISHNAMURTI: You cannot exist except in relationship with persons, with environment, with tradition, with the background of the past. To be is to exist in relationship. Either you can make relationship vital, strong, expressive, harmonious, or you can turn it into conflict and pain. It is suffering which forces you to withdraw from relationship, and as you cannot exist without being in relation with something, you begin to cultivate detachment, a self-protective reaction against sorrow. If you love, you are in right relationship with environment; but if love turns into hatred, into jealousy, and creates conflict, then relationship becomes burdensome and painful, and you begin the artificial process of detaching yourself from that which gives you pain. You can intellectually create a self-protective barrier of detachment and live in this self-created prison, which slowly destroys the fullness of mind-heart. To live is to be in relationship. There cannot be harmonious and vital relationship if there are any self-protective desires and reactions which bring about sorrow and conflict.

Question: If I understand you rightly, awareness alone and by itself is sufficient to dissolve both the conflict and the source of it. I am perfectly aware, and have been for a long time, that I am "snobbish." What prevents my getting rid of snobbishness?

KRISHNAMURTI: The questioner has not understood what I mean by awareness. If you have a habit, the habit of snobbishness for instance, it is no good merely to overcome this habit by another, its opposite. It is futile to fight one habit by another habit. What rids the mind of habit is intelligence. Awareness is the process of awakening intelligence, not creating new habits to fight the old ones. So you must become conscious of your habits of thought, but do not try to develop opposite qualities or habits. If you are fully aware, if you are in that state of choiceless observation, then you will perceive the whole process of creating a habit and also the opposite process of overcoming it. This discernment awakens intelligence which does away with all habits of thought. We are eager to get rid of those habits which give us pain or which we have found to be worthless, by creating other habits of thought and assertions. This process of substitution is wholly unintelligent. If you will observe you will find that mind is nothing but a mass of habits of thought and memories. By merely overcoming these habits by others, the mind still remains in prison, confused and suffering. It is only when we deeply comprehend the process of self-protective reactions, which become habits of thought, limiting all action, that there is a possibility of awakening intelligence which alone can dissolve the conflict of opposites.

Question: Will you kindly explain the difference between change in *will and change of* will?

KRISHNAMURTI: Change *in* will is merely the result of duality in consciousness, and change *of* will takes place in the plenitude of one's whole being. One is a change in degree and the other is a change in kind. The conflict of want, or the change in the object of want, is merely a change in will, but with the cessation of all want there is a change of will.

The change in will is submission to the authority of ideal and conduct. The change of will is discernment, intelligence, in which there is not the conflict of antitheses. In the latter there is deep and spontaneous adjustment; in the former there is compulsion through ignorance, want, and fear.

Question: Is the renewal of the individual sufficient for the solution of the problems of the world? Does intelligence comprise action for the liberation of all?

KRISHNAMURTI: What are the problems of the world? Bread, unemployment, wars, conflicts, opposing political groups, the enjoyment by the few of the riches of the world, class divisions, starvation, death, immortality—these are the problems of the world. Are not these also individual problems? The problems of the world can be understood only through that process which is focused in each one, the 'I' process. Why create this artificial division of the individual and the world? We are the world, we are the mass. If you, as an individual, comprehend the process of division as nationalism, class conflict, and racial antagonisms, if you are no longer Dutch, French, German, or English, with all the absurdities of separativeness, then surely you become a center of intelligence. You are then fighting stupidity wherever you are, though it may lead you to hunger and struggle. If we fully comprehend this through action, we can be as oases in the midst of deserts. The process of hatred and division is as old as the centuries. You cannot withdraw from it, but in the midst of it you can be clear, simple, true, without all the encrustations of past stupidities. Then you will see what great understanding and joy you can bring to life. But unfortunately in the moment of great upheavals and wars, you are swept off your feet. Your own potential hatreds and fears are aroused and carry you away. You are not the tranquil oasis to which suffering humanity can come.

So it is of the utmost importance to comprehend the process which engenders these limitations, hatreds, sorrows. Action born of integral understanding will be a liberating force, though the effects of such action may not show themselves in your lifetime or within a set period. Time is of no consequence. A bloody revolution does not bring about lasting peace or happiness for all. Instead of merely desiring immediate peace in this world of confusion and agony, consider how you, the individual, can be a center, not of peace, but of intelligence. Intelligence is essential for order, harmony, and man's well-being.

There are many organizations for peace, but there are very few individuals who are free, who are intelligent in the true sense of the word. You must begin as individuals to comprehend reality; then the flame of understanding will spread over the face of the earth.

July 29, 1936

Fifth Talk at Ommen

Our minds have become the battleground of ideals, fears and illusions, desires and denials, hopes and frustrations, regimentation and spontaneity. Can we bring the conflict in the mind to an end without creating at the same time emptiness, aridity, and frustration? You can suppress conflict for a while by forcing the mind into a certain mold, but this merely creates illusions and maladjustments in life. Most of us try to subjugate our desires, or give them full freedom, but conflict is not thereby ended.

Is there a way by which we can end conflict and sorrow without destroying creative intelligence and integral completeness? Can there ever be choiceless living, that is, can there ever be action without denial or aggressive want? Can there be action which is spontaneous and thus free of the conflict of opposites? Can there ever be a life of fullness without the withering process of dis-

cipline, denial, fear, and frustration? Is such a state of deep comprehension ever possible? I wonder how many of you are vitally conscious of this conflict in the battlefield of the mind.

A life of fullness, a life of choiceless action, a life free from the withering process of subjugation and substitution, is possible. How is this state to be realized? Systems and methods cannot produce this happy state of mind. This condition of choiceless life must come about naturally, spontaneously; it cannot be sought after. It is not to be understood or realized or conquered through a discipline, through a system. One can condition the mind through training, discipline, and compulsion, but such conditioning cannot nourish thought or awaken deep intelligence. Such a trained mind is as the soil that is barren.

Few of us are deeply conscious of conflict, with its suffering, its subtle, evasive uncertainties, and at the same time of that struggle for certainties on which the mind relies for its security and comfort. The deep and vital consciousness of conflict is as the tilling of the soil. There must only be the process of tilling the soil, there must only be the choiceless awareness of conflict. Now, when there is conflict there is either the desire to escape from it or there is the desire to utilize it for future achievement. But there must be only the deep consciousness of suffering, of conflict, which is but the tilling of the soil, and the mind must not allow itself to search for remedies, substitutions, and escapes. There must be the tilling of the soil, the upheaval, the revolution of the mind, and yet, at the same time, there must be stillness, silent perception, without denial, acceptance, or resignation. Mind, when it is in conflict, immediately seeks a remedy and thereby creates artificially an escape for itself, thus hindering the full comprehension of suffering; but through spontaneous discernment alone can there be that direct comprehension, which brings about choiceless adjustment to life. Where there is imitation there must also be fear, and action which is imitative is unintelligent. The discipline of compulsion, of fear, leads to the slow withering of the mind, and there cannot be that choiceless and spontaneous relationship to environment, which alone is right action.

There can be right action only when there is the comprehension of the whole process of the 'I', which is but the process of ignorance. As long as there is not the discernment of the process of consciousness, of this vast complex of ignorance, memories, wants, tendencies, conflicts, the mere imitation of conduct cannot possibly bring about intelligent and harmonious order in the world, and happiness to man. Such imitation may produce a superficial order of economic industrialism, but it cannot create intelligence. To comprehend the full significance of the 'I' process, intelligent persistency is essential, not casual awareness at odd moments.

Action born of want or fear can only intensify ignorance and increase limitation and thereby maintain the 'I' process. Through the voluntary cessation of want and fear, intelligence is awakened. The awakening of intelligence is the beginning of true action. This intelligence alone can bring about spontaneous adjustment in life without the compulsion of choice.

Question: How can I awaken intelligence?

KRISHNAMURTI: Where there is no intelligence, there must be suffering. Intelligence can be awakened through choiceless perception of the mind that it is creating for itself escapes by dividing itself into different parts, into different wants. If the mind is aware of these illusory divisions with their values, then there is the awakening of intelligence. The process of choice is merely one want

overcoming another, one illusion dispelling another, one set of values substituting itself for another. This duality in consciousness perpetuates conflict and sorrow, and conflict is the lack of integral action.

Question: I realize that the liberation of the individual is essential, but how can lasting social order be established without mass effort?

KRISHNAMURTI: In all my talks I have been pointing out the utter necessity of individual comprehension. Social order is the outcome of individual comprehension. The emphasis on individual liberation is not an encouragement to selfish activities or narrow self-expression. Only by liberating thought from the limitations which now cripple the mind, can intelligence be awakened, and intelligence alone can bring about true social order. To be responsible for one's actions and to be integral in one's thought implies completeness of being, especially in a world where mass movement seems to be of the greatest importance. It is comparatively easy to create mass enthusiasm for concerted action, but it is very difficult to comprehend oneself and to act rightly. Out of deep comprehension alone can there be cooperation and lasting social order.

These talks are not meant to induce mass effort or concerted action; they can only help to create individual comprehension and effort and so free the individual from the prison of self-created limitations. The awakening of integral comprehension of oneself, which is choiceless discernment, will alone bring about true social order in a world free of exploitation and hatred.

Question: Does art belong to the world of illusion or to reality? What relation has art to life?

KRISHNAMURTI: Art divorced from life has no reality. Art should not be a superficial expression of man's dual life, but it should be an integral expression of indivisible man. At the present time, art expresses but one aspect of man and so merely emphasizes division. Thus there is a strange separation between actual life and art. When art is the true integral expression of man, his life and activities, then it is of reality, then it has direct relationship with us and our environment.

Question: When faced with the agony of the death of someone we love greatly, it is difficult to maintain that life is the most essential thing and that the consideration of the hereafter is futile. On the other hand, one wonders whether life is, after all, anything more than the physiological and biological processes conditioned by heredity and environment, as some scientists maintain. In this confusion what is one to do? How should one think and act to know what is true?

KRISHNAMURTI: As the questioner himself points out, some scientists maintain that heredity explains man's individual tendencies and peculiarities, and others assert that he is the result of environment, merely a social entity. From these confusing assertions, what are we to choose? What is man? How can we understand the significance of death and the deep agony that comes with it? By merely accepting the various assertions, can we solve the sorrow and the mystery of death? Are we capable of choosing, among these explanations, the one that is true? Is it a matter of choice?

What is chosen cannot be true. In opposites, the real cannot be found, for opposites are merely the interplay of reactions. If what is true is not to be found in opposites, and that which is chosen does not lead to the comprehension of truth, then what

is one to do? You must comprehend for yourself the process of your own being, and not merely accept the investigation of scientists or the assertions of religions. In fully discerning the process of your own being, you will be able to comprehend suffering and the agony of loneliness that comes with the shadow of death. Until you perceive the process of yourself profoundly, the consideration of the hereafter, the theory of reincarnation, the explanations of the spiritists must remain superficial, giving temporary consolation which only prevents the awakening of intelligence. Discernment is essential for the comprehension of the 'I' process. Through discernment alone can be solved the many problems which the 'I' process is ever creating for itself.

You try to get rid of suffering by explanations, drugs, drink, amusement, or resignation, and yet suffering continues. If you would bring sorrow to an end, you must understand the process of division in consciousness which creates conflict and makes the mind a battlefield of many wants. Through choiceless discernment, there is awakened that creative intuition, intelligence, which alone can free the mind-heart from the many subtle processes of ignorance, want, and fear.

August 1, 1936

Sixth Talk at Ommen

Question: What, according to you, are the basic principles on which to bring up and educate children? Should we always be justified in assuming that children are capable of knowing what is good and what is right for them, and that the less interference and guidance from adults, the better?

KRISHNAMURTI: The many problems concerning the education of children can only be solved comprehensively, integrally. Humanity is being educated and regimented according to certain industrial, philosophical, and religious ideas. If man is nothing but the result of environment and heredity, if he is merely a social entity, then surely the more there is of regimentation, guidance, imposition, and compulsion, the better. If this be so, then from a very tender age, the child must be controlled, and its innermost reactions to life must be corrected and disciplined according to industrial necessity and biological morality.

Opposed to this conception stands faith, which maintains that there is only one transcendental, universal force, which is God, and everything is part of it, and nothing is unknown to it. Then man is not free and his destiny is predetermined. In faith also there is regimentation of thought through belief and ideal. What we call religious education is merely the forcing of the individual to adapt himself to certain ideas, moralities, and conclusions laid down by religious organizations.

If you examine both these opposites, the assertions of faith and of science, you will see that though they are in opposition, they both shape man, grossly or subtly, each according to its own pattern. Before we can know how to bring up children, or ourselves, we must comprehend the significance of these opposites. We have created through faith, fear, and compulsion a system of thought and conduct which we call religion and to which we are constantly adjusting ourselves; or, by continual assertion that man is merely a social entity, a product of environment and heredity, we have created a superficial morality which is hollow and barren. So before we can educate children or ourselves, we have to comprehend what man is.

Our thought and action spring sometimes from faith and at other times from the reactions of biological or industrial necessity. When there is burning anxiety, fear, uncertainty, we turn to God, we assert that there is a transcendental force which is guiding us, and with the morality of faith we try to live in a world of opportunism, hatred, and cruelties. So inevitably there is conflict between the system of faith and the system of egotistic morality. Through either of these systems which are opposed to each other, what man is cannot be discerned.

How, then, are we going to discover what man is? We must first become aware of our thought and action and free them from faith, fear, and compulsion. We must disentangle them from the reaction and conflict of opposites in which they are at present held. By being alert and constantly aware, we shall discover for ourselves the true process of consciousness. I have tried to explain this process in my various talks.

Instead of belonging to either of the opposite systems of thought—faith and science—we must go above and beyond them, and then only shall we discern that which is true. Then we shall see that there are many energies whose processes are unique, and that there is not one universal force which puts into motion these separate energies. Man is this unique, self-active energy which has no beginning. In its self-active development there is consciousness, from which arises individuality. This process is self-sustaining through its own activities of ignorance, prejudice, want, fear. So long as the process of ignorance and want exists, there must be fear with its many illusions and escapes; from this process arise conflict and suffering.

If we truly discern this self-sustaining process of ignorance, then we shall have a wholly different attitude towards man and his education. Then there will not be the compulsion of faith or of superficial morality, but the awakening of intelligence which will adjust itself to all the provocations of life. Until we really understand the significance of all this, mere search for another system of education is utterly futile. To awaken creative intelligence so that each human being is capable of spontaneous adjustment to life, there must be the deep discernment of the process of oneself. No philosophical system can aid one to understand oneself. Comprehension comes only through the discernment of the 'I' process with its ignorance, tendencies, and fears. Where there is deep and creative intelligence, there will be right education, right action, and right relationship with environment.

Question: Does not experience lead to the fullness of life?

KRISHNAMURTI: We see many people going through experience after experience, multiplying sensation, living in past memories with future anticipation. Do such people live a life of plenitude? Do accumulative memories bring about the fullness of life? Or is there the plenitude of life only when the mind is open, vulnerable, utterly denuded of all self-protective memories?

When there is integral action without the division of many wants, there is fullness, intelligence, the depth of reality. Mere accumulation of experience, or living in the sensation of experience, is but a superficial enrichment of memory, which gives an artificial sensation of fullness, through stimulation. Mere enrichment of memory is not fullness of life; it only builds further self-protective walls against the movement of life, against suffering. Self-protective walls of memory prevent the spontaneity of life and increase resistance and thereby intensify sorrow and conflict. Accumulative memories of experience do not bring about comprehension or the strength of deep pliability.

Memory guides us through experiences. We approach each new experience with a conditioned mind—a mind that is already burdened with self-protective memories of fears, prejudices, tendencies. Memory is ever conditioning the mind and creating for it an environment of values in which it becomes a prisoner. As long as self-protective memories exist and give continuity to the 'I' process, there cannot be the plenitude of life.

So we must understand the process of experience and perceive how the mind is ever gathering lessons out of experience, which become its guide. These lessons, these ideals and guides, which are but self-protective memories, constantly help the mind to escape from actuality. Though the mind seeks to escape from suffering aided by these memories, it thereby only accentuates fear, illusion, and conflict. Plenitude of life is possible only when the mind-heart is wholly vulnerable to the movement of life, without any self-created and artificial hindrances. Richness of life comes when want, with its illusions and values, has ceased.

Question: Please speak to us about the beauty and ecstasy of freedom. Is it possible to attain that happy state without the use of meditation or other methods suitable to our stage?

KRISHNAMURTI: Why do you want me to speak to you about the beauty and ecstasy of freedom? Is it in order to have a new sensation, a new imaginative picture, a new ideal, or is it because you hope to create in yourself through my description an assurance, a certainty? You desire to be stimulated. As when you read a poem you are carried away by the momentary vision of the poet's fancy, so you want the stimulation of my description. When you look at a beautiful painting, you are transported for a while by its loveliness from your daily conflict, misery, and fear. You escape, but soon you return to your sorrow. Of what avail is my describing to you the indescribable? No words can measure it. So let us not ask what is truth, what is freedom.

You will know what is freedom when you are deeply conscious of the walls of your prison, for that very awareness dissolves the self-created limitations. When you ask what is truth, what is the ecstasy of freedom, you are only demanding a new escape from the weary burden of everyday struggle, passion, hatred. Occasionally we are aware of the loveliness of the indescribable, but these moments are so rare that we cling to them in memory and try to live in the past, with actuality ever present. This but creates and perpetuates conflict and illusion. Do not let us live through imagination in an anticipated future, but let us be conscious of our everyday struggles and fears.

There are the few who, comprehending the self-sustaining process of ignorance, have brought it voluntarily to an end. And there are the many who have almost escaped from the actual; they cannot discern the real, the ever-becoming. No system, philosophical or scientific, can lead them to the ecstasy of truth. No system of meditation can free them from self-engendered, self-active illusions, conflicts, and miseries, which are so insistent that they help to create those conditions which prevent the fruition of intelligence. You mean by meditation a set of rules, a discipline, which, if followed, you hope will help you to awaken intelligence. Can compulsion, either of reward or of punishment, bring about creative intuition of reality? Must you not be conscious, deeply aware of the process of ignorance, want, which is creating further want and so ever engendering fear and illusion? When you really begin to be aware of this process, that very awareness is meditation, not the artificial meditation for a few minutes of the day in which you withdraw from life to contemplate life. We think that by withdrawing from life, even for a minute, we shall understand life. To under-

stand life we must be in the flow of life, in the movement of life. We must be cognizant of the process of ignorance, want, and fear, for we are that very process itself.

I am afraid that many of you who hear me often but do not experiment with what I say will merely acquire a new terminology, without that fundamental change of will which alone can free the mind-heart from conflict and sorrow. Instead of asking for a method of meditation, which is but an indication of wanting an escape from actuality, discern for yourself the process of ignorance and fear. This deep discernment is meditation.

Question: You say that discipline is futile, whether external or self-imposed. Nevertheless, when one takes life seriously, one submits oneself inevitably to a kind of voluntary self-discipline. Is there anything wrong in this?

KRISHNAMURTI: I have tried to explain that conduct born of compulsion, whether it be the compulsion of reward or of punishment, of fear or of love, is not right conduct. It is merely an imitation, a forcing and training of the mind according to certain ideas in order to avoid conflict. This kind of discipline, imposed or voluntary, does not lead to right conduct. Right conduct is possible only when we understand the full significance of the self-active process of ignorance and the re-forming of limitation through the action of want. In deeply discerning the process of fear, there is the awakening of that intelligence which brings about right conduct. Can intelligence be awakened through discipline, imposed or voluntary? Is it a question of training thought according to a particular pattern? Is intelligence awakened through fear which makes you subjugate yourself to a standard of morality? Compulsion of any kind, whether externally or voluntarily imposed, cannot awaken intelligence, for imposition is the outcome of fear. Where there is fear there cannot be intelligence. Where intelligence is functioning there is spontaneous adjustment without the process of discipline. So the question is not whether discipline is right or wrong, or whether it is necessary, but how the mind can be free from self-created fear. For when there is freedom from fear, there is not the sense of discipline, but only the plenitude of life.

What is the cause of fear? How is fear engendered? What is its process and expression? There must be fear so long as there is the 'I' process, the consciousness of want, which limits action. All action born of the limitation of want only creates further limitation. This constant change of want, with its many activities, does not free the mind from fear; it but gives to the 'I' process an identity and a continuity. Action springing from want must ever create fear and thereby hinder intelligence and the spontaneous adjustment to life.

Instead of asking me if it is right or wrong to discipline yourself, be conscious of your own want, and then you will see how fear comes into being and perpetuates itself. Instead of wanting to get rid of fear, be deeply conscious of want, without compulsion of any kind. Then there will be the cessation of fear, the awakening of intelligence, and the deep plenitude of life.

August 2, 1936

Seventh Talk at Ommen

To discern reality mind must be infinitely pliable. Most of us imagine that beyond and above the mind there is reality, that beyond and above this consciousness of conflict and limitation, pleasure and sorrow, there is truth. But to understand reality mind must comprehend its own creations, its own limita-

tions. To discern the process of consciousness, which is conceptual as well as actual, to go deeply into its tremendous subtleties, mind must be exquisitely pliable, and there must be integral thought. Integral thought is not the result of training, control, or imitation. A mind that is not divided into opposites, that is able to perceive directly, cannot be the result of training. It is not the outcome of one will dominating another will, one want overcoming another want. All antithesis in thought must be false. Mind consciously or unconsciously plays a trick on itself by dividing itself. Training and control indicate a process of duality in want, which brings about conflict in consciousness. Where there is conflict, subjugation, overcoming, a battle of antitheses, there cannot be pliability, mind cannot be subtle, penetrating, discerning. Through the conflict of opposites mind becomes conditioned; and conditioned thought creates further limitations and thus the process of conditioning is continued. This process prevents pliability.

How is one to bring about that state which is not the result of the conflict of opposites? We must become aware of the conflict of opposites taking place in each one of us, without identifying ourselves with one of the opposites or interfering with the conflict. Conflict stirs up the mind, and as the mind dislikes being agitated, it seeks an artificial way out of that disturbed condition. Such a way must be an escape or an opposite, which but creates for the mind further limitation. To be in conflict and at the same time to be vibrantly still, neither accepting nor denying it, is not easy. Being in a state of conflict and at the same time seeking no remedy or escape brings about integral thought. This is right effort.

To free the mind from the conflict of the opposites, you must become cognizant of the process of overcoming one part of consciousness by another, one division by another.

This process you call training the mind; but it is nothing more than the formation of a habit born of the opposites.

Let us consider the mind caught up in authority. There is the authority of outward compulsion, of groups, leaders, opinions, traditions. You may yield to this authority without fully comprehending it and assert that it is from voluntary choice; but if you really examine yourself, you will see that in that choice there is a deep desire for security, which creates fear, and to overcome that fear you submit yourself to authority. Then there is the subtle, subjective authority of accumulative memories, prejudices, fears, antipathies, wants, which have become values, ideals, standards. If you deeply examine it you will see that the mind is constantly accepting and rejecting authority and conditioning itself by new values and standards born of craving for self-protection and security. You may say to yourself that you are not in any way seeking security which creates the many subtle forms of authority, but if you observe you will see that you are seeking insecurity in order that you may become convinced of the falseness of security. So the idea of insecurity becomes only another form of security and authority. When you reject authority and seek freedom from it, you are but seeking the antithesis; whereas true freedom, the intelligent and awakened state of mind, is beyond opposites. It is that vibrant stillness of deep thought, of choiceless awareness, that creative intuition, which is the plenitude of life.

Question: If I am in conflict with family, friends, employers, and state laws, in fact, with the various forms of exploitation, will not seeking liberation from all bondage make life practically impossible?

KRISHNAMURTI: I am afraid it would, if you were merely seeking liberation as an opposite of conflict and so an escape from actuality. If you desire to make life practical, and vital, then you must understand the whole process of exploitation, both the obvious and the insidious. Mere escape from conflict with family, friends, and environment will not free you from exploitation. It is only in comprehending the significance of the whole process of exploitation that there is intelligence. Intelligence makes life possible, practical, and vital. I mean by intelligence, not the superficial intellectual process, but that change of will which is brought about by the integral completeness of one's whole being.

We are well acquainted with the obvious forms of exploitation, but there are the many subtle forms of which we are unconscious. If you would really comprehend exploitation in its obvious and subtle forms, you must discern the 'I' process—that process which is born of ignorance, want, fear. All action born of this process must entail exploitation. Many people withdraw from the world to contemplate reality, and hope to bring the 'I' process to an end. You should not withdraw from life to consider life. This escape does not bring the 'I' process of ignorance, want, and fear to an end. To live is to be in relationship, and when that relationship begins to be irksome, limited, it creates conflict, suffering. Then there is the desire for the opposite, an escape from relationship. One does very often escape, but only into a shallow, arid life of fear and illusion, which intensifies conflict and brings about slow decay. It is this escape which is impractical and confusing. If you would strip life of all its ugliness and cruelty you must, through right effort, bring the self-sustaining process of ignorance to an end.

Question: If truth is beyond and above all limitations, it must be cosmic and hence embrace within it every expression of life.

Should not such cosmic consciousness, therefore, include the understanding of every aspect and activity of life and exclude none?

KRISHNAMURTI: Do not let us concern ourselves about what is cosmic consciousness, truth, and so on. That which is real will be known when the various forms of illusions have ceased. As the mind is capable of such subtle deceptions and has the power to create for itself many illusions, our concern should not be about the state of reality, but to dispel the many delusions that are consciously or unconsciously springing up. By belonging to a religious organization with its dogmas, beliefs, creeds, or by being one of these new dogmatic nationalists, you hope to realize God, truth, or human happiness. But how can the mind comprehend reality if it is twisted by beliefs, prejudices, dogmas, and fears? Only when these limitations are dissolved can there be truth. Do not preconceive *what is* and then adjust to that conception your wants.

To love man you think you must belong to some nationality; to love reality you think it is necessary to belong to some organized religion. As we have not the capacity to discern truth among the many illusions that crowd our mind, we deceive ourselves by thinking that the false as well as the true, hate as well as love, are essential parts of life. Where there is love, hatred cannot exist. To comprehend reality you need not go through all the experiences of illusion.

Question: How can we solve the problems of sex?

KRISHNAMURTI: Where there is love the problem of sex does not exist. It becomes a problem only when love has been displaced by sensation. So the question really is how to control sensation. If there were the vital flame of love, the problem of sex would cease. Now sex has become a problem through sensation, habit, and stimulation, through the many absurdities of modern civilization. Literature, cinemas, advertisements, talk, dress—all these stimulate sensation and intensify the conflict. The problem of sex cannot be solved separately, by itself. It is futile to try to understand it through behavioristic or scientific morality. Artificial restrictions may be necessary, but they can only produce an arid and shallow life.

We all have the capacity for deep and inclusive love, but through conflict and false relationship, sensation and habit, we destroy its beauty. Through possessiveness with its many cruelties, through all the ugliness of reciprocal exploitation, we slowly extinguish the flame of love. We cannot artificially keep the flame alive, but we can awaken intelligence, love, through constant discernment of the many illusions and limitations which now dominate our mind-heart, our whole being. So what we have to understand is not what kind of restrictions, scientific or religious, should be placed on wants and sensations, but how to bring about deep and enduring fulfillment. We are frustrated on every side; fear dominates our spiritual and moral life, forcing us to imitate, conform to false values and illusions. There is no creative expression of our whole being, either in work or in thought. So sensation becomes monstrously important and its problems overwhelming. Sensation is artificial, superficial, and if we do not penetrate deeply into want and comprehend its process, our life will be shallow and utterly vain and miserable. The mere satisfaction of want or the continual change in want destroys intelligence, love. Love alone can free you from the problems of sex.

Question: You say that we can become fully aware of that 'I' process which is focused in each one of us individually. Does that mean that no experience can be of any value except to the person who has it?

KRISHNAMURTI: If you are conditioning thought by your own experience, how can the experience of another liberate it? If you have conditioned your mind through your own volitional activities, how can the comprehension of another free you? It may stimulate you superficially, but such help is not lasting. If you comprehend this, then the whole system of what is called spiritual help, through worship and discipline or through messages from the hereafter, has very little significance. If you discern that the 'I' process is maintaining itself through its own volitional activities, born of ignorance, want, and fear, then the experience of another can have very little significance. Great religious teachers have declared what is moral and true. Their followers have merely imitated them and so have not fulfilled. If you say that we must have ideals by which to live, this but indicates that there is fear in your mind-heart. Ideals create duality in consciousness, and so merely continue the process of conflict. If you perceive that the awakening of intelligence is the ending of the 'I' process, then there is spontaneous adjustment to life, harmonious relationship with environment, instead of the compulsion of fear or the imitation of an example, which but increases the 'I' process of ignorance, want, fear.

Now if each one of you really perceived this, I assure you, there would be a vital change in your will and attitude towards life. People often ask me, "Should we not have authority? Should we not follow Masters? Should we not have discipline?" There are others who say, "Do not talk to us about authority because we have gone beyond it." So long as the 'I' process continues, there must be the many subtle forms of authority, of want, with its fears, illusions, and compulsion. Authority of example implies that there

is fear, and as long as we do not understand the 'I' process, mere examples will only become hindrances.

Question: Is there any such being as God, apart from man? Has the idea of God any value to you?

KRISHNAMURTI: Why are you asking me this question? Do you want me to encourage you in your faith or support you in your disbelief? Either there is God or there is not. Some assert that there is, and some deny. Man is perplexed by these contradictions.

To discern the actual, the real, mind must be free of opposites. I have explained that the world is made up of unique forces without a beginning, which are not propelled by one supreme force or by one transcendental, unique energy. You cannot understand any other process of energy except that which is focused in you, which is you. This unique energy in its self-active development becomes consciousness creating its own limitations and environment, both conceptual and actual.

The 'I' process is self-sustaining through its own volitional activities of ignorance, want. So long as the 'I' process continues, there must be conflict, fear, and duality in action. In bringing the volitional activities to an end, there is bliss, the love of the true. When you suffer, you do not consider the cause of the whole process of suffering, but only desire to escape into an illusion which you call happiness, reality, God. If all illusion is perceived and there is deep discernment of the cause of suffering, which awakens right effort, then there is the immeasurable, the unknowable.

Question: Has the idea of predestination any actual validity?

KRISHNAMURTI: Action arising each moment from limitation, ignorance, modifies and renews the 'I' process, giving to it continuity and identity. This continuity of action through limitation is predestination. By your own acts you are being conditioned, but at any moment you can break the chain of limitation. So you are a free agent at all times, but you are conditioning yourself through ignorance, fear. You are not the plaything of some entity, of some mysterious force, good or evil. You are not at the mercy of some erratic forces in the world. You are not merely controlled by heredity or environment.

When we think about destiny, we imagine that our present and future are determined by some external force and so we yield to faith. We accept, on the authority of faith, that some unique energy, intelligence, God, has already settled our destiny. In opposition to faith we have science, with its mechanistic explanations of life.

What I say cannot be understood through the opposites. Thought is conditioned by ignorance and fear, and through its own volitional activities, consciousness sustains itself and maintains its identity. Action born of limitation must create further conditioning of the mind; that is, ignorance of oneself forms a chain of self-limiting actions. This process of self-determining and self-limiting thought-action gives identity and continuity to consciousness as the 'I.'

The past is the background of conditioned thought-action which is dominating and controlling the present and thereby creating a predetermined future. An act born of fear creates certain memories or self-protective resistances which determine future action. Thus the past controlling the present is overshadowing the future. So there is a chain formed which holds thought in bondage. The choiceless awareness of this process is the beginning of true freedom.

If the mind is cognizant of the process of ignorance, it can liberate itself from it at any moment. If you deeply comprehend this you will see that thought need not ever be conditioned by cause and effect. If this is understood, lived, there is vital freedom, without fear, without the superficiality of antithesis.

August 3, 1936

Eighth Talk at Ommen

I hope you have spent these ten days in purposeful thought, for now you have to return to face the daily routine of conflicts and problems in a world gone mad with hatred. We have been trying during these few days to understand in what way we can deal with the many complex problems of man. Without deep penetration into the whole process of human struggle, mere superficial response to reactions can only lead to greater conflict and suffering. This camp, I hope, has given each one of us an opportunity to think integrally, fully, and truly. Going out into the world again, each one of us has to cope with the many problems of his religious, social, and economic environment, with its conflicting and sorrowful divisions.

By tracing each problem back to its cause, shall we be free from conflicts? By studying reactions, can we perceive the cause of all action? Science and religion with their conflicting assertions have only created division in the mind. How are we with our intricate, subtle human problems to know what is the true center or cause of all action with its conflict and suffering? Until we discover for ourselves this center of action and discern it comprehensively, integrally, the mere analysis of reactions or the reliance on faith will not free the mind from ignorance and sorrow.

If we fully discern the center of all action, we will bring about a tremendous change in our outlook and activities. Without understanding the process of action, mere tinkering with social reforms or economic changes is utterly useless; it may produce results, but they can only be superficial remedies.

There are many unique separative forces or energies at work in the world, which we cannot wholly understand. We can only understand fundamentally and integrally the unique energy which is focused in each one of us, which is the 'I'. It is the only process we can understand.

To understand the process of this unique energy, the 'I', you need deep discernment, not the study of intellectual deductions and analysis. You must have a mind that is capable of great pliability. A mind that is burdened with want and fear, which creates opposites and from which arises choice, is incapable of discerning the subtle process of the 'I', the center of all action. As I have explained, this energy is unique; it is conditioning and conditioned at the same time. It is creating its own limitation through its own action born of ignorance. This unique energy, without a beginning, has in its self-active development become consciousness, the 'I' process.

This consciousness, which is conditioning itself through its own volitional activities, this 'I' process of ignorance, wants, fears, illusions is the center of action. This center is continually re-forming itself and creating anew its own limitation through its own volitional activities, and so there is always conflict, pain, sorrow. There must be a fundamental change in consciousness, in this very center of action; mere discipline and the authority of ideals cannot bring about the cessation of suffering and sorrow. You have to discern that the 'I' process, with its fear and illusion, is transient and so can be dissolved.

Many of you subtly believe that the 'I' is eternal, divine, and that without the 'I' there cannot be activity, there cannot be love, and

that with the cessation of the 'I' process, there can only be annihilation. So you must first discern profoundly for yourselves if the 'I' process is ever enduring, or if it is transient. You must know what is its nature, its being. This is a very difficult task, for most of you have been brought up through faith in the religious tradition which makes you cling to the 'I' and prevents you from perceiving its true essence. Some of you, who have cast aside religious beliefs only to accept scientific dogmas, will equally find it difficult to know the true nature of the center of action. Superficial inquiry into the nature of the 'I', or casual assertion of its divinity, merely indicates an essential lack of understanding of the true nature of the 'I' process.

You can discern for yourself what it is, as I know for myself its real nature. When I say this, it is not to encourage a belief in my comprehension of the 'I' process. Only when you know for yourself what it is, can this process be brought to an end.

With the cessation of the 'I' process, there is a change of will, which alone can end suffering. No system, no discipline, can bring about the change of will. Become aware of the 'I' process. In choiceless awareness, duality which exists only in the action of want, fear, and ignorance ceases. There is simply the perception of the actor, with his memories, wants, and fears, and his actions— the one center perceiving itself without objectifying itself.

Mere control or compulsion, one want overcoming another want, mere substitution, is but a change in will, which can never bring suffering to an end. The change in want is a change in limitation, further conditioning thought, which results in superficial reformation. If there is change of will through the comprehension of the 'I' process, then there is intelligence, creative intuition, from which alone can come harmonious relationship with individuals, with environment. Through discernment of the 'I' process of ignorance, there comes awareness. It is choiceless spontaneity of action, not action born of discrimination which is weighing one act against another, one reaction against another, one habit of thought against another. When there is the full comprehension and so the cessation of the 'I' process, there comes a choiceless life, a life of plenitude, a life of bliss.

Question: When one encounters those who are caught up in the collective thought and mass psychology which are responsible for much of the chaos and strife around us, how can one extricate them from their mass mentality and show them the necessity of individual thought?

KRISHNAMURTI: First extricate yourself from mass psychology, from collective thoughtlessness. This extrication of thought from the stupidities of ages is a very difficult task. Thoughtlessness and stupidity of the mass exist in us. We are the mass, conscious of some of its stupidities and cruelties but mostly unconscious of its overpowering prejudices, false values, and ideals. Before you can extricate another, you must free yourself from the great power of those wants and fears. That is, you must know for yourself what are the stupidities, what are those values which condition life and action. Some of you are conscious of the obviously false values of hatred, national divisions, and exploitation, but you have not discerned the process of these limitations and freed yourselves from them. When you begin to perceive the false values that hold you and discern their significance, then you will know what a tremendous change takes place in you. Then only can you truly help another. Though you may not become a leader of great multitudes, though you may not accomplish spectacular reforms, if you really

grasp the significance of what I am saying, you will become as an oasis in a burning desert, as a flame in darkness.

The ending of the 'I' process is the beginning of wisdom which alone can bring intelligent order and happiness to this chaotic world.

Question: Some of us have listened to you for ten years, and while, as you encouragingly remark, we may have changed a little, we have not changed radically. Why is this? Must we wait for the urge of suffering?

KRISHNAMURTI: I do not think you need to wait for the urge of suffering to change you radically. You are suffering now. You may be unconscious of conflict and sorrow, but you are suffering. What brings about superficial change is thought that is seeking superficial remedies, escapes, and security. Profound change of will can come about only when there is the deep comprehension of the 'I' process. In that alone is there the plenitude of intelligence and love.

Question: What is your idea of evolution?

KRISHNAMURTI: Obviously there is simplicity and there is great complexity; simplicity and great complexity of form; simplicity and great subtlety of thought; the simple wheel of many thousands of years ago and the complex machinery of today. Is the simple becoming complex, evolution? When you talk about evolution, you are not thinking merely about the evolution of form. You are thinking about the subtle evolution of consciousness which you call the 'I'. From this there arises the question: Is there growth, a future continuance, for individual consciousness? Can the 'I' become all-comprehensive, permanent, enduring?

That which is capable of growth is not eternal. That which is enduring, true, is ever becoming. It is choiceless movement. You ask me if the 'I' will evolve, become glorious, divine. You are looking to time to destroy and diminish sorrow. So long as the mind is bound to time, there will be conflict and sorrow. So long as consciousness is identifying itself, renewing and re-forming itself through its own activities of fear, which are time binding, there must be suffering. It is not time that will free you from suffering. Craving for experience, for opportunity, comparing memories cannot bring about the plenitude of life, the ecstasy of truth. Ignorance seeks the perpetuation of the 'I' process; and wisdom comes into being with the cessation of the self-active renewal of limited consciousness. Mere complexity of accumulation is not wisdom, intelligence. Mere accumulation, growth, time, does not bring about the plenitude of life. To be without fear is the beginning of understanding, and fear is ever in the present.

Question: As a living example of one who has attained liberation, you are a tremendous source of encouragement to us who are still involved in suffering. Is there not a danger that in spite of ourselves this very encouragement might become a hindrance to us?

KRISHNAMURTI: I hope I am not becoming an example for you to follow because I speak of the process of suffering and ignorance, the illusion of the mind, the false values created by fear, the freedom of truth. An example is a hindrance, it is born of fear which leads to compulsion and imitation. Imitation of another is not the comprehension of oneself.

To know oneself there can be no following of another; there cannot be compulsive memories which prevent the 'I' process from revealing itself. When the mind has ceased to escape from suffering into illusions and false values, then that very suffering brings understanding, without the false motives of reward and punishment. The center of action is ignorance and its result is suffering. The following of another or the disciplining of the mind according to the authority of an ideal will not bring about plenitude of life nor the bliss of reality.

Question: Is there any way in the world by which we can end the stupid horror which again we see perpetrated in Spain?

KRISHNAMURTI: War is the problem of humanity. How are we going to end mass and individual barbarities? To arouse mass action against the horrors, cruelties, and absurdities of the present civilization, there must be individual comprehension.

Begin with yourself. Root out the appallingly cruel prejudices and wants, and you will know a happy world. Root out your personal ambitions and subtle exploitations, acquisitiveness and the craving for power. Then you will have an intelligent and orderly world. As long as there is cruelty and violence in the individual, collective hatred, patriotism, and strife must continue.

When you realize your individual responsibility in action, then there will be the possibility of peace and love and harmonious relationship with your neighbor. Then there will be the possibility of ending the horror of strife, the horror of man killing man.

August 4, 1936

Madras, India, 1936

*

First Talk in Madras

In this world of conflict and suffering, right comprehension alone can bring about intelligent order and lasting happiness. To awaken intelligent thought there must be right effort on the part of each individual—effort which is not induced by personal reactions and fancies, by beliefs and ideals. Such thought alone can produce right organization of life and true relationship between the individual and society. I shall try to help you, the individual, to think directly and simply, but you must have the intense desire for comprehension. You must free yourself from the prejudice of loyalty to particular beliefs and dogmas, from the prejudices of habitual conduct molded by traditions of thoughtlessness. You must have the burning desire for experimentation and action, for only through action can you truly perceive that authority, beliefs, ideals are definite hindrances to intelligence, to love.

But I am afraid most of you come merely by habit to listen to these talks. This is not a political meeting. Nor do I wish to incite you to some economic, social, or religious action. I do not want a following nor do I seek your worship. I do not want to become a leader or create a new ideology. I desire only that we should attempt to think together clearly, sanely, intelligently; and from this process of true thinking, action will inevitably follow; thought is not to be separated from action.

Right comprehension of life cannot come about if, in any form, there is fear, compulsion. Creative understanding of life is prevented when thought and action are constantly impeded by authority—the authority of discipline, of reward, and punishment. By the directness of creative action you will discern that the ruthless search for individual security must inevitably lead to exploitation and suffering. Only through dynamic thoughtaction can there come about that complete inward revolution with its possibility of true human relationship between the individual and society.

What, then, is our individual answer to the present complex problem of living? Do we meet life with the particular point of view of religion, science, or economics? Do we cling to tradition, whether old or new, without thought? Can this prodigiously subtle, complex thing called life be understood by dividing it into different parts, as political, social, religious, scientific; by laying emphasis on one part and disregarding the others?

It is the fashion nowadays to say, "Solve the economic problem first, and then all other problems will be solved." If we regard life merely as an economic process, then living becomes mechanical, superficial, and destructive. How can we grasp the subtle, unknown, psychological process of life by merely saying that we must solve first the question of bread? The mere repetition of slogans does not demand much thought.

I do not mean to say that bread is not a problem; it is an immense problem. But by laying emphasis on it and by making it our chief interest, we approach the complexity of life with narrowness of mind and thereby only further complicate the problem.

If we are religious, that is, if our minds are conditioned by beliefs and dogmas, then we merely add further complexity to life. We must view life comprehensively with deep intelligence, but most of us try to solve life's problems with conditioned minds burdened with tradition. If you are a Hindu you seek to understand life through the particular beliefs, prejudices, and traditions of Hinduism. If you are a Buddhist, a socialist, or an atheist, you try to comprehend life only through your special creed. A conditioned, limited mind cannot understand the movement of life.

Please do not look to me for a panacea, a system, or a mode of conduct because I regard systems, modes of conduct, and panaceas as hindrances to the intelligent comprehension of life.

To understand the complexity of life, mind must be extremely pliable and simple. Simplicity of mind is not the emptiness of negation, renunciation, or acceptance; it is the fullness of comprehension. It is the directness of perception, of integral thought, unhindered by prejudice, fear, tradition, and authority. To free the mind from these limitations is arduous. Experiment with yourself and you will see how difficult it is to have integral thought, unconditioned by provocative memory with its authority and discipline. And yet with such thought alone can we comprehend the significance of life.

Please see the importance of a pliable mind, a mind that knows the intricacies of fear with its illusions and is wholly free from them, a mind that is not controlled by environmental influences. Before we can comprehend the full significance of life, its vital processes, thought unconditioned by fear is necessary; and to awaken that creative thought, we must become conscious of the complex, the actual.

What do I mean by "being conscious"? I mean not only the objective perception of the interrelated complexity of life, but also the complete awareness of the hidden, subtle, psychological processes from which arise confusion, joy, struggle, and pain. Most of us think that we are conscious of the objective complexity of life. We are conscious of our jobs, of our bosses, of ourselves as employers or as the employed. We are conscious of friction in relationship. This perception of the mere objective complexity of life is not, to me, full consciousness. We become fully conscious only when we deeply relate the psychological to the objective complexity. When we are able to relate through action the hidden with the known, then we are beginning to be conscious.

Before we can awaken in ourselves this full consciousness from which alone can come true creative expression, we must become aware of the actual, that is, of the prejudices, fears, tendencies, wants, with their many illusions and expressions. When we are thus aware, we shall know the relationship of the actual to our action which limits and conditions thought-emotion with its reactions, hopes, and escapes. When we are conscious of the actual, there is the immediate perception of the false. That very perception of the false is truth. Then there is no problem of choice, of good and evil, false and true, the essential and unessential. In perceiving *what is,* the false and the true are known, without the conflict of choice.

Now, you think you are able to choose between the false and the true. That choice is based on prejudice; it is induced by preconceived ideals, by tradition, hope, and so the choice is only a modification of the false. But, if you are able to perceive the actual without any desire or identification, then in that very perception of the false, there is the beginning of the true. That is intelligence, which is not based on prejudice, tradition, want, and that alone can dissolve the subtle essence of all problems spontaneously, richly, and without the compulsion of fear.

Let us find out, if we can, what is the actual, without interpretation, without identification. When I speak of your beliefs and theories, your worships, your Gods, your ideals and leaders, when I speak of the disease of nationalism, of systems, of gurus and Masters, do not project defensive reactions. All that I am trying to do is to point out what I consider to be the cause of conflict and suffering.

Action from integral thought, without identification and interpretation, will awaken creative intelligence. If you are deeply observant you will begin to see what is true; then you will awaken intelligence without the continual conflict of choice. Mere conduct according to a standard is imitative, not creative. Intelligent action is not imitation. Only the conditioned mind is always adjusting itself to standards, because it is afraid to know *what is*. If you perceive the actual in all its clarity, as it is, without interpretation and identification, then at the very instant of perception, there is the dawning of new intelligence. This intelligence alone can solve the tremendously complicated, conflicting, and painful problems of life.

What is the picture of ourselves and of the world? The division as ourselves and the world seems actual, though such division disappears when we deeply examine the individual and the mass. The actual is the conflict between the individual and the mass, but the individual is the mass and the mass is the individual. Individuality or the mass ceases when the characteristics of the individual or the mass disappear. The mass is ignorance, want, fear, in the individual. All the unexplored regions of consciousness, the half-awakened states of the individual, form the mass. It is only when the individual and the mass, as conflicting forces, cease to exist that there can be creative intelligence. It is this division of the mass and the individual, which is but an illusion, that is creating confusion and misery. You are not a complete individual nor are you wholly the mass; you are both the individual and the mass.

In the minds of most people there is this unfortunate division as the individual and the mass; there is the idea that by organizing the mass you will bring about creative, individual freedom and expression. If you are thinking of organizing the mass in order to help the creative release of the individual, then such organizing becomes the means of subtle exploitation.

There are two forms of exploitation, the obvious and the subtle. The obvious has become habitual, which we know and pass by, but it requires deep perception to recognize the subtle forms of exploitation. One class, which has the wealth, exploits the mass. The few who control industry exploit the many who work. Wealth concentrated in the hands of the few creates social distinctions and divisions; and through these divisions we have economic and sentimental nationalism, the constant threat of war with all its terrors and cruelties, the division of peoples into races and nations with their fierce struggle for self-sufficiency, the hierarchical systems of graded cunning and privilege.

All this is obvious, and as it is obvious, you have become accustomed to it. You say nationalism is inevitable; so each nation asserts and prepares for war and slaughter. As individuals you are unconsciously helping war by emphasizing your national separativeness. Nationalism is a disease, whether in this country, in Europe, or America. Separative individual or national search for security only intensifies conflict and human suffering.

The subtle form of exploitation is not easily perceived because it is an intimate process of our individual existence. It is the result of the search for certainty, for comfort in the present and in the hereafter. Now this search, which we call the search for truth, for God, has led to the creating of systems of exploitation which we call beliefs, ideals, dogmas, and to their perpetuation by priests, gurus, and guides. Because you as individuals are in confusion and doubt, you hope that another will bring enlightenment to you. You hope to overcome suffering and confusion by following another, by following a system of discipline or some ideal. This attempt to conquer misery and pain by submitting yourself to another, by regulating your conduct according to a standard, is merely a flight from actuality. So, in your search for escape from the actual, you go to another to be enriched and comforted, and thereby you engender the process of subtle exploitation. Religion, as it is, thrives on fear and exploitation.

How many of you are conscious that you are seeking security—an escape from the constant gnawing of fear, from confusion, and sorrow? The desire for security, for psychological certainty, has encouraged a subtle form of exploitation through discipline, compulsion, authority, tradition.

So, you must discern for yourself the process of your own thought-action, born of ignorance and fear, which brings about cruel exploitation, confusion, and sorrow. When there is the comprehension of the actual, without the struggle of choice, there is love, the ecstasy of truth.

December 6 and 25, 1936

Second Talk in Madras

Amongst the many conflicting remedies, theories, ideals, what is the true cure for our social complexities and cruelties, for the deep misunderstandings that are creating confusion and chaos in the world?

There are many teachers with their methods, many philosophers with their systems. How is one to choose what is true? Each system, each teacher, lays emphasis on some part of the whole existence of man.

How is one, then, to comprehend the whole process of life, and how is one to free the mind, so that there can be the perception of what is true? Each leader has his own group of people, in conflict with another group, with another leader. There is disagreement, confusion, chaos. Some groups become ruthless, and others try to become tolerant, liberal, for their leaders say to them, "Cultivate tolerance, for all paths lead to reality." So, in trying to develop the spirit of tolerance, brotherliness, they gradually become indifferent, sluggish, even brutal.

In a world of confusion, disagreement, when people take their beliefs and ideals seriously, vitally, can there be true cooperation between groups that believe differently and work for varying ideals? If you believed firmly in an idea, and another through his ardent faith worked in opposition to you, could there be tolerance, friendship between you and the other? Or is the conception of each one going his own way false? Is the idea of cultivating brotherliness and tolerance in the midst of conflict impossible and hypocritical? In spite of your strong beliefs, convictions, and hopes, can you establish a superficial relationship of friendliness and tolerance with another who is diametrically opposed to your conception of life? If you can, there must be compromise, a lessening of that which is true to you, and so you yield to another who is circumstantially more powerful than you. This but creates more confusion. The cultivation of tolerance is only an intellectual feat and so is without any deep significance, leading to thoughtlessness and poverty of being.

If you examine the propaganda that is being made throughout the world by nations, classes, groups, sects, individuals, you will see that in various ways they are all determined to convert you to their particular point of view or belief. Can rival propagandists be friendly and tolerant, deeply, truly? If you are Hindu and another is a Mohammedan, you a capitalist and another a socialist, can there be deep relationship between you? Is this possible? It is impossible. The cultivation of tolerance is an intellectual, and so an artificial, process which has no reality. This does not mean that I am advocating persecution or some cruel act for the sake of beliefs. Please follow what I am saying.

While there is conversion, incitement, the subtle forcing of another to join a particular group or subscribe to a particular set of beliefs while there are opposite, contradictory ideas, there cannot be harmony and peace, though we may pretend intellectually to be tolerant and brotherly. For each one is so interested, so enthusiastic about his own ideas and methods that he desires urgently that another shall accept them, and so creates a condition of conflict and confusion. This is obvious.

If you are thoughtful and not a propagandist, you are bound to see the superficiality of this jargon of tolerance and brotherliness and face the fierce battle of contradictory ideas, hopes, and faiths. In other words, you must perceive the actual, the disagreement, the confusion that is now about us. If we can put aside this easy jargon of tolerance and brotherhood, we may then see the way to comprehend disagreement. There is a way out of the chaos, but it does not lie through artificial brotherhood or intellectual tolerance. Only through right thinking and action

can the conflict of opposing groups and ideas be ended.

What do I mean by right thinking? Thought must be vital, dynamic, not mechanical or imitative.

A system of disciplining the mind according to a particular mode is considered to be positive thinking. You first create or accept an intellectual image, an ideal, and to accord with that you twist your thought. This conformity, imitation, is mistaken for comprehension, but in reality it is only the craving for security born of fear. The prompting of fear only leads to conformity, and discipline born of fear is not right thinking.

To awaken intelligence you must perceive what impedes the creative movement of thought. That is, if you can perceive for yourself that ideals, beliefs, traditions, values are constantly twisting your thought-action, then by becoming aware of these distortions, intelligence is awakened. There can be no creative thinking so long as there are conscious or unconscious hindrances, values, prejudices, that pervert thought. Instead of pursuing imitativeness, systems, and gurus, you must become conscious of your impediments, your own prejudices and standards, and in discerning their significance there will be that creative intelligence which alone can destroy confusion and bring about deep agreement of comprehension.

The most stubborn of all impediments is tradition. You may ask, "What will happen to the world if tradition is destroyed? Will there not be chaos? Will there not be immorality?" Confusion, conflict, pain exist now, in spite of your honored traditions and moral doctrines.

What is the process by which the mind is ever accumulating values, memories, habits, which we call tradition? We cannot discern this process so long as mind is conditioned by fear and want which are constantly creating anchorages in consciousness that become tradition.

Can the mind ever be free of these anchorages of values, traditions, memories? What you call thinking is merely moving from one anchorage or center of bias to another, and from this center, judging, choosing, and creating substitutions. Anchored in limitation, you contact other ideas and values, which superficially modify your own conditioned beliefs. You then form another center of new values, new memories, which again condition future thought and action. So always from these anchorages you judge, calculate, and react. As long as this movement from anchorage to anchorage continues, there must be conflict and suffering, there cannot be love. Superficial cultivation of brotherhood and tolerance only encourages this movement and intensifies illusion.

Can the mind-heart ever free itself from the center of conditioned thought-emotion? If the mind-heart does not create for itself these anchorages of self-protection, then there can be clear thought, love, which alone will solve the many problems that now create confusion and misery. If you begin to be conscious of these centers, you will discern what a tremendous power they are for disagreement, for confusion. When you are not conscious of them, you are exploited by organizations, by leaders, who promise you new substitutions. You learn to talk easily of brotherhood, kindliness, love—words that can have no significance at all as long as you merely move from one bias to another.

Either you discern the process of ignorance with its tradition, and so there is immediate action, or you are so accustomed to the drug of substitution that perception becomes impossible, and so you begin to seek a method of escape. Perception is action, they are not divisible. What you call intellectual perception creates an artificial separation between thought and action. You then struggle

to bridge this division, an effort that has no significance, for it is the lack of comprehension that has created this illusory division. Either you are aware of the process or you are not. If you are not, let us consider this process deeply, enthusiastically, but do not let us seek a method. This eagerness to comprehend becomes the flame of awareness which burns away the desire for substitution.

Question: Can I forever be rid of sorrow, and by what method?

KRISHNAMURTI: Sorrow is the companion of all—the rich and the poor, the believer and the nonbeliever. In spite of all your beliefs and doctrines, in spite of your temples and Gods, suffering is your constant companion. Let us understand it and not merely think of being rid of it. When you have fully comprehended sorrow, then you will not seek a way to overcome it.

Do you want to be rid of joy, ecstasy, bliss? No. Then why do you say you must be rid of sorrow? The one gives pleasure, the other pain, and the mind clings to that which is pleasurable and nourishes it. All interference on the part of the mind to stimulate joy and overcome sorrow must be artificial, ineffective. You are seeking a way out of your misery, and there are those who will help you to forget sorrow by offering you the dope of belief, doctrine, and future happiness. If mind does not interfere either with joy or pain, then that very joy, that very sorrow, awakens the creative flame of awareness.

Sorrow is but an indication of conditioned thought, of mind limited by beliefs, fears, illusions, but you do not heed the incessant warning. To forget sorrow, to overcome it, to modify it, you seek refuge in beliefs, in the anchorage of self-protection and security. It is very difficult not to interfere with the process of sorrow, which does not mean that you must be resigned to it or that you must accept it as inevitable, as karma, as punishment. As you do not wish to change a lovely form, the glow after sunset, the vision of a tree in a field, so also do not obstruct the movement of sorrow. Let it ripen, for in its own process of fulfillment there is comprehension. When you are aware of the wound of sorrow, without acceptance, resignation, or denial, without artificially inviting it, then suffering awakens the flame of creative intelligence.

The very search for an escape from sorrow creates the exploiter, and the mind yields to exploitation. So long as the artificial process of interference with sorrow continues, sorrow must be your constant companion. But if there is vital awareness, without choice, without detachment, then there is intelligence which alone can dispel all confusion.

Question: With what special significance do you use the word intelligence? *Is it graded and therefore capable of constant evolution and variation?*

KRISHNAMURTI: I am using the word *intelligence* to convey the vital completeness of thought-action. Intelligence is not the outcome of intellectual effort nor of emotional fervor. It is not the product of theories, beliefs, and information. It is the completeness of action arising from the undivided comprehension of thought-emotion. In rare moments of deep love we know completeness.

Creative intelligence cannot be invited or measured, but the mind seeks definition, description, and is ever caught in the illusion of words. Awareness without choice reveals, in the very moment of action, the concealed distortions of thought and emotion and their hidden significance.

"Is it graded, and therefore capable of constant evolution and variation?" What is discerned completely cannot be variable, cannot evolve, grow. The comprehension of the process of the 'I', with its many centers of self-protection, the discernment of the significance of anchorages, cannot be changeable, cannot be modified through growth. Ignorance can vary, develop, change, grow. The various self-protective centers of the mind are capable of growth, change, and modification. The process of substitution is not intelligence, it is but a movement within the circle of ignorance.

The flame of intelligence, love, can be awakened only when the mind is vitally aware of its own conditioned thought, with its fears, values, wants.

December 13, 1936

Third Talk in Madras

I have tried to explain what is clear, creative thinking and how tradition, anchorages, fear, and security constantly impede the free movement of thought. If you would awaken intelligence, your mind must not escape into ideals and beliefs nor can it be caught in the accumulative process of self-protective memories. You must be conscious of the escape from the actual, and of living in the present with the values of the past or of the future.

If you observe yourself you will see that the mind is building up for itself security, certainty, in order to be free from fear, from apprehension, danger. The mind is ever seeking anchorages from which its choice and action may spring.

Mind is ever seeking and developing various forms of security, with its values and illusions: the security of wealth with its personal advantages and power; the security of belief and ideal; and the security which the mind seeks in love. A mind that is secure develops its own peculiar stupidities, puerilities, which cause much confusion and suffering.

When the mind is bewildered and fearful, it seeks impregnable certainties which become ideals, beliefs. Why does the mind create and cling to these anchorages of beliefs and traditions? Is it not because, perplexed by conflict and constant change, it seeks a finality, a deep assurance, a changeless state? And yet, in spite of these anchorages, suffering and sorrow continue. So mind begins to seek new substitutes, other ideals and beliefs, hoping again for security and happiness. The mind goes from one hope of certainty to another, from one illusion to another. This wandering is called growth.

When the conditioned mind becomes conscious of sorrow and uncertainty, it soon begins to stagnate by escaping into beliefs, theories, hopes. This process of substitution, of escape, only leads to frustration.

The search for security is but the expression of fear which distorts the mindheart. When you see the significance of your search for security through belief and ideal, you become conscious of its falseness. Then the mind seeks through reaction against belief and ideal an antithesis in which it hopes again to find certainty and happiness, which is but another form of escape from actuality. Mind has to become aware of its habit of developing antitheses.

Why is the mind guarding itself strongly against the movement of life? Can a mind that is not vulnerable, that is looking to its own advantages through its self-created values, ever know the ecstasy of life and the completeness of love? The mind is making itself impregnable so as not to suffer, and yet this very protection is the cause of sorrow.

Question: I can see that intelligence must be independent of intellect and also of any form of discipline. Is there a way by which *we can quicken the process of awakening intelligence and making it permanent?*

KRISHNAMURTI: There cannot be love, creative intelligence, so long as there is fear in any form. If you are fully aware of fear with its many activities and illusions, that very awareness becomes the flame of intelligence.

When the mind discerns for itself the hindrances that are preventing clear thought, then no artificial impetus is necessary for the awakening of intelligence. A mind that seeks a method is not aware of itself, of its ignorance, fears. It merely hopes that perhaps a method, a system of discipline, will dissipate its fears and sorrows. Discipline can only create habit, and so deaden the mind. To be aware without choice, to be conscious of the many activities of the mind, its richness, its subtleties, its deceptions, its illusions, is to be intelligent. This awareness itself dispels ignorance, fear. If you make an effort to be aware, then that effort creates a habit, impelled by the hope of escape from sorrow. Where there is deep and choiceless awareness, there is self-revelation which alone can prevent the mind from creating illusions for itself and thereby putting itself to sleep. If there is constant alertness of mind without the duality of the observer and the observed, if mind can know itself as it is without denial, assertion, acceptance, or resignation, then out of that very actuality there comes love, creative intelligence.

Question: Why are there many paths to truth? Is this idea an illusion, cleverly conceived to explain and justify differences?

KRISHNAMURTI: To clear thinking can there be many paths? Can any system lead to creative intelligence? There is only creative intelligence, not systems to awaken it. There is only truth, not paths leading to truth. It is only ignorance which divides itself into many paths and systems. Each religion maintains that it alone has the truth and that through it alone God can be realized; various organizations assert or imply that through their special methods truth can be known; each sect maintains that it has the special message, that it is the special vehicle of truth. Individual prophets and spiritual messengers offer their panaceas as direct revelations of God. Why do they claim such authority, such efficacy for their assertions? Is it not obvious? Vested interests, in the present or in the hereafter. They have to maintain their delusions of prestige and power, or else what will happen to all the creations of their terrestrial glory? Others, because they have impoverished themselves by denial and sacrifice, imagine themselves grown in grandeur and so assume the spiritual right of guiding the worldly. It is one of the facile explanations of spiritual interests to say that there are many paths to truth, thus justifying their own organized activities and attempting at the same time to be tolerant to those who maintain similar systems.

Also, we are so entrenched in prejudice, in tradition with its special beliefs and dogmas, that we repeat dogmatically, readily, that there are many paths to truth. To bring about tolerance between the many divisions of antagonistic and conditioned thought, the leaders of organized interests try to cover up, in weighty phrases, the inherent brutality of division. The very assertion of paths to truth is the denial of truth. How can anyone point out a way to truth—which has no abode, which is not to be measured, or sought after? That which is fixed is dead, and to that there may be paths. Ignorance creates the illusion of many ways and methods.

Through your own conditioned thought, through your own desire for certainty, finality, through your own fears which are constantly creating safety, you fabricate mechanical, artificial conceptions of truth, of perfection. And having invented these, you seek ways and means to maintain them. Each organization, group, sect, knowing that divisions deny friendship, tries to bring about artificial unity and brotherhood. Each says, "You follow your religion and I will follow mine; you have your truth and I will have mine; but let us cultivate tolerance." Such tolerance will only lead to illusion and confusion.

A mind that is conditioned by ignorance, fear, cannot comprehend truth, for out of its own limitation it creates for itself further limitations. Truth is not to be invited. Mind cannot create it. If you comprehend this fully, then you will discern the utter futility of systems, practices, and disciplines.

Now you are so much a part of the intellectual and mechanical process of living that you cannot perceive its artificiality; or you refuse to see it, for perception would mean action, hence the poverty of your own being. When you begin to be aware of the process of thought and become conscious that it is creating for itself its own emptiness and frustration, then that very awareness will dispel fear. Then there is love, completeness of life.

Question: Do you not see, sir, that your ideas can lead us but to one result—the blankness of negation and ineffectiveness in our struggle with the problems of life?

KRISHNAMURTI: What are the problems of life? To earn a living, to love, to have no fear, no sorrow, to live happily, sanely, completely. These are the problems of our life. Am I saying anything that can lead you to negation, to emptiness, that can prevent you from comprehending your own misery and struggle? Do you not ask me this question because your mind is accustomed to seek what is called positive instruction? That is, you want to be told what to do, advised to practice certain disciplines, so that you may lead a life of happiness and realize God. You are accustomed to conform, in the hope of a greater and fuller life. I say, on the contrary, conformity is born of fear, and this imitation is not the positive way of life. To point out the process in which you are caught, to help you to become aware of the prison of limitation which the mind has created for itself, is not negation. On the contrary, if you are aware of the process that has brought you to this present condition of sorrow and confusion, and if you understand the full significance of it, then that very comprehension dispels ignorance, fear, want. Then only can there be a life of fullness and true relationship between the individual and society. How can this lead you to a life of negation and ineffectiveness?

What have you now? A few beliefs and ideals, some possessions, a leader or two to follow, an occasional whisper of love, constant struggle and pain. Is this richness of life, fulfillment and ecstasy? How can the bliss of reality exist when the mind-heart is caught up in fear? How can there be enlightenment when the mind-heart is creating its own limitation and confusion? I say, consider what you have, become aware of these limitations, and that very awareness will awaken creative intelligence.

Question: Is freedom from conflict possible for anyone at any time, regardless of evolution? Have you come across another instance, besides yourself, in which the possibility has become an actuality?

KRISHNAMURTI: Do not let us inquire whether someone else has freed himself from ignorance and conflict. Can you, burdened with illusion and fear, free yourself from sorrow at any time? Can you, with many beliefs

and values, free yourself from ignorance and want? The idea of eventual perfection is but an illusion. A slothful mind clings to the satisfying idea of gradual growth and has accumulated for itself many comforting theories.

Can the movement from experience to experience bring about creative intelligence? You have had many experiences. What is the result? From such experiences you have only accumulated self-protective memories, which guard the mind from the movement of life.

Can the mind become aware, at any moment, of its own conditioning and begin to free itself from its own limitation? Surely, this is possible.

You may intellectually admit this, but it will have no significance whatsoever so long as it does not result in action. But action entails friction, trouble. Your neighbor, your family, your leader, your values, all these create opposition. So the mind begins to evade the actual and develop clever, cunning theories for its own protection. The conditioned mind, fearing the result of its effort, subtly escapes into the illusion of postponement, of growth.

December 20, 1936

Fourth Talk in Madras

In my talks I use words without the special significance which has been given to them by philosophers or psychologists.

What comprehension have these talks brought to you? Are you still asserting that there is a divinity, a love that is beyond human life? Are you still groping for partial remedies, superficial cures? What is the state of your mind and heart?

To bring about intelligent order there must be right thinking, right action. When the mind is capable of comprehending its own process of struggle, limitation, when thought is capable of revealing itself without the conflict of division, then there is the completeness of action. If the mind prepares itself for action, then such preparation must be based on the past, on self-protective memories, and must therefore prevent the fullness of action. Mere analysis of past action cannot yield its full significance. Mind that is consciously or unconsciously conforming to an ideal, which is but the projection of personal security and satisfaction, must limit action and so become conditioned. It is merely developing self-protective memories and habits to resist life. So there is constant frustration.

From the accumulation of self-protective memories there arises identity, the conception of the 'I' and its continuance, its evolution towards perfection, towards reality. This 'I' seeks to perpetuate itself through its own volitional activities of ignorance, fear, want. As long as the mind is not aware of these limitations, the effort to evolve, to succeed, only creates further suffering and increases the unconscious. Effort thus becomes a practice, a discipline, a mechanical adjustment, and conformity.

Most of us think that time and evolutionary progress are necessary for our fulfillment. We think that experiences are essential for our growth and unfoldment. Many accept this idea readily, as it comforts them to think that they have many lives through which they can perfect themselves; they hold that time is essential for their fulfillment. Is this so? Does experience truly liberate or merely limit thought? Can experience free the mind with its self-protective memories, from ignorance, fear, want? Self-protective memories and desires use experiences for their perpetuation. So we are time-bound.

What do we mean by experience? Is it not the accumulation of values, based on self-protective memories, which give us a mode of behavior prompted by personal advantage? It is the process of like and dislike, of choice. The accumulation of self-protective memories is the process of experience, and relationship is the contact between two individualized and self-protective memories, whose morality is the agreement to guard what they possess.

You are your own way and your own life. Out of your own right effort will be awakened creative intelligence. Until there is this creative intelligence, born of choiceless awareness, there must be chaos, there must be contention, hatred, conflict, sorrow.

Question: You have said that the comprehension of truth is possible only through experimentation. Now experimentation means action, which if it is to have any value must be born of mature thought. But if, to start with, my thinking is itself conditioned by memories and reactions, how can I act or experiment rightly?

KRISHNAMURTI: To experiment rightly, mind must first be aware that its thought is conditioned. One may think one is experimenting; but, if one is not aware of the limitation, then one is still acting within the bondage of ignorance, fear. Conditioned thought cannot know itself as conditioned; the desire to escape from this limitation, through analysis, through the artificial process of compulsion, denial, or assertion, will not bring you comprehension, freedom. No system or compulsion of will can reveal to the mind its own limitation, its own bondage.

When there is suffering, mind seeks an escape and therefore only creates for itself further illusions. But if the mind is fully aware of suffering and does not seek an escape, then that very awareness destroys illusion; that awareness is comprehension. So instead of inquiring how to free thought from fear, from want, be conscious of sorrow. Sorrow is the indication of a conditioned mind, and mere escape from it only increases limitation. In the moment of suffering, begin to be aware; then mind itself will perceive the illusory nature of escape, of self-protective memories and personal advantages.

Question: Should one be dutiful?

KRISHNAMURTI: Who asks this question? Not a man who is seeking comprehension, truth, but the man whose mind is burdened with fear, tradition, ideals, and racial loyalties. Such a mind coming into contact with the movement of life only creates friction and suffering for itself.

Question: Are elders guilty of exploitation when they expect respect and obedience from the young?

KRISHNAMURTI: The showing of respect to the aged is generally a habit. Fear can assume the form of veneration. Love cannot become a habit, a practice. There is no respect in the aged for the young nor in the young for the aged, but only the show of authority and the habit of fear.

The organization of phrases, the cultivation of respect, is not culture, but a trap to hold the thoughtless. Our minds have become so slavish to habitual values that we have lost all affection and deep respect for human life. Where there is exploitation there can be no respect for human dignity. If you demand respect just because you are aged and have authority, it is exploitation.

Question: If a man is in ignorance or at a loss to know what to do, is there no need of a guru to guide him?

KRISHNAMURTI: Can anyone help you to cross this aching void of daily life? Can any person, however great, help you out of this confusion? No one can. This confusion is self-created; this turmoil is the result of one will in conflict with another will. Will is ignorance.

I know the pursuit of gurus, teachers, guides, Masters is the indoor sport of many, the sport of the thoughtless all over the world. People say, "How can we prevent this chaotic misery and cruelty unless those who are free, the enlightened, come to our aid and save us from our sorrow?" Or they create a mental image of a favored saint and hang all their troubles round his neck. Or they believe that some super physical guide watches over them and tells them what to do, how to act. The search for a guru, a Master, indicates an avoidance of life.

Conformity is death. It is but the formation of habit, the strengthening of the unconscious. How often we see some ugly, cruel scene and recoil from it. We see poverty, cruelty, degradation of every kind; at first we are appalled by it, but we soon become unconscious of it.

We become used to our environment, we shrug our shoulders and say, "What can we do? It is life." Thus we destroy our sensitive reactions to ugliness, to exploitation, cruelty, and suffering, also our appreciation and deep enjoyment of beauty. Thus there comes a slow withering of perception.

Habit gradually overcomes thinking. Observe the activity of your own thought and you will see how it is forming itself into one habit after another. The conscious is thus becoming the unconscious and habit hardens the mind through will and discipline. Forcing the mind to discipline itself through fear, which is often mistaken for love, brings about frustration.

The problem of gurus exists when you seek comfort, when you desire satisfaction. There is no comfort, but understanding; there is no satisfaction, but fulfillment.

Question: You seem to give a new significance to the idea of will, that divine quality in man. I understand you to regard it as a hindrance. Is this so?

KRISHNAMURTI: What do you mean by will? Is it not an overcoming, a conquering, a determining effort? What have you to conquer? Your habits, resistances developed by fear, the conflict of your desires, the struggle of the opposites, the frustration of your environment. So you develop will. The will to be, in all its significance, is but a process of resistance, a process of overcoming, prompted by self-protective craving.

Will is really an illusory necessity of fear, not a divine quality. It is but the perpetuation of self-protective memories. Out of fear you make yourself invulnerable to love, to truth; and the development of the process of self-protection is called will. Will has its roots in egotism. The will to exist, the will to become perfect, the will to succeed, the will to acquire, the will to find God, is the urge of egotism.

When the action of fear, ambition, security, personal virtue, and character yields to intelligence, then you will know how to live completely, integrally, without the battle of will.

Will is only the insistent prompting of self-protective memories, the result of individualized ignorance and fear. The cessation of will is not death, it is only the cessation of illusion, born of ignorance. Action devoid of fear and personal advantage will alone bring about harmonious, creative relationship with another, with society.

December 26, 27, and 28, 1936

Ommen, Holland, 1937

*

First Talk at Ommen

Amidst the changing circumstances of life, is there anything permanent? Is there any relation between ourselves and the constant change about us? If we accepted that everything is change, including ourselves, then there would never be the idea of permanency. If we thought of ourselves as in a state of continual movement, then there would be no conflict between the changing circumstances of life and the thing we now think of as being permanent.

There is a deep, abiding hope or a certainty in us that there is something permanent in the midst of continual change, and this gives rise to conflict. We see that change exists about us. We see everything decaying, withering. We see cataclysms, wars, famines, death, insecurity, disillusionment. Everything about us is in constant change, becoming and decaying. All things are worn out by use. There is nothing permanent about us. In our institutions, our morals, our theories of government, of economics, of social relationship—in all things there is a flux, there is a change.

And yet in the midst of this impermanency, we feel that there is permanency; being dissatisfied with this impermanency, we have created a state of permanency, thereby giving rise to conflict between that which is supposed to be permanent and that which is changing, the transient. But if we realized that everything, including ourselves, the 'I', is transient and the environmental things of life are also impermanent, surely then there would not be this aching conflict.

What is it that demands permanency, security, that longs for continuity? It is on this demand that our social, moral relationship is based.

If you really believed or deeply felt for yourself the incessant change of life, then there would never be a craving for security, for permanency. But because there is a deep craving for permanency, we create an enclosing wall against the movement of life.

So conflict exists between the changing values of life and the desire which is seeking permanency. If we deeply felt and understood the impermanency of ourselves and of the things of this world, then there would be a cessation of bitter conflict, aches, and fears. Then there would be no attachment from which arises the social and individual struggle.

What then is this thing that has assumed permanency and is ever seeking further continuity? We cannot intelligently examine this until we analyze and understand the critical capacity itself.

Our critical capacity springs from prejudices, beliefs, theories, hopes, and so on, or from what we call experience. Experience is based on tradition, on accumulated memories. Our experience is ever tinged by the past. If you believe in God, perhaps you may have what you call an experience of Godhood. Surely this is not a true experience. It has been impressed upon our minds through centuries that there is God, and according to that conditioning we have an experience. This is not a true, firsthand experience.

A conditioned mind acting in a conditioned way cannot experience completely. Such a mind is incapable of fully experiencing the reality or the nonreality of God. Likewise a mind that is already prejudiced by a conscious or an unconscious desire for the permanent cannot fully comprehend reality. To such a prejudiced mind all inquiry is merely a further strengthening of that prejudice.

The search and the longing for immortality is the urge of accumulated memories of individual consciousness, the 'I', with its fears and hopes, loves and hates. This 'I' breaks itself up into many conflicting parts: the higher and the lower, the permanent and the transient, and so on. This 'I', in its desire to perpetuate itself, seeks and uses ways and means to entrench itself.

Perhaps some of you may say to yourselves, "Surely with the disappearance of these cravings, there must be reality." The very desire to know if there is something beyond the conflicting consciousness of existence is an indication that the mind is seeking an assurance, a certainty, a reward for its efforts.

We see how resistance against each other is created, and that resistance through accumulative memories, through experience, is more and more strengthened, becoming more and more conscious of itself.

Thus there is your personal resistance and that of your neighbor, society. Adjustment between two or more resistances is called relationship, upon which morality is built.

Where there is love, there is not the consciousness of relationship. It is only in a state of resistance that there can be this consciousness of relationship, which is merely an adjustment of opposing conflicts.

Conflict is not only between various resistances, but also within itself, within the permanent and the impermanent quality of resistance itself.

Is there anything permanent within this resistance? We see that resistance can perpetuate itself through acquisitiveness, through ignorance, through conscious or unconscious craving for experience. But surely this continuance is not the eternal; it is merely the perpetuation of conflict.

What we call the permanent in resistance is only part of resistance itself and so part of conflict. Thus in itself it is not the eternal, the permanent.

Where there is incompleteness, unfulfillment, there is the craving for continuance which creates resistance, and this gives to itself the quality of permanency.

The thing that the mind clings to as the permanent is in its very essence the transient. It is the outcome of ignorance, fear, and craving.

If we understand this, then we see the problem is not that of one resistance in conflict with another, but how this resistance comes into being and how it is to be dissolved. When we face this problem deeply, there is a new awakening, a state which may be called love.

August 1, 1937

Second Talk at Ommen

Conflict invariably must arise when there is a static center within one, and about one there are changing values. This static center must be in battle with the living quality of life.

Change implies that there is nothing permanent to which the mind can attach itself, but it constantly desires to cling to some form of security. The form of attachment is undergoing a constant change, and this change is considered progress, but attachment still continues.

Now this change implies that there can be no personal center which is accumulating, storing up memories as safeguards and virtues, no center which is constantly gathering to itself experiences, lessons for the future. Though intellectually we may grasp this, emotionally each one clings to a personal, static center, identifying himself with it. In reality there is no center as the 'I' with its permanent qualities. We must understand this integrally, not merely intellectually, if we are to alter fundamentally our relationship with our neighbor, which is based on ignorance, fear, wants.

Now do we, each one of us, think that this center, from which most of our action takes place—do we think that this center is impermanent?

What does thinking mean to you? Are you merely stimulated by my word-picture, by an explanation which you will examine intellectually at your leisure and make into a pattern, into a principle to be followed and to be lived? Does such a method bring about an integral living? Mere explanation of suffering does not cause it to disappear, nor following a principle or a pattern, but what does destroy it is integral thought and emotion.

If you are not suffering, then the word-picture of another about suffering—his explanation concerning it—may for the moment be stimulating and might make you think that you should suffer. But such suffering has no significance.

There are two ways of thinking. One is through mere intellectual stimulation, without any emotional content; but when the emotions are deeply stirred, there is an integral thought process which is not superficial, intellectual. This integral thought-emotion alone can bring about lasting comprehension and action.

If what I am saying acts merely as a stimulation, then there arises the question of how to apply it to your daily life with its pains and conflicts. The how, the method, becomes all-important only when explanations and stimulations are urging you to a particular action. The how, the method, ceases to be important only when you are aware, integrally.

When the mind reveals to itself its own efforts of fears and wants, then there arises integral awareness of its own impermanency which alone can set the mind free from its binding labors. Unless this is taking place, all stimulation becomes further bondage.

All artificially cultivated qualities divide; all intellectual cultivation of morality, ethics, is cruel, born of fear, only creating further resistance of man against man.

The quality of resistance is ignorance. To be acquainted with many intellectual theories is not freedom from ignorance. A man who is not integrally aware of the process of his own mind is ignorant.

To free thought from acquisitiveness through discipline, through will, is not a release from ignorance, for it is still held in the conflict of opposites. When thought integrally perceives that the effort to rid itself of acquisitiveness is also part of acquisitiveness, then there is a beginning of enlightenment.

Whatever effort the mind makes to rid itself of certain qualities, it is still caught up in ignorance; but when the mind discerns that all effort it makes to free itself is still within the process of ignorance, then there is a possibility of breaking through the vicious circle of ignorance.

The will of satisfaction breaks up the mind into many parts, each in conflict with the other, and this will cannot be destroyed by a superior will, which is but another form of the will of satisfaction. This circle of ignorance breaks, as it were, from within only when the mind ceases to be acquisitive.

The will of satisfaction destroys love.

Question: How are we to distinguish between revelation, which is true thought, and experience? To me, experience, because of our untruthful methods of living, becomes limited and so is not pure revelation. They should be one.

Question: You mean experience is a memory, a memory of something done?

KRISHNAMURTI: Experience may further condition thought or it may release it from limitations. We experience according to our conditioning, but that conditioning may be broken through, which may give to one's whole being an integral freedom. Morality, which should be spontaneous, has been made to follow a pattern, a principle which becomes right or wrong according to the beliefs that one holds. To alter this pattern some resort to violence, hoping to create a "true" pattern, and others turn to law to reshape it. Both hope to create "right" morality through force and conformity. But such enforcement is no longer morality.

Violence in some form is considered as a necessary means to a pacific end. We do not see that the end is controlled and shaped by the means we employ.

Truth is an experience disassociated with the past. The attachment to the past with its memories, traditions, is the continuance of a static center which prevents the experience of truth.

When the mind is not burdened with belief, with want, with attachment, when it is

creatively empty, then there is a possibility of experiencing reality.

August 3, 1937

Third Talk at Ommen

All strife is one of relationship, an adjustment between two resistances, two individuals. Resistance is a conditioning, limiting or conditioning that energy which may be called life, thought, emotion. This conditioning, this resistance, has had no beginning. It has always been, and we can see that it can be continued. There are many and complex causes for this conditioning.

This conditioning is ignorance, which can be brought to an end.

Ignorance is the unawareness of the process of conditioning, which consists of the many wants, fears, acquisitive memories, and so on.

Belief is part of ignorance. Whatever action springs from belief only further strengthens ignorance.

The craving for understanding, for happiness, the attempt to get rid of this particular quality and acquire that particular virtue—all such effort is born of ignorance, which is the result of this constant want, so in relationship strife and conflict continue.

As long as there is want, all experience further conditions thought and emotion, thus continuing conflict.

Where there is want, experience cannot be complete, thus strengthening resistance. A belief, the result of want, is a conditioning force; experience based on any belief is limiting, however wide and large it may be.

Whatever effort the mind makes to break its own vicious circle of ignorance must further aid the continuance of ignorance. If one does not understand the whole process of ignorance and merely makes an effort to get rid of it, thought is still acting within the circle of ignorance.

So what is one to do, discerning that whatever action, whatever effort one makes only strengthens ignorance? The very desire to break through the circle of ignorance is still part of ignorance. Then what is one to do?

Now, is this an all-important, vital question to you? If it is, then you will see that there is no direct, positive answer, for positive answers can only bring about further effort, which but strengthens the process of ignorance. So there is only a negative approach, which is to be integrally aware of the process of fear or ignorance. This awareness is not an effort to overcome, to destroy or to find a substitute, but is a stillness of neither acceptance nor denial, an integral quietness of no choice. This awareness breaks the circle of ignorance from within, as it were, without strengthening it.

Question: How can one know for certain whether the mind is unconditioned, because there is a possibility of illusion there?

KRISHNAMURTI: Do not let us be concerned about the certainty of an unconditioned mind, but rather be aware of the limitations of thought-emotion.

Question: There is a real difference between being unaware of our conditioning and imagining that we are unconditioned.

KRISHNAMURTI: Surely that is obvious. To inquire into the unconditioned state when one's mind is limited is so utterly futile. We have to be concerned with those causes which hold thought-emotion in bondage.

Question: We know there is reality and unreality, and from the unreal we must move to the real.

KRISHNAMURTI: Surely that is another form of conditioning. How do you know that there is the real?

Question: Because it is there.

KRISHNAMURTI: You have stopped thinking, if I may say so, when you assert that it is there.

Question: I think we realize continually that we are conditioned, because we are always suffering and in conflict.

KRISHNAMURTI: So conflict, suffering, the strain of relationship, indicates a conditioning. There may be many causes for conditioning, but are you aware of at least one of them?

Question: Fear and desire are the causes of limitation.

KRISHNAMURTI: When you make that statement are you conscious that, in your life, fear and desire cause strife, misery?

When you say that fear is conditioning your life, are you aware of that fear? Or is it because you have read of it or heard me talk about it that you repeat, "Fear is conditioning"? Fear cannot exist by itself, but only in relation to something.

Now when you say you are conscious of fear, is it caused by something outside of yourself, or is it within you? One is afraid of an accident, or of the neighbor, or of some immediate relation, or of some psychological reaction, and so on. In some cases it is the outward things of life which are making us afraid, and if we can free ourselves from them, we think that we shall be without fear.

Can you free yourself from your neighbor? You may be able to escape from a particular neighbor, but wherever you are, you are always in relation with someone. You may be able to create an illusion into which you can withdraw, or build a wall between your neighbor and yourself and thereby protect yourself. You may separate yourself through social division, through virtues, beliefs, acquisitions, and so free yourself from your neighbor. But this is not freedom.

Then there is the fear of contagious diseases, accidents, and so forth, against which one takes natural precautions without unduly exaggerating them.

The will to survive, the will to be satisfied, the will to continue—this is the very root cause of fear.

Do you know this to be so? If you do, then what do you mean by "knowing"? Do you know this merely intellectually, as a word-picture, or are you aware of it integrally, emotionally?

You know of fear as a reaction when your resistance is weakened, when the walls of your self-protection have been broken into; then you are conscious of fear and your immediate reaction is to patch up again those walls, to strengthen them so as to be secure.

Question: Will you tell us what fear is?

KRISHNAMURTI: Will I tell you what fear is! Don't you know what it is?

If in your house there is nothing of value to which you are attached, then you are not afraid of your neighbor—your windows and doors are open. But fear is in your heart when you are attached; then you bar your windows, then you lock your doors. You isolate yourself.

The mind has gathered certain values, treasures, and it intends to guard them. If the worth of these possessions is questioned, there is an awakening of fear. Through fear we guard them more closely, or sell out the old and acquire the new which we protect more cunningly. This isolation we call by various names.

I am asking you if you have anything precious in your mind, in your heart, that you are guarding. If you have, then you are bound to create walls against fear, and this resistance is called by many names—love, will, virtue, character.

Have you anything precious? Have you anything that may be taken away from you— your position, your ambitions, desires, hopes?

What is it that you have, actually? You may have worldly possessions which you try to safeguard. To protect them you have imperialism, nationalism, class distinctions. Each individual, each nation is doing that, breeding hate and war. Can the fear of loss be utterly removed? Every sign indicates this fear cannot be taken away by greater protection, greater nationalism, greater imperialism. Where there is attachment, there is fear.

Question: Is it by letting the objects go, or by setting up a different relationship between ourselves and them, that fear is dissipated?

KRISHNAMURTI: Surely we have not yet come to the question of how to rid ourselves of fear. We are trying to find out what are the precious things that each one of us holds so cunningly, and then only can we discover the means of getting rid of fear.

Question: It is very difficult to know. I do not know what I am holding on to.

KRISHNAMURTI: Yes, that is one of the difficulties, but unless you know that, fear must continue, though you may desire to get rid of it. Are you conscious with your whole being that you are protecting yourself in some form or other through belief, acquisitions, virtue, ambition?

When you begin to consider deeply, you will perceive how belief or any other form of exclusion is segregating you either as a group or as an individual, and that belief acts as a resistance against the movement of life.

Some of you may say that the mind is not guarding a belief, but that it is part of the mind itself, that without some form of belief mind, thought, cannot exist. Or you may say that belief is not really a belief, but intuition, to be guarded, to be encouraged.

Question: With me it seems that belief is there, and I do not know what to do about it. I do not know whether I am guarding it or not.

KRISHNAMURTI: That is just it. It is part of you, you say. Why is it there? Why is it part of you? You have been conditioned through tradition, education; you have acquired belief consciously or unconsciously as a protection against various forms of fear, or through propaganda you have accepted a belief as a cure-all. You may not have a belief in a particular theory, but you may have in a person. There are various forms of belief. The desire for comfort, for security, forces one to some kind of belief, which one guards, for without it one feels utterly lost. So there is the constant attempt to justify one's belief or to find a substitute in the place of the old.

Where there is attachment there is fear, but the freedom from fear is not a reward of nonattachment. Suffering makes one decide to be utterly detached, but this detachment is really a form of protection against suffering. Now as the majority of us have something— love, possessions, ideals, beliefs, conceptions—to protect, which go to make up that resistance which is the 'I', the 'me', it is futile to ask how to get rid of the 'I', the

'me', with its many layers of wants, fears, without fully comprehending the process of resistance. The very desire to free oneself from them is another and safer form of self-protection.

If you are aware of this process of protection, of building up walls to guard that which you are and have, if you are conscious of this, then you will never ask what is the way, the method, to free yourself from fear, from craving. Then you will find in the stillness of awareness the spontaneous breaking up of the various causes that condition thought-emotion.

You are not going to be aware by merely listening to one or two talks. It is as a fire which must be built, and you must build it. You must begin, however little, to be conscious, to be aware, and this you can be when you talk, when you laugh, when you come into contact with people, or when you are still. This awareness becomes a flame, and this flame consumes all fear which causes isolation. The mind must reveal itself spontaneously to itself. And this is not given only to a few, nor is it an impossibility.

August 4, 1937

Fourth Talk at Ommen

Ignorance is the unawareness of the process of one's own thought and emotion. I have tried to explain what I mean by awareness.

Will experience dissolve this ignorance? What do we mean by experience? Action and reaction according to conditioned thought and emotion. The mind-heart is conditioned through conclusions, habits of thought, preconceptions, beliefs, fears, wants.

This mass of ignorance cannot be dissolved merely by experience. Experience can give to ignorance new meaning, new values, new illusions; but it is still ignorance. Mere experience cannot dissolve ignorance; it can only re-form it.

Can the mere control and change of environment dissolve ignorance? What do we mean by environment? Economic habits and values, social divisions, the morality of conformity, and so on. Will the creation of a new environment, brought about through compulsion, violence, through propaganda and threat, dissolve this ignorance or merely reshape it again in a different way?

Through external domination, can this ignorance be dissolved? I say it cannot. This does not mean that the present barbarity of wars, of exploitation, cruelties, class dominations, should not be changed. But mere change of society will not alter the fundamental nature of ignorance.

We have looked to two different processes of dissolving ignorance: the one to control the environment and the other to destroy ignorance through experience. Before you accept or deny the impossibility of doing away with ignorance through these methods, you must know the reality of each process. Do you know it? If not, you must experiment and find out. No artificial stimulation can yield reality.

Ignorance cannot be dissolved either through experience or through the mere control of environment, but it spontaneously, voluntarily withers away if there is that awareness in which there is no desire, no choice.

Question: I am conscious that I love and that death will take away the one I love, and the suffering is a difficult thing for me to comprehend. I know it is a limitation and I know that I want something else, but I do not know what.

KRISHNAMURTI: Death brings great sorrow to most of us, and we want to find a way out of that suffering. We either turn to belief in immortality, taking comfort in this, or try to forget sorrow by various means, or cultivate a superior form of indifference, through rationalization.

All things decay, everything is worn away by usage, all comes to an end. Perceiving this, some rationalize away their sorrow. By an intellectual process they deaden their suffering. Others seek to overcome this suffering through postponement, through a belief in the hereafter, through a concept of immortality. This also deadens suffering, for belief gives shelter, comfort. One may not be afraid of the hereafter or the death of oneself, but most of us do not want to bear the agony of the loss of someone we love. So we set about to discover ways and means of frustrating sorrow.

The intellectual explanations of how to do away with suffering make one indifferent to it. In the disturbance caused by becoming aware of one's own impoverishment through the death of someone whom one loves, there comes the shock of suffering. Again the mind objects to sorrow, so it seeks ways and means to escape from it: it is satisfied with the many explanations of the hereafter, of continuity, of reincarnation, and so forth. One man rationalizes away suffering so as to live as undisturbed as possible, and another in his belief, in his postponement, takes shelter and comfort so as not to suffer in the present. These two are fundamentally the same; neither wants to suffer, it is only their explanations that differ. The former scoffs at all beliefs, and the latter is deeply immersed either in bolstering up his belief in reincarnation, in immortality, and so on or in finding out "facts," "reality" about them.

Question: I do not see why the refuge itself is false. I think taking refuge is silly. Reincarnation may be a fact.

KRISHNAMURTI: If one is suffering and there is the supposed fact of reincarnation, what fundamental value has this fact if it ceases to be a refuge, a comfort? If one is starving, what good is it to know that there is overproduction in the world? One wants to be fed, not facts, but much more nourishing substance.

We are not disputing as to whether reincarnation is a fact or not. To me this is utterly irrelevant. When you are diseased, hungry, facts do not relieve suffering, do not satisfy hunger. One can take hope in a future ideal state, but hunger will still continue. The fear of death and the sorrow it brings will continue even in spite of the supposed fact of reincarnation, unless, of course, one lives in complete illusion.

Why do you take shelter in a supposed fact, in a belief? I am not asking you how you know that it is a fact. You think that it is, and for the moment let us leave it at that. What prompts you to take shelter? As a man takes refuge in the rationalized conclusion that all things must decay, and thereby softens his suffering, so by taking refuge in a belief, in a supposed fact, you also deaden the action of sorrow. Because of the sharpness of misery, you desire comfort, an alleviation, and so you seek a refuge, hoping that it is enduring and real. Is it not for this fundamental reason that we seek refuge, shelter?

Question: Because we are not able to face life, we seek a substitute.

KRISHNAMURTI: Merely asserting that you are seeking substitutions does not solve the problem of suffering. They prevent us from thinking and feeling deeply.

Those of you who have suffered and are suffering, what has been your experience?

Question: Nothing.

KRISHNAMURTI: Some of you do nothing, bearing it indifferently. Some try to escape from it through drink, amusement, forgetting themselves in action, or taking shelter in a belief.

What is the actual reaction in the case of death? You have lost the person whom you love and you would like to have him back; you do not want to face loneliness. Realizing the impossibility of having him back, you turn, in your emptiness and sorrow, to fill your mind and heart with explanations, with beliefs, with second-hand information, knowledge, and experiences.

Question: There is a third possibility. You show us only those two possibilities, but I feel quite distinctly that there is another way to meet sorrow.

KRISHNAMURTI: There may be many ways of meeting sorrow, but if there is a fundamental desire to seek comfort, all the methods resolve themselves into these two definite approaches—either to rationalize or to seek refuge. Both these methods only assuage sorrow; they offer an escape.

Question: What if a man remarries?

KRISHNAMURTI: Even if he does, the problem of suffering still remains unsolved. This is also a postponement, a forgetting. One gives himself intellectual, rational explanations because he does not want to suffer. Another takes shelter in a belief, also to avoid suffering. Another takes refuge in the idea that if he can find truth there will be at last a cessation of suffering. Another, through cultivation of irresponsibility, avoids suffering. All are attempting to escape from suffering.

Do not object to the words *shelter, refuge.* Substitute your own word—belief, God, truth, remarriage, rationalization, and so on. But as long as there is a conscious or unconscious craving to escape from sorrow, illusion in many forms must exist.

Now, why should you not suffer? When you are happy, when you are joyous, you do not say you must not be happy. You do not run away from joy, you do not seek a refuge from it. When you are in a state of ecstasy, you do not resort to beliefs, to substitutions. On the contrary, you destroy all things which stand in its way—your gods, your moralities, your values, your beliefs, everything—to maintain this ecstasy.

Now why don't you do the same thing when you are suffering? Why don't you destroy all things that interfere with sorrow—the mind's many explanations, escapes, fears and illusions? If you sincerely and deeply put this question to yourself, you will see that beliefs, gods, hopes no longer matter. Then your life has a new and fundamental meaning.

In the flame of love, all fear is consumed.

August 5, 1937

Fifth Talk at Ommen

Though intellectually we may perceive the cause of suffering, it has but little influence on our lives. Though we may intellectually agree that so long as there is attachment there is fear and sorrow, yet our desire is so strongly possessive that it overcomes all reasoning. Even though we may know the cause of suffering, suffering will continue, for mere intellectual knowledge is not sufficient to destroy the cause. So when the mind through analysis discovers the cause of suffering, that very discovery itself may become a refuge. The hope that by discovering the cause of sorrow, suffering will cease, is an illusion.

Why does the mind seek the cause of sorrow? Obviously to overcome it. Yet in the moments of ecstasy there is no search for its cause; if there were, ecstasy would cease. In craving for ecstasy, we grope after those causes that stand in the way. This very craving for ecstasy and the intense desire to overcome sorrow prevent their fulfillment.

A mind that is burdened with the desire for reality, for happiness, for love, cannot free itself from fear. Fear deadens sorrow as also it distorts joy. Is our whole being in direct contact with sorrow as it is with happiness, with joy?

We are aware that we are not integral with sorrow; that there is a part of us which is trying to run away from it. In this process the mind has accumulated many treasures to which it clings desperately. When we realize this process of accumulation, then there is an urge to put a stop to it. Then we begin to seek methods, the way to get rid of these burdens. The very search for a method is another form of escape.

The choice of methods, of a way to rid yourself of those accumulated burdens, which cause resistance—this very choice is born of a desire not to suffer and is therefore prejudicial. This prejudice is the outcome of the desire for refuge, comfort.

Question: I think that nobody has thought what you have said just now. It is too complicated.

KRISHNAMURTI: We are trying to perceive, to feel truth which shall liberate man, not merely to find out what are the causes of sorrow. If what I have said, which may sound complicated, is the truth, then it is liberating.

The discovery of truth is a complex process, for the mind has enveloped itself in many illusions.

The dawning of truth does not lie in the choice of the essential as against the unessential. But when you begin to perceive the illusion of choice itself, then that revelation is liberating, spontaneously destroying the illusion upon which the mind nourishes itself.

Is it love that, when it is thwarted, suffers, and there is bitterness, there is emptiness? It is the exposure of one's own smallness of love that is hurting.

Whenever the mind chooses, its choice must be based on self-protective prejudice, and as we desire not to suffer, its acts are based on fear. Fear and reality cannot exist together. One destroys the other. But it is one of the illusions of the mind that creates the hope of something beyond its own darkness. This something, this hoped-for reality, is another form of refuge, another escape from sorrow. The mind perpetuates its own conditioned state through fear.

Question: What you say leads to a very materialistic form of life.

KRISHNAMURTI: What do you mean by a materialistic form of life? That there is only this life, that there is no reality, no God, that morality must be based on social and economic convenience, and so on. Now, what is the nonmaterialistic attitude towards life? That there is God, that there is a soul which continues, that there is a hereafter, that the individual holds within himself the spark of the eternal. What is the difference between the two, the materialistic and the religious?

Question: Both are beliefs.

KRISHNAMURTI: But why then do you despise the materialistic form of life?

Question: Because it denies persistence.

KRISHNAMURTI: You are merely reacting to prejudice. Your religious life is fundamentally an irreligious one. Though you may cover it up by talking about God, love, the hereafter, in your heart it means nothing, just so many phrases which you have learned as the materialistic man has learned his ideas and phrases. Both the religious and the materialistic mind are conditioned by their own prejudices which prevent the integral comprehension of truth and the communion with it.

Question: Yesterday you asked us to say why we tried to escape from suffering, and suddenly I saw the whole significance of it. If we give ourselves over to suffering instead of trying to escape from it, we break up the resistance within us.

KRISHNAMURTI: Yes, if it is not the effort of the will. But is not this giving oneself over to sorrow artificial, an effort of the intellect to gain something? Surely you do not give yourself over to ecstasy? If you do, it is not ecstasy.

Question: I did not mean that. I meant that instead of trying to escape, you just suffer.

KRISHNAMURTI: Why do you feel that you must suffer? When you say to yourself that you must not escape, you are hoping that out of suffering you will achieve something. But when you are integrally aware of the illusion of all escape, then there is no will to resist the desire to escape nor the will to achieve something through suffering.

Question: Yes, I see that.

Question: Will you please repeat what you have just now said.

KRISHNAMURTI: One does not give oneself over to joy. There is no duality in ecstasy. It is a state which spontaneously comes into being without our willing it. Suffering is an indication of duality. Without understanding this, we perpetuate duality through the many intellectual efforts and processes of overcoming it, giving oneself over to its opposite, developing virtues, and so forth. All such attempts only strengthen duality.

Question: Do not the resistances which we put up against suffering also act as resistances against ecstasy?

KRISHNAMURTI: Of course. If there is a lack of sensibility to ugliness, to sorrow, there must also be deep insensitiveness to beauty, to joy. Resistance against sorrow is also a barrier to happiness.

What is ecstasy? That state of being when the mind and heart are in complete union, when fear does not tear them asunder, when the mind is not withholding.

Question: Is there a better way of suffering? A better way of living?

KRISHNAMURTI: There is, and this is what I have been trying to explain. If each one becomes aware of his own conditioned state, then he will begin to free himself from hate, ambition, attachment, from those fears which cripple life.

If the mind destroys one conditioned state only to enter into another, life becomes utterly vain and hopeless. This is what is happening to most of us, wandering from cage to cage, thinking that each is more free than the one before, while in reality each is but a dif-

ferent kind of limitation. That which is free cannot grow from the less to the more.

Question: I accept the conditioned state in the same manner as that the globe is revolving, as a necessary part of development.

KRISHNAMURTI: Then we are not using intelligence. By merely asserting that all existence is conditioned, we shall never find out if there is a state that may not be conditioned. By becoming integrally aware of the conditioned state, each one will then begin to comprehend the freedom that comes through the cessation of fear.

August 6, 1937

Sixth Talk at Ommen

Relationship may be limited, between two individuals, or it may be with many, in an ever-widening sphere. Limited or wide, the importance lies in the character of relationship.

What do we mean by relationship? It is an adjustment between two individualistic desires. In this relationship there is strife of opposing ambitions, attachments, hopes, wants. Thus almost all relationship becomes one of strain and conflict. There is relationship not only with people and external values but also with those values and conceptions within us.

We are aware of this strife between friends, between neighbors, between ourselves and society.

Must this conflict ever continue? We may adjust our relationship with another so cunningly that we never come into contact with each other vitally; or adjustment being impossible, two people may be forced to separate. But as long as there is any kind of activity, there must be relationship between the individual and society, which may be one or many. Isolation is possible only in a complete state of neurosis. Unless one acts mechanically, unthinking and unfeeling, or is so conditioned that there is only one pattern of thought and feeling, all relationship is one of adjustment—either of strife and resistance, or of yielding.

Love is not of relationship nor of adjustment; it is of a wholly different quality.

Can this strife in relationship ever cease? We cannot, through mere experience, bring about a relationship without strife. Experience is a reaction to previous conditioning which in relationship produces conflict. The mere domination of environment with its social values, habits, and thoughts, cannot bring about a relationship which is free from strife.

There is conflict between the conditioning influences of desire and the swift, lively current of relationship. It is not, as most people think, relationship that is limiting, but it is desire that conditions. It is desire, conscious or unconscious, that is ever causing friction in relationship.

Desire springs from ignorance. Desire cannot exist independently; it must feed on previous conditioning, which is ignorance.

Ignorance can be dissipated. It is possible. Ignorance consists of the many forms of fear, of belief, of want, of attachment. These create conflict in relationship.

When we are integrally aware of the process of ignorance, voluntarily, spontaneously, there is the beginning of that intelligence which meets all conditioning influences. We are concerned with the awakening of this intelligence, of this love, which alone can free the mind and heart from strife.

The awakening of this intelligence, this love, is not the result of a disciplined, systematized morality, nor is it an achievement to be sought after, but it is a process of constant awareness.

Question: Relationship is also a contact between habits, and through habit there is the continuity of activity.

KRISHNAMURTI: In most cases action is the result of habit, habit based on tradition, on thought and desire patterns, and this gives to action an apparent continuity. Generally, then, habit rules our action and relationship.

Is action merely habit? If action is the outcome of mere mechanical habit, then it must lead to confusion and sorrow. In the same way, if relationship is merely the contact of two individualized habits, then all such relationship is suffering. But unfortunately we reduce all contact with each other to a dull and weary pattern through incapacity of adjustment, through fear, through lack of love.

Habit is conscious or unconscious repetition of action which is guided by memory of past incidents, of tradition, of thoughtdesire patterns, and so forth. One often realizes that one is living in a narrow groove of thought and, breaking away from it, slips into another. This change from habit to habit is often called progress, experience, or growth.

Action, which may once have followed full awareness, often becomes habitual, without thought, without any depth of feeling.

Can true relationship exist when the mind is merely following a pattern?

Question: But there is a spontaneous response, which is not habit at all.

KRISHNAMURTI: Yes, we know of this, but such occasions are rare, and we would like to establish a relationship of spontaneity. Between what we would like to be and what we are, there is a wide gap. What we would like to be is a form of ambitious attachment which has no significance to one who is searching out reality. If we can understand what we are, then perhaps we shall know *what is*.

Can true relationship exist when the mind is merely following a pattern? When one is aware of that state called love, there is a dynamic relationship that is not of a pattern, that is beyond all mental definitions and calculations. But, through the conditioning influence of fear and desire, such relationship is reduced to mere gratification, to habit, to routine. Such a state is not true relationship but a form of death and decay. How can there be true relationship between two individualized patterns, though there may be mechanical response from each?

Question: There is a continual adjustment between these two habits.

KRISHNAMURTI: Yes, but such adjustment is merely mechanical, which conflict and suffering enforce; such enforcement does not break down the fundamental desire to form habit patterns. Outside influences and inward determinations do not break down the formation of habit, but only aid in superficial and intellectual adjustment which is not conducive to true relationship.

Is this state of patterns, of ideals, of conformity, conducive to fulfillment, to creative and intelligent life and action? Before we can answer this question, do we realize or are we aware of this state? If we are not aware of it, there is no conflict, but if we are, then there is anxiety and suffering. From this we try to escape or try to break down old habits and patterns. In overcoming them, one merely creates others; the desire for mere change is stronger than the desire to be aware of the whole process of the formation of habit, of patterns. Hence we move from habit to habit.

Question: Yes, I know habit is foolish, but can I break away from it?

KRISHNAMURTI: Before you ask me how to overcome a particular habit, let us find out what is the thing that is creating habit, because you may break away from one habit, one pattern, but in that very process you may be forming another. This is what we generally do, go from one habit to another. We will go on doing this indefinitely unless we find out why it is that mind ever seeks to form habits, follow thought-desire patterns.

All true relationship requires constant alertness and adjustment not according to pattern. Where there is habit, the following of patterns, ideals, this state of pliability is impossible. To be pliable demands constant thought and affection, and as the mind finds it is easier to establish behavior patterns than to be aware, it proceeds to form habits; and when it is shaken from a particular one, through affliction and uncertainty, it moves on to another. Fear for its own security and comfort compels the mind to follow thoughtdesire patterns. Society thus becomes the maker of habit, patterns, ideals, for society is the neighbor, the immediate relation with which one is ever in contact.

August 8, 1937

Seventh Talk at Ommen

Suffering is the indication of the process of thought and desire patterns. This suffering the mind seeks to overcome by putting itself to sleep again through the development of other patterns and other illusions. From this self-imposed limitation the mind is again shaken, and again it induces itself to thoughtlessness, until it so identifies itself with some thought-desire pattern or belief that it can no longer be shaken or allow itself to suffer. This state many realize and consider as the highest achievement.

Once you develop the will that merely overcomes all habit, conditioning, that very will itself becomes thoughtless and repetitive.

We must understand both the habitual action and the ideal or conceptual action, before we can comprehend action without illusion. For reality lies in actuality.

Awareness is not the development of an introspective will, but it is the spontaneous unification of all the separative forces of desire.

Question: Is awareness a matter of slow growth?

KRISHNAMURTI: Where there is intense interest there is full awareness. As one is mentally lazy and emotionally crippled with fear, awareness becomes a matter of slow growth. Then it is not really awareness but a process of carefully building up walls of resistance. As most of us have built up these self-protecting walls, awareness appears to be a slow process, a growth, thus satisfying our slothfulness. Out of this laziness we carve theories of postponement—eventually but not now, enlightenment is a process of slow growth, of life after life, and so on. We proceed to rationalize this slothfulness and satisfactorily arrange our lives according to it.

Question: This process seems inevitable. But how is one to awaken quickly?

KRISHNAMURTI: Is it a slow process for individuals to change from violence to peace? I think not. If one really perceives the whole significance of hate, affection spontaneously comes into being; what prevents this immediate and deep perception is our unconscious fear of intellectual and desire commitments and patterns. For such a perception might involve a drastic change in our

daily life: the withering away of ambition, the putting away of all nationalistic class distinctions, attachments, and so on. This fear is prompting us, warning us, and we consciously or unconsciously yield to it and thereby increase our safeguards, which only engenders further fear. So long as we do not comprehend this process, we shall ever be thinking in terms of postponement, of growth, of overcoming. Fear cannot be dissolved in the future; only in constant awareness can it cease to be.

Question: I think we must come quickly to peace.

KRISHNAMURTI: If you hate because your intellectual and emotional well-being is threatened in many ways and if you merely resort to further violence, though you may successfully, for the moment at least, ward off fear, hate will continue. It is only by constantly being aware that fear and hate can disappear. Do not think in terms of postponement. Begin to be aware, and if there is interest, that itself will bring about, spontaneously, a state of peace, of affection.

War, the war in you, the hate of your neighbor, of other peoples, cannot be overcome by violence in any form. If you begin to see the utter necessity of deeply thinking-feeling about it now, your prejudices, your conditioning, which are the cause of hate and fear, will be revealed. In this revelation there is an awakening of affection, love.

Question: I think that it will take all our life to overcome fear, hate.

KRISHNAMURTI: You are again thinking in terms of postponement. Does each one feel the appallingness of hate and perceive its consequences? If you deeply feel this, then you are not concerned with when hate will cease, for it has already yielded to something in which alone there can be deep human contact and cooperation.

If one is conscious of hate or violence in different forms, can that violence be done away with through the process of time?

Question: No, not by the mere passing of time. One would have to have a method to get rid of it.

KRISHNAMURTI: No, the mere passage of time cannot resolve hate; it may be covered over heavily or carefully watched over and guarded. But fear, hate, will still continue. Can a system help you get rid of hate? It may help you to subjugate it, control it, strengthen your will to combat it, but it will not bring about that affection which alone can give man abiding freedom. If you do not feel deeply that hate is inherently poisonous, no system, no authority, can destroy it for you.

Question: You may intellectually see that hate is poison, but still you feel hate.

KRISHNAMURTI: Why does this happen? Is it not because intellectually you are over-developed and still primitive in your desires? There cannot be harmony between the beautiful and the ugly. The cessation of hate cannot be brought about through any method but only through constant awareness of the conditionings that have brought about this division between love and hate.

Why does this division exist?

Question: Lack of love.

Question: Ignorance.

KRISHNAMURTI: Don't you see, by merely repeating that if one really lived rightly, this division would not exist; that by not being ignorant, it would disappear; that habit is the cause of this division; that if we were not conditioned, there would be perfect love—don't you see that you are merely intoning certain phrases that you have learned? Of what value is this? None. Is each one of you conscious of this division? Please, don't answer. Consider what is taking place in yourself.

We see that we are in conflict, that there is hate and yet at the same time a disgust for it. There is this division. We can see how this division has come into being, through various conditioning causes. The mere consideration of the causes is not going to bring freedom from hate, fear. The problem of starvation is not solved by merely discovering its causes—the bad economic system, over-production, maldistribution, and so on. If you, personally, are hungry, your hunger will not be satisfied merely by your knowing the causes of it. In the same way, merely knowing the causes of hate, fear, with its various conflicts, will not dissolve it. What will put an end to hate is choiceless awareness—the cessation of all intellectual effort to overcome hate.

Question: We are not conscious enough of this hate.

KRISHNAMURTI: When we are conscious, we object to the conflict, to the suffering involved in this conflict, and proceed to act, hoping to overcome all conflict. This only further strengthens the intellect. You have to be aware of all this process, silently, spontaneously, and in this awareness there comes a new element which is not the result of any violence, any effort, and which alone can free you from hate and those conditionings that cripple.

August 9, 1937

Eighth Talk at Ommen

Hate is not dissolved through experience, nor through any accumulation of virtue, nor can it be overcome by the practice of love. All these merely cover up fear, hate. Be aware of this, and then there will be a tremendous transformation in your life.

Question: What relationship has the illusion of this psychological growth to the growth which we see around us?

KRISHNAMURTI: We see that which is capable of growth is not enduring. But to our psychological growth each one of us clings, as something permanent. If we felt deeply and so were aware that all things are in continual change, a constant becoming, then perhaps we should be able to free ourselves from the conflict which exists in ourselves and so with the neighbor, with society.

Question: It seems to me I cannot jump from hate to love, but I can transform my antipathy slowly into a feeling of understanding and like.

KRISHNAMURTI: We cannot wipe the mind clean of past conditioning and start anew.

But we can be aware what it is that maintains fear, hate. We can be aware of the psychological causes and reactions that prevent us from acting integrally. The past is dominating us, with its beliefs, hopes, fears, conclusions, memories; this prevents us from integral action. We cannot wipe out the past, for in its essence the mind is of the past. But by being aware of the accumulations of the past and their effect on the present, we shall begin to free ourselves without violence from those values which cripple the mind and heart.

Is this, the past with its dominating influences, fears, an acute problem to you, personally?

Life as it is, breeding wars, hatreds, divisions, despoiling unity—is this a problem to you? If it is, then, as you are a part of it, you will comprehend it only through your own sufferings, ambitions, fears. The world is you and its problem is your intimate problem. If it is an acute problem, as I hope it is with each one of you, then you will never escape into any theories, explanations, "facts," illusions. But that requires great alertness—one has to be intensely aware—so we prefer the easier way, the way of escape. How can you solve this problem if your mind and heart are being diverted from it?

I do not say that this problem is simple. It is complex. So you must give your mind and heart to it. But how can you give your whole being to it if you are running away from it, if you are being diverted through various escapes which the mind has established for itself?

Question: But we do not see it at the moment of escape.

KRISHNAMURTI: We are attempting to understand ourselves, to open up the hidden corners of the mind, to see the various escapes, so that spontaneously we shall face life, deeply and fully. Any form of overcoming one habit by another, overcoming hate by virtue is a substitution, and the cultivation of opposites does not do away with those qualities from which we desire to free ourselves. We have to perceive hate, not as an antithesis of love, but as in itself poisonous, an evil.

Question: Don't you think that we can see the different escapes? We can know that hatred is poisonous, and at the same time we know that we are going on with it. But I think that if we would comprehend it fully, then we must be willing to leave everything—home, wife, everything; we must shake hands and say goodbye and go to a concentration camp.

KRISHNAMURTI: Do not think of the consequences of being without hate, but consider if you can free yourself from it. Do you say to yourself that you are incapable of getting rid of hate?

Question: We can only try; we do not know.

KRISHNAMURTI: Why do you say you do not know?

Question: Because it is not our actual problem.

KRISHNAMURTI: Though hate exists in the world, in you and about you, yet you say that it is not an acute problem to you. You are not conscious of it. Why are you not conscious of it? Either because you are free from it or you have so entrenched yourself, so cunningly protected yourself, that you have no fear, no hate, for you are certain of your own security.

Question: We do not feel hate at this moment.

KRISHNAMURTI: When you are not here, then you do feel it, then it is a problem to you. Here you have momentarily escaped from it, but the problem still exists. You cannot escape from it, either here or in any other place. It is a problem to you, whether you want it or not. Though it is a problem, you have put it away, you have become unconscious of it. And therefore you say that you do not know how you will act with regard to it.

Question: We often wish that life itself would directly act and take away from us those things we cherish though we know their worthlessness. Is this also an escape?

KRISHNAMURTI: Some people seem relieved in time of war. They have no responsibilities; their life is directed by the war office. In this lies one of the main reasons why authority, temporal or spiritual, flourishes and is worshipped. Death is preferable to life.

We have been trained to think that hate is inevitable, that we must go through this stage, that is part of human heritage, instinct.

We are used to thinking that hate cannot be got rid of immediately, that we must go through some kind of discipline to overcome hate. Thus there is a dual process going on within us, violence and peace, hate and affection, anger and kindliness.

Our effort goes towards bridging these two separate forces, or overcoming one by the other, or concentrating on one so that its opposite shall disappear.

Whatever effort you make to destroy hate by love is in vain, for violence, fear reveal themselves in another form. We have to go much deeper than mere discipline; we have to find out why this duality of hate and affection exists within us. Until this dual process ceases, the conflict of opposites must continue.

Question: Perhaps hate does not really belong to me?

Question: Is our love too poor then?

KRISHNAMURTI: These questions are very revealing; they show how the mind is conditioned. Whatever effort the mind makes must be part of that from which it is trying to get away.

The mind finds that it does not pay to hate, for it has discovered that there is too much suffering involved in it, and so it makes an effort to discipline itself, to overcome hate by love, to subdue violence and fear by peace. All this indicates the fundamental desire merely to escape from suffering; that is, to guard itself in those virtues and qualities that will not give it pain, that will not cause disturbance. Until this desire, this craving for self-protective security ceases, fear must continue, with all its consequences. Mind cannot get rid of fear. In its attempt to do so it cultivates the opposites, which is part of fear itself. Thus the mind divides itself, creates within itself a dual process. All effort on the part of the mind must maintain this duality, though it may develop tendencies, characteristics, virtues, to overcome that very duality.

Question: I do not quite see how the mind has divided itself into love and hate.

KRISHNAMURTI: There is good and evil, the light and the dark. Light and darkness cannot exist together. One destroys the other.

If light is light, then darkness, evil, ceases to exist. Effort is not necessary, it is then nonexistent. But we are in a state of continual effort because that which to us is light is not light—it is only the light, the good of the intellect.

We are making constant effort to overcome, to acquire, to possess, to be detached, to expand. There are moments of clarity amidst the enveloping confusion. We desire this clarity and cling to it, hoping that it will dissolve the conflicting wants. This desire for clarity, this desire to overcome one quality by another, is waste of energy; for the will that craves, the will

that overcomes, is the will of success, satisfaction, the will of security. This will must ever continue creating and maintaining fear, even though it is asserting that it is seeking truth, God. Its clarity is the clarity of escape, of illusion, but not the clarity of reality.

When the will destroys itself spontaneously, then there is that truth which is beyond all effort. Effort is violence; love and violence cannot exist together.

The conflict in which we exist is not a struggle between good and evil, between the self and the not-self. The struggle is in our own self-created duality, between our various self-protective desires. There cannot be a conflict between light and darkness; where light is, darkness is not. As long as fear exists, there must continue conflict, though that fear may disguise itself under different names. And as fear cannot free itself through any means, for all its efforts spring from its own source, there must be the cessation of all intellectual safeguards. This cessation comes, spontaneously, when the mind reveals to itself its own process. This takes place only when there is integral awareness, which is not the result of a discipline, or of a moral or economic system, or of enforcement.

Each one has to become aware of the process of ignorance, the illusions that one has created.

Intellect cannot lead you out of this present chaos, confusion, and suffering. Reason must exhaust itself, not by retreating, but through integral comprehension and love of life.

When reason no longer has the capacity to protect you through explanations, escapes, logical conclusions, then when there is complete vulnerability, utter nakedness of your whole being, there is the flame of love.

Truth alone can free each one from the sorrow and confusion of ignorance. Truth is not the end of experience, it is life itself. It is not of tomorrow, it is of no time. It is not a result, an achievement, but the cessation of fear, want.

August 10, 1937

Ommen, Holland, 1938

✳

First Talk at Ommen

Have you ever tried to communicate to a friend something which you feel very deeply? You must have found it very difficult, however intimate that friendship may be. You can imagine how difficult it is for us here to understand each other, for our relationship is peculiar. There is not that friendship which is essential for deep communication and understanding. Most of us have the attitude either of a disciple towards a teacher, or of a follower, or of one who tries to force himself to a particular point of view, and communication becomes very difficult. It is further complicated if you have a propagandist attitude, if you come merely in order to propagate certain ideas of a particular society or sect, or an ideology that is popular at the moment. Free communication is possible only when both the listener and the talker are thinking together on the same point.

During these days of the camp there should not be this attitude of a teacher and a disciple, of a leader and a follower, but rather a friendly communication with each other, which is impossible if the mind is held in any belief or in any ideology. There is never a friendship between a leader and a follower, and hence deep communication between them is impossible.

I am talking about something which to me is real, in which I take joy, and it will be of very little significance to you if you are thinking of something quite different. If we can somehow go beyond this absurd relationship that we have established through tradition and legend, through superstition and all kinds of fantasies, then perhaps we shall be able to understand each other more naturally.

What I want to say seems, to me at least, very simple, but when these thoughts and feelings are put into words, they become complicated. Communication becomes more difficult when you, with your particular prejudices, superstitions, and barriers, try to perceive what I am trying to say, instead of attempting to clear your own mind of those perversions that prevent full understanding—which alone can bring about a critical and affectionate attitude.

As you know, this camp is not meant for propaganda purposes, for either right or left, or for any particular society or ideology. I know there are many here who regularly come to the camp to do propaganda for their societies, for their nationality, for their church, and so on. So I would seriously ask you not to indulge in this kind of pastime. We are here for more serious purposes. Those who have an itch for this kind of pastime have plenty of opportunity elsewhere. Here, at least, let us try to find out what we individually think and feel, and then, perhaps, we will begin to understand the chaos, the hate that exists in and about us.

Each one of us has many problems: whether one should become a pacifist, or how far one should go towards pacifism; whether one should fight for one's country; social and economic problems, and the problems of belief, conduct, and affection. I am not going to give an answer which will immediately solve these problems. But what I should like to do is to point out a new approach to them, so that when you are face to face with these problems of nationalism, war, peace, exploitation, belief, love, you will be able to meet them integrally and from a point of view which is real.

So please do not at the beginning of these talks expect an immediate solution for your various problems. I know Europe is a perfect madhouse, in which there is talk of peace and at the same time preparation for war, in which frontiers and nationalism are being strengthened while at the same time there is talk of human unity; there is talk of God, of love, and at the same time hate is rampant. This is not only the problem of the world, but your own problem, for the world is you.

To face these problems you must be unconditionally free. If you are in any way bound, that is, if in any way you have fear, you cannot solve any of these problems. Only in unconditioned freedom is there truth; that is, in that freedom alone can you be truly yourself. To be integral in one's whole being is to be unconditioned. If in any way, in any matter, you have doubt, craving, fear, these create a conditioned mind which prevents the ultimate solution of the many problems.

I want to explain in what manner to approach the freedom from conditioning, fear, so that you can be yourself at all times and under all circumstances. This state without fear is possible, in which alone can there be ecstasy, reality, God. Unless one is fully, in-tegrally free from fear, problems merely increase and become suffocating, without any meaning and purpose.

This is what I want to say: that only in unconditioned freedom is there truth, and to be utterly oneself, integral in one's whole being, is to be unconditioned, which reveals reality.

So what is it—to be oneself? And can we be ourselves at all times? One can be oneself at all times only if one is doing something that one really loves and if one loves completely. When you are doing something which you cannot help doing with your whole being, you are being yourself. Or when you love another completely, in that state you are yourself, without any fear, without any hindrance. In these two states one is completely oneself.

So one has to find out what it is that one loves to do. I am using the word *love* deliberately. What is it that with your whole being you love to do? You do not know. We do not know what it is wise to do, and what is foolish, and the discovery of what is wise and what is foolish is the whole process of living. You are not going to discover this in the twinkling of an eye.

But how is one to discover it? Is it to be discovered—what is wise and what is foolish—mechanically, or spontaneously? When you do something with your whole being, in which there is no sense of frustration or fear, no limitation, in this state of action you are yourself, irrespective of any outward condition. I say, if you can come to that state, when you are yourself in action, then you will find out the ecstasy of reality, God.

Is this state to be mechanically achieved, cultivated, or does it come into being spontaneously? I will explain what I mean by the mechanical process. All action imposed from without must be habit-forming, must be mechanical, and therefore not spontaneous.

Can you discover what it is to be yourself through tradition?

Let me here digress a little and say that we will try, as we did last year, to talk over these ideas during the following meetings. We will try to take up the various points—not arguing with each other, but in a friendly manner finding out what we individually think about these things. In my first talk I want to give a brief outline of what, to me, is the real process of living.

Can you be yourself if your being is in any way touched by tradition? Or can you find yourself through example, through precept?

Question: What is precept?

KRISHNAMURTI: Through a precept, through a saying—that evil is all that which divides and good all that which unites—by merely following a principle, can you be yourself? Will living according to a pattern, an ideal, following it ruthlessly, meditating upon it, bring you to the discovery of yourself? Can that which is real be perceived through discipline or will? That is, by exertion, by an effort of the intellect, curbing, controlling, disciplining, guiding, forcing thought in a particular direction, can you know yourself? And can you know yourself through behavior patterns; that is, by preconceiving a mode of life, of what is good, the ideal, and following it constantly, twisting your thought and feeling to its dictates, putting aside what you consider evil and ruthlessly following what you consider to be good? Will this process reveal to you that which you are, whatever that is? Can you discover yourself through compulsion? It is a form of compulsion, this ruthless overcoming of difficulties through will, discipline—this subduing and resisting, a withholding and a yielding.

All this is the exertion of will, which I consider to be mechanical, a process of the intellect. Can you know yourself through these means—through these mechanical means? All effort, mechanical or of the will, is habit-forming. Through the forming of habit you may be able to create a certain state, achieve a certain ideal which you may consider to be yourself, but as it is the result of an intellectual effort or the effort of the will, it is wholly mechanical and hence not true. Can this process yield the comprehension of yourself, of what you are?

Then there is the other state, which is spontaneous. You can know yourself only when you are unaware, when you are not calculating, not protecting, not constantly watching to guide, to transform, to subdue, to control; when you see yourself unexpectedly, that is, when the mind has no preconceptions with regard to itself; when the mind is open, unprepared to meet the unknown.

If your mind is prepared, surely you cannot know the unknown, for you are the unknown. If you say to yourself, "I am God," or "I am nothing but a mass of social influences or a bundle of qualities"—if you have any preconception of yourself, you cannot comprehend the unknown, that which is spontaneous.

So spontaneity can come only when the intellect is unguarded, when it is not protecting itself, when it is no longer afraid for itself; and this can happen only from within. That is, the spontaneous must be the new, the unknown, the incalculable, the creative, that which must be expressed, loved, in which the will as the process of intellect, controlling, directing, has no part. Observe your own emotional states and you will see that the moments of great joy, great ecstasy, are unpremeditated; they happen mysteriously, darkly, unknowingly. When they are gone, the mind desires to recreate those moments, to recapture them, and so you say to yourself, "If I can follow certain laws, form certain habits, act in this way but not in that, then I shall have those moments of ecstasy again."

There is always a war between the spontaneous and the mechanical. Please do not adapt this to suit your own religious, philosophic terms. To me, what I am saying is vitally new and cannot be twisted to suit your particular prejudices of the higher and the lower self, the transient and the permanent, the self and the not-self, and so on. Most of us have, unfortunately, almost destroyed this spontaneity, this creative joy of the unknown from which alone there can be wise action. We have sedulously cultivated through generations of tradition, of morality based on will, of compulsion, the mechanical attitude of life, calling it by sweet-sounding words; in essence it is purely mechanical, intellectual. The process of discipline, of violence, of subjugation, of resistance, of imitation—all this is the outcome of the development of the mere intellect, which has its root in fear. The mechanical is overwhelmingly dominant in our lives. On this is based our civilization and morality—and at rare moments when the will is dormant, forgotten, there is the joy of the spontaneous, the unknown.

I say that in this state of spontaneity alone can you perceive that which is truth. In this state alone can there be wise action, not the action of calculated morality or of will.

The various forms of moral and religious disciplines, the many impositions of social and ethical institutions, are but the outcome of a carefully cultivated mechanical attitude towards life, which destroys spontaneity and brings about the destruction of truth.

Through no method—and all methods must inevitably be mechanical—can you unravel the truth of your own being. One cannot force spontaneity by any means. No method will give you spontaneity. All methods can but create mechanical reactions. No discipline will bring about the spontaneous joy of the unknown. The more you force yourself to be spontaneous, the more spontaneity retreats, the more hidden and obscure it becomes and the less it can be understood. And yet that is what you are trying to do when you follow disciplines, patterns, ideals, leaders, examples, and so forth. You must approach it negatively, not with the intention of capturing the unknown, the real.

Is each one aware of the mechanical process of the intellect, of the will, which destroys the spontaneous, the real? You cannot answer immediately, but you can begin to think about the intellect, the will, and especially feel its destructive quality. You can perceive the illusory nature of the will, not through any compulsion, not through any desire to achieve, to attain, to understand, but only when the intellect allows itself to be denuded of all its protective sheaths.

You can know yourself only when you love completely. This, again, is the whole process of life, not to be gathered in a few moments from a few words of mine. You cannot be yourself when love is dependent. It is not love when it is merely self-gratification, though it may be mutual. It is not love when there is a withholding; it is not love when it is merely a means to an end; when it is merely sensation. You cannot be yourself when love is at the behest of fear; it is then fear, not love, that is expressing itself in many ways, though you may cover it up by calling it love. Fear cannot allow you to be yourself. Intellect merely guides fear, controls it, but can never destroy it, for intellect is the very cause of fear.

As fear cannot allow you to be yourself, how then is one to overcome this fear—fear of all kinds, not of one particular type? How is one to free oneself from this fear, of which one may be conscious or unconscious? If you are unconscious of fear, become conscious of it; become aware of your thoughts and actions, and soon you will be conscious of fear. And if you are conscious of it, how are you going to be free from it? Are you going to free yourself from fear mechanically, through will; or will it begin to dissolve of its own accord, spontaneously? The mechanical or the will process can but hide away fear more and more, guard it and carefully withhold it, allowing only the reactions of controlled morality. Below these controlled behavior patterns, fear must ever continue. This is the inevitable result of the mechanical process of the will, with its disciplines, desires, controls, and so on.

Until one frees oneself from the mechanical, there cannot be the spontaneous, the real. Craving for the real, for that flame which bursts from within, cannot bring it about.

What will free you from the mechanical is the deep observation of the process of the will, being one with it, without any desire to be free from it. Now you observe the mechanical attitude towards life with a desire to get rid of it, to alter it, transform it. How can you transform will when desire is of the will itself?

You must be aware of the whole process of will, of the mechanical, of its struggles, its escapes, its miseries; and as the farmer allows the soil to lie fallow after a harvest, so must you allow yourself to be silent, negative, without any expectation. It is not easy. If in the hope of gaining the real, you mechanically allow yourself to be silent, force yourself to be negative, then fear is the reward. As I have said, this creative emptiness is not to be run after or sought by devious ways. It must happen. Truth is. It is not the result of organized morality, for morality based on will is not moral.

We have many problems, individual as well as social, and for these problems there is no solution through the intellect, through the will. As long as the process of will con-

tinues in any form, there must be confusion and sorrow. Through will you cannot know yourself, nor can there be the real.

August 4, 1938

Second Talk at Ommen

You may remember that I was trying to explain the difference between spontaneity and mechanical action, the mechanical being the morality of the will, and the spontaneous that which is born out of the depth of one's own being. This morning I will talk about one or two things concerning this, and then let us discuss them.

I was saying that fear in any form creates habit, which prevents unconditioned freedom in which alone there is reality, in which alone there can be the integrity of oneself. Fear prevents spontaneity.

Now it would be rather ridiculous, and impossible, to consider what it is to be spontaneous, or to judge who is spontaneous and who is not, and to consider also the qualities, the characteristics of spontaneity. Each one will know what it is to be spontaneous, to be real, when there is the right inward condition. You will know for yourself when you are truly spontaneous, when you are really yourself. To judge another to see if he is spontaneous means, really, that you have a standard of spontaneity, which is absurd. The judgment of what is spontaneous reveals a mind that is merely reacting mechanically to its own habit and moral patterns.

So it is futile and a waste of time, leading to mere opinion, to consider what it is to be real, spontaneous, to be oneself. Such consideration leads to illusion. Let us concern ourselves with what is the necessary condition that will reveal the real.

Now what is the right condition? There is no division as the inner and the outer condition; I am dividing it as the inner and the outer only for purposes of observation, to understand it more clearly. This division does not exist in reality.

From the right inward state alone can the outer conditions be changed, ameliorated, and fundamentally transformed. The approach from the merely superficial, that is, from the outer, in creating right conditions, will have little significance in understanding truth, God.

One has to understand what is the right inner condition, but not from any superficial compulsion or authority. The deep inward change will always intelligently deal with the outward conditions. Once and for all, let us fully perceive the importance of this necessary inward change and not merely rely on the change of outer circumstances. It is ever the inward motive and intentions that change and control the outer. Motives, desires, are not fundamentally altered by merely controlling the outer.

If a man is inwardly peaceful and is affectionate, without greed, surely such a man does not need laws imposing peace on him, police to regulate his conduct, institutions to maintain his morality.

Now we have given great significance to the outer, to maintain peace; through institutions, laws, police, armies, churches, and so on, we seek to maintain a peace which does not exist. By imposition and domination, opposing violence by violence, we hope to create a peaceful state.

If you really comprehend this, deeply, honestly, then you will see the importance of not approaching the many problems of life as the outer and the inner, but only from the comprehensive and the integral.

So what is the inward condition necessary to be oneself, to be spontaneous? The first necessary inward condition is that the habit-forming mechanism must cease. What is the motive power behind this mechanism?

Before we answer this we must first find out whether our thoughts and feelings are the result of mere habit, traditions, and are following ideals and principles. Most of us, if we really think about it intelligently, honestly, will see that our thoughts and feelings usually spring from various standardized patterns, whether they be ideals or principles.

The continuation of this mechanical habit and its motive power is the desire to be certain. The whole mechanism of tradition, of imitation, of example, the building up of a future, of the ideal, of the perfect and its achievement, is the desire to be secure; and the development of various supposedly necessary qualities is for its assurance, for its success.

Desire gives a false continuity to our thinking, and mind clings to that continuity whose actions are the mere following of patterns, ideals, principles, and the establishment of habit. Thus experience is never new, never fresh, never joyous, never creative—and hence the extraordinary vitality of dead things, of the past.

Now let us take a few examples and see what I mean. Take the habit of nationalism, which is now becoming more and more strong and cruel. Is not nationalism really a false love of man? One who is at heart a nationalist can never be a complete human being. To a nationalist, internationalism is a lie. Many insist that one can be a nationalist and at the same time be of no nation: this is an impossibility and only a trick of the mind.

To be attached to one particular piece of earth prevents the love of the whole. Having created a false and unnatural problem of nationalism, we proceed to solve it through clever and complex arguments for the necessity of nationalism and its maintenance through armaments, hate, and division. All such answers must be utterly stupid and false, for the problem itself is an illusion and a perversion. Let us understand this question of nationalism, and in this respect at least let us remain sane in a world of brutal regimentation and insanity.

Is not the organized love of one's country, with its regimented hate and affection, cultivated and imposed through propaganda, through leaders, merely a vested interest? Does not this so-called love of one's country exist because it feeds one's own egotism through devious ways? All enforcement and gratification must inevitably create mechanical habits which must constantly come into conflict with one's own integrity and affections. Prejudice, hate, fear, must create division, which inevitably breeds war—war not only within oneself, but also between peoples.

If nationalism is merely a habit, what is one to do? Not having a passport does not make you free of the nationalistic habit. Mere superficial action does not liberate you from the brutal inner conviction of a particular racial superiority. When you are confronted with feelings of nationalism, what is your reaction? Do you feel that they are inevitable, that you must go through nationalism to come to internationalism, that you must pass through the brutal to become pacific? What is your reasoning? Or do you not reason at all, but merely follow the flag because there are millions doing this absurd thing? Why are you all so silent? But how eager you will be to discuss with me about God, reincarnation, or ceremonies!

This question of nationalism is knocking at your door whether you will or not, and what is your answer?

Question: Is it not possible to look upon nationalism as improvement on provincialism and therefore the first step towards internationalism?

Question: It is the same thing, surely.

Question: I find nationalism an extended provincialism.

Question: It does seem to me, sir, that you perhaps overemphasize the nationalist position. It seems to me that there is less national feeling today in some quarters of the globe than there was fifty years ago, and that as time goes on the national feeling may become less among more and more people, and that internationalism may therefore have more chance. I think it is most important to have time for the moderate elements in the population to increase their international thoughts and feelings, and to prevent, if possible, some explosion which would sweep away the good in the present civilization along with the bad.

KRISHNAMURTI: The point is this, is it not: Can you at any time come to peace through violence—whether you call it provincialism, nationalism, or internationalism? Is peace to be achieved through slow stages? Love is not a matter of education or of time. The last war was fought for democracy, I believe, and look, we are more prepared for war than ever before, and people are less free. Please do not indulge in mere intellectual argumentations. Either you take your feelings and thoughts seriously and consider them deeply, or you are satisfied by superficial intellectual answers.

If you think you are seeking truth or creating in the world a true human relationship, nationalism is not the way; nor can this human relationship of affection, of friendship, be established by means of guns. If you love deeply there is neither the one nor the many. There is only that state of being which is love, in which there may be the one, but it is not the exclusion of the many. But if you say to yourself that through the love of the one there will be the love of the many, then you are not considering love at all but merely the result of love, which is a form of fear.

Now let us take another example of the process of the habit-forming mechanism which destroys creative living. You must be made new to understand reality.

Take the question of the way we treat people. Have you noticed how you yourself treat people—one whom you think to be superior, with great consideration, and the inferior with offensive contempt and indifference? Have you noticed it? (Yes) It is obvious in this camp: the way you treat me and the way you treat one of your fellow campers or those who help in running the camp: the way you behave to a titled person, and to a commoner; the respect you pay to money, and the respect you do not pay to the poor, and so on. Is not this the result of mere habit, of tradition, of imitation, of the desire to succeed, the habit of gratifying one's own vanity?

Please just think about this and perceive how the mind lives and continues in habit, though it is asserting that it must be spontaneous, free. What is the good of your listening to me if the obvious thing is escaping your consideration? Again you are silent because this is a common event in your lives, and so you are a bit nervous of approaching it, for you do not want to be exposed too radically.

If this habit exists—and it is merely a habit and not a deliberate, conscious action except in the case of a few—when you become conscious of it, it will disappear if you really love this whole process of living. But if you are not interested, you will listen to me, and you may be intellectually excited for a few minutes, but you will continue in the same old manner. But those of you who are deeply interested, who love to understand truth, to you I say: Observe how this or any other habit creates a chain of memories which becomes more and more strong, until

there is only the 'I', the 'me'. This mechanism is the 'I', and as long as this process exists, there cannot be the ecstasy of love, of truth.

Let us take another example—that of meditation. Now I see you are beginning to take interest. Nationalism, the way we treat people, love, meditation—all these are part of the same process; they all spring from the one source, but we are examining each separately to understand them better.

Perhaps you will talk over with me this question of meditation, for most of you, in one way or another, practice this thing called meditation, don't you? (Yes and No) Some do; some do not. Those of you who do, why do you do it? And those of you who do not, why don't you? Those who do not meditate, what is their motive? Either their attitude is one of complete thoughtlessness, indifference, or they are afraid of becoming involved in all this rubbish, or they fear to reveal themselves to themselves, or there is the fear of acquiring new and inconvenient habits, and so on. Those who do meditate, what is their motive?

Question: Egotism.

KRISHNAMURTI: Are you putting forward this word as an explanation? I can give you also a very good explanation, but we are trying to go beyond mere explanations. Mere explanations usually put a stop to thinking. What are we trying to do in talking this matter over? We are exposing ourselves. We are helping each other to see what we are. You are acting as a mirror to me, and I as a mirror to you, without distortion. But if you merely give an explanation, just throw off a few words, you cloud the mirror, which prevents clear perception.

We are trying to find out why we meditate, and what it means. Those of you who meditate, you do it presumably because you feel that you need certain poise and clarity, through self-recollectedness, to deal with the problems of life. So you set aside some time for this purpose, and you hope during this period to come into contact with something real, which will help to guide you during the day. Is this not so? (Yes) During this period you begin to discipline yourself, or during the whole day you discipline your thoughts and feelings, and so your actions, according to the established pattern of those few moments of so-called meditation.

Question: No, I consider it a step on the pathway to the liberation of the self, a footstep only.

KRISHNAMURTI: Surely you are saying the same thing as I am pointing out, only you put it in your own words. Through discipline can you liberate thought, liberate emotion? This is the point which the questioner raises. Can one discipline oneself in order to become spontaneous, to comprehend the unknown, the real? Discipline implies a pattern, a mold which is shaping, and that which is truth must be the unknown and cannot be approached by the known.

Question: I think I meditate because I want to know myself, because I am afraid of myself, because I hate myself as I hate my neighbor, and I want to know myself to protect myself. I hate my neighbor, and I love him. I hate him because he threatens my habits, my well-being. I love him because I want him. And I am a nationalist because I am afraid of those across the frontier. I protect myself in every way possible.

KRISHNAMURTI: You are saying that you meditate in order to protect yourself. (Yes) That is so, but we should go more deeply into this question of discipline, not only the

discipline imposed by the outside world through various institutions of organized morality, through particular social systems, but also the discipline that desire develops.

Discipline imposed from without, by society, by leaders, and so on, must inevitably destroy individual fulfillment; I think this is fairly obvious. For such discipline, compulsion, conformity, merely postpones the inevitable problem of the individual fear with its many illusions.

Now there are many reasons for disciplining oneself; there is the desire to protect oneself in various ways, by achievement, by trying to become wiser, nobler, by finding the Master, by becoming more virtuous, by following principles, ideals, by wanting and craving for truth, for love, and so on. All this indicates the working of fear, and the noble reasons are but the coverings of this innate fear.

You say to yourself, "In order to reach God, to find out reality, to put myself in communion with the absolute, with the cosmic"—you know all the phrases—"I must begin to discipline myself. I must learn to be more concentrated. I must practice awareness, develop certain virtues." When you are asserting these things and disciplining yourself, what is happening to your thoughts and emotions?

Question: Do you mean it is a form of self-glorification?

Question: We are forming habits.

KRISHNAMURTI: Suppose one conceives a pattern of what is good, or it has been imposed through tradition, education, or one has learned that evil is that which divides; and if this is the ideal, the pattern for life's conduct that one pursues through meditation, through self-imposed discipline, then what is happening to one's own thoughts and emotions? One is forcing them, violently or lovingly, to conform, and thereby establishing a new habit instead of the old. Is this not so? (Yes)

Thus intellect, will, is controlling and shaping morality; will based on the desire to protect oneself. The desire to protect oneself is born of fear, which denies reality. The way of discipline is the process of fear, and the habit created by so-called meditation destroys spontaneity, the revelation of the unknown.

Question: Is it not possible to form a habit of love without losing spontaneity?

KRISHNAMURTI: Habit is of the mind, of the will, which merely overcomes fear without doing away with it. Emotions are creative, vital, new, and therefore cannot be made into a habit however much the will tries to dominate and control them.

It is the mind, the will, with its attachments, desires, fears, that creates conflict between itself and emotion. Love is not the cause of misery; it is the fears, desires, habits of the mind that create pain, the agony of jealousy, disillusionment. Having created conflict and suffering, the mind with its will for satisfaction finds reasons, excuses, escapes, which are called by various names—detachment, impersonal love, and so on. We must understand the whole process of the habit-forming mechanism and not ask which discipline, pattern, or ideal is best. If discipline is coordination, then it is not to be realized through enforcement, through any system. The individual must comprehend his own profound complexity and not merely look to a pattern for fulfillment.

Do not practice discipline, follow patterns and mere ideals, but be aware of the process of forming habits. Be conscious of the old grooves along which the mind has run and also of the desire to create new ones.

Seriously experiment with this; perhaps there will be greater confusion and suffering, for discipline, moral laws, have merely acted to hold down the hidden desires and purposes. When you are aware integrally, with your whole being, of this confusion and suffering, without any hope of escape, then there will arise spontaneously that which is real. But you must love, be enthused by that very confusion and suffering. You must love with your own heart, not with another's.

If you begin to experiment with yourself, you will see a curious transformation taking place. In the moment of highest confusion there is clarity; in the moment of greatest fear there is love. You must come to it spontaneously, without the exertion of will.

I suggest seriously that you experiment with what I have been saying and then you will begin to see in what manner habit destroys creative perception. But it is not a thing to be wished for and cultivated. There cannot be a groping after it.

August 6, 1938

Third Talk at Ommen

I have been trying to explain what is the right inward condition in which one can truly be oneself; that so long as the habit-forming mechanism exists, one cannot truly be oneself, even if it is considered good. All habit must prevent clarity of perception and must conceal one's own integrity. This mechanism has been developed as a means of escape, a process of concealment, of covering up one's own confusion and uncertainties; it has been developed to cover up the futility of one's own actions and the routine of work, of occupation; or to escape from emptiness, sorrow, disappointment, and so on.

We are trying to escape, run away from ignorance and fear through forming habits that will counteract them, that will resist them—habits of ideals and morality. When there is discontentment, sorrow, the intellect mechanically comes forward with solutions, explanations, tentative suggestions, which gradually crystallize and become habits of thought. Thus suffering and doubt are covered over.

So fear is the root of this habit-forming mechanism. We must understand its process. By understanding I do not mean the mere intellectual grasp of it, but the becoming aware of it as an actual process that is taking place, not superficially, but as something that is happening every day of one's life. Understanding is a process of self-revelation, of being aware not merely objectively, mechanically, but as a part of our very existence.

To understand this mechanism of escape through habit, we must first find out the concealed motive—the motive that drives us to certain actions, which brings in its wake what we call experience. As long as we do not understand the motive power of this mechanism that creates escape, merely to consider the escapes is of little value.

Experience is a process of accumulation and denudation, of revelation and a strengthening of old habits, a breaking down and building up of that which we call the will. Experience either strengthens the will or at moments destroys it, either builds up purposive desires or breaks those desires we have stored up, only to create new ones. In this process of experiencing, living, there is the gradual formation of will.

Now there is no divine will, but only the plain, ordinary will of desire—the will to succeed, to be satisfied, to be. This will is a resistance, and it is the fruit of fear which guides, chooses, justifies, disciplines. This will is not divine. It is not in conflict with the so-called divine will, but because of its very existence, it is a source of sorrow and conflict, for it is the will of fear. There cannot be conflict between light and darkness; where the one is, the other is not. However much we may like to clothe this will with divinity, with high-sounding principles and names, will in its essence is the result of fear, of desire.

Some are aware of this will of fear, with all its permutations and combinations. Perhaps some realize this will as fear and attempt to break it down by pursuing it along its many expressions, thus only creating another form of will, breaking down one resistance only to create another.

So before we begin to inquire into the ways and means of breaking down fear through discipline, through forming new habits, and so on, we must first understand the motive power that lies behind the will. I have explained what I mean by understanding. This understanding is not an intellectual, analytical process. It is not of the drawing-room or of the specialist, but has to be understood in everyday actions, in our daily relationships. That is, the process of living will reveal to us, if we are awake at all, the functioning of this will, of this habit, the vicious circle of creating one resistance after another, which we can call by different names—ideals, love, God, truth, and so forth.

The motive power behind the will is fear, and when we begin to realize this, the mechanism of habit intervenes, offering new escapes, new hopes, new gods. Now it is at this precise moment, when the mind begins to interfere with the realization of fear, that there must be great awareness not to be drawn off, not to be distracted by the offerings of the intellect, for the mind is subtle and cunning. When there is only fear without any hope of escape, in its darkest moments, in the utter solitude of fear, there comes from within itself, as it were, the light which shall dispel it.

Whatever attempts we make superficially, intellectually, to destroy fear through various forms of discipline, behavior patterns, only create other forms of resistances; and it is in this habit that we are caught. When you ask how to get rid of fear, how to break down habits, you are really approaching it from outside, intellectually, and so your question has no significance. You cannot dissolve fear through will, for will is the child of fear; nor can it be destroyed through "love," for if love is used for the purposes of destruction, it is no longer love but another name for will.

Question: Please, what is samadhi? *Those who have reached it maintain that it is a true realization. Is it not, on the contrary, only a kind of suicide, the final result of an artificial way? Is there not an absolute lack of all creative activity? You point out the necessity of being oneself, whereas this is a mere killing of oneself, is it not?*

KRISHNAMURTI: Any process that leads to limitation, to resistance, to cutting oneself off, as it were, in an intellectual or an ideal state, is destructive of creative living. Surely this is obvious. That is, if one has an ideal of love—and all ideals must be intellectual and therefore mechanical—and one tries to practice it, make love into a habit, one reaches certainly a definite state. But it is not that of love, it is only a state of an intellectual achievement.

This pursuit of the ideal is attempted by all peoples; the Hindus do it in their way, and the Christians and other religious bodies also do it. Fear creates the ideal, the pattern, the principle, for the mind is pursuing satisfaction. When this satisfaction is threatened the mind escapes to the ideal. Fear, having created the pattern, molds thought and desire, gradually destroying spontaneity, the unknown, the creative.

Question: The greatest fear I have is that the life of another, or my own, should be spoiled.

KRISHNAMURTI: Is not each one, in his own way, spoiling his own life? Are we not destroying our own integrity? By our own desires, by our own conditionings, we are spoiling our own individual lives. Having control of another, and having the capacity to spoil our own life, we proceed to twist the life of another, whether it is a child, a dependent, or a neighbor.

There are institutions, governmental and religious, to which we are willingly or unwillingly forced to conform. So to which kind of spoiling does the questioner refer? The deliberate perversion of one's own life, or the twisting of one's life by powerful institutions? Our natural reaction is to say that institutions, great and small, are corrupting our lives. One's reaction is to put the blame on the outer, on circumstances.

To put it in a different way, here we are in a world of regimentation, of compulsion, of the clever technique of governments and organized religions to wear down the individual—and what is one to do? How is an individual to act? I wonder how many of you have seriously put this question to yourselves. Some may have realized the brutality of all this and joined societies or groups which promise to alter certain conditions. But in the process of alteration, the organization of the party, of the society, has grown to vast proportions and has become of the greatest importance. So the individual is again caught in its machinery.

How are we to approach this question? From the outside or from within? There is no division as the outer and the inner, but merely changing the outer cannot fundamentally alter the inner. If you are aware that you are spoiling your own life, how can you look to an institution or to an outward pattern to help you?

If you deeply feel that violence in any form can only lead to violence, though you may not stop wars, you will at least be a center of sanity as a doctor in the midst of disease. So in the same way, if you integrally perceive in what manner you are spoiling your life, that very perception begins to straighten out those things that are crooked. Such an action is not an escape.

Question: Must we return to the past? Must I be aware of what I have been? Must I know my karma?

KRISHNAMURTI: By being aware, both the past and the present are revealed, which is not some mysterious process, but in trying to understand the present, the past fears and limitations are revealed.

Karma is a Sanskrit word whose verb means to act. A philosophy of action has been created around the central idea, "As you sow, so shall you reap," but we need not go into all that now. We see that any action born of the idea of reward or of punishment must be limiting, for such action springs from fear. Action brings either clarity or confusion, depending on one's conditioning. If one is brought up to worship success, either here or in the so-called spiritual sphere, there must be the pursuit of reward with its fears and hopes, which conditions all action, all living. Living becomes then a process of learning, of the constant accumulation of knowledge. Why do we lay up this so-called knowledge?

Question: Are we not to have in ourselves some standard for action?

KRISHNAMURTI: Now we come to the fundamental question: "Must one live by standards, whether outer or inner?" We easily recognize the outer standard as one of compulsion and therefore preventing individual fulfillment. We look to an inner standard which each one has created through action and reaction, through judgment of values, desires, experiences, fears, and so on. What is this inner standard based upon, though it is constantly varying? Is it not based upon self-protective desire and its many fears? These desires and fears create a pattern of behavior, of morality, and fear is the constant standard, assuming different forms under different conditions. There are those who take shelter in the intellectual formula, "Life is one," and others in the love of God, which is also an intellectual formula, and they make these into patterns, principles, for their daily life. Morality of will is not moral but the expression of fear.

August 8, 1938

Fourth Talk at Ommen

Each one of us has a peculiar and particular problem of his own. Some are concerned with death and the fear of death and what is to happen in the hereafter; some are so lonely in their occupations that they are seeking a way to overcome this emptiness; some are sorrow laden; some have the routine and boredom of work, and others the problem of love with its complexities. How can all these problems or the particular problem of each one be solved? Is there only one problem or are there many separate problems? Is each one to be solved separately, disconnected from the others, or are we to trace each problem and so come to the one problem? Is there, then, only one problem, and by tracing each difficulty, shall we come to the one problem through which, if we understand it, we can solve all others?

There is only one fundamental problem, which expresses itself in many different ways. Each one of us is conscious of a particular difficulty and desires to grapple with that difficulty by itself. In solving one's peculiar difficulty, one may eventually come upon the central problem, but during the process of getting there, the mind becomes weary and has acquired knowledge, formulas, standards, which really stand in the way of its understanding the one central problem. Some of us try to trace each problem to its source, and in the process of examination and analysis, we are learning, we are accumulating so-called knowledge. This knowledge gradually becomes formulas, patterns. Experience has given us memories and values which guide and discipline and which must inevitably condition.

Now it is these self-protective standards and memories, this stored-up knowledge, these formulas, that prevent us from grasping the fundamental problem and solving it. If we are confronted with a vital experience and try to understand it with dead memories, values, we merely pervert it, absorbing it into the dead accumulation of the past.

To solve this problem of living you must have a fresh, new mind. A new birth must take place. Life, love, reality are ever new, and a fresh mind and heart are needed to understand them. Love is ever new, but this freshness is spoiled by the mechanical intellect with its complexities, anxieties, jealousies, and so on.

Are we made anew, is there a new birth each day? Or are we merely developing the capacity of resistance through will, through habit, through values?

We are merely strengthening the will of resistance in different and subtle forms. So experience, instead of liberating us, giving us freedom to be reborn, to be made anew, is further conditioning us, further binding us to the dead accumulations of the past, to the stored-up knowledge, which is really ignorance and fear. This perverts and destroys the liberating force of experience.

This is the fundamental problem—how to be reborn or made anew. Now, can you be made anew through formulas, through beliefs? Is it not absurd, the very idea that you can be made anew by patterns, ideals, standards? Can discipline, enforced or self-imposed, bring about a rebirth of the mind? This also is an impossibility, is it not? Through slogans, repetitive words, institutions, through the worship of another can you be made anew? Perhaps momentarily, while you are listening to me, you feel the impossibility of being made anew through a method, through a person, and so on.

Then what will make us anew? Do you perceive the vital necessity of being renewed, of being reborn? To understand life, with all its complex problems, and reality, the unknown, there must be a constant death and a new birth. Otherwise you meet new problems, new experiences, with dead accumulations, which only bind, causing confusion and suffering.

We are, then, confronted with these accumulated memories and formulas, beliefs and values, which are constantly acting as a shield, as a resistance. Now if we try to remove these resistances, these safeguards, merely through will, discipline, the mind is not being made anew. And yet we have the power, the only force which can liberate and which can make anew, and that is love—the love, not of the ideal, not of the formula, but the love of man and man. But we have hedged this love about with the morality of the will because there is the desire for satisfaction, and its fear. So love becomes destructive, binding, instead of liberating, renewing.

We see this process of bondage and pain in our daily life. It is only in daily life, with its relationships and its conflicts, its fears and its ambitions, that you begin to perceive the renewing force of love. This love is not sentiment. Sentiment, after all, is merely the incapacity to feel deeply, integrally, and therefore to alter fundamentally.

Question: I should like to know why I am sometimes too lazy to be fresh and new?

KRISHNAMURTI: You may be lazy because of the lack of proper diet, but possessing a healthy body—does that ensure a rebirth of the mind? You may be quiet, apparently lazy, and yet be extraordinarily alive.

Question: To be made anew we must exert ourselves.

KRISHNAMURTI: You cannot be made anew with the dead weight of the past, and perceiving this you think you must make an effort to get rid of it. Being caught in confusion, you feel that to become disentangled from it, you must discipline yourself, you must make an effort to overcome it, or otherwise confusion will increase and continue. This is what you mean, isn't it? Either you make an effort to keep still and observe in order to find ways and means of overcoming this confusion and conflict, or you make an effort to see its causes so that you may overcome them; or you are intellectually interested only to observe—but we need not be concerned with the so-called intellectuals. Either you accept the chaos, the struggle, or you try to overcome suffering; both involve effort. If you examine the motive for this exertion, you will perceive that there is the desire not to suffer, the desire to escape, to be satisfied, to protect oneself, and so on. Effort is being made to overcome, to understand, to transform that which we are into that which we want to be or think we ought to be. Does not all such effort really produce

a series of new habits instead of the old? The old habits, the old values have not given you the ideal, the satisfaction, and so you make an effort to establish new ideals, a new series of habits and values and satisfactions. Such effort is considered worthy and noble. You are making an effort to be or not to be something according to a preconceived formula, pattern. So there cannot be a rebirth, but only a continuation of the old desire in a new form which soon creates confusion and sorrow. Again there is the exertion of the will to overcome this conflict and pain; one is again caught up in the vicious circle of effort, whether it is the effort to find the cause of suffering or the effort to overcome it.

Effort is made to overcome fear through discovering its causes. Why do you want to discover the cause? Is it not because you do not want to suffer, you are afraid to suffer? So you hope that, through fear yielding to fear, all fear will be overcome. This is an impossibility.

Now do you make an effort to discover the cause of joy? If you do, then joy ceases to be and only its memories and habits exist.

Question: So by analyzing, fear should also disappear in the same way that pleasure does when examined. But why does it not?

KRISHNAMURTI: Joy is spontaneous, unsought, and uninvited, and when the mind analyzes it to cultivate or to recapture it, then it is no longer joy. Whereas fear is not spontaneous except in sudden, unforeseen incidents, but it is sedulously cultivated by the mind in its desire for satisfaction, for certainly. So if you make an effort to get rid of fear by discovering its causes, and so on, you are merely covering up fear, for effort is of the will, which is resistance created by fear.

If you integrally, with your whole being, understand this process, then in the midst of this flame of suffering, when there is no desire to escape, to overcome—out of this very confusion there arises a new comprehension spontaneously springing up out of the soil of fear itself.

August 10, 1938

Fifth Talk at Ommen

I have tried to explain that renewal, rebirth, must be spontaneous and not the result of effort.

Before finding out if effort is moral or immoral, important or unimportant, we must first consider desire. In understanding desire, each one will discover for himself whether effort is moral or immoral with regard to the renewal, the rebirth of the mind. If one had no desire, there would be no effort. So we must know its process, the motive power behind effort, which is always desire; by whatever name you like to call it—righteousness, the good, the God in us, the higher self, and so on—nevertheless it is still desire.

Now desire is always for something; it is always dependent and therefore always productive of fear. In being dependent there is always uncertainty which breeds fear. Desire cannot exist by itself, it must always be in relation to something. You can observe this in your daily, psychological reactions. Desire is always dependent, related to something. It is only love which is not dependent.

There is the desire to be something, to become, to succeed, not to suffer, to find happiness, to love and to be loved, to find truth, reality, God. There is the positive desire to be something and the negative desire not to be something. If we are attached, there is agony, suffering, and from that we learn—what we call learn—that attachment gives pain. So we desire not to be attached and cultivate that negative quality, detachment. Desire is prompting us to be this and not that.

We are familiar with the positive and the negative desire, to be and not to be, to become and not to become. Now desire is not emotion; desire is the result of a mind that is ever seeking satisfaction, whose values are based on satisfaction. To be satisfied is the motive behind all desire. The mind is ever seeking satisfaction at any cost, and if it is thwarted in one direction, it seeks to achieve its purpose in another. All effort, all directive power of the mind, is that it may be satisfied. So satisfaction becomes a mechanical habit of the mind. In moments of great emotion, of deep love, there is no dependency of desire, nor its search for satisfaction.

To be satisfied, the mind develops its own technique of resistance and nonresistance, which is the will. And when the mind discovers that in the process of satisfaction there is suffering, then it begins to develop desirelessness, detachment. Thus there is the positive and the negative will ever exerting, ever seeking satisfaction. The desire to be satisfied creates will, which maintains itself by its own continual effort. And where will is, there must always follow fear—fear of not being satisfied, of not achieving, of not becoming. Will and fear always go together. And again to overcome this fear, effort is made, and in this vicious circle of uncertainty, the mind is caught. Will and fear go always hand in hand, and will maintains its continuity from satisfaction to satisfaction, through memory which gives to consciousness its continuity, as the 'I'.

Will and effort, then, is merely the mechanism of the mind to be satisfied. Thus desire is wholly of the mind. Mind is the very essence of desire. Habit is established by constant search for satisfaction, and the sensation which the mind stimulates is not emotion.

All effort then, springing from the will either to be satisfied or not to be satisfied, must ever be mechanical, habit-forming, and so cannot bring about rebirth, renewal. Even when the mind inquires into the cause of suffering, it is doing so primarily because it desires to escape, to do away with that which is not satisfactory and to gain that which is.

Now this whole process in which the mind is caught up is the way of ignorance. Will that is maintaining itself through effort to be satisfied, to be gratified, through various ways and methods—this will of satisfaction must of its own accord cease, for any effort to put an end to satisfaction is only another way of being satisfied.

So this process of satisfaction, of gratification, is continually going on and all effort can only give strength to it. Perceiving that all effort is the desire for satisfaction and therefore of fear itself, how is one to bring this process to an end? Even this very desire for its cessation is born of the will to be satisfied. This very question of how to be free of desire is prompted by desire itself.

If you feel integrally this whole process as ignorance, then you will not ask for a way to be free from desire, fear. Then you will not seek any method, however promising, however hopeful. There is no method, no system, no path to truth. When you understand the full inward significance of all methods, that very comprehension is beginning spontaneously to dissolve desire, fear, which is seeking satisfaction.

Only in deep emotion is there no craving for satisfaction. Love is not dependent on satisfaction and habit. But the will of desire ever seeks to make of love a mechanical habit, or tries to control it through moral laws, through compulsion, and so on. Hence there is a constant battle by the mind, with its will of satisfaction, to control, dominate love; and the battle is almost always won by the mind, for love has no conflict within itself and so with another. Only when desire, with its will of fear, ceases of its own spontaneous accord—not through compulsion or

the promise of reward—is there a renewal, a rebirth of one's whole being.

Question: Can I trust or have faith in this love, or is this also a way of self-protection?

KRISHNAMURTI: Is not faith another refuge in which mind takes satisfaction and shelter? You may have faith in love, another in God, and so on. All such faith is an anchorage for the mind. Any refuge, any attachment, whatever its name, must be one of self-protection, satisfaction, and therefore the result of fear.

One perceives appalling cruelty about one, utter chaos and barbarity, and one takes refuge in an ideal, in belief, or in some form of consolation. Thus one escapes into an illusion; but the conflict between the actual and the illusory must continue until either the unreal overcomes the actual or the actual breaks through all safeguards, all escapes, and begins to reveal its deep significance.

Question: By merely insisting on individual fulfillment are you not putting aside the social question? How can the individual, who is ever in relation with society, be the only important factor? Why do you emphasize the individual?

KRISHNAMURTI: Without the individual, society cannot exist; this social entity is not independent of the individual. Society is the relationship of one individual with another. Society is personal but it has become an independent machine with a life of its own which merely uses the individual. Society has become merely an institution which controls and dominates the individual through opinion, moral laws, vested interests, and so on. As institutions are never important but only the individual, we must consider his fulfillment, which cannot be brought about by mere change of environment, however drastic the change may be. The mere alteration of the superficial will not bring about the deep fulfillment of man, but only mechanical reactions. This division as the individual and the environment is mechanical and false; when fundamentally each one understands this to be so, then the individual will act integrally, not as an individual nor as merely the mechanical product of society, but as an integrated human being.

Question: This surely will take many centuries, will it not? So must we not make new social laws and conditions now?

KRISHNAMURTI: How are we going to bring about this change which we all desire? Either through force or each individual beginning to awaken to the necessity of fundamental change. Either through enforcement, revolution, domination or through the awakening of the individual to reality.

If we want to produce a merely mechanical world of moral systems, law, impositions, then violence may be sufficient, force of every description; but if we want peace and brotherhood, relationship based on love, then violence in any form cannot be the way. Through violence you cannot come to peace, to love, but only to further violence. Violence is complex and subtle, and until the individual is free from its obvious and its hidden domination, there cannot be peace nor lasting brotherhood.

Question: Then must we let cruel people go on being cruel?

KRISHNAMURTI: To save humanity must you first destroy the human? Is that what you are asking me? Because you have certain ideologies, certain beliefs, must the individual be sacrificed to them? No, my friends, we do not want to help the world, we only want to impose on others a certain ideology, a certain faith, a certain belief. We want the tyranny of ideas to prevail, and not love.

Each one is pursuing his own particular problem, or his own ideal of man, or his own conception of the state, or his belief in God, and so on. But if you who are listening to me fundamentally grasp what I am saying, then you will be concerned with the root problems—that of desire with its fear and efforts—which prevents individual fulfillment, rebirth.

August 12, 1938

Sixth Talk at Ommen

I have been trying to explain the habit-forming mechanism of fear, which destroys renewal, rebirth, in which alone there can be reality. The desire for satisfaction creates fear and habit. As I explained, desire and emotion are two different and distinct processes—desire being entirely of the mind, and emotion the integral expression of one's whole being. Desire, the process of the mind, is ever accompanied by fear, and emotion is devoid of fear. Desire must ever produce fear, and emotion has no fear at any time for it is of one's whole being. Emotion cannot conquer desire, for emotion is a state of fearlessness which can be experienced only when desire, with its fear and will of satisfaction, ceases. Emotion cannot overcome fear; for fear, as desire, is of the mind. Emotions are wholly of a different character, quality and dimension.

Now what we are trying to do, the majority of us, is to overcome fear either by desire or by what we call "emotion"—which is really another form of desire. You cannot overcome fear by love. To overcome fear through another force which we call emotion, love, is not possible, for the desire to overcome fear is born of desire itself, of the mind itself, and is not of love. That is, fear is the result of desire, satisfaction, and the desire to overcome fear is of the nature of satisfaction itself. It is not possible to overcome fear by love, as most people find out for themselves. Mind, which is of desire, cannot destroy part of itself. This is what you try to do when you talk of "getting rid" of fear. When you ask, "How am I to get rid of fear, what am I to do about the various forms of fear?" you are merely wanting to know how to overcome one set of desires by another—which only perpetuates fear. For all desire creates fear. Desire breeds fear, and in trying to overcome one desire by another, you are only yielding to fear. Desire can only recondition itself, reshape itself to a new pattern, but it will still be desire, giving birth to fear.

We know that our present habits of thought and morality are based on individual security and gain, and that thus we have created a society which is maintained through our own desire. Realizing this, there are those who try to create new habits, new virtues, in the hope of creating a new society based on nongain, and so on. But desire still persists in different forms, and until we realize the whole process of desire itself, the mere transformation of outside conditions, values, will have little significance.

To change the form of desire from the old to the new is merely to recondition the mind, for it will still be of desire, and thus it will always be a source of fear. So we must understand the process of the mind itself. Is not the mind, as we know it, an instrument developed for survival, for satisfaction, for self-protection, for resistance, and therefore the instrument of fear? Let us put aside the consideration that the mind is the instrument of God, the highest moral guide, and so on, for all such assumptions are merely traditional or are mere hopes. Mind is essentially an instrument of fear. From desire spring reason, conclusion, action—whose values and moralities are based on the will to survive, to be satisfied. Thus the mind, thought, breaks itself up into many parts, as the conscious and the unconscious, the high and the low, the real and the false, the good and the evil. That is, the mind, seeking satisfaction, has broken itself up into many parts, each part being in conflict with the other, but the central and essential pursuit of each part and of the whole is one of self-satisfaction, under different forms. So the mind is ever engendering its own fear.

There are various forms of fear: fear of one's own future, fear of death, of life, of responsibility, and so forth. So the mind is ever trying to make itself secure through beliefs, hopes, illusions, knowledge, ideals, patterns. There is a constant struggle between the known and the unknown. The known is the past, the accumulated, habit, and the unknown is that which is the uncertain, the unconquerable, the spontaneous, the creative.

The past is ever trying to overcome the future; habit proceeds to make the unknown into the habitual so that fear may cease. Thus there is the constant conflict of desire, and fear is ever present. The process is to absorb, to be certain, to be satisfied, and when this is not possible, the mind resorts to satisfying explanations, theories, beliefs. Thus death, the unknown, is made into the known; truth, the unconquerable, is made into the attainable.

So the mind is a battlefield of its own desires, fears, values, and whatever effort it makes to destroy fear—that is, to destroy itself—is utterly vain. That part which desires to get rid of fear is ever seeking satisfaction; and that from which it craves to free itself has been in the past a means of satisfaction. Thus satisfaction is trying to get rid of that which has satisfied; fear is trying to overcome that which has been the instrument of fear. Desire, creating fear in its search for satisfaction, tries to conquer that fear, but desire itself is the cause of fear. Mere desire cannot destroy itself, nor fear overcome itself, and all effort of the mind to rid itself of them is born of desire. Thus the mind is caught in its own vicious circle of effort.

We must understand deeply the inward nature of the mind itself, and this understanding is not born of a day; it needs immense awareness of our whole being. The mind, as I said, is a battlefield of various desires, values, hopes, and any effort on its part to free itself from them can only accentuate the conflict. Struggle exists so long as desire in any form continues; when one desire discriminates against another, one series of values against another, one ideal against another, this conflict must continue. This discriminative power of desire, choice, must cease, and this can happen only when one understands, inwardly feels the blind effort of the intellect. The deep observation of this process, without want, without judgment, without prejudice, and so without desire, is the beginning of that awareness which alone can free the mind of its own destructive fears, habits, illusions.

But with the majority of us, the difficulty is to pierce through those forms of emotion which are really the stimulations of desire, fear, for such emotions are destructive of love. They prevent integral awareness.

Question: Are desire and interest, as we know them now, the same?

KRISHNAMURTI: If interest is merely the result of desire, to gain, to be satisfied, to succeed, then interest is the same as desire and therefore destructive of creative life.

Question: How can I attain the quality of desirelessness without having the desire to attain it?

KRISHNAMURTI: Sir, this is exactly what I have been talking about this morning. Why do you want to attain desirelessness? Is it not because you have found through experience that desire is painful, desire brings fear, desire creates conflict or a success that is cruel? So you crave to be in a state of desirelessness, which can be achieved, but it is of death, for it is merely the result of fear. You want to be free from all fear, and so you make desirelessness the ideal, the pattern to be pursued. But the motive behind that ideal is still desire and so still of fear.

Question: Is mind, life itself? Because one cannot divide up life as mind and emotion?

KRISHNAMURTI: As I have explained, the mind has merely become an instrument of self-protection of various forms, and it has divided itself into emotion and thought—not that life has divided it nor that emotions have separated themselves from the mind, but the mind, through its own desires, has broken up itself into different parts. The mind has discovered that by being desireless, it will be less prone to suffering. It has learned through experience, through knowledge, that desirelessness might bring the ultimate comfort, which it hopes is truth, God, and so on. So it makes an effort to be without desire and therefore divides itself into different parts.

Question: Is it possible to be without desire when one has a body?

KRISHNAMURTI: What do you say, sir? This is a problem that you have to face, that we all have to face. Mind, as I said, is ever seeking satisfaction through various forms.

Necessity has thus become a means of gratification. This expresses itself in many ways—greed, power, position, and so forth. Can one not exist in this world without desire? You will find this out in your daily life. Do not separate needs from desire, which would be a false approach to the understanding of desire. When needs are glorified as a means for self-importance, then desire starts the complex process of ignorance. If you merely emphasize needs and make a principle of it, you are again approaching the question of desire from a most unintelligent point of view, but if you begin to consider the process of desire itself, which breeds fear and ignorance, then needs will have their significant value.

Question: Please give us your views or anything you care to say on the subject of how to bring up children.

Question: It is not the child that is the problem; we are the problem.

KRISHNAMURTI: Are you saying that we must first resolve our own problems and then we shall be able to deal with the child? Is this not a very one-sided conception? Is not child education a very complex problem? You want to help the child grow to its own fullest integral capacity, but as there are not adequate teachers and schools for this purpose, education becomes a problem. You as a parent may have certain definite ideas that will help the child to be intelligently critical and to be spontaneously himself at all times, but unfortunately at school, nationalism, race hatred, leadership, tradition, example, and so on are inculcated in the child, thus counteracting all that you may be doing at home. So either you have to start a school of your own where prejudices of race, country, examples, religious superstitions, beliefs are not inculcated in the children—which means that an intelligent human being as a teacher is necessary; and one is rarely found. Or you must send the child to the schools that already exist, hoping for the best, and counteracting at home all the stupid and pernicious things he learns at school by helping him to be intelligent and critical. But generally you have not time to do this, or you have too much money, so you employ nurses to look after your children.

It is a complex problem which each parent must deal with according to his capacity, but unfortunately this is paralyzed by his own fears, superstitions, beliefs.

Question: At least we can give the child a right environment at home.

KRISHNAMURTI: Even that is not enough, is it? For the pressure of opinion is very great. A child feels out of it if he does not put on some kind of uniform or carry a wooden gun when the majority of them are doing it. There is the demand of the so-called nation whose government, with its colossal power, forces the individual to a certain pattern, to carry arms, to kill, to die. Then there is the other institution, organized religion, which through belief, dogma, and so on equally tries to destroy the individual. Thus the individual is being continually thwarted of his fulfillment.

This is a problem of our whole life, not to be solved through mere explanations and assertions.

August 14, 1938

Ojai, California, 1940

※

First Talk in The Oak Grove

The world is ever in pain, in confusion; it has ever this problem of struggle and sorrow. We become conscious of this conflict, this pain, when it affects us personally or when it is immediately about us, as now. The problems of war have existed before, but most of us have not been concerned with them as they were remote and not affecting us personally and deeply; but now war is at our door and that seems to dominate the minds of most people.

Now I am not going to answer the questions that must inevitably arise when one is immediately concerned with the problems of war, what attitude and action one should take with regard to it, and so on. But perhaps we shall talk over together a much deeper problem, for war is only an outward manifestation of inward confusion and struggle of hate and antagonism. The problem that we should discuss, which is ever present, is that of the individual and his relationship with another, which is society. If we can understand this complex problem, then perhaps we shall be able to avoid the many causes that ultimately lead to war. War is a symptom, however brutal and diseased, and to deal with the outer manifestation without regard to the deeper causes of it, is futile and purposeless; in changing fundamentally the causes, perhaps we can bring about a peace that is not destroyed by outer circumstances.

Most of us are apt to think that through legislation, through mere organization, or through leadership, the problems of war and peace and other human problems can be solved. As we do not want to be responsible, individually, for this inner and outer turmoil in our lives, we look to authorities, groups, and mass action. Through these outward methods one may have temporary peace, but one can have that abiding, lasting peace only when the individual understands himself and his relationship with another, which makes society. Peace is within and not without; there can only be peace and happiness in the world when the individual—who is the world—sets about definitely to alter the causes within himself which produce confusion, sorrow, hate, and so on. I want to deal with these causes and how to change them deeply and lastingly.

The world about us is in constant flux, constant change; there is incessant sorrow and pain. Amidst this mutation and conflict can there be lasting peace and happiness, independent of all circumstances? This peace and happiness can be discovered, hewn out of whatever circumstances the individual finds himself in. During these talks, I shall try to explain how to experiment with ourselves and thus free thought from its self-imposed limitations. But each one must experiment and live strenuously and not merely live on superficial action and phrases.

This earnest experiment must begin with ourselves, with each one of us, and it is vain merely to alter the outward conditions without deep, inward change. For what the individual is, society is; what his relationship is with another is the social structure of society. We cannot create a peaceful, intelligent society if the individual is intolerant, brutal, and competitive. If the individual lacks kindliness, affection, thoughtfulness, in his relationship with another, he must inevitably produce conflict, antagonism, and confusion. Society is the extension of the individual; society is the projection of ourselves. Until we grasp this and understand ourselves profoundly and alter ourselves radically, the mere change of the outer will not create peace in the world, nor bring to it that tranquillity that is necessary for happy social relationship.

So let us not think of only altering the environment; this will and must take place if our whole attention is directed to the transformation of the individual, of ourselves, and our relationship with another. How can we have brotherhood in the world if we are intolerant, if we hate, if we are greedy? Surely this is obvious, isn't it? If each of us is driven by a consuming ambition, striving for success, seeking happiness in things, surely we must create a society that is chaotic, ruthless, and destructive. If all of us here understand and agree deeply on this point—that the world is ourselves and what we are the world is—then we can proceed to think how to bring about the necessary change in ourselves. So long as we do not agree on this fundamental thing, but merely look to the environment for our peace and happiness, it assumes that immense importance which it has not, for we have created the environment, and without radical change in ourselves, it

becomes an intolerable prison. We cling to the environment, hoping to find security and self-identified continuity in it, and thus resist all change of thought and values. But life is in continual flux, and so there is constant conflict between desire, which must ever become static, and that reality which has no abode.

Man is the measure of all things, and if his vision is perverted, then what he thinks and creates must inevitably lead to disaster and sorrow. Out of what he thinks and feels, the individual builds the society. I personally feel that the world is myself, that what I do creates either peace or sorrow in the world that is myself, and as long as I do not understand myself, I cannot bring peace to the world; so my immediate concern is myself—not selfishly, not merely to alter myself in order to gain greater happiness, greater sensations, greater successes—for, as long as I do not understand myself, I must live in pain and sorrow and cannot discover an enduring peace and happiness.

To understand ourselves, we must first be interested in the discovery of ourselves, we must become alert about our own process of thought and feeling. With what are our thoughts and feelings mostly concerned? They are concerned with things, with people, and with ideas. These are the fundamental things in which we are interested—things, people, ideas.

Now why is it that things have assumed such an immense importance in our lives? Why is it that things—property, houses, clothes, and so on—take such a dominant place in our lives? Is it because we merely need them, or is it that we depend upon them for our psychological happiness? We all need clothes, food, and shelter. This is obvious. But why is it that they have assumed such tremendous importance, significance? Things assume such disproportionate value and significance because we psychologically depend on them for our well-being. They feed our vanity; they give us social prestige; they give us the means for procuring power. We use them in order to achieve purposes other than what they in themselves signify. We need food, clothes, shelter, which is natural and not perverting, but when we depend upon things for our gratification, when things become psychological necessities, they assume an altogether disproportionate value and importance—and hence the struggle and conflict to possess and the various means to hold those things upon which we depend.

Ask yourself this question: Am I dependent on things for my psychological happiness, satisfaction? If you earnestly seek to answer this apparently simple question, you will discover the complex process of your thought and feeling. If things are a physical necessity, then you put an intelligent limitation on them, then they do not assume that overwhelming importance which they have when they become a psychological necessity. In this way you begin to understand the nature of sensation and gratification; for the mind that would understand truth must be free of such bondages. To free the mind from sensation and satisfaction, you must begin with those sensations with which you are familiar, and there lay the right foundation for understanding. Sensation has its place, and by comprehending it, it does not assume the stupid distortion which it has now.

Many think that if the things of the world were well-organized so that all had enough of them, then it would be a happy and peaceful world, but I am afraid this will not be so if individually we have not understood their true significance. We depend on things because inwardly we are poor and we cover up that poverty of being with things, and these outward accumulations, these superficial possessions, become so vitally important that for them we are willing to lie, cheat, battle, and destroy each other. For things are a means to

power, to self-glory. Without understanding the nature of this inward poverty of being, mere change of organization for fair distribution of things, however necessary, will create other ways and means of gaining power and self-glory.

Most of us are concerned with things, and to understand our right relationship to them requires intelligence. It is not asceticism nor acquisitiveness, it is not renunciation nor accumulation, but a free, intelligent awareness of needs without the clawing dependence upon things. When you understand this there is not the sorrow of giving up nor the pain of competitive struggle. Is one capable of critically examining and understanding the difference between one's needs and the psychological dependence on things? You are not going to answer this question within this hour. You will answer it only if you are persistently earnest, if your purpose is unwavering and clear.

Surely we can begin to discover what is our relationship to things. It is based on greed, is it not? But when does need become greed? Is it not greed when thought, perceiving its own emptiness, its own worthlessness, proceeds to invest things with an importance greater than their own intrinsic worth and thereby create a dependence on them? This dependence may produce a sort of social cohesion, but in it there is always conflict, pain, disintegration. We must make our thought process clear, and we can do this if in our daily life we become aware of this greed, with its appalling results. This awareness of need and greed will help to lay the right foundation to our thinking. Greed in one form or another is ever the cause of antagonism, ruthless national hatred, and subtle brutalities. If we do not understand and grapple with greed, how can we understand, then, reality which transcends all these forms of struggle and sorrow? We must begin with ourselves, with our relationship to things and to people. I took things first because most of us are concerned with them. To us they are of tremendous importance. Wars are about things and our social and moral values are based on them. Without understanding the complex process of greed, we shall not understand reality.

Question: We are in imminent danger of being involved in the war. Why not give us some concrete suggestions of how to fight against it?

KRISHNAMURTI: There is really only one war, the war within ourselves, which produces external wars. I am only concerned with the war that is within ourselves. If we can understand and transcend intelligently that war within us, then perhaps there will be a peace in the world. I say perhaps, because there can be peace in the world only when each one of us is integrally peaceful. One can have this integrated peace within oneself if one is earnest and intelligently aware. The conflict that creates this hate is within yourself, and that is your first problem. If you are in the process of solving it, you will know what that tranquillity is, but merely to have suggestions or instructions given by another—what you should do under this or that circumstance—does not bring about peace. Great intelligence and deep understanding, not mere assertions, not blind acceptance of any theory, but continual awareness, strenuous questioning with delicacy and care, will create within us abiding peace. So our first task is with ourselves, for the world is ourselves in extension. We try to alter the circumference without fundamentally altering the center; we are concerned with the periphery without understanding the core. When there is peace at the center, then there is a possibility of it in the world.

Question: Would you please explain more fully in what sense you use the word sensation.

KRISHNAMURTI: The process of living is partly sensation; seeing, tasting, touching, thinking, and so on. If we seek pleasure through sensation or use sensation for increasing gratification, then thought becomes a slave of desire. There is a sort of psychological satisfaction in possessing and in being possessed. When the sensation of possession is satisfied, then thought seeks other types of sensation and pleasure, so desire is continually changing its object of gratification until reality is assumed to be a form of pleasure which is hoped to be permanent. The constant desire for greater and greater sensation must inevitably lead to pain and sorrow; one does not often realize this, and one craves for an enduring satisfaction, a final security in an idea, person, or things. This craving for a finality is the result of a series of satisfactions and disappointments, but the desire for permanency is still a form of sensation and gratification. If each one of us can understand the process of sensation and pleasure with regard, let us say, to things, then we shall begin to be aware when needs become the means of greater satisfaction, and the pursuit of this greater satisfaction, we shall perceive, is greed. This intelligent perception or awareness places a natural limit to sensation, without the conflict of control. So without deeply and fully understanding the process of sensation and outgoing desires, if we try to seek reality, peace, happiness, then what we may find, though we may call it the eternal and so on, will only be the result of pleasure and craving and therefore not real.

Question: What is the wisest step to take to understand oneself most unselfishly?

KRISHNAMURTI: Do you think there are two ways of understanding oneself, selfishly and unselfishly? You just understand yourself, not selfishly or unselfishly. If you try to understand yourself selfishly, you don't understand yourself at all because your being is of the self. If you say to yourself, I must unselfishly understand myself, you are presupposing a condition; you are establishing a concept which may be utterly false. So, to understand yourself, you must see yourself as you are, not biased by the selfish or the unselfish thought. To understand yourself you must create a mirror that reflects accurately what you are. We do not like to create for ourselves such a faculty that reflects purely, without bias, for we are concerned with judgment and alteration. Alteration depends on the background in which we have been brought up. If we are religious persons we will change ourselves according to our religious concepts and dogmas. If we think in social terms we will alter ourselves according to social morality. But to understand ourselves clearly and fully, we must perceive ourselves as we are, without prejudice, without condemnation. To perceive so clearly, without bias, requires constant alertness, a peculiar, alert passivity that needs patience and care. But this is difficult, as most of us are carried away by our sensations and desires; we want to keep, store up, that which is pleasant in us and reject that which is unpleasant. The desire to hold on and the desire to deny is not conducive to the understanding of yourself, but when you see yourself clearly, without any distortion, then you begin to find out why distortion has taken place. Then you begin to discover the cause, and that, again, requires keen alertness, serious purpose. In the process of understanding yourself, mind must not be burdened with craving, however subtle, for a result. If you are seeking a result, then you are not concerned with the process of understanding yourself; you are after gain, achievement, success, which has its own sorrow and reward. To understand yourself, you must have a mind-heart that is clear, without fear, without the entanglements of hope.

Question: How can one alter oneself without creating resistance?

KRISHNAMURTI: In the very idea of altering oneself, there is implied a preconceived pattern which prevents critical understanding. If you have a preconception of what you want to be, of what you should be, then surely your awareness of what you are is not critical, as you are then only concerned with conforming or with denying. We want to be this or that, and hence we are incapable of real critical examination of what we are, and therefore when we alter in relationship with what we want to be, we are bound to create resistances and so fundamental change does not take place at all.

Instead of being concerned with the change that must take place in ourselves, let us see if we have preconceived ideas of what we should be. As we have them, our attentions should be turned to the inquiry of how and why they have come into being. If we seriously inquire, we shall find that fear creates various patterns, preconceived ideas of ourselves and what we should be. Without these preconceptions, what are you? And so, having concepts and images of what you should be, you are striving after them, which only distorts your critical comprehension of yourself, thus building up resistances. But if you are capable of looking at yourself as you are, then there is a possibility of radical change which is not brought about through comparison. All comparative change is a change only in resistance.

Question: What about a school for children? This is a present need.

KRISHNAMURTI: This is not only a present need but a need of all times. It becomes important and immediate when we have our own children and circumstances are critical. Circumstances are ever critical to the thoughtful. If the parents, the guardians, are themselves in confusion, how can they establish schools in which children shall be brought up without confusion, without hate and ignorance? Surely this again is the same old problem, is it not, that you must begin with yourself, and because of your interest, you create or help to create schools in which there may grow up a generation which is not bound by fear and hate.

May 26, 1940

Second Talk in The Oak Grove

To those who have come here today for the first time I shall briefly explain what we talked about last Sunday. Those of you who are earnestly following these talks should not become impatient, for we are trying to paint in words as complete a picture of life as possible. We must understand the whole picture, the complete attitude towards life, and not merely a part of it.

I was saying last week that there cannot be peace or happiness in the world unless we as individuals cultivate that wisdom which brings forth tranquillity. There are many who think that without considering their own inward nature, their own clarity of purpose, their own creative understanding, by somewhat altering the outer conditions they can bring about peace in the world. That is, they hope to have brotherhood in the world though inwardly they are racked with hatred, envy, ambition, and so on. That this peace cannot be unless the individual, who is the

world, brings about a radical change within himself is pretty obvious to those who think deeply.

We see chaos about us, and extraordinary brutality after centuries of preaching of kindliness, brotherhood, love; we are easily caught up in this whirlpool of hatred and antagonism, and we think that by altering the outward symptoms we shall have human unity. Peace is not a thing to be brought from the outside, it can only come from within; this requires great earnestness and concentration, not on some single purpose, but on the understanding of the complex problem of living.

I took greed as one of the principal causes of conflict in ourselves and so in the world—greed, with its fear, with its craving for power and domination, social as well as intellectual and emotional. We tried to differentiate between need and greed. We need food, clothes, and shelter, but that need becomes greed, a driving psychological force in our lives when we, through craving for power, social prestige, and so on, give to things disproportionate value. Until we dissolve this fundamental cause of conflict or clash in our consciousness, mere search for peace is vain. Though through legislation we may have superficial order, the craving for power, success, and so on will constantly disturb the cement that holds society together and destroy this social order. To bring about peace within ourselves and so within society, this central clash in consciousness caused by craving must be understood. To understand there must be action.

There are those who see that the conflict in the world is caused by greed, by individual assertion for power and domination, through property, and so they propose that individuals shall not hold the means of acquiring power; they propose to bring this about through revolution, through state control of property—state being those few individuals whose hands hold the reins of power. You cannot destroy greed through legislation. You may be able to destroy one form of greed through compulsion but it will take inevitably another form which will again create social chaos.

Then there are those who think greed or craving can be destroyed through intellectual or emotional ideals, through religious dogmas and creeds; this again cannot be, for it is not to be overcome through imitation, service, or love. Self-forgetfulness is not a lasting remedy for the conflict of greed. Religions have offered compensation for greed, but reality is not a compensation. The pursuit of compensation is to remove the cause of conflict which is greed, craving, to another level, to another plane, but the clash and sorrow are still there.

Individuals are caught up in the desire to create social order or friendly human relationship between people through legislation, and to find reality which religions promise as a compensation for the giving up of greed. But, as I pointed out, greed is not to be destroyed through legislation or through compensation. To grapple anew with the problem of greed, we must be fully aware of the fallacy of mere social legislation against it and of the religious compensatory attitude that we have developed. If you are no longer seeking religious compensation for greed, or if you are not caught up in the false hope of legislation against it, then you will begin to understand a different process of dissolving this craving wholly, but this requires strenuous earnestness without emotionalism, without the deceits of the cunning intellect.

Every human being in the world needs food, clothes, and shelter, but why is it that this need has become such a complex, painful problem? Is it not because we use things for psychological purposes rather than for mere needs? Greed is the demand for gratification, pleasure, and we use needs as a means to achieve it and thereby give them far greater importance and worth than they have. So long as one uses things because one needs them, without being psychologically involved in them, there can be an intelligent limitation to needs, not based on mere gratification.

The psychological dependence on things manifests itself as social misery and conflict. Being poor inwardly, psychologically, spiritually, one thinks of enriching oneself through possessions, with ever-increasing complex demands and problems. Without fundamentally solving the psychological poverty of being, mere social legislation or asceticism cannot solve the problem of greed, craving. How is this to be overcome fundamentally, not merely in its outward manifestation, on the periphery? How is thought to be liberated from craving? We perceive the cause of greed—desire for satisfaction, gratification—but how is it to be dissolved? Through the exertion of will? Then what type of will? Will to overcome, the will to refrain, the will to renounce? The problem is, is it not, being greedy, avaricious, worldly, how to disentangle thought from greed?

For thought is now the product of greed, and therefore transitory, and so cannot understand the eternal. That which can understand the immortal must also be immortal. The permanent can be understood only through the transitory. That is, thought born of greed is transient, and whatever it creates must surely also be transient, and so long as the mind is held within the transient, within the circle of greed, it cannot transcend nor overcome itself. In its effort to overcome, it creates further resistances and gets more and more entangled in them.

How is greed to be dissolved without creating further conflict if the product of conflict is ever within the realm of desire, which is transitory? You may be able to overcome greed through the mere exertion of the will of denial, but that does not lead to understanding, to love, for such a will is the product of conflict and therefore cannot free itself from greed. We recognize that we are greedy. There is satisfaction in possession. It fills one's being, expands it. Now why do you need to struggle against it? If you are satisfied with this expansion, then you have no conscious problem. Can satisfaction ever be complete, is it not ever in a state of constant flux, craving one gratification after another?

Thus thought becomes entangled in its own net of ignorance and sorrow. We see we are caught up in greed and also we perceive, at least intellectually, the effect of greed; how then is thought to extricate itself from its own self-created cravings? Only through constant alertness, through the understanding of the process of greed itself. Understanding is not brought about through the mere exertion of a one-sided will but through that experimental approach which has that peculiar quality of wholeness. This experimental approach lies in the actions of our daily life; in becoming keenly aware of the process of craving and gratification there comes into being that integral approach to life, that concentration which is not the result of choice but which is completeness. If you are alert, you will observe keenly the process of craving; you will see that in this observation there is a desire for choice, a desire to rationalize, but this desire is still part of craving. You have to be sharply aware of the subtlety of craving, and through experiment there comes into being the wholeness of understanding which alone radically frees thought from craving. If you are so aware, there is a different type of will or understanding which is not the will of conflict or of renunciation, but of wholeness, of completeness that is holy. This understanding is the approach to reality which is not the product of the will to

achieve, the will of craving and conflict. Peace is of this wholeness, of this understanding.

Question: Since it is as true that the individual is a product of society as that society is a product of the individual who composes it; and since the change in social organization affects large numbers of individuals, is it not as important to stress the need for changing society as it is to emphasize the need for changing individuals; and since the major causes of catastrophe in the world arise from malfunctioning social organization, is there not danger in over-emphasizing the need for the individuals to change themselves, even though the change is ultimately necessary?

KRISHNAMURTI: What is society? Is it not the relationship of one individual with another? If individuals in themselves are ignorant, cruel, ambitious, and so on, their society will reflect all that they are in themselves. The questioner seems to suggest that the conflicting relationship of individuals, which is society, with its many organizations, should be changed. We all see the necessity, the importance, of social change. Wars, starvation, ruthless pursuit of power, and so on—with these we are all familiar, and some earnestly desire to change these conditions. How are you going to change them? By destroying the many or the few who create the disharmony in the world? Who are the many or the few? You and I, aren't we? Each one is involved in it because we are greedy, we are possessive, we crave for power. We want to bring order within society, but how are we to do it? Do you seriously think there are only a few who are responsible for this social disorganization, these wars and hatreds? How are you going to get rid of them? If you destroy them, you use the very means they have employed and so make of yourself also an instrument of hatred and brutality. Hate cannot be destroyed by hate, however much you may like to hide your hate under pleasant sounding words. Methods determine the ends. You cannot kill in order to have peace and order; to have peace you must create peace within yourself and thereby in your relationship with others, which is society.

You say that more emphasis should be laid on changing the social organization. Superficial reforms can, perhaps, be made, but surely radical change or lasting peace can be brought about only when the individual himself changes. You may say that this will take a long time. Why are you concerned about time? In your eagerness you want immediate results, you are concerned with results and not with the ways and means; thus in your haste you become a plaything of empty promises. Do you think that the present human nature which has been the product of centuries of maltreatment, ignorance, fear can be altered overnight? A few individuals may be able to change themselves overnight, but not a crystallized society. This does not mean a postponing, but the man who thinks clearly, directly, is not concerned with time.

Social organization may be an independent mechanism, but it has to be run by us. We have created it and we are responsible for it, and we can be independent of it only when we, as individuals, do not contribute to the general hate, greed, ambition, and so on. In our desire to change the world, we always meet with opposition—groups are formed for and against, which only further engender antagonism, suspicion, and competition in conversion. Agreement is almost impossible except when there is common hate or fear; all actions born of fear and hate must further increase fear and hate. Lasting order and peace can be brought about only when the individual voluntarily and intelligently consents to think without hate, greed,

ambition, and so on. Only in this way can there be creative peace within you and therefore in your relationship with another, which is called society.

This requires strenuous and directed attention without emotionalism, but as most of us are lazy, we hope that through some miraculous happenings, social organization will be changed. Thus we yield to sentiment and not to clear thought. We consider self-assertion, aggressiveness as manly, for we have made of religion a thing of sentiment; we have denied critical, experimental thought in the most serious thing that matters, religion and reality, and then naturally we become brutal, destructive with regard to the things of this world.

Question: How is emotion to be controlled?

KRISHNAMURTI: Let us understand this problem of control. What do we mean by control? What is involved in control? We see in our thinking process a dual force at work, the desire to hold, to grasp, and also the desire not to grasp, not to hold. Isn't that so? There is in thought that which is and also that which it wants to be—the pleasant, called the good, and the unpleasant, the evil. So there is continual conflict between these dual processes, the one trying to overcome the other, through discipline, assertion, denial, and so on. So in the idea of control there is always duality. Thought, having divided itself into two processes—that which is pleasurable and that which is not pleasurable—creates conflict in itself, and it tries to overcome this conflict through various means, ideals, denials, concentration, and so on. So the central point is not how to control but why do we create and cling to this dual process? What makes one angry first and later discover the pain of anger which induces one to learn to control oneself? What makes one brutal and then try to cultivate compassion? In becoming aware of the process of duality, we shall awaken that understanding, wholeness, completeness, which will eliminate the conflict of resistance. What makes our life, thought, so disjointed, so uncoordinated? Why have we in our thought process created this duality, not that there is not duality?

At the precise moment of anger there is no reaction of its opposite, we are merely angry. Then later on come all our reactions to it depending on our previous conditioning, and according to this, we control ourselves, training ourselves not to be angry, and by exerting will, we throw up resistances against anger, which is not the dissolution of anger; we cover it up and thus duality still exists. Now why are we angry? For many reasons. It may be that our social or financial security is threatened, or it may be due to some physiological reason. Now without understanding fully the physiological and psychological reasons for anger, and thereby intelligently and wholly becoming aware of them, we are only concerned deeply with the idea of getting rid of anger. Merely to get rid of anger is comparatively easy, but this does not completely dissolve its causes; but if you are fully aware of the causes, physiological as well as psychological, aware without the desire to be free from anger, then in this fullness of understanding not only the effect, anger, but also the causes fade away, giving place to a quality that only experience can reveal. All overcoming is a form of ignorance and violence; only understanding can free thought from bondage.

Question: Will you please explain more fully "The world is the extension of the individual, you are the world."

KRISHNAMURTI: Through experimental approach one discovers that man is the measure of all things; or, accepting authority, there is another measure beyond man, God or whatever you choose to call it. The world of the past is the world of today, of the 'I' and the future 'I' of tomorrow. The past is the world of our ancestors, the previous generations, with their ignorance, fears, and so on which limit the present, the 'I' of today and gives birth to the 'I' of tomorrow, the future. Each one of us is this accumulated past, with which is incorporated the present with its reactions and experiences. Individuals are the result of varied forms of influence and limitation, and the relationship of one individual with another creates the world—the world of values. The world is the social, moral, spiritual structure based on values created by us, isn't it? The social world, as well as the so-called spiritual world, is created by us individuals through our fears, hopes, cravings, and so on. We see the world of hate taking its harvest at the present. This world of hate has been created by our fathers and their forefathers and by us. Thus ignorance stretches indefinitely into the past. It has not come into being by itself. It is the outcome of human ignorance, a historical process, isn't it? We as individuals have co-operated with our ancestors, who, with their forefathers, set going this process of hate, fear, greed, and so on. Now, as individuals, we partake of this world of hate so long as we, individually, indulge in it.

The world, then, is an extension of yourself. If you as an individual desire to destroy hate, then you as an individual must cease hating. To destroy hate, you must dissociate yourself from hate in all its gross and subtle forms, and so long as you are caught up in it, you are part of that world of ignorance and fear. Then the world is an extension of yourself—yourself duplicated and multiplied. The world does not exist apart from the individual. It may exist as an idea, as a state, as a social organization, but to carry out that idea, to make that social or religious organization function, there must be the individual. His ignorance, his greed, his fear maintain the structure of ignorance, greed, and hate. If the individual changes, can he affect the world—the world of hate, greed, and so on? First make sure, doubly sure, that you, the individual, do not hate. Those who hate have no time for thought—they are consumed with their own intense excitement and with its results. They won't listen to calm, deliberate thought; they are carried away by their own fear; and you cannot help these people, can you, unless you follow their method, which is to force them to listen, but such force is of no avail. Ignorance has its own sorrow. After all, you are listening to me because you are not immediately threatened, but if you were, probably you would not be; you would not be thoughtful. The world is an extension of yourself as long as you are thoughtless, caught up in ignorance, hate, greed; but when you are earnest, thoughtful, and aware, there is not only a dissociation from those ugly causes which create pain and sorrow, but also in that understanding there is a completeness, a wholeness.

June 2, 1940

Third Talk in The Oak Grove

I was trying to explain last week the difference between greed and need. If we don't understand the difference between them, there will be a constant conflict of choice. There is a different approach to the problem of craving and need instead of the usual control, denial, and choice; it is to understand the process of greed, to become aware of craving. Psychologically, inwardly, being impoverished, we want to enrich ourselves through accumulations and possessions, and thereby give to things a disproportionate

value. In being aware, there is a deep understanding of the causes of this psychological poverty, of this lack of creative enrichment, and so there is a freedom from greed and its conflicts. In this process of awareness, in this inward search to understand the dependence upon things for one's satisfactions, pleasures, you will perceive, if you will experiment, that there is a different kind of will—not the will of conflicting resistances, but the will of understanding which is whole, complete. To experiment one must become aware of craving, greed, not theoretically, but in our daily life of relationship and action. It is only when we are really inwardly free from greed, not merely in our outward relationship and action, that there can be peace and disinterested action.

We have been trying to understand our craving for things, and now let us go into the question of our relationship with people, and through understanding this complex problem, the richness of life is revealed.

Is not all existence a question of relationship? To be is to be related. In our relationship there is conflict, not only between individuals, but also between the individual and society. Society is, after all, the relationship of the individual with the many; it is the extension, the projection, of the individual. If the individual does not understand his relationship with regard to things or with people he is immediately concerned with, his actions will produce conflict—personal as well as social. There is conflict in relationship and also there is the desire to isolate oneself, to withdraw from a relationship that causes pain. This isolation takes the form of either accepting new and pleasant relationships instead of the old, or withdrawing oneself into the world of ideas. If life is a series of events that will ultimately produce an isolation of the individual, then relationship is a means towards that end. But one cannot withdraw, for all existence is a form of relationship. So until one understands and is free from the causes of conflict within oneself, wherever one is, whatever the circumstances are, there must always be conflict. The idea of progressive isolation which man in his conflict longs for, calling it reality, unity, love, and so on, is an escape from reality which is to be understood only in relationship. There is in relationship conflict, and at the same time thought is seeking to withdraw from that conflict. One finds many ways of escape, but the cause of conflict is still there.

Why is there conflict between people? What is the reason of this conflict even among those who say they love each other? Now, is not all relationship a process of self-revelation? That is, in this process of relationship, you are being revealed to yourself, you are discovering yourself—all the conditions of your being, the ugly and the pleasant. If you are aware, relationship acts as a mirror, reflecting more and more the various states of your thoughts and feelings. If we deeply understand that relationship is a process of self-revelation, then it has a different significance. But we don't accept relationship to be a revealing process, for we are not willing to be shown what we are, and hence there is constant conflict. In relationship we are seeking gratification, pleasure, comfort, and if there is any deep opposition to it, we try to change our relationship. So relationship, instead of being a progressive action of constant awareness, tends to become a process of self-isolation. The way of desire leads to self-isolation and limitation.

When we are seeking merely gratification in relationship, critical awareness becomes impossible, yet it is only in this alert awareness any adjustment or understanding is possible. Responsibility in relationship, then, is not based on satisfaction but on understanding and love. Not finding satisfaction in human relationship, we often try to establish

it in the realm of theories, beliefs, concepts. Love, then, becomes merely an emotion, a sensation, an ideal conception, and not a reality to be understood in human relationship. Because in human relationship there is friction, pain, we try to idealize love and call it cosmic, universal, which is but an escape from reality. To love wholly, without fear, without possessiveness, demands an intense awareness and understanding which can only be realized in human relationship when thought is freed from craving and possessiveness. Then only can there be the love of the whole.

If we understand the cause of conflict and sorrow in our relationship without fear, there comes into being a quality of completeness which is not mere expansiveness nor the aggregation of many virtues. We hope to love man through the love of God, but if we do not know how to love man, how can we love reality? To love man is to love reality. We find that to love another is so painful, so many complex problems are involved in it, that we think it is easier and more satisfying to love an ideal, which is an intellectual emotionalism, not love.

We depend on sensation for the continuance of so-called love, and when that gratification is withheld, we try to find it in another. So what most often we are seeking is satisfaction of desire in our human relationship. Without understanding craving, there cannot be completeness of love. This again requires constant and intense awareness. To understand this completeness, this wholeness, we must begin to be aware of desire as greed and possessiveness. Then we shall understand the complex nature of desire and thus there will not only be a freedom from greed but also completeness that transcends intellect and its resistances. If we are able to do this with regard to things, then perhaps we shall be able to grasp a much more complex form of craving, which exists in human relationship. We must begin not from the heights of aspiration, hope, and vision, but with things and people with whom we are in daily contact. If we are incapable of deep understanding of things and of people, we shall not understand reality, for reality lies in the understanding of the environment, things, and people. This environment is the product of our relationship to things and people; if the result is based on craving and its gratification, as it is now, to escape from it and seek reality is to create other forms of gratification and illusion. Reality is not the product of craving; that which is created through craving is transient; that which is eternal can be understood only through the lasting.

Question: Is it not sometimes very difficult to differentiate between natural human needs and the psychological desires for satisfaction?

KRISHNAMURTI: It is very difficult to differentiate. To do this, there must be clarity of perception. To be aware of the process of all outgoing desires, and in fully understanding them, natural human needs will intelligently be regulated without undue emphasis. But you see, individually we are not interested in understanding the process of desire. We are not eager enough to find out if we can differentiate between human needs and psychological desires. One can discover this through critical awareness, through patient probing, but another's understanding of this problem is of little value to you; you will have to understand it for yourself. If you say that you will limit yourself to the minimum of things, you are not understanding the complex problem of desire; you are then merely interested in achieving certain results, which is to seek gratification on another level; but this does not solve the problem which desire creates.

What we are trying to do here is to understand the process of desire, not to put a boundary to craving. In understanding craving, there comes a natural limitation of things, not a predetermined limitation brought about by the exertion of will. It is craving that gives to things their disproportionate values. Those values are based on psychological demands. If one is psychologically poor, one seeks satisfaction in things; therefore, property, name, family become urgent and important, resulting in social chaos. As long as one has not solved this conflict of greed, mere limitation of things cannot bring about either social order or that tranquillity of freedom from craving. Through social legislation, greed cannot be destroyed; you may limit its expression in certain directions, but even those limitations are overcome if craving is still the motive for man's action. Compensations that are offered by religions for giving up worldly things are still forms of craving. To be free from craving, one must patiently, tactfully, without prejudice, understand its complex process.

Question: Last Sunday you said that if we could find out why we are angry instead of trying to control anger, we would free ourselves from it. I find I am angry when my comfort, my opinions, my security, and so forth, are threatened; and why am I angry when I hear of injustice that concerns someone I don't know?

KRISHNAMURTI: We have all, I am sure, tried to subdue anger, but somehow that does not seem to dissolve it. Is there a different approach to dissipate anger? As I said last Sunday, anger may spring from physical or psychological causes. One is angry, perhaps, because one is thwarted, one's defensive reactions are being broken down, one's security which has been carefully built up is being threatened, and so on. We are all familiar with anger. How is one to understand and dissolve anger? If you consider that your beliefs, concepts, opinions are of the greatest importance, then you are bound to react violently when questioned. Instead of clinging to beliefs, opinions, if you begin to question whether they are essential to one's comprehension of life, then through the understanding of its causes there is the cessation of anger. Thus one begins to dissolve one's own resistances which cause conflict and pain. This again requires earnestness. We are used to controlling ourselves for sociological or religious reasons or for convenience, but to uproot anger requires deep awareness and constancy of intention.

You say you are angry when you hear of injustice. Is it because you love humanity, because you are compassionate? Do compassion and anger dwell together? Can there be justice when there is anger, hatred? You are perhaps angry at the thought of general injustice, cruelty, but your anger does not alter injustice or cruelty; it can only do harm. To bring about order, you yourself have to be thoughtful, compassionate. Action born of hatred can only create further hatred. There can be no righteousness where there is anger. Righteousness and anger cannot dwell together. Anger under all circumstances is the lack of understanding and love. It is always cruel and ugly. What can you do if someone else acts unjustly, with hatred and prejudice? That act is not wiped away by your anger, by your hatred.

You are really not concerned with injustice—if you were you would never be angry. You are angry because there is an emotional satisfaction in hatred and anger—you feel masterful through hating and being angry. If in our human relationship there is compassion and forgiveness, generosity and kindliness, how can there also be brutality and hatred? If we have no love, how can there be order and peace? We desire to reform

another when we ourselves are in need of it most. It is not another that is cruel, unjust, but ourselves. To understand this we have to be aware constantly. The problem is ourselves and not another. And I tell you that when you look at anger in yourself and are beginning to be aware of its causes and expressions, then in that understanding there is compassion, forgiveness.

Question: In being completely dissociated from violence, is it possible that my action can be dissociated? For example, if I am attacked, I kill for self-preservation as a part of violence. If I refuse to kill and let myself be killed, am I not still a part of violence? Is dissociation a matter of attitude rather than action?

KRISHNAMURTI: Questions about violence in all its various forms will be understood if we can grasp the central cause of hatred, of the desire to hurt, of vengeance, of fear, and so on. If we can understand this, then we shall know spontaneously how to deal with those who hate us, who wish to do violence to us. Our whole attention should be directed not to what we should do with regard to violence aimed at us, but to understand the cause of our own fear, hate, arrogance, or partisanship. In understanding this in our daily life, the problems created by another cease to have much significance. You will solve the outward problem of violence by understanding the central problem of craving, envy, through constant critical awareness of your thought, of your relationship with another.

Question: To be fully aware, to be pliable, there must always be a great feeling of love. Not by effort can one feel love nor become fully aware, so what should one do?

KRISHNAMURTI: Now what is the effort involved in understanding, for example, our psychological cravings and natural needs? To understand deeply that all psychological dependence, whether on things or on people, creates not only social but personal conflict and sorrow, to understand the complex causes of conflict and the desire to be free from it, requires not the mere will to be free, but constant awareness in our daily life. If that awareness is the outcome of the desire to achieve a certain result, then the effort to be aware only produces further resistance and conflict. Awareness comes into being when there is the interest to understand, but interest cannot be created through mere will and control. If you give true value to things only in order not to have conflict, you are living in a state of illusion, for then you do not understand the process of craving which creates conflict and pain.

June 9, 1940

Fourth Talk in The Oak Grove

In the last three talks I tried to explain the experimental approach to the problem of greed, an approach that is neither denial nor control but an understanding of the process of greed, which alone can bring lasting freedom from it. So long as one depends on things for one's psychological satisfaction and enrichment, greed will continue, creating social and individual conflict and disorder. Understanding alone will free us from greed and craving which have created such havoc in the world.

We shall now consider the problem of relationship between individuals. If we understand the cause of friction between individuals and therefore with society, that understanding will help to bring about freedom from possessiveness. Relationship is now based on dependence, that is, one depends on another for one's psychological satisfaction, happiness, and well-being. Generally we do not realize this but if we do, we pretend that we are not dependent on another or try to disengage ourselves artificially from dependence. Here again let us approach this problem experimentally.

Now for most of us relationship with another is based on dependence, economic or psychological. This dependence creates fear, breeds in us possessiveness, results in friction, suspicion, frustration. Economic dependence on another can perhaps be eliminated through legislation and proper organization, but I am referring especially to that psychological dependence on another which is the outcome of craving for personal satisfaction, happiness, and so on. One feels, in this possessive relationship, enriched, creative, and active; one feels one's own little flame of being is increased by another and so in order not to lose this source of completeness, one fears the loss of the other, and so possessive fears come into being with all their resulting problems. Thus in this relationship of psychological dependence, there must always be conscious or unconscious fear, suspicion, which often lies hidden in pleasant-sounding words. The reaction of this fear leads one ever to search for security and enrichment through various channels, or to isolate oneself in ideas and ideals, or to seek substitutes for satisfaction.

Though one is dependent on another, there is yet the desire to be inviolate, to be whole. The complex problem in relationship is how to love without dependence, without friction and conflict; how to conquer the desire to isolate oneself, to withdraw from the cause of conflict. If we depend for our happiness on another, on society, or on environment, they become essential to us; we cling to them and any alteration of these we violently oppose because we depend upon them for our psychological security and comfort. Though, intellectually, we may perceive that life is a continual process of flux, mutation, necessitating constant change, yet emotionally or sentimentally we cling to the established and comforting values; hence there is a constant battle between change and the desire for permanency. Is it possible to put an end to this conflict?

Life cannot be without relationship, but we have made it so agonizing and hideous by basing it on personal and possessive love. Can one love and yet not possess? You will find the true answer not in escape, ideals, beliefs but through the understanding of the causes of dependence and possessiveness. If one can deeply understand this problem of relationship between oneself and another, then perhaps we shall understand and solve the problems of our relationship with society, for society is but the extension of ourselves. The environment which we call society is created by past generations; we accept it, as it helps us to maintain our greed, possessiveness, illusion. In this illusion there cannot be unity or peace. Mere economic unity brought about through compulsion and legislation cannot end war. As long as we do not understand individual relationship, we cannot have a peaceful society. Since our relationship is based on possessive love, we have to become aware, in ourselves, of its birth, its causes, its action. In becoming deeply aware of the process of possessiveness with its violence, fears, its reactions, there comes an understanding that is whole, complete. This understanding alone frees thought from dependence and possessiveness. It is within oneself that harmony in relationship can be found, not in another, nor in environment.

In relationship, the primary cause of friction is oneself, the self that is the center of unified craving. If we can but realize that it is not how another acts that is of primary importance, but how each one of us acts and reacts, and if that reaction and action can be fundamentally, deeply understood, then relationship will undergo a deep and radical

change. In this relationship with another, there is not only the physical problem but also that of thought and feeling on all levels, and one can be harmonious with another only when one is harmonious integrally in oneself. In relationship the important thing to bear in mind is not the other but oneself, which does not mean that one must isolate oneself but understand deeply in oneself the cause of conflict and sorrow. So long as we depend on another for our psychological well-being, intellectually or emotionally, that dependence must inevitably create fear from which arises sorrow.

To understand the complexity of relationship there must be thoughtful patience and earnestness. Relationship is a process of self-revelation in which one discovers the hidden causes of sorrow. This self-revelation is only possible in relationship.

I am laying emphasis on relationship because in comprehending deeply its complexity, we are creating understanding—an understanding that transcends reason and emotion. If we base our understanding merely on reason, then in it there is isolation, pride, and lack of love; and if we base our understanding merely on emotions, then in it there is no depth—there is only a sentimentality which soon evaporates, and no love. From this understanding only can there be completeness of action. This understanding is impersonal and cannot be destroyed. It is no longer at the behest of time. If we cannot bring forth understanding from the everyday problems of greed and of our relationship, then to seek such understanding and love in other realms of consciousness is to live in ignorance and illusion.

Without fully understanding the process of greed, merely to cultivate kindliness, generosity, is to perpetuate ignorance and cruelty; without integrally understanding relationship, merely to cultivate compassion, forgiveness, is to bring about self-isolation and to indulge in subtle forms of pride. In understanding craving fully, there is compassion, forgiveness. Cultivated virtues are not virtues. This understanding requires constant and alert awareness, a strenuousness that is pliable; mere control with its peculiar training has its dangers as it is one-sided, incomplete, and therefore shallow. Interest bring its own natural, spontaneous concentration in which there is the flowering of understanding. This interest is awakened by observing, questioning the actions and reactions of everyday existence.

To grasp the complex problem of life with its conflicts and sorrows, one must bring about integral understanding. This can be done only when we deeply comprehend the process of craving which is now the central force in our life.

Question: In speaking of self-revelation, do you mean revealing oneself to oneself or to others?

KRISHNAMURTI: One often does reveal oneself to others, but what is important—to see yourself as you are or to reveal yourself to another? I have been trying to explain that if we allow it, all relationship acts as a mirror in which to perceive clearly that which is crooked and that which is straight. It gives the necessary focus to see sharply, but as I explained, if we are blinded by prejudice, opinions, beliefs, we cannot, however poignant relationship is, see clearly, without bias. Then relationship is not a process of self-revelation.

Our primary consideration is: What prevents us from perceiving truly? We are not able to perceive because our opinions about ourselves, our fears, ideals, beliefs, hopes, traditions—all these act as veils. Without understanding the causes of these perversions, we try to alter or hold on to what is perceived and this creates further resistances and further sorrow. Our chief consideration should be not the alteration or the acceptance of what is perceived, but to become aware of the many causes that bring about this perversion. Some may say that they have not the time to be aware, they are so occupied, and so on, but it is not a question of time but rather of interest. Then in whatever they are occupied with, there is the beginning of awareness. To seek immediate results is to destroy the possibility of complete understanding.

Question: You have used several times the word training *in the past talks. As the idea of training with many of us is associated with control leading eventually to the possibility of rigidity and lifelessness, could you give a definition of this term? Is it to be understood in the sense of unflagging will, of alertness, adaptability, and constant pliability?*

KRISHNAMURTI: Do we control ourselves out of fear? Do we control in order not to be hurt, to gain certain results and rewards? Is control the outcome of the search for greater and more lasting satisfaction and power? If it is, then it must lead to rigidity and lifelessness. Mere self-control does ultimately result in the sterility of understanding and love. Those who have, merely by the exertion of will, brought about self-control will know of its dire results.

I am talking of understanding which transcends reason and emotion. In this understanding there is a natural and creative adaptability, an alert awareness and infinite pliability, but mere control does not create understanding. If we try to cultivate virtue, it is no longer virtue. Virtue is a byproduct of understanding and love. Those who are greedy may train themselves not to be greedy through the mere exertion of will, but thereby they have not deeply understood the process of greed and so are not free from greed.

They think by the aggregation of many virtues they will come to the whole. They seek to confine the whole vast expanse of life in virtues. To understand, there must be the clarity of purpose not established by another but which comes into being when one comprehends one's relationship to things and people. This experimental approach brings about that understanding which is not the result of mere control. If this inquiry is earnest and constant, then there will be a natural restraint without fear, without the will of expansive desires. This understanding is not partial but complete. Through constant awareness of the many obvious and subtle problems of greed, there comes a definite and delicate pliability which, as I said, is a by-product of understanding and love.

Question: How does one cultivate virtues?

KRISHNAMURTI: All cultivated virtues are no longer virtues. Understanding and love are of primary importance and virtues are of secondary importance. Duty, courage, charity, as virtues, are in the likeness of their own opposites, and therefore, without understanding and love, they may be misused and become a source of grave danger. Take for example duty as a virtue. This can be and is being brutally and tragically misused. Without understanding and love, virtues can become the instruments of barbarity and cruelty. Most of us have been conditioned by virtues, and as they are not of deep thought and understanding, those of us who are so limited are exploited by cunning and ambitious people. Without understanding the nature of greed, merely to cultivate its opposite does not free us from greed. What frees us from greed is to understand the process of craving, and in doing this we will find that virtues naturally come into being. What is of primary importance then is understanding, in whose wake follows compassion.

Question: What do you mean by self-reliance?

KRISHNAMURTI: Organized religions have not made us self-reliant, for they have taught us to look for our salvation through another—through saviors, Masters, deified personalities, through ceremonies, priests, and so on. Modern tendencies also encourage us to be psychologically non-self-reliant by insisting that collective action is of greater importance. Psychological regeneration cannot be brought about through the authority of tradition, group, or of another, however great; there cannot be self-reliance which alone can help us to understand reality if we retain mass psychology. But there is a grave danger of this self-reliance turning into individualistic action, each for himself. Because the present social structure has been the result of this individualistic, aggressive action, we have its reaction in collectivism, the worship of the state. True collective and cooperative action can come into being only when psychologically the individual is self-reliant. As long as the individual is greedy, possessive in his relationship and depends for his psychological enrichment on beliefs, dogmas, and so forth, cooperative action, urged through economic necessity, only makes him more cunning, more subtle in his individualistic appetites for power and achievement.

We think that self-expression is a form of creativeness; we have intense longing to express ourselves, and so self-expression has assumed a great importance. I am trying to explain some of the problems involved in self-reliance, and we must understand fully, if we can, the underlying significance in all this. When we rely psychologically on another, on a group, or on a leader for our understanding, for our hope, what takes place in us? Does it not create fear? Or being afraid, do we not depend on others for our well-being? So fear is engendered or continues in both cases. But where there is fear, conscious or unconscious, intelligent understanding of life become impossible. Fear can only breed fear and so ignorance continues. This fear cannot be understood and dissolved except through one's own strenuous awareness.

If you think that understanding, love, can be given to you by another, then authority and belief become most important. Then dogma takes the place of self-reliant understanding. Where there is dogma there must be narrowness of mind and heart. The clash of dogma, belief, creates intolerance, cruelty. Self-reliance, in the deep psychological sense, is denied when you are pursuing compensatory religious or worldly promises and rewards. It is only when you are completely self-reliant, wholly independent of any savior, Master, is there serenity, wisdom, reality. Likewise, when you merely rely for your social well-being on a particular group or organization, then you will become mere instruments in cunning and ambitious hands. This does not mean that social organizations should not exist, which would be absurd, but true cooperative social organizations of intelligent consent can exist only when there is deep, psychological self-reliance.

We are the result of the past, and without the critical comprehension of it, if we merely express it, then such self-expression or action can only continue ignorance and conflict. The ideas which we now have partly come from others who thought them and partly arise through present action and reaction. They are the result of craving, fear, possessiveness, and greed. As we are concerned with self-expression, we must ask ourselves what it is that is expressing itself. If I am a Hindu, I have certain beliefs, dogmas, social restrictions, a certain heritage, the result of my father's and my forefathers' craving, acquisitiveness, fear, and success, to which I have added my own conditioned experiences and knowledge. If I try to express myself as originally and fully as possible, what am I expressing? Surely, am I not repeating, perhaps with modification and variations, essentially the limited thoughts and feelings of the past which I consider to be myself?

The expression of the self seems so vitally important to most of us. We are trying to express ourselves according to space and time, and as we do not deeply understand what it is that is expressing itself, we are bound to create confusion, sorrow, antagonism, and competition. In other words, ignorance is expressing itself, creating further ignorance; and if thwarted in one of its expressions, we try to overcome that resistance through violence, anger, or other impetuous action. In its fullest scope and expression, the self, which is born of ignorance, must when it acts from itself create its own bondages and sorrow. Without understanding the full implication of self-expression, self-reliance becomes merely the means to greater and greater expression of narrow individualistic and ignorant action.

Until we begin to break down this vicious circle of ignorance which only creates further ignorance, self-reliance cannot bring about release from sorrow. Yet to understand this continuity of ignorance and sorrow, each one must become utterly self-reliant to be able to probe into craving, fear, tendencies, memories, and so on. Mere self-expression is not creativeness, and to be truly creative, one must understand the process of the self and so be free from it. Through earnest awareness as to what it is that is expressing itself, we begin to understand the limited causes of the past which control the present, and in this strenuous understanding there comes a freedom from the cause of ignorance. True self-reliance, not the self-reliance for the purpose of mere aggressive expression of the self, can come about only through understanding the process of craving, with its limiting values, fears, and hopes; then self-reliance has great significance, for through one's own strenuous awareness there is a wholeness, a completeness.

June 16, 1940

Fifth Talk in The Oak Grove

During the last four Sundays we have been trying to understand what we mean by greed and some of the problems involved in relationship. We divided craving into greed, possessive love, and dependence on beliefs, but in fact, there is no such division; we did it to understand craving more fully. There is only a complex unity of craving and its artificial division is for convenience only. We said that craving expresses itself in three ways: through worldliness, through possessive love, and through the desire for personal immortality. Perhaps some of you have thought it over and have seen the significance of what I have been saying and have become aware of how it expresses itself in relationship. Of course, there are many problems involved in it, such, for instance, as earning a living. To earn a livelihood in a humane and intelligent way seems almost impossible, as social organization is based on personal gain, but we cannot hope to bring about a complete change in the system until there is a complete change in our own consciousness. To bring about that necessary change, we, as individuals, have to abandon our interest in ourselves. For, as I tried to explain, the individual is the world; his activities, his thoughts, his affections, and conflicts produce the environment which is but his own reflection. As it seems almost impossible under existing conditions to earn a livelihood humanely and honestly, the primary thing is to understand the process of greed and thereby free thought from those

psychological cravings which distort our lives.

To transcend the conditions that limit thought and hold it in constant conflict, we must understand craving expressed in our relationship with another, with society. I explained in what manner this is to be done—not through mere control, not through mere discipline or denial, but through constant awareness of the process of craving. This demands strenuous application, patience, and constant alertness. In becoming actively aware of the process of craving, you will perceive that craving, as possessiveness of things and people, undergoes a fundamental change. Also, I tried to explain that the expression of greed has created a society in which great importance is placed on things, on property, on material and otherworldliness, which is partly the cause for separative conflicts, racial antagonisms, and wars.

Also, we saw how craving expresses itself in relationship as sensation, gratification, possessiveness. Possessiveness cannot be love, it is the result of fear. Fear and sorrow permeate our being through our unawareness of the process of craving. Craving for pleasure and gratification necessitates the possessing of the other—thus creating and continuing fear and sorrow. Where there is fear there cannot be understanding, compassion. Until we solve this individual problem of relationship, we cannot solve our social problem, for society is but the extension of the individual, his thoughts and activities.

So, craving expresses itself through worldliness and through possessive love. When thought is limited by greed, by that possessive desire which we call love, surely there must be sorrow and conflict; and in order to escape from this conflict and sorrow, we invent various beliefs and hopes which we imagine will endure and so be satisfying, unaware that they are still the creation of craving and therefore transient.

Our ideas, beliefs, hopes, are so deeply imbedded in us that they escape our critical observation. Yet, without the knowledge of their cause and origin, there cannot be true understanding. If our ideas and beliefs spring from ignorance and fear, then our life and action must be limited and ever in conflict and sorrow. But ignorance is difficult to eradicate.

What is the basis of our thought? What is the origin of the mind? Those of you who have experimented with greed will have become aware of its process and the various expressions of craving; also you will have become aware of the origin of possessive love. Now in the same way, perhaps we can discover for ourselves from what source the process of our daily thought begins. Mere control of the many expressions of thought will not reveal its true source.

What is the basis, the root, of our thought-process? It is important to discover this, is it not? If the root of a tree is diseased or decayed, what value is there in trimming its branches? Likewise, should we not first discern the origin of our thinking before concerning ourselves with its varied expressions and alterations? In understanding truly the source, through deep awareness, our human thought will become free of illusion and fear. Each one has to discover this source for himself, and with vital awareness transform radically the process of thinking.

Has not our thought its source in craving? Is not what we call the mind the result of craving? Through perception, contact, sensation, and reflection, thought divides itself into like and dislike, hate and affection, pain and pleasure, merit and demerit—the series of opposites, the process of conflict. It is this process which is the content of our consciousness, the unconscious as well as the conscious, and which we call the mind. Being caught up in this process and fearing uncertainty, cessation, death, each one craves after permanency and continuity. We seek to establish this continuity through property, name, family, race, and dubiously perceiving their insecurity, again we seek this continuity and permanency through beliefs and hopes, through the concepts of God and soul and immortality.

Having accumulated various experiences, many memories, and achievements, we identify ourselves with them, but there is ever within us the gnawing of uncertainty and the apprehension of death, for everything decays, passes away and is in a continual flux. So, some begin to justify to themselves their complete abandonment to the pleasures of this world and their ruthless self-expansion; others, believing in continuity, become watchful, anxious, and live their lives dreading a future punishment or hoping for a reward in the hereafter, perhaps in heaven or perhaps in another life on earth.

There are various forms of subtle craving for immortality, reward, and success. Thought is deeply and actively concerned with the idea of continuity of itself in different forms, gross and subtle. Is this not our main preoccupation in life, the continuity of the self in possessions, in relationship, in ideas? We crave for certainty, but craving ever creates ignorance and illusion and establishes instruments of faith and authorities who will reward and punish. The pursuit of self is death.

The basis of our thinking is craving, which creates the self, and thought expresses itself in worldliness, in possessive love, and in the belief of self-continuity. What happens to a mind that is occupied with itself and its expressions, consciously or unconsciously? It will limit itself and so give importance to itself. Thought, thus occupied, must engender confusion, conflict, sorrow. Being caught in its own net, it tries to escape into the future or into those activities that assure immediate forgetfulness—the so-called social service, worship of state or person, racial and social antagonism, and so on. Thus thought gets more and more entangled in the net of its own desires and escapes. As long as thought is preoccupied with its own personal importance and continuity, it is incapable of becoming aware of its own process.

How are we to become aware? Alertly and disinterestedly observe the working of the mind without immediate correction, without controlling, denying, or judging it. The present eagerness to judge, to correct, is not from understanding; it springs from craving, fear. There is a deep and fundamental transformation of the self when there is understanding of the process of craving. Understanding transcends mere reason or emotion. Mind-intellect is now the instrument of craving, with its rationalization and expansive outgoing desires; to rely solely on either for understanding and love is to continue in ignorance and suffering.

Question: What do you mean by experimenting?

KRISHNAMURTI: If consciously or unconsciously we are merely seeking results, we are not experimenting. Experimentation with one's own thought and feeling becomes impossible if we are merely adjusting ourselves to a pattern, ancient or modern. We may think we are experimenting, but if our thought is influenced and limited, say by a belief, then experimentation is not possible and most of us are blind to our own limitations. True experimenting consists in understanding through our own alert watchfulness, awareness, the causes that condition thought. Why is thought conditioned? Being uncertain, fearful, it clings to certainties, definite results, and achievements, either those of someone whom it considers great or of its own assured memories. That is, thought moves from the known to the known, from

one certainty to another, from one assurance to another, from one substitute to another. Reality is not the known. What is conceived cannot be the real when the mind is the instrument of craving. Craving always breeds ignorance and sorrow follows. True experimenting consists not in trying to discover the unknown but rather in understanding the forces, the causes, that make thought cling to the known. In the understanding of this process, ever deeply, patiently, there comes a new element which has transcended mere reason and emotion.

Question: What should my attitude be towards violence?

KRISHNAMURTI: Does violence cease through violence, hate through hate? If you hate me and I hate you in return, if you act violently towards me and I act likewise towards you, what is the result—more violence, more hatred, more bitterness, is it not? Is there any other consequence than this? Hate begets hate, ill will begets ill will. Very often in our relationship, individual or social, this spirit of retaliation breeds only more violence and more antagonism.

The spirit of vengeance is rampant in the world. Can you have any other attitude towards violence? We feel powerful in being violent. To use a commercial phrase—there are larger and quicker dividends in hate. The individual has created the existing social structure because of hatred within him, because of his desire to retaliate and to act violently. The world about us is in this feverish condition of hate and violence because of its cunning and purposeful strength; unless we, ourselves, are free of hate, we are easily carried away by the brutal current. If you are free of it, then the question of what attitude one should have towards the many expressions of hate does not arise. If you were deeply aware of hate itself and not merely of its cunning expressions, you would see that hate only begets hate. If you have hatred within you, you will respond to the hate of another, and since the world is you, you are bound to react to its fears, ignorance, and greed. Surely, you are bound to hate, to act vengefully, if your thought is confined to the self. Greed and possessive love must breed ill will, and if thought does not free itself from them, there must be the constant action of hate and violence. As I pointed out, our beliefs and hopes are the result of craving, and when doubt is cast on them, resentment and anger arise. In understanding the cause of hate, there comes into being forgiveness, kindliness. Love and understanding come through being constantly aware.

Question: Is it not natural to love the Masters, knowing instinctively without analyzing it that their response to us vivifies our love because we are one? This is not an effort to expand, for love is life itself.

KRISHNAMURTI: There are two types of gurus, Masters, or teachers—those with whom the pupil is directly in contact on this plane of existence, and those with whom the pupil is supposed to be in contact indirectly. The teacher with whom the pupil is in contact directly, physically, observes the pupil while helping and guiding him. This is exacting and difficult enough for the pupil. Now the "Masters" are not in direct, physical contact with the pupil except apparently with those who claim that they are intermediaries. In this relationship, which has its own rewards and anxieties, the mind can deceive itself limitlessly.

Now, the questioner wants to know if our love for a Master does not vivify our love? Why do you seek a Master to love when you don't know how to love human beings? Why do you claim unity with Masters and not with human beings? To love an ideal, a

Master, a god, a state is easier, is it not? For they can be created in our image, according to our hopes, fears, illusions. It is more convenient, though perhaps exacting in a different way, to have an ideal, a far-off image to love, for between that and ourselves there can be no unpleasant, personal reaction, which causes such sorrow in human relationship. Such love is not love but an intellectual creation called love. Not being directly in contact with a Master, one must depend on either an intermediary or on one's own so-called intuition. Dependence on an intermediary destroys understanding and love and further conditions the mind; and so-called intuition has its grave dangers for it may be only a self-deceiving wish.

Now, why do you want to depend on a mediator or on an intuition? To learn not to be greedy, to have no ill will, to be compassionate? Why do you want to look at a distant ideal when understanding and love can be awakened only through human relationship? When we love another, our passions, our possessive love, and jealousies are aroused; we find sorrow and conflict in this relationship, and because we cannot resolve this ache here, we try to run away from it.

Because we do not know how to love human beings, we love Masters, ideals, gods. But you might say that to love a Master is also to love humanity—to love the highest is to love also the lowly. But this generally does not happen. Is this not odd, complicated, and artificial? If we cannot love another without possessiveness, without constant conflict and pain, with which we are all so familiar, if we don't understand this, how can we hope to understand and love something else, especially when in this something there is a great possibility of self-deception? Where is love to begin—with gods and Masters and ideals or with human beings? How can there be love when we take pride in our individual prejudices, racial antagonisms, national hatreds, and economic conflicts? How can we love another when we are mainly concerned with our own security, with our own growth, with our own well-being? This so-called love of ideals, Masters, gods is romantic and false; I do not think one sees the brutality of this. The worship of Masters, ideals, is idolatry and destructive of understanding and love.

Love and understanding are not the products of the intellect. Love is not to be divided artificially as the love of God and the love of man. If it can be so divided, it is no longer love. Love completely, wholly, without the thought of self, and thereby free yourself truly from fear which necessitates various forms of escape and forgetfulness.

Question: What would you do if your child were attacked?

KRISHNAMURTI: I have no answer to hypothetical problems. How one will react instantly to violence will depend upon the conditioning of one's mind. If you have been conditioned to meet violence with violence, then you will act violently, but, if you have become aware of the cause and the process of violence, then your action will depend upon the depth of your awareness and the fullness of your understanding and love. Our problem is: Can thought dissipate the center of violence which is in oneself? It can, through constant awareness and understanding. Then if violence comes upon you unexpectedly, you will know how to act, but mere speculation of how one should act in the future is vain. The problem is not how we shall act when violence is upon us but how can we now be free of violence in our thoughts and feelings? Most of us are unaware of our own state of being; we act thoughtlessly and sorrow overtakes us.

Question: Can one be self-reliant in spite of frustrated self-expression? Is not the process of self-revelation part of the necessary self-reliance?

KRISHNAMURTI: We must discover for ourselves what it is in us that is expressing itself before we give such importance to self-expression. There can be no frustration if we understand the nature of the self that is craving to express itself. Giving importance to self-expression causes frustration. The individual expresses himself through his conditioning, and that limitation which he insists is his self-expression, is but sorrow and frustration. What is it that is constantly seeking expression in our daily action? Craving, is it not, in different forms, as power, success, satisfaction?

I said relationship is a process of self-revelation. If thought allows itself, without any hindrance, to perceive its own process in the action and interaction of relationship, then there is the beginning of understanding of the causes of conflict and sorrow; this understanding is true self-reliance. Until one fully understands the process of craving with its self-protective fear which is very often revealed in relationship with another or with society, self-expression only becomes a barrier between man and man. This comprehensive awareness demands strenuous interest and discernment, which is true meditation.

June 23, 1940

Sixth Talk in The Oak Grove

Those of you who have been to these meetings regularly will have to have a little patience, as I am going to make a short résumé of what I have been saying to the newcomers.

During the last five weeks we have been trying to understand the problem of greed and relationship. I tried to explain that as long as one depends psychologically on things, on property, there must be greed, which creates many individual and social problems. The natural need of man is not greed, but it is greed when things assume a psychological significance and importance. Being caught up in greed, how can thought free itself from it? This freedom does not come from mere renunciation or denial but from fully understanding the process of craving. Understanding is not control or restraint but a process that transcends both reason and emotion through discerning awareness.

After dealing with greed and its complexities, I went into the question of human, personal relationship, in which, as most of us are aware, there is constant conflict. I tried to explain that relationship is a process of self-revelation—revelation of oneself through contact with others. That is, if we allow it, others can help us to see ourselves as we are, but this revelation is denied to us if we depend upon them or use them for our gratification and happiness, whether physiological or psychological. For, the condition of dependence is caused by fear which gives rise to possessive love. In this state of fear there cannot be self-revelation or the understanding of oneself. Relationship is deep; it needs constant adjustment which becomes impossible if one is always seeking satisfaction and certainty. If the individual does not understand his relationship with another and the causes of conflict involved in it, then his relationship with society will inevitably lead to friction and antisocial action. The extension of the individual is society.

Last Sunday we saw how dependence upon ideas creates beliefs, dogmas, creeds, and cults which divide man against man. Can thought ever be free from all dependence, either of the past or the future? Dependence is an indication of fear which prevents the understanding of the real. When thought depends for its well-being on things, on people, there must be fear which creates illusion and sorrow. Likewise, dependence on various beliefs and ideals which one has created for oneself prevents the understanding of human relationship and unity of man. We see this process ever at work in the world through social and religious divisions; each group is anxious to preserve, at all cost, its own separative identity and seeks to convert other groups, or to overcome their resistance to its own security. Thus the world is torn apart by beliefs, ideals, dogmas, and creeds. As I explained last week, thought ever seeking security, moves from one anchorage to another; but in each anchorage there is uncertainty, yet it hopes for ultimate certainty. So it creates an ideal reality, a god that is of ultimate satisfaction. Against the background of the known, mind tries to find the unknown, thus creating duality. The mind has become a storehouse of experiences and memories, it is the past with its traditions and accumulative certainties, limiting the present and so the future. With this burden, thought tries to understand the unknown. What is known is not reality.

From what source does our thought spring? It begins surely, does it not, from craving, from expansive and outgoing desire. Perception, contact, sensation give rise to reflection; then craving generates these outgoing desires in which thought becomes entangled. Then begins the conflict of the opposites—the pleasurable and the painful, the transient and the permanent. Our consciousness is held in the conflict of the opposites of pain and pleasure, of denials and identification, of the self and the not-self. The content of our consciousness, which we regard as our whole being, is made up of these dual and contradictory values, both mental and emotional.

Observe your own process of thinking and you will see that it springs from some fear or other, from craving, affection, hope, from the sensation of what is mine and not mine. In other words, thought is enslaved by craving. This dependent thought divides itself into the high and the low, the conscious and the subconscious, and there is conflict between the two. The conscious influenced by the subconscious creates that faculty which we call the intellect—the faculty to discern, to discriminate, to choose. Memory, tradition, value imposed by society, religion, and personal experience influence our discernment. Thought, in our daily life, is occupied with the creation of tradition, the continuance of tradition, and the modification of tradition. To do away with the conflict that is there, to prevent it from arising, and to create a state in which there will be no conflict; to overcome any sorrow that is there, to prevent any future sorrow from arising, and to find peace that is enduring—this is the desire of most of us, is it not? The will of outgoing desires, with its conflict and pain; the will to refrain or to deny, and the will to renounce—all these forms of will are still within the limitation of craving. If one can grasp the full significance of all these forms of will and how they arise in life, in action, then through intense and discerning awareness there is an understanding which is not the result of mere control, denial, or renunciation. This understanding is the natural outcome of deep awareness of the process of craving in its different forms. This demands keen interest out of which comes spontaneous concentration. Understanding is not a reward; in the very moment of awareness it is born.

The outgoing desires with their various layers of memories, the divisions of the high and the low, and the different types of will form the content of our consciousness. The intellect, the faculty to discern, to choose, is influenced by the past, and if we merely rely on that faculty to understand, to love, then our understanding, our love, will be limited.

Reality, or whatever one may choose to call it, for most of us, is the product of the intellect or of the emotion and so must inevitably be illusion. But if we can become keenly aware of the process of craving, understanding will naturally come into being. This awareness is not morbid self-introspection but a keen, joyous perception, in which conflict of choice is no longer taking place. The conflict of choice arises when the intellect—with its fears, and limitations of mine and another's, of merit and demerit, of failure and success—begins to project itself into the solution of our human problems. What we have to become aware of is craving in its different forms; this craving is not to be denied or renounced, but to be understood. Through mere denial or renunciation thought does not free itself from fear and its limitations.

Question: How do we keep intelligence awakened?

KRISHNAMURTI: Surely, this is a wrong way of putting the question, is it not? Either you are awake or you are not. Is there not the subtle thought implied in this question that you are fundamentally intelligent, that deep within you is reality or God and that this abiding intelligence in you is guiding, shaping your life? And, at the same time, being caught up in ignorance and sorrow, how are you to keep awake to its beauty and its promptings?

Now, where there is darkness there cannot be light, where there is ignorance there cannot be understanding or love. If you are God then you are not suffering, you are not afraid, brutal, covetous; but you *are* suffering, you *are* afraid, so that must be false, and to assert that you are not suffering because you are truth or God is to deceive yourself and be in illusion.

Alert and discerning awareness alone can awaken intelligence. In becoming aware of your environment, you begin to perceive the creator of that environment, which is yourself; you see how you have separated yourself from it and thereby started a dual process of conflict between the 'I' and the not 'I'. But through this awareness you begin to understand the cause of your own prejudices, your fears, your national and racial antagonisms, your craving. In trying to understand the environment, you come upon yourself, the investigator, and you find that you yourself are limited. Then how is thought to free itself from its own limitations? It can do so only by becoming intensely aware of its own process of greed, possessive love, and its craving for its own continuity. This strenuous awareness creates its own understanding.

Question: What may I hope?

KRISHNAMURTI: Does not the questioner mean, "What is there for me in the future"? One is seeking blessedness in the future and thereby creates imaginatively, ideally, or romantically, a state after which one constantly aspires with a nostalgic feeling of otherness. Hope indicates a future. That is, having been frustrated in one's desires and ambitions and being caught up in this world of brutal struggle and sorrow, one hopes for a happy, peaceful future state. Is there a blessedness in the future beyond all these transitory states?

Time is the continuous past, present, and future. Hope, the outcome of the present influenced by the past, is concerned with the future. Future hope implies the postponement of the present. Looking to the future is a denial of the present. When you are concerned with the future, you must have satisfying theories about it—what you will be, will not be, and so on. You must create theories that will help you to overcome the present, with its aches and fears. So one

begins to procrastinate; but looking to the future is an avoidance of the present. Or if you do not look to the future, then you look to the immediate alteration of the present. When you are concerned with gaining blessedness in the present, there must be haste, a restlessness, a quick, eager, thoughtless acceptance of assurances to gain what you crave for. Both these aspects of time, postponement and haste bring about illusion.

To look to the future for hope or to the present for immediate fulfillment is to create delusion from which sorrow arises. Blessedness is ever in the present. It can never be in the future. Even in the future there is always the present. If you cannot understand the present, you will not understand it in the future. If we don't understand now, how can we understand in the future? If we are not keenly aware now, how can we realize it in the future? Blessedness is ever in the present, and to understand it requires constant interest and awareness. Peace is ever in the present, but to understand it one must not be concerned with time. Thought must free itself from the continuous past, present, and future; in that freedom, *what is* is immortal, timeless. Blessedness is not a reward. One has to be alert, aware, in a state of continual understanding, never letting one thought or one word pass by without seeing its significance. This state of awareness, which is happiness, is not to be confused with self-introspective, morbid analysis. Blessedness is ever in the present, and to know it one must be free of the bondage of time.

Question: Do you believe in karma and reincarnation?

KRISHNAMURTI: I hear some of you groaning. Why? Do you understand the problem of karma and reincarnation so well, or are you bored with it, or are you tired?

Comment: No.

KRISHNAMURTI: Now let us go into this question fairly thoroughly because I think it is important to understand it, for consciously or unconsciously most of us think in terms of rebirth, continuity, and personal immortality. Let us take first the idea of karma. It is a Sanskrit word, its basic meaning is to act, to do, to work. If thought is fettered, limited, then all action springing from it is also fettered, limited. An acorn will produce an oak tree; the seed holds the future tree. A cause must produce a certain effect, a certain result. We experience this in our daily life. We do something without understanding, either greedily or viciously. It brings its own result. If you hate, the result of this is further hate and violence. If thought is narrow, personal, it must always create, with modification and variation, further ignorance, further limitation, and it cannot escape from its results. The result can always be changed or modified according to our understanding and the integrity of our thought. A cause may not necessarily produce a definite, expected result, for there are always factors and influences tending to modify or change the effect. Thought cannot escape from its limited action and reaction until it understands deeply and fully the cause and the process of its own bondage.

Suppose one is a Hindu—the thought that is expressed by him is limited by the beliefs and traditions of a Hindu, which are the results of accumulated craving, ignorance, fear, and convenience. When this thought expresses itself in action, then that action creates further limitation of thought. Into this very drastic and simple reality, reward and punishment have been introduced to deter so-called wrong action. If one is good—the good depending upon the limitation of thought, not upon understanding—then in the future or in the next life one will be suitably rewarded, and if one is not, one will be suitably punished. This element of fear, as reward and punishment, destroys understanding and love. If thought is influenced by reward and punishment, gain and loss, achievement and failure, then it cannot understand the craving that seeks reward and avoids punishment. Thought can only understand its own process if it does not identify itself with and cling to any of its own creations, any of its outgoing desires. To dissociate our thought from the idea of reward and punishment requires earnest awareness and in this process each one will discover his own particular form of conditioning. Mere discovery of the cause is not understanding; action, born of understanding alone, frees thought from limitation.

The idea of reincarnation involves the rebirth of the 'I' which is regarded as a spiritual essence, the soul—and this implies a timeless state—or as the various sheaths which cover up the reality in man. This 'I' is supposed to continue being born over and over again until it reaches perfection, reality, liberation. We are trying to understand the idea; we are not condemning the theory, so please do not be on the defensive.

If you think that you are a spiritual entity or reality, what does it mean? Does it not imply a timeless, deathless state? If it is the eternal, then it has no growth; for that which is capable of growth is not eternal. If the soul is spiritual essence, above and beyond all physical conditioning, apart from this thing called the 'I', then the 'I' is of no importance. Then why do we cling to it so desperately? Why are we caught up in its perpetuity, in its activities, in its ambitions and achievements, in its expansive desires? So when we say there is a spiritual entity independent of all influence and conditioning, surely such an idea is an illusion, is it not? And also, if that spiritual entity is beyond and above and yet in us, if it cannot be contaminated, if nothing can be added to it, then why do we exert ourselves to understand, why do we struggle to make ourselves more perfect? If this spiritual essence is supposed to be love, intelligence, truth, then how can it be surrounded by this confusing darkness, by this violence and hate, by this feverish pursuit of the demands of the self? Yet it is. This does not mean that I am denying reality which can only be comprehended through understanding illusion and not by inventing illusions. We have accepted this idea of a spiritual entity, apart from the 'I', for such an idea is very gratifying, comforting.

Now what is this 'I'? We see continuation of character, the 'I' being different from another 'I'. As I explained, conditioned thought must continue to create further limitations for itself. The 'I' is not only a particular physical form with its name, but beyond its outer appearance, there is the psychological 'I'. What is this 'I'? A representative of previous influences and limitations, being born in a certain family, belonging to a certain group, a particular race, with its prejudices, its hates and superstitions, fears, and so on. These fears and conditioning originate in ignorance, in craving. These limitations have been transmitted from father to son right through until I am also that father, that past.

Comment: This is interesting.

KRISHNAMURTI: You say that this is interesting; if you saw the implication in it, you would understand its real significance and not merely be intellectually interested. My father is also myself. The ideas and the beliefs which my forefathers had, and which have come down to me, combine with the present action and reaction and become the 'I' of the present. Thus character is preserved and continued—myself as today being reborn as another in the future. Without sentimen-

tality and false emotion and prejudice, one can perceive the deep significance and reality of what I am saying—that our ancestors, through their desires, fears, and hopes created a certain pattern of thought, and this thought is partly continuing in us; these ideas, in combination with the present, have created that narrow and limited thought which is the 'I'. This 'I', this ignorance, this myself, will go on in the future as another. So the world, mankind, is myself. If I, being the world, the you, act thoughtlessly, I must increase and perpetuate ignorance with all its effects, fears, and hates. So what I do matters greatly, not in terms of reward and punishment. But when I am deeply concerned about my rebirth, my immortality, the continuance of my experiences of achievement and sorrow, such concern must lead to wrong and thoughtless conclusions. The 'I' is a conditioned, limited state, and so it is unreal. Reality is that state which is free from the self.

Now, most of us are apt to think that cause and effect are cyclic. If it were thus in the past, it must be so in the present, and so in the future. But this is not so, for there is always a continuous change taking place and thus modifying the effect. Understanding the past influences and limitations, and discerning their effect, thought can transform itself in the present and need not be bound by the past. Thought can free itself in the present from the bondages of the past through intense awareness. Take, for example, a Hindu or Christian with his social and religious background; thoughtlessly he lives in a limited state and so in sorrow, and he attributes this sorrow to karma, to the past and not to his thoughtlessness. It is indolence, a form of conceit, that makes us cling to our past. Blessedness is not in the past or in the future but in the present for those who through joyous awareness understand, and so, are free from the cause of ignorance, which is craving.

If you will seriously reflect upon what I have been saying, then understanding will come out of your own earnestness. Knowledge is utterly valueless if you do not relate it to your daily life. If we are worldly, psychologically depending on things for our personal happiness, if our love is possessive and our thought crippled by beliefs and fears, then life becomes an increasing sorrow. In joyous and strenuous awareness, thought frees itself from its limitations; out of self-reliant, exercised understanding, there comes peace.

June 30, 1940

Seventh Talk in The Oak Grove

The world, especially at the present time, is in a state of confusion and conflict and in deep sorrow. One can create a theoretical conception of what the world should be and try to adjust oneself to that idea, but in the long run that would not contribute to our understanding of the complex problem of life, though momentarily it might alleviate our suffering. Intellect is the faculty to discern, and when it is limited, as it is now, theoretical hopes are of little use. When so many people are caught up in hate, in ruthless ambition, which is creating such havoc and misery, you, at least as an individual, can liberate yourself from these causes and help to bring about a happier and a saner world. If you have a desire to help the world, you must begin with yourself for the world is yourself. The present condition of the world has been brought about consciously or unconsciously by each one of us, and in order to alter it fundamentally, we must deliberately and intelligently direct our minds and hearts to bring about a complete change in ourselves. If we do not deeply understand this

and try to organize merely a better economic or social system, our efforts will not, I feel, create a saner and happier world. Unless the individual is harmonious in himself, he is bound to be antisocial in his relationship with another, which is after all society.

We have been trying to understand what it is that creates in us and so about us confusion and misery. The disproportionate value we give to things when we psychologically depend upon them creates greed. Human needs do not corrupt our thoughts and feelings if psychologically we do not become dependent upon things, possessions. As long as our relationship with another is possessive, there must conflict, for conflict arises when there is physiological and psychological dependence. I explained how the world is broken up and divided through individuals and groups depending upon beliefs, dogmas, theories, whether they be political, social, or religious. These beliefs and dogmas have their origin in the craving of each individual for security, not only economic, but also psychological and spiritual.

Thus we are in a world divided in itself, racially, socially, economically, nationally, and religiously. We are aware of this. Then what are we to do? How are we to break through this vicious circle of greed, possessive love, and personal immortality? Is it possible to break through completely and not fall into other subtle forms of avarice, power, and possessiveness? How are we to set about removing the cause of so much suffering and illusion?

We must become aware, thoughtful. I am going to explain what I mean by awareness. We have to become conscious of what we are. How do we become conscious of what we are? By being interested. That is, in being interested, there is a natural concentration which produces will. Concentration is the focusing of all energies on something in which we are interested. For instance, when our interest is in making money, and in the power money gives, or when we are absorbed in a book or in some creative activity, there is natural concentration. Will is created when there is interest. When there is no interest, there is diffusion of thought, contradiction of desire. The beginning of awareness is the natural concentration of interest in which there is no conflict of desires and choice, and therefore there is a possibility of understanding different and opposing desires. If thought is seeking a certain definite result, then there is exclusion or aggregation, which leads to incompleteness and is not the awareness of which I speak. You cannot understand the whole complex process of your being if you are seeking results or trying to achieve a state which you think is peace or reality or liberation. Awareness is the understanding of the whole process of the conscious and the unconscious desire. In the very beginning of awareness, there is the perception of what is true; truth is not a result or an achievement, but it is to be understood. In the very process of understanding, say for example, greed, there is the realization of what is true. This understanding is not born of mere reason or emotion but is the outcome of awareness, the completeness of thought-action.

When we are conscious, we are aware of a dual process at work in us—want and non-want, expansive desires and refraining desires. The outgoing desires have their own form of will. The concentration on outgoing desires, and their action, create a world of competition and division in worldliness, of possessive love and the craving for personal continuity. Perceiving the consequences of these outgoing desires, which cause pain and sorrow, there is the desire to refrain, with its own type of will. So there is conflict between the outgoing will and the will to refrain. This conflict creates either understanding or confusion and ignorance. The outgoing will and the will to refrain are the cause of duality, which is not to be denied.

Though opposites have a similar common cause, we cannot slur over them or put them aside; we have to understand them and so be free from the conflict of opposites. Being envious and therefore conscious of conflict and pain, we try to cultivate its opposite, but there is no freedom from envy. The motive for cultivating the opposite matters greatly; if it is a desire to escape from the struggle and pain of envy, then its opposite becomes identical with itself, and so there is no freedom from envy. Whereas, if you consider deeply the intrinsic cause of envy and become aware of its various forms, with their urges, then in that understanding there is a freedom from envy, without creating its opposite. The concentration that comes into being in the process of awareness is not the result of self-interest or of morbid self-introspection. As I said, to be interested is to be creative, which is happiness. This concentration of interest comes naturally when there is awareness. When there is an understanding of the process of outgoing desires, with its so-called positive will and the will of restraint, then there comes a completeness, a wholeness which is not the creation of the intellect. Intellect, the faculty of discernment, is the instrument of understanding and not an end in itself. Understanding transcends reason and emotion.

Question: What is the best attitude towards this terrible war in Europe? Can we do anything by thought? I feel the horror and suffering of this war. Can I escape from it? Can I escape from it if I dissociate myself from it? Will you consider the present world conditions in your talk?

KRISHNAMURTI: We often mistakenly think that the world's chaos and misery arise from a single cause and by overcoming it we shall bring order and happiness to the world. Life is a complex process and we must have wide and deep understanding to grasp its vastness. War is the result of our daily life, of our acquisitiveness, of our general attitude towards our fellow men in so-called peacetime. In our daily life we are competitive, aggressive, nationalistic, vengeful, self-seeking, which inevitably culminates in war; intellectually and emotionally we are influenced and limited by the past which produces the present reaction of hate, antagonism, and conflict. Intellectually we are incapable of clear discernment, and so we are confused; we are incapable of critical discernment because our faculty to think has become dulled by previous influences and limitations. Until thought is freed from them, struggle and war, pain and sorrow will continue. Until our own lives are no longer aggressive and greedy, and psychologically we cease seeking security, and so breaking up the world into different classes, races, nationalities, religions, there cannot be peace.

Though, superficially, there might be a cessation of this carnage, yet until we direct our minds and hearts earnestly and strenuously to understand and so free ourselves from those psychological causes of acquisitiveness—possessive love—and continuity of self struggle and misery must ever be. Peace is from within, not from without. This understanding of peace requires deep thought and earnestness.

You ask if you can escape from war if you dissociate yourself from it. How can you dissociate yourself from war? For you are the cause of war. Why are you associated with this war that is going on? Either because your relations are involved in it or you are emotionally caught up in it. If your relations are involved in it, such a sorrow is understandable, but merely to be emotionally involved in it is thoughtless. If you merely dissociate

yourself from this form of excitement, you will undoubtedly turn to other forms. So unless you understand why you depend upon sensation, upon this constant search for excitement, which becomes vulgar and degrading, you will ever find new forms of excitement, satisfaction. The cause is deep and you have to understand it to be free from its superficialities.

Do not think by merely wishing for peace you will have peace, when in your daily life of relationship you are aggressive, acquisitive, seeking psychological security here or in the hereafter. You have to understand the central cause of conflict and sorrow and then dissolve it and not merely look to the outside for peace. But you see, most of us are indolent. We are too lazy to take hold of ourselves and understand ourselves, and being lazy, which is really a form of conceit, we think others will solve this problem for us and give us peace, or that we should destroy the apparently few people that are causing wars. When the individual is in conflict within himself, he must inevitably create conflict without, and only he can bring about peace within himself and so in the world, for he is the world.

Question: Should we refrain from taking on new responsibilities in order not to have cause for new desires?

KRISHNAMURTI: Surely that depends on how one has acquitted oneself with regard to the old responsibilities. If one has not understood the past responsibilities fully and has merely broken away from them, taking on new ones is merely the continuation of the old in a different form. Must I explain this further?

Comment: Yes, please.

KRISHNAMURTI: What we consider new responsibilities are really the continuation of the old under different conditions. So, before one takes on new responsibilities, one must consider how one has fulfilled the old; if one has not, but has merely broken away through anger, through thoughtlessness or obstinacy, then one has to consider why one takes on the new. The assumption of the new may only be the continuation of craving for sensation, for comfort, for the old desire has not been fully understood and solved. Desire is ever seeking further expression and expansion and merely taking on new responsibilities will not fulfill desire, for there is no end to desire, to craving. But in understanding the process of desire, through becoming aware of its implications and causes, you will know for yourself whether to take on new responsibilities or not. I cannot, naturally, tell you what you should do, but you can find out for yourself definitely.

Question: Please tell us what is your conception of God.

KRISHNAMURTI: Now, why do we want to know if there is God? If we can understand deeply the intention of this question, we shall comprehend a great deal. Belief and nonbelief are definite hindrances to the understanding of reality; belief and ideals are the results of fear; fear limits thought and to escape from conflict we turn to various forms of hopes, stimulations, illusions. Reality is authentic, direct, experience. If we depend on the description of another, reality ceases, for what is described is not the real. If we have never tasted salt, no description of its taste is of any value. We have to taste it for ourselves to know it. Now, most of us want to know what God is because we are indolent, because it is easier to depend upon the experience of another than upon our own understanding; it also cultivates in us an irresponsible attitude, and then all we have to do is to imitate another, mold our life after the pattern, or the experience of another, and by following the example, we think we have arrived, attained, realized. To understand the highest, there must be liberation from time—the continuous past, present, and future—from the fears of the unknown, of failure, and success. You are asking this question because you want either to compare your image of God with mine and so bolster up yourself or to condemn, which only leads to contention and wallowing in opinions. This way does not lead to understanding.

God, truth, or whatever you may choose to call reality cannot be described. That which can be described is not the real. It is vain to inquire if there is God, for reality comes into being when thought frees itself from its limitations, its cravings. If we are brought up in the belief of God or in opposition to that, thought is influenced, a habit is formed from generation to generation. Both belief and nonbelief in God prevent the understanding of God. Being anchored in belief, any experience that you may have in accordance with your belief can only strengthen your previous conditioning. Mere continuation of limited thought is not an understanding of reality. When we assert that through our own experience there is or there is no God, we are continuing and repeating experiences influenced by the past. Experiences, without our understanding the causes of bondage, do not give us wisdom. If we continue to repeat a certain influence which we call experience, such experience only strengthens our limitations and so does not bring about freedom from them. The mind, as I pointed out in my talk, is the result of craving and therefore transient, and when the mind conceives a theory of God or of truth, it is bound to be the product of its own conceit, and so it is not real. One has to become aware of the various forms of craving, fear, and so on, and through constant inquiry and discernment, a new understanding comes into being which is not the result of the intellect or of the emotion. To understand reality, there must be constant and earnest awareness.

Question: What is the significance of Christ or the problem of Christianity in our present age?

KRISHNAMURTI: What is happening in our present age? There is confusion, hate, fear, greed, war. Now, what is the answer to all this? Is there a Christian or a Hindu or a Buddhist answer to this, or is there only one true solution? Each religion and each dogmatic group thinks that it alone has the key to the solution of the present chaos. There is competition between religions, with their systems, and priests. The solution of the present chaos lies in yourself and not in another. Through self-reliance you can bring about peace within yourself, and so in the world, which is an extension of yourself. No leader can give you peace. The important thing is to understand how your own thought and action create the present chaos and misery, and only through your own self-reliant and discerning awareness can there be freedom from this ever-recurring agony and confusion.

Question: Is there any relationship between reality and myself?

KRISHNAMURTI: You hopefully imply, do you not, that there should be a relationship between reality and yourself? You believe that reality or God or whatever you like to call it is in you, but is covered over by ignorance; then you ask what is the relationship between this ignorance and reality. Can there be any relationship between ignorance and understanding? Now what are these

coverings, these sheaths, that are supposed to hide reality? What is the 'I' that is asking this question? Is not the 'I' a certain form, a name, a certain bundle of qualities, memories that have divided themselves into the high and the low, into the spiritual and non-spiritual, and so on? All of this is the 'I'.

Now you want to know if there is any relationship between this 'I' and reality. What is reality? You don't know, but you have a hope, a longing for it. Can there be any relationship between the known, the 'I', and the unknown? You can find out if there is any relationship only by understanding what you are, not by supposing or asserting that there is a relationship between the 'I' and reality. Surely, if the 'I' is transient, and it is transient as we can observe it from day to day, then what is the relationship between the transient and something which is not? None whatsoever. In thoroughly comprehending the process of the 'I' and its transiency and being unattached to it, there is an understanding of reality. The 'I' is this bundle of desires, of greed, of possessive love, of craving for immortality, here or in the hereafter; and through earnest awareness, the process of craving can be transformed into peace which is not a theoretical hope but a reality.

Question: You say we must be alert and watchful every moment and that this watchfulness isn't the same as introspection. Will you please explain how they differ.

KRISHNAMURTI: Between awareness and introspection there is a difference. Introspection is a kind of self-analysis in which thought is measuring its own action and its results, according to pleasure and pain, reward and punishment, thus forming a judgment, a pattern. That is, having examined the action of the past, thought tries to carry out what it has learned through the present action and so determines how it shall act in the future. Observe what takes place as you try to analyze yourself. You are always analyzing a past action; you cannot analyze an action that is being lived. If you have done something which has caused pain or conflict, you want to understand it in order not to act again in the same manner. So when you do this, you are trying to understand a past action, a dead action, with present intention, hoping to produce a future result. That is, thought is occupied, in this introspective process, with the result, with how it should act.

Now, awareness is different. In awareness there is only the present—that is, being aware, you see the past process of influence which controls the present and modifies the future. Awareness is an integral process, not a process of division. For example, if I ask the question, "Do I believe in God,"—in the very process of asking, I can observe, if I am aware, what it is that is making me ask that question; if I am aware I can perceive what has been and what are the forces at work which are compelling me to ask that question. Then I am aware of various forms of fear—those of my ancestors who have created a certain idea of God and have handed it down to me, and combining their idea with my present reactions, I have modified or changed the concept of God. If I am aware I perceive this entire process of the past, its effect in the present and in the future, integrally, as a whole.

If one is aware, one sees how through fear one's concept of God arose; or perhaps there was a person who had an original experience of reality or of God and communicated it to another who in his greediness made it his own, and gave impetus to the process of imitation. Awareness is the process of completeness, and introspection is incomplete. The result of introspection is morbid, painful, whereas awareness is enthusiasm and joy.

Question: Do you advise meditation?

KRISHNAMURTI: It all depends on what you call meditation. There is a great deal involved in this question. Have you ever done any so-called meditation? Perhaps some of you have in one form or another. Perhaps you have reflected deeply when there was a pressing human problem that demanded an answer; this can be considered to be a form of meditation. Through continual dwelling upon a certain idea which helps to eliminate other intruding ideas, you will learn concentration; this also is considered to be a form of meditation. You want to awaken certain powers, the so-called occult powers, because you hope by having these powers you will find greater understanding. These practices are also considered a form of meditation.

To be constantly alert and aware, to be thoughtful, is the beginning of meditation, for without the true foundation of discernment, mere concentration and other forms of so-called meditation become dangerous and are without any deep significance. As I pointed out, when you are aware you will find that the mind is seeking a result, a conclusion, desiring achievement, security. To pursue a predetermined conclusion is no longer meditation, for thought then is caught in it own net of images.

Let us consider the process of meditation a little more fully. It is very difficult to steady the wandering and trembling thought; it moves from one object of sensation to another, from one interest to another. In this process one becomes aware of the extreme sensitiveness of thought. Thought wanders from one set of ideas to another, either because of interest or merely because it is sluggish and indifferent. If thought merely controls itself from wandering, it becomes narrow, limited, and destructive. If thought is interested in wandering, then merely controlling itself is useless because that will not reveal why it is interested in the dissipation of its own energy. But if you are interested to find out why it is wandering, then you are beginning to discern and be aware and there is then a natural, spontaneous concentration. So, first you must observe that thought is wandering, then discern why it wanders. When thought perceives that it is indolent, lazy, it is already beginning to be active, but merely controlling thought does not bring about creative action.

When there is a natural concentration of interest, not mere control, you begin to discover that thought is in a process of constant imitation and that it is ever wandering through its many layers of memories, precepts, examples; or, having had a stimulating sensation or experience during moments of concentration, it recreates it and tries to vivify the past sensation, but thereby it only stultifies its own creative process; or, apart from daily life, thought tries to develop various qualities in order to control its daily actions, and living loses its inherent significance, and standard becomes most important.

All this then is merely a form of approximation and not creative meditation. If you are aware in your daily activities—when you are talking, when you are walking, when you are making money or seeking pleasure—in that awareness, depending on your earnestness, there begins an understanding, a love, which is not at the behest of intellect or of emotion. So, meditation is a process of awareness in action. From the reality of life must spring meditation, and then meditation is a process of self-liberation. Meditation is not the approximation of a pattern. The stilling of the mind through will, choice, may achieve certain calmness, but this calmness is of death, producing languor. This is not meditation. But the understanding of choice, which is a very delicate and strenuous process, is meditation in which there is calmness without a trace of languor or contentment. There must be alert and strenuous discernment in meditation. Meditation is a process of completeness, wholeness, not a series of achievements culminating in reality.

Question: What has diet to do with the mental process or intelligence?

KRISHNAMURTI: Certainly, a great deal. Understanding reality does not necessarily depend on the kind of food one eats; one may be a vegetarian and be vicious and dull, or a meat-eater and be intelligent in the widest sense. If one overeats, it is an indication of thoughtlessness; moderate and rational diet is necessary to alert thought. Too much fasting also dulls the mind. Not to be angry, not to be disparaging in our talk, not to be ruthless, obstinate, not to flatter, not to receive flattery—these are more important than the consideration of what we eat. Of primary importance are your thoughts and feelings. Cleanliness of food is not cleanliness of thought. Again we begin at the wrong end, with the external, hoping to grasp that state of inward peace, which cannot be realized through the mere alteration of environment. We hope to have psychological peace through discipline and denial, through imitation and isolation; we begin at the periphery, hoping to create inward peace and compassion, but we must begin from the center—the center from which arise conflict and sorrow. We must become aware of the process of craving and its outward expressions; in discerning these, there is a natural restraint not imposed through fear.

July 7, 1940

Eighth Talk in The Oak Grove

We are all well aware of the appalling chaos and misery that exist at the present time, not only in the world about us but also in ourselves. To this problem there must be a complete solution. Certain groups and systems of thought maintain that only their particular panacea will solve the problem. Any partial remedy to the complexity of life, however facile and logical, must inevitably bring in its wake other complications. Let us see if we cannot find a complete solution to this problem, which is economic, psychological, and spiritual. We must understand this struggle, this suffering, as comprehensively as possible, not partially through the limitation of any particular system; we must have a free mind that is capable of facing the problem as a whole.

There must be some cause for this confusion and misery not only in ourselves but also in our relationship with mankind which we call society. If we can understand the fundamental cause, then perhaps this problem will be forever solved.

We will consider two different approaches to the problem of conflict and sorrow. This division is artificial, for convenience only. The one is the approach from the outside, and the other from within. If we attempt to solve this problem of struggle and pain entirely from the outside, we shall not understand it, nor shall we understand it if we deal with it only from within. For the sake of clarity only, do we divide life as the outer and the inner, but to understand the complex problem of life, we must have an integrated understanding.

In all my talks I have been trying to explain this integrated approach to our daily problems of relationship, not only with another, but also with our work and our ideas. When we try to solve the problem of existence from the outside, as it were, we soon realize that there must be a complete social and economic change; we see that there must be the elimination of barriers, racial, national, economic. We perceive also that we must be free of religious barriers, with their separative dogmas and beliefs,

which cause different groups to be formed in antagonistic competition with one another. Organized religions have separated man from man, they have not united mankind. If we approach this problem of existence from the outside, emphasis must be laid on institution, on legislation, on the importance of the state, with its resultant dangers. Though the action of the state may momentarily give satisfactory results, there is inherent in it great possibilities of corruption and brutality; for the sake of an ideology, man will sacrifice man.

In this external approach there is a possibility of losing oneself in an ideology, in service, in the state, and so on; one hopes unconsciously that through this forgetfulness, one's own sorrows, anxieties, responsibilities, and conflicts will disappear. And yet, in spite of the attempt to sacrifice oneself to the outer, there still remains the 'I' with its personal, limited ambitions, hopes, fears, passions, and greed. One may forget oneself in the state, but as long as the 'I' remains, the state becomes the new means for its expansion, for its glory, and cunning thought will again bring about new chaos and misery. Competition for property is primarily for the power it gives, and power will ever be sought as long as the 'I' exists. Competition is the outward manifestation of the inner conflict of ambition, envy, and the worship of success.

The other approach to the problem of suffering and conflict is from within—to overcome the many causes that create conflict in relationship between individuals, and so with society. We try to overcome one cause by another cause, one substitution by another substitution, and so thought gets entangled in its own vicious net. We try to remove the cause of conflict and misery by mere assertions, by logical and rational conclusions. We worship God or an idea or a pattern in order to forget ourselves and be free of our daily struggles through our sacrifice and love.

There is the idea that the individual is a spiritual essence, and if through constant assertion and control he can discipline thought and emotion according to a particular idea, he will be able to identify himself with that spiritual essence and thus escape his daily conflict in relationship and action. Thus the pattern, the belief, becomes more important than the understanding of life. There is ever competition between religious groups; their leaders are thinking in terms of conversion and so cannot coalesce. Behind the weight of tradition, escape, and worship, there is ever the 'I' with its worldliness, possessive love, and craving for its own immortality.

Though we may try to lose or forget ourselves in beliefs and dogmas, yet behind this effort there is an intense craving for completeness, wholeness. Without thoroughly understanding this craving, merely to multiply or change beliefs and dogmas is utterly in vain.

There is a complete answer to our problem of suffering and conflict, which is not based on dogmatism or on theories. This answer is to be found when we approach the problem integrally from the center; that is, we must understand the process of the 'I' in its relationship with another, with action, with belief. In the voluntary transformation of the process of the 'I', intelligently and sanely and without compulsion, lies the complete solution of our conflict and sorrow. As most of us are unwilling to concentrate thought on the fundamental alteration in the center, legislation and institutions force us to adjust ourselves to an outward pattern in the hope of achieving social harmony, but this does not eradicate the cause of conflict and suffering. Compulsion does not create understanding, whether it is from outside or from within.

The complete answer to this problem of conflict and suffering lies in understanding the process of craving, not through mere control and introspection, but through becoming aware of its expression in our daily thought and action. That is, by becoming aware of greed, possessive love, and the desire for personal continuity, there comes into being a comprehensive understanding without the conflict of choice. This needs experimental approach and earnest application. As most of us are slothful, environmental influences and external impositions, as values, traditions, opinions, control our lives and so keep our thought in bondage.

Unless we thoroughly understand and so transcend the process of craving, however well the outer is planned and made orderly, this inward process will ever overcome the outer and bring about disorder and confusion. However carefully and sanely the social and economic conditions are arranged, as long as individual thought is acquisitive, possessive, seeking security for itself, either here or in the hereafter, these well-arranged social orders will constantly be disintegrated. The inner is ever overcoming the outer and until we transcend craving, the superficially well-arranged social order is in vain.

We as individuals must direct our thought to that freedom in which there is no sense of the 'I', the freedom from the self. This freedom from the self can only come about when we understand the process of craving as acquisitiveness, possessive love, and personal immortality. For, the world is the extension or projection of the individual, and if the individual looks to authority and legislation to bring about a drastic change within himself, he will be caught in a vicious circle of thoughtlessness from which there is no release.

Through constant and alert awareness, thought must free itself from worldliness and discern greed from need; thought must free itself from possessive love, and love completely, without fear, without the thought of self; thought must free itself from the craving for personal immortality through property, family, or race, or through the continuation of the individual 'I'. As long as craving, expressing itself in these three complex ways, is the motive of action, peace and human unity cannot be realized. When thought is not conditioned by acquisitiveness, possessive love, and the desire for personal continuation, there is true disinterestedness which alone can bring about a sane and happy social order. This depends on each one of us, and each one of us has to become actively and discerningly aware of the expressions of the self and so free thought from its bondage.

Question: Can continued effort in meditation lead to full awareness?

KRISHNAMURTI: Without true discernment mere concentration on an idea, image, or virtue leads to barrenness of thought and to the destruction of love. Discernment comes through constant awareness of our daily thought, speech, and action; without this true corrective element, meditation becomes an escape, a source of delusion. Without understanding and love, any form of meditation must lead to illusion; without true awareness, any form of meditation is an escape from reality.

When there is awareness we observe that thought is ever approximating itself to a pattern, to a memory, to a past experience; it is measuring itself against an opinion or a standard. Though mind may reject outward patterns, standards, values, yet it may cling to its own so-called experience; this experience without true discernment may be the continuation of narrow and prejudiced thought and unless mind frees itself from its bondages, meditation only strengthens its own limitation. So through alert awareness of daily thought, speech, and action, thought must free itself from its fetters; this freedom is the true beginning of meditation.

When thought is occupied with approximation, then it is concerned with achievement, with success, and so it is no longer capable of true discernment, for the desire to gain, to attain, springs from fear which prevents true perception. Fear cannot yield understanding, but in becoming intensely aware of the causes of fear in our daily life, interest and discernment are born. Interest is natural concentration without the conflict of opposing desires. We force ourselves to concentrate without this interest, and so it becomes artificial, painful, and has no deep significance. Understanding does not come through compulsion or through mere control but through constant and earnest awareness of our daily thoughts and activities, of our speech and work. Meditation must spring from this awareness. The cultivation of so-called occult powers, trances, and so forth is of very little importance. Without true discernment mere concentration on images, standards, and ideals does not lead to comprehension. Creative stillness of the mind is necessary for the understanding of reality.

Question: You are in a happy position, all you need is given to you by friends. We have to earn money for ourselves and our families, we have to contend with the world. How can you understand us and help us?

KRISHNAMURTI: Each one of us has to contend with some particular environment. Each has his own limitations and tendencies wherever his sphere of existence may be. Being envious of another does not help us to comprehend the aches and sorrows of our own life; to be envious is part of our heritage, part of our social structure. If we succumb to our limitation, then there is no possibility of understanding another; but if we, wherever we find ourselves, try earnestly to understand our environment and free thought from our particular tendencies and limited experiences, then we will comprehend life as a whole, and not be bound by the prejudices, the traditions, and values of our particular environment.

Whatever the circumstances of our life may be, we have to understand and so transcend them. Thought must dig deep into its own conscious and subconscious states and liberate itself from those influences and bondages that make it personal, greedy, possessive, and cruel. Truth is to be understood in our daily thoughts, conduct, and activities. It is foolish to be envious of another, for the other is ourselves.

Question: In one of your recent talks you stressed the importance of action. Is what I do of tremendous importance?

KRISHNAMURTI: I said that if thought is limited by memories, traditions, prejudices, by the past, then any action springing from it can only create further ignorance and sorrow. If one thinks in terms of a particular race or religion, then such thinking must be limited, separative. Sanely and deliberately, as individuals we can set about to free thought from those causes that bring about limitation. Then what one thinks and does greatly matters. If one acts thoughtlessly then one increases and perpetuates limitation and sorrow. But by becoming aware of the past and the causes of conditioning, if one is interested and therefore concentrated, one can free thought from its bondages. This demands earnestness and integral awareness. Also you are the world, and by your particular action or inaction, you can increase or help to diminish ignorance.

Question: By being ambitious, do I destroy my purpose?

KRISHNAMURTI: If our purpose is the outcome of the desire for self-aggrandizement, conscious or unconscious, to achieve it ambition is necessary. Such ambition, being the expression of craving for personal success, must produce antisocial action and sorrow in relationship. One must grasp the underlying significance of ambition; ambition is an ardent desire for personal distinction and achievement, which in action becomes competitive and ruthless. We give such importance to self-expression without fully and deeply understanding what it is that is being expressed. In modern society to be ambitiously self-expressive is considered not to be antisocial and is even honored. This form of ambition is condemned by those who are spiritually ambitious; that is, they condemn worldliness but yet they crave for achievement, success, in other spheres. Both forms of ambition are the same, both imply the expansion of the 'I', the self.

So unless we grasp the meaning of self-expression, its purpose, and its action, merely to aspire towards an ideal becomes a subtle form of self-aggrandizement. Unless we see the inward significance of craving, mere outward legislation and religious promises cannot curb the desire for dominance, for personal power, and success. In becoming intensely aware of the process of craving, with its many ambitions and pursuits, there is born not only the will to refrain but also understanding, whose creative expression is not of the self.

Question: I would like to devote my life to awakening men to a desire for freedom. Your dissertations, writings, seem to be the best instrumentality, or should each develop his own technique?

KRISHNAMURTI: Before we awaken another, we must be sure that we ourselves are awake and alert. This does not mean that we must wait until we are free. We are free insofar as we begin to understand and transcend the limitations of thought. Before one begins to preach awareness and freedom to another, which is fairly easy, one must begin with oneself. Instead of converting others to our particular form of limitation, we must begin to free ourselves from the pettiness and narrowness of our own thought.

Question: You said, if I remember rightly, that we must tackle the problem of inner insufficiency. How can one tackle that problem?

KRISHNAMURTI: Why does one accumulate things, property, and so on? In oneself there is poverty and so one tries to enrich oneself through worldly things; this enrichment of oneself brings social disorder and misery. Observing this, certain states and religious sects prohibit individuals from possessing property and being worldly, but this inner poverty, this aching insufficiency still continues, and it must be filled. So thought seeks and craves for enrichment in other directions. If we do not find enrichment through possessions, we try to seek it in relationship or in ideas, which leads to many kinds of delusion. So long as there is craving, there must be this painful insufficiency; without understanding the process of craving, the cause, we try to deal with the effect, insufficiency, and get lost in its intricacies. By becoming aware of the fallacy of accumulative sufficiency, thought begins to free itself of those possessions which it has accumulated for itself through fear of incompleteness. Completeness, wholeness, is not the aggregation of many parts or the expansion of the self; it is to be realized through understanding and love.

Question: Will you explain again the relationship between awareness and self-analysis.

KRISHNAMURTI: I thought I explained this last Sunday, but that was a week ago.

For most people it is difficult to concentrate with interest for more than half an hour or so. Added to this difficulty, many are anxious to take notes. Unless they are experts they cannot listen with attention and at the same time take notes. These talks will be printed, so it is more important to listen now than to take notes. You would not be taking notes if you were interestedly listening to a friend.

The purpose of these talks has been not to give a system of thought, but to help each one of us to become aware of ourselves, of our daily action and relationship, and thus naturally discern our prejudices, fears, cravings; through this awareness, there is a natural concentration, induced by interest, which brings about the will to refrain; this will is not the result of mere fear and control but of understanding.

July 14, 1940

Eddington, Pennsylvania, 1940

✳

Notes of Sarobia Discussions, Eddington, PA

Opinions, ideologies, and theories are dividing the world; no agreement is possible as long as we cling to them in any form whatsoever, for they breed thoughtlessness and obstinacy. Agreement is only possible when we have disentangled thought from them and experience for ourselves. We cannot agree if our thought is perverted; genuine, direct experience cannot create contention. To be capable of an original experience we must slough off the many bondages, the limiting influences, on our thoughts and feelings, and we shall attempt to do this during this gathering. This is essential and it is only possible if each one of us becomes aware, and understands the component parts that go to create our background, the 'I'.

We must have knowledge about the material before we can transform it. The material is the intellectual, emotional state of our being, also the religious, artistic, scientific, physical. Any form of limitation must be a hindrance to completeness. For this attempt, deep and wide intelligence is necessary. Intelligence is the discovery, by each one, of what is of primary importance and the capacity to pursue it.

If one pursues the path of knowledge— "What must I know?"—one has to submit to authority, which must engender fear and various forms of idolatry; then Masters, guides, intermediaries, priests, in different forms, become necessary. This path is the way of the intellect and any action that comes from the mere pursuit of knowledge must be imitative and not liberating. For them action must conform to a preconceived pattern of knowledge which hinders direct experience. But if we put to ourselves this question: "What can I do?"—then direct experience is knowledge and this knowledge is not a limiting process. With action comes knowledge which is not imitative and so is liberating. The pursuit of "What can I know?" destroys self-reliance, but the pursuit of "What can I do?" creates self-reliance which is essential for the comprehensiveness of reality— "What can I do with regard to life, things, people, and ideas?"

✳   ✳   ✳

Greed in its many forms puts man against man, bringing disunion and contention. Balance, coordination, is necessary for completeness; mere control or denial of the objects of craving does not free thought from greed, envy. Only through understanding the process of craving, by becoming aware of it, is there a possibility of thought freeing itself from it. Awareness is not mere analysis or self-examination. Meditation is interested concentration, the awareness in which the conflict of opposites ceases.

* * *

Greed breeds envy and hate. Imitation is the result of envy. Our social structure is based on envy and imitation. One of the main causes of division in society is envy and the craving for success; each is imitating the one above him. Many of us desire to belong to the socially elect. This imitative process keeps the social division going from generation to generation.

This same attitude and action exist in the so-called spiritual realm. There too we think in terms of progressive hierarchical achievement. Such attitude is born of greed and envy, which produces imitation and fosters fear; the idea that one day you will become a Master or a higher being is similar to your becoming one day a knight or a duke. It is repulsive and not ennobling to a man of thought.

There is expansion, growth, in greed and envy but not in freedom from them. There may be growth or evolution of the outer, of the periphery, but not of what is true. The freedom from greed and envy is not progressive; you are either free or not free from them. This freedom is not the result of evolution, growth. If we understand need utterly dissociated from greed, craving, and envy, then social and personal conflicts cease, then thought is free from worldliness.

What can I do about my needs? The answer will be found when we put to ourselves the question: "How is thought to free itself of greed, from the very center and not merely from the outside?" First, one must be conscious or aware of being greedy or envious or imitative; then be aware also of its opposite reactions. That is, be aware of the very strong will of outgoing desires, cultivated through generations, which has a very strong momentum; and also become aware of the will to refrain, to deny, which has also been cultivated through moral and religious injunctions. Our mind is the battleground of these two opposing forces, of want and nonwant. We hope by pursuing and cultivating an opposite, we shall transcend all opposites; that which is achieved through the cultivation of the opposites is still within the opposite, though one may think that the state one has achieved has transcended the opposites.

There is duality, good and evil, greed and nongreed. Being greedy, to cultivate its opposite is not freedom from greed, nor does thought transcend an opposite by the cultivation of its opposite. Thought can only free itself from the opposites, duality, when it is not caught up in them and is capable of understanding *what is* without the reaction of the opposite. That is, being envious, to cultivate its opposite does not free thought from envy, but if we do not react in opposition to it, but are capable of understanding the process of envy itself, then there is a lasting freedom from it. In the very center there is a freedom from greed and not merely from the outside. This experience is truly religious and all experiences of opposites are nonreligious.

* * *

All comparative change is a change in resistance; all comparative thinking and acting do not free thought from its limiting influences. Freedom from greed, envy, and imitation lies not in the mere change of the outside, but in understanding and transcending the will of outgoing desires, which brings lasting transformation in the very center itself. Relationship with people divides itself— though there is no such real division—as superficial and deep; as superficial contact and contact of interest and affection.

* * *

Love is hedged about with fear, possessiveness, jealousy, and with peculiar tendencies inherited and acquired. We have to become aware of these barriers, and we can become aware of them most poignantly and significantly in relationship, whether superficial or deep. In relationship the 'I' generally forms the center and from this, action radiates. There cannot be compassion if thought is perverted by partisanship, by hate, by prejudices of class, of religion, of race, and so on.

All relationship, if allowed, becomes a process of self-revelation; but most of us do not allow ourselves to discover what we are, as this involves pain. In all relationship there is the 'I' and the 'other'; the 'other' may be one or the many, the society, the world.

Can there be individuality in the widest and deepest sense if one belongs to society? What is society? It is the many, cemented together through necessity, convenience, affection, greed, envy, fear, standards, values, imitation, that is, essentially through craving; the many with their peculiar organizations and institutions, religions, and moralities. If one is born a Hindu, one is brought up in a certain social and religious environment with its special dogmas and prejudices. As long as one remains conditioned as a Hindu, one has consciously identified oneself with a particular race, a class, a set of ideas, and so one is really not an individual. Though within that limited conditioning, called Hinduism, one may struggle to achieve, to create; though one may have a functional purpose which gives a sense of independence, utility, importance, yet within the circle of its conditioned influence, there can be no true individuality.

The world is broken up into these different forms of restricting groups, Hindu, English, German, Chinese, and so on, each fighting and killing or coercing the other. It is possible to be a true individual in the highest sense only if one is not identified with any special conditioning. The conflict of society is between those who are liberating themselves from the mass, from a particular identification, and those who are still part of a particular group. Those who escape from particular influences and limitations are soon deified or put in prison or neglected.

Relationship is a process of self-revelation and liberation. To inquire within the circle of limitation about the soul, reality, God, immortality is vain, for these words, images, and ideas belong to the world of hate, greed, fear, craving. When one has liberated oneself from society, group, race, family, and from all separative conditioning, and has become an undivided, integral being, the problems which now torment the citizens of various particularized states will have utterly lost their significance. As long as man belongs to particular groups, classes, creeds, there cannot be love, there must be antagonism, war.

* * *

Individual thought is influenced, limited, by society, by inherited and acquired tendencies. These tendencies are revealed in relationship, superficial and intimate. By becoming aware of them and not through mere self-analysis does thought free itself without falling into other forms of narrowness, pettiness. This requires interested watchfulness and clear discernment. This discernment is not comparative, nor is it the result of choice. Intellect, the instrument of craving, is itself narrow, conditioned, and therefore what it chooses is bound to be also limited.

We need things for our physical existence, this need is natural and not harmful, but when things become psychological necessities, then begin greed, envy, imitation, from which conflict and other unnatural desires ensue. If we "need" people, then there is a dependence upon them. This dependence shows itself in possessiveness, fear, domination. When we use people, as we use inanimate things, consciously or unconsciously, to satisfy our craving for comfort or security, true human relationship ceases. Then relationship, superficial or deep, is no longer a process of self-revelation or of liberation.

* * *

Love is the only lasting answer to our human problems. Do not divide love artificially as the love of God and the love of man. There is only love, but love is hedged about by various barriers. Compassion, forgiveness, generosity, and kindliness cannot exist if there is no love. Without love, all virtues become cruel and destructive. Hate, envy, and ill will, prevent completeness of thought-emotion, and in this completeness alone can there be compassion, forgiveness.

Relationship acts as a mirror to reflect all the states of our being if we allow it; but we do not allow it as we want to conceal ourselves; revelation is painful. In relationship, if we become aware, both the unconscious and the conscious states are revealed. This self-revelation ceases when we use people as needs, when we depend upon them, when we possess them. Mostly, relationship is used to cover our inner poverty; we try to enrich this psychological poverty by clinging to each other, flattering each other, limiting love to each other, and so on. There is conflict in relationship, but instead of understanding its cause and so transcending it, we try to escape from it and seek gratification elsewhere.

We use our relationship with people, with society, as we use things—to cover up our shallowness. How is one to overcome this shallowness? All overcoming is never transcending, for that which is overcome only takes another form.

Poverty of being is revealed when we try to overcome it by covering it up with possessions, with the worship of success, and even with virtues. Then things, property, come to have great significance; then class, social position, country, pride of race assume great importance and have to be maintained at all costs; then name, family, and their continuance become vital.

Or we try to cover up this emptiness with ideas, beliefs, creeds, fancies; then opinion, goodwill, and experience of others take on powerful import; then ceremonies, priests, Masters, saviors become essential and destroy self-reliance; then authority is worshipped.

Thus the fear of what one is creates illusion, and poverty of being continues. But if one becomes intensely aware of these indications in oneself, both in the conscious and the unconscious, then through strenuous discernment there comes about a different state which has no relation to the poverty of being. To overcome shallowness is to continue to be shallow.

Self-analysis and awareness are two different things; the one is morbid, but awareness is joyous. Self-analysis takes place after action is past; out of that analysis mind creates a pattern to which a future action is forced to conform. Thus there comes about a rigidity of thought and action. Self-analysis is death and awareness is life. Self-analysis only leads to the creation of pattern and imitation, and so there is no release from bondage, from frustration. Awareness is at the moment of action; if one is aware, then one understands comprehensively, as a whole, the cause and effect of action, the imitative process of fear, its reactions, and so on. This awareness frees thought from those causes and influences which limit and hold it without creating further bondages, and so thought becomes deeply pliable, which is to be deathless. Self-analysis or introspection takes place before or after action, thus preparing for the future and limiting it. Awareness is a constant process of liberation.

* * *

We should approach life, not from the point of "What can I know?" but "What can I do?'' The path of ''What can I know?'' leads to the worship of authority, fear, and illusion; but in understanding ''What can I do?'' there is self-reliance which alone brings forth wisdom.

From what source does our thought process come? Why do I think that I am separate? Am I really separate? Before we can transcend what we are, we must first understand ourselves. So what am I? Can I know this for myself or must I rely for this knowledge on others? To rely on others is to wallow in opinion; the acceptance of opinion, information, is based on like and dislike which lead to illusion. Am I really separate? Or is there only a variation, a modification of a central craving or fear, expressing itself in different ways? Does the expression of the same fundamental craving, ignorance, hate, fear, affection in different ways make us truly different, truly individuals? As long as we are expressing ignorance, however differently, we are essentially the same. Then why do we separate ourselves into nations, classes, families, and why do we concern ourselves with our soul, our immortality, our unity? As long as we cling to the separateness of the expression of ignorance, of fear, there can never be the lasting unity of mankind.

Separateness is an illusion and a vanity. To think of myself as separate, different in consciousness, is to identify myself with fundamental ignorance; to cling to my achievement, my work, or my soul is to continue in illusion. What are we? We are the result of our parents, who were, like their parents, influenced and limited by climatic, social, and psychological values based on ignorance, fear, and craving. Our parents passed on to us those values. We are the result of the past; our forefathers' beliefs, ideas, hopes, in combination with the present action and reaction, are our thoughts. We cherish illusion and try to find unity, hope, love, in it. Illusion can

never create human unity nor awaken that love which alone can bring peace. Love cannot be transmitted, but we can experience its immensity if we can become free of our prejudices, fears, greed, and craving.

We are concerned with things, people, and personal continuity—continuity in different forms; continuity through things, property, family, race, nationality; continuity through ideals, beliefs, dogmas. The craving for personal immortality breeds fear, illusion, and the worship of authority. When the craving for personal immortality ceases, in all its forms, there is a state of deathlessness.

What is our mind? What is our thought process? What are the contents of our consciousnesses and how have they been created? Perception, contact, sensation, and reflection lead to the process of like and dislike, attachment and nonattachment, self and not-self. Mind is the outcome of craving; and intellect, the power to discern, to choose, is influenced and limited by the past in combination with the present action and reaction. Thus the instrument of discernment itself is cunningly perverted. Thought must free itself from the past, from the accumulations of self-protective instincts; intellect must make straight its own wanton crookedness.

* * *

What is the origin of our thinking? Seeing, contacting, sensing, reflecting. Like and dislike, pleasure and pain, the many pairs of opposites are the outcome of reflection; the desire for the continuance of the one and the denial of the other is part of reflection. Sensation, craving, dominates most of our thinking. Our thought is influenced and limited by the past generations of people who in their suffering, in their joys, in their aspirations, in their escapes, in their fear of death, in their longing for continuity created ideas, images, symbols, which gave them hope, assurance. These they have passed on to us. When we use the word *soul,* it is their word to convey that intense longing for continuity, for something permanent, enduring beyond the transiency of the physical, of the material. Because we also crave for certainty, security, continuity, we cling to that word and all that it represents. So our consciousness—both the conscious and the subconscious—is the repository of ideas, values, images, symbols of the race, of the past generations. Our daily thought and action are controlled by the past, by the concealed motives, memories, and hidden cravings. In all this there is no freedom but only continued imitation caused by fear.

Within consciousness, there are two opposing forces at work which create duality—want and nonwant, pain and pleasure, outgoing desires and refraining desires. Instincts, motives, values, prejudices, and passions control and direct the conscious.

Is there, in consciousness, any part that is not contaminated by the past? Is there anything original, uncorrupted, in our consciousness? Have we not to free thought from the past, from instincts, from symbols, images, in order to understand that which is incorruptible, untrammelled?

The known cannot understand the unknown; death cannot understand life. Light and darkness cannot exist together. God, reality, is not to be realized through the known. What we are is of the past in combination with the present action and reaction according to various forms of influence, which narrows down thought, and through this limitation we try to understand that which is beyond all transiency. Can thought free itself from the personal, from the 'I'? Can thought make itself anew, original, capable of direct experience? If it can, then there is the realization of the eternal.

*　*　*

What is the content of consciousness? Both the conscious and the subconscious tendencies, values, memories, fears, and so on. The past, the hidden causes, control the present. Is there not in us, in spite of this limited consciousness, a force, a something, that is unconditioned? To assume that there is, is a part of our past influence; we have been brought up, through many generations, to think and believe and hope that there is. This tradition, this memory, is part of our racial heredity, part of our ignorance, but also, merely to deny it is not to discover for ourselves if there is. To assert or to deny, to believe or not to believe that there is an uncontaminated, spiritual essence, unconditioned in us, is to place a barrier to our discovery of what is true.

There is suffering, conflict, between want and nonwant, between the will of outgoing desires and the will to restrain. Of this conflict we are all conscious.

When we do not understand the makeup of our background, the cause of our tendencies and limitations, experience only further strengthens them; but in becoming aware of them in our daily thought and action, experience acts as a liberating force.

Neither postponement nor trying to seek an immediate solution to our human problems can free thought from bondage. Postponement implies thoughtlessness and this sluggishness produces comforting theories, beliefs, and further complication and suffering; and if thought is concerned with the immediate now, with the idea that we live but once, then there is restlessness, haste, and a shallowness that destroys understanding. But without imagining a future or clinging to the past, we can understand the fullness of each flowing moment. Then *what is* is immortal.

Masters, gurus, teachers cannot help to free thought from its own self-imposed bondage and suffering; neither ceremonies, nor priests, nor organizations can liberate thought from its attachments, fears, cravings;

these may force it into a new mold and shape it, but thought can free itself only through its own critical awareness and self-reliance.

Extrasensory perception, clairvoyance, occult powers, cannot free thought from confusion and misery; sensitive awareness of our thoughts and motives, from which spring our speech and action, is the beginning of lasting understanding and love. Mere self-control, discipline, self-punishment, or renunciation cannot liberate thought; but constant awareness and pliability give clarity and strength. Only in becoming aware of the cause of ignorance, in understanding the process of craving and its dual and opposing values, is there freedom from suffering. This discerning awareness must begin in our life of relationship with things, people, and ideas, with our own hidden thoughts and daily action.

* * *

The way we think makes our life either complete or contradictory and unbalanced. Through the awareness of craving, with its complex process, there comes an understanding which brings detachment and serenity. Detachment or serenity is not an end in itself. In this world of frenzied buying and selling, whose economy is based on craving, unless thought is persistently aware, greed and envy bring the confusing and conflicting problems of possessions, attachment, and competition. Our private thoughts and motives can bring either harmony in our relationship or disturbance and pain. It depends on each one what he makes of relationship with another or with society. There can never be self-isolation, however much one may crave for it; relationship is ever continuous; to be is to be related.

The trembling and wavering thought is difficult to steady; mere control does not lead to understanding. Interest alone creates natural, spontaneous adjustment and control. If thought becomes aware of itself, it will perceive that it goes from one superficial interest to another, and merely to withdraw from one and try to concentrate on another does not lead to understanding and love. Thought must become aware of the causes of its various interests, and by understanding them, there comes a natural, concentrated interest in that which is most intelligent and true.

Thought moves from certainty to certainty, from the known to the known, from one substitution to another, and thus it is never still, it is ever pursuing, ever wandering; this chattering of the mind destroys creative understanding and love, but these cannot be craved for. They come into being when thought becomes aware of its own process, of its cravings, fears, substitutions, justifications, and illusions. Through constant, discerning awareness, thought naturally becomes creative and still. In that stillness there is immeasurable bliss.

We have all many and peculiar problems of our own; our craving to solve them only hinders the comprehension of the problems. We must have that rare disinterested awareness which alone brings understanding. When death causes us great sorrow, in our eagerness to overcome that sorrow, we accept theories, beliefs, in the hope of finding comfort which only becomes a bondage. This comfort, though satisfying for a passing moment, does not free thought from sorrow; it is only covered up and its cause continues. Likewise when one feels frustrated, instead of craving for fulfillment, one must understand what it is that feels itself frustrated. There will be frustration as long as there is craving; instead of understanding what is deeply implied in craving, we struggle anxiously to fulfill ourselves, and so the ache of frustration continues.

* * *

These discussions are not meant to be for intellectual amusement. We have discussed together in order to clear our thought so as to be able to apply ourselves more acutely and disinterestedly to the problems of our everyday life. It is only through disinterested application, through strenuous and discerning awareness, and not through following this or that belief, ideology, leader, or group that thought can liberate itself from those self-imposed bondages and influences.

Being incomplete, one craves for completeness, which is only a substitution, but if one understands the causes of incompleteness, then there comes a freedom through that understanding, the ecstasy of which is not to be described or compared. We must begin low to climb high, we must begin near to go far.

We all have to live in this world; we cannot escape from it. We must understand it and not run away from it into illusory comforts, hopeful theories, and fascinating dreams. We are the world and we must intelligently and creatively understand it. We have created this world of devastating hate, this world that is torn apart by beliefs and ideologies, by religions and gnawing cults, by leaders and their followers, by economic barriers and nationalities. We have created this world through our individual craving and fear, through our ambition and ignorance. We ourselves must change radically, free ourselves of these bondages, so that we can help to create a truly sane and happy world.

Then let us live happily without attachment and envy; let us love without possessiveness and be without ill will towards anyone; do not let us separate ourselves into narrow and conflicting groups. Thus through our own strenuous and constant awareness will our thought be transformed from the limited into the complete.

September 9–21, 1940

Ojai, California, 1944

✳

First Talk in The Oak Grove

Amidst so much confusion and sorrow it is essential to find creative understanding of ourselves, for without it no relationship is possible. Only through right thinking can there be understanding. Neither leaders nor a new set of values nor a blueprint can bring about this creative understanding; only through our own right effort can there be right understanding.

How is it possible then to find this essential understanding? From where shall we start to discover what is real, what is true, in all this conflagration, confusion, and misery? Is it not important to find out for ourselves how to think rightly about war and peace, about economic and social conditions, about our relationship to our fellow men? Surely there is a difference between right thinking and right or conditioned thought. We may be able to produce in ourselves imitatively right thought, but such thought is not right thinking. Right or conditioned thought is uncreative. But when we know how to think rightly for ourselves, which is to be living, dynamic, then it is possible to bring about a new and happier culture.

I would like during these talks to develop what seems to me to be the process of right thinking so that each one of us is truly creative, and not merely enclosed in a series of ideas or prejudices. How shall we then begin to discover for ourselves what is right thinking? Without right thinking there is no possibility of happiness. Without right thinking our actions, our behavior, our affections have no basis. Right thinking is not to be discovered through books, through attending a few talks, or by merely listening to some people's ideas of what right thinking is. Right thinking is to be discovered for ourselves through ourselves.

Right thinking comes with self-knowledge. Without self-knowledge there is no right thinking. Without knowing yourself, what you think and what you feel cannot be true. The root of all understanding lies in understanding yourself. If you can find out what are the causes of your thought-feeling, and from that discovery know how to think-feel, then there is the beginning of understanding. Without knowing yourself, the accumulation of ideas, the acceptance of beliefs and theories have no basis. Without knowing yourself you will ever be caught in uncertainty, depending on moods, on circumstances. Without knowing yourself fully you cannot think rightly. Surely this is obvious. If I do not know what my motives, my intentions, my background, my private thoughts-feelings are, how can I agree or disagree with another? How can I estimate or establish my relationship with another? How can I discover anything of life if I do not know myself? And to know myself is an enormous task requiring constant observation, meditative awareness.

This is our first task even before the problem of war and peace, of economic and social conflicts, of death and immortality. These questions will arise, they are bound to arise, but in discovering ourselves, in understanding ourselves, these questions will be rightly answered. So, those who are really serious in these matters must begin with themselves in order to understand the world of which they are a part. Without understanding yourself you cannot understand the whole.

Self-knowledge is the beginning of wisdom. Self-knowledge is cultivated through the individual's search of himself. I am not putting the individual in opposition to the mass. They are not antithetical. You, the individual, are the mass, the result of the mass. In us, as you will discover if you go into it deeply, are both the many and the particular. It is as a stream that is constantly flowing, leaving little eddies, and these eddies we call individuality, but they are the result of this constant flow of water. Your thoughts-feelings, those mental-emotional activities—are they not the result of the past, of what we call the many? Have you not similar thoughts-feelings as your neighbor?

So when I talk of the individual, I am not putting him in opposition to the mass. On the contrary, I want to remove this antagonism. This opposing antagonism between the mass and the you, the individual, creates confusion and conflict, ruthlessness and misery. But if we can understand how the individual, the you, is part of the whole, not only mystically but actually, then we shall free ourselves happily and spontaneously from the greater part of the desire to compete, to succeed, to deceive, to oppress, to be ruthless, or to become a follower or a leader. Then we will regard the problem of existence quite dif-

ferently. And it is important to understand this deeply. As long as we regard ourselves as individuals, apart from the whole, competing, obstructing, opposing, sacrificing the many for the particular or the particular for the many, all those problems that arise out of this conflicting antagonism will have no happy and enduring solution; for they are the result of wrong thinking-feeling.

Now, when I talk about the individual, I am not putting him in opposition to the mass. What am I? I am a result; I am the result of the past, of innumerable layers of the past, of a series of causes-effects. And how can I be opposed to the whole, the past, when I am the result of all that? If I, who am the mass, the whole, if I do not understand myself, not only what is outside my skin, objectively, but subjectively, inside the skin, how can I understand another, the world? To understand oneself requires kindly and tolerant detachment. If you do not understand yourself, you will not understand anything else; you may have great ideals, beliefs, and formulations, but they will have no reality. They will be delusions. So you must know yourself to understand the present and through the present, the past. From the known present, the hidden layers of the past are discovered and this discovery is liberating and creative.

To understand ourselves requires objective, kindly, dispassionate study of ourselves, ourselves being the organism as a whole— our body, our feelings, our thoughts. They are not separate, they are interrelated. It is only when we understand the organism as a whole that we can go beyond and discover still further, greater, vaster things. But without this primary understanding, without laying right foundation for right thinking, we cannot proceed to greater heights.

To bring about in each one of us the capacity to discover what is true becomes essential, for what is discovered is liberating, creative. For what is discovered is true. That is, if we merely conform to a pattern of what we ought to be or yield to a craving, it does produce certain results which are conflicting, confusing, but in the process of our study of ourselves, we are on a voyage of self-discovery, which brings joy.

There is a surety in negative rather than positive thinking-feeling. We have assumed in a positive manner what we are, or we have cultivated positively our ideas on other people's or on our own formulations. And hence we depend on authority, on circumstances, hoping thereby to establish a series of positive ideas and actions. Whereas if you examine you will see there is agreement in negation; there is surety in negative thinking, which is the highest form of thinking. When once you have found true negation and agreement in negation, then you can build further in positiveness.

The discovery that lies in self-knowledge is arduous, for the beginning and the end is in us. To seek happiness, love, hope, outside of us leads to illusion, to sorrow; to find happiness, peace, joy within requires self-knowledge. We are slaves to the immediate pressures and demands of the world, and we are drawn away by all that and dissipate our energies in all that, and so we have little time to study ourselves. To be deeply cognizant of our motives, of our desires to achieve, to become, demands constant, inward awareness. Without understanding ourselves, superficial devices of economic and social reform, however necessary and beneficial, will not produce unity in the world but only greater confusion and misery.

Many of us think that economic reform of one kind or another will bring peace to the world; or social reform or one specialized religion conquering all others will bring happiness to man. I believe there are something like eight hundred or more religious sects in this country, each competing, proselytizing. Do you think competitive religion will bring peace, unity, and happiness to mankind? Do you think any specialized religion, whether it be Hinduism, Buddhism, or Christianity, will bring peace? Or must we set aside all specialized religions and discover reality for ourselves? When we see the world blasted by bombs and feel the horrors that are going on in it; when the world is broken up by separate religions, nationalities, races, ideologies, what is the answer to all this? We may not just go on living briefly and dying and hope some good will come out of it. We cannot leave it to others to bring happiness and peace to mankind; for mankind is ourselves, each one of us. Where does the solution lie, except in ourselves? To discover the real answer requires deep thought-feeling, and few of us are willing to solve this misery. If each one of us considers this problem as springing from within and is not merely driven helplessly along in this appalling confusion and misery, then we shall find a simple and direct answer.

In studying and so in understanding ourselves, there will come clarity and order. And there can be clarity only in self-knowledge, which nurtures right thinking. Right thinking comes before right action. If we become self-aware and so cultivate self-knowledge from which springs right thinking, then we shall create a mirror in ourselves which will reflect, without distortion, all our thoughts-feelings. To be so self-aware is extremely difficult as our mind is used to wandering and being distracted. Its wanderings, its distractions are of its own interests and creations. In understanding these—not merely pushing them aside—comes self-knowledge and right thinking. It is only through inclusion and not by exclusion, not through approbation or condemnation or comparison, that understanding comes.

Question: What is my right in my relationship to the world?

KRISHNAMURTI: It is an interesting and instructive question. The questioner seems to put himself in opposition to the world and then asks himself what are his rights in relationship to it. Is he separate from the world? Is he not part of the world? Has he any right apart from the whole? Will he, by setting himself apart, understand the world? By giving importance to and strengthening the part, will he comprehend the whole? The part is not the whole, but to understand the whole, the part must not set itself in opposition to it. In understanding the part, the whole is comprehended. When the individual is in opposition to the world, then he claims his rights; but why should he put himself in opposition to it? The attitude of opposition, of the 'I' and the not 'I', prevents comprehension. Is he not part of the whole? Are not his problems the problems of the world? Are not his conflicts, confusions, and miseries those of his neighbor, near or far? When he becomes aware of himself, he will know that he is part of the whole. He is the result of the past with its fears, hopes, greeds, aspirations, and so on. This result seeks a right in its relationship to the whole. Has it any right so long as it is envious, greedy, ruthless? It is only when he does not regard himself as an individual but as a result and a part of the whole that he will know that freedom in which there is no opposition, duality. But as long as he is of the world with its ignorance, cruelty, sensuality, then he has no relationship apart from it.

We should not use the word *individual* at all, nor the words *mine* and *yours* because they have no meaning, fundamentally. I am the result of my father and my mother and the environmental influence of the country and society. If I put myself in opposition, there is no understanding; the combination of opposites does not produce understanding. But if I become aware and observe the ways of duality, then I will begin to feel the new

freedom from opposites. The world is divided into the opposites, the white and the dark, the good and the bad, mine and yours, and so on. In duality there is no understanding, each antithesis contains its own opposite. Our difficulty lies in thinking of these problems anew, to think of the world and yourself from a different point of view altogether, observing silently, without identifying and comparing. The ideas which you think are the result of what others have thought in combination with the present. Real uniqueness lies in the discovery of what is true and being in that discovery. This uniqueness, joy, and liberation which comes from this discovery is not to be found in the pride of possessions, of name, physical attributes, and tendencies. True freedom comes through self-knowledge which brings about right thinking; through self-knowledge there is the discovery of the true, which alone puts an end to our ignorance and sorrow.

Through self-awareness and self-knowledge peace is found, and in that serenity there is immortality.

May 14, 1944

Second Talk in The Oak Grove

Last Sunday I was trying to explain what is right thinking and how to set about it. I said that unless there is self-awareness, self-knowledge of all the motives, intentions, and instincts, thought-feeling has no true foundation, and that without this foundation there is no right thinking. Self-knowledge is the beginning of understanding. And as we are—the world is. That is, if we are greedy, envious, competitive, our society will be competitive, envious, greedy, which brings misery and war. The state is what we are. To bring about order and peace, we must begin with ourselves and not with society, not with the state, for the world is ourselves. And it is not selfish to think that each one must first understand and change himself to help the world. You cannot help another unless you know yourself. Through self-awareness one will find that in oneself is the whole.

If we would bring about a sane and happy society, we must begin with ourselves and not with another, not outside of ourselves but with ourselves. Instead of giving importance to names, labels, terms—which bring confusion—we ought to rid the mind of these and look at ourselves dispassionately. Until we understand ourselves and go beyond ourselves, exclusiveness in every form will exist. We see about us and in ourselves exclusive desires and actions which result in narrow relationship.

Before we can understand what kind of effort to make in order to know ourselves, we must become aware of the kind of effort we are now making. Our effort now consists, does it not, in constant becoming, in escaping from one opposite to another? We live in a series of conflicts of action and response, of wanting and not wanting. Our effort is spent in becoming and not becoming. We live in a state of duality. How does this duality arise? If we can understand this then perhaps we can transcend it and discover a different state of being. How does this painful conflict arise within us between good and bad, hope and fear, love and hate, the 'I' and the not 'I'? Are they not created by our craving to become? This craving expresses itself in sensuality, in worldliness, or in seeking personal fame or immortality. In trying to become, do we not create the opposite? Unless we understand this conflict of the opposites, all effort will bring about only different and changing sorrowful conditions. So we must use right means to transcend this conflict. Wrong means will product wrong ends; only right means will produce right ends. If we want peace in the world, we must use peaceful methods, and yet we seem invariably to use wrong methods hoping to produce right ends.

Unless we understand this problem of opposites with its conflicts and miseries, our efforts will be in vain. Through self-awareness, craving to become, the cause of conflict, must be observed and understood; but understanding ceases if there is identification, if there is acceptance or denial or comparison. With kindly dispassion, craving must be deeply understood and so transcended. For a mind that is caught in craving, in duality, cannot comprehend reality. Mind must be extremely still, and this stillness cannot be induced, disciplined, compelled through any technique. This stillness comes about only through the understanding of conflict. And you cannot compel conflict to cease. You cannot by will bring it to an end. You may cover it up, hide it away, but it will come up again and again. A disease must be cured, but to treat merely the symptom is of little use. Only when we become aware of the cause of conflict, understand and transcend it, can we experience that which is. To become aware is to think out, feel out the opposites as much as you can, as widely and deeply as possible, without acceptance or denial, with choiceless awareness. In this extensional awareness you will find there comes a new kind of will or a new feeling, a new understanding which is not begotten out of the opposites.

Right thinking ceases when thought-feeling is bound, held in the opposites. If you become aware of your thoughts and feelings, your actions and responses, you will find that they are caught in the conflict of opposites. As each thought-feeling arises, think it out feel it out fully, without identification. This extensional awareness can take place only when you are not denying, when you are not rejecting nor accepting nor comparing. Through this extensional awareness there will be discovered a state of being which is free from the conflict of all opposites.

This creative understanding is to be discovered, and it is this understanding which frees the mind from craving. And it is this extensional awareness in which there is no becoming, with its hope and fear, achievement and failure, with its self-enclosing pain and pleasure, that will free thought-feeling from ignorance and sorrow.

Question: How is it possible to learn real concentration?

KRISHNAMURTI: In this question many things are involved, so one must be patient and listen to the whole of it. What is real meditation? Is it not the beginning of self-knowledge? Without self-knowledge can there be true concentration, right meditation? Meditation is not possible unless you begin to know yourself. To know yourself you must become meditatively aware, which requires a peculiar kind of concentration—not the concentration of exclusiveness which most of us indulge in when we think we are meditating. Right meditation is the understanding of oneself with all one's problems of uncertainty and conflict, misery and affliction.

I suppose some of us have meditated or have tried to concentrate. What happens when we are trying to concentrate? Many thoughts come, one after the other, crowding, uninvited. We try to fix our thought upon one object or idea or feeling and try to exclude all other thoughts and feelings. This process of concentration or one-pointedness is generally considered necessary for meditation. This exclusive method will inevitably fail, for it maintains the conflict of the opposites; it may momentarily succeed, but as long as duality exists in thought-feeling, concentration must lead to narrowness, obstinacy, and illusion.

Control of thought does not bring about right thinking; mere control of thought is not right meditation. Surely we must first find out why the mind wanders at all. It wanders or is repetitive either because of interest or of habit or of laziness or because thought-feeling has not completed itself. If it is of interest then you will not be able to subdue it; though you may succeed momentarily, thought will return to its interests and hence its wanderings. So you must pursue that interest, thinking it out, feeling it out, fully, and thus understand the whole content of that interest, however trivial and stupid. If this wandering is the result of habit, then it is very indicative; it indicates, does it not, that your mind is caught up in mere habit, in mere patterns of thought and so is not thinking at all. A mind that is caught up in habit or in laziness indicates that it is functioning mechanically, thoughtlessly, and of what value is thoughtlessness, though well under control? When thought is repetitive, then it indicates that thought-feeling has not fulfilled itself, and until it has it will go on recurring. Through becoming aware of your thoughts-feelings, you will find there is a general disturbance, a stirring up; from the awareness of the causes of disturbances, there comes a self-knowledge and right thinking which are the basis for true meditation. Without self-knowledge, self-awareness, there is no meditation, and without meditation there is no self-knowledge.

True concentration comes with self-knowledge. You can create noble fixations and wholly be absorbed in them, but this does not bring about understanding. This does not lead to the discovery of the real. It may produce kindliness or certain desirable qualities, but noble fixations only further strengthen illusion, and a mind that is caught in the opposites cannot understand the whole. Instead of developing the exclusive, contracting process, let your thought-feeling flow, understand every flutter, every movement of it. Think it out, feel it out as widely and deeply as possible. Then you will discover that out of this awareness there comes extensional concentration, a meditation which is no longer a becoming but a being. But this extensional awareness is strenuous, to be carried on throughout the day and not only during a set period. You must become strenuous and experiment, for it is not to be picked out of books or through attending meetings or following a technique. It comes through self-awareness, through self-knowledge. The real significance of what meditation is becomes of enormous importance. This process of self-awareness is not to be limited to certain periods of the day but to be continuous. Out of this meditative awareness comes deep stillness in which alone there is the real. This stillness of the mind is not the result of exclusiveness, of contraction, of setting aside of every thought and feeling and concentrating on making the mind still. You can enforce stillness on the mind, but it is the stillness of death, uncreative, stagnant, and in that state it is not possible to discover that which is.

Question: How is one to be free from any problem which is disturbing?

KRISHNAMURTI: To understand any problem we must give our undivided attention to it. Both the conscious and the unconscious, or the inner mind, must take part in solving it, but most of us unfortunately try to dissolve it superficially, that is, with that little part of the mind which we call the conscious mind, with the intellect only. Now our consciousness or our mindfeeling is like an iceberg, the greater part of it hidden deep down, only a fraction of it showing outside. We are acquainted with that superficial layer, but it is a confused acquaintance; of the greater, the deep unconscious, the inner part,

we are hardly aware. Or, if we are, it becomes conscious through dreams, through occasional intimations, but those dreams and hints we translate, interpreting according to our prejudices and to our ever-limited intellectual capacities. And so those intimations lose their deep, pure significance.

If we wish to really understand our problem, then we must first clear up the confusion in the conscious, in the superficial mind, by thinking and feeling it out as widely and intelligently as possible, comprehensively and dispassionately. Then into this conscious clearing, open and alert, the inner mind can project itself. When the contents of the many layers of consciousness have been thus gathered and assimilated, only then does the problem cease to be.

Let us take an example. Most of us are educated in nationalistic spirit. We are brought up to love our country in opposition to another, to regard our people as superior to another and so on. This superiority or pride is implanted in the mind from childhood and we accept it, live with it and condone it. With that thin layer which we call the conscious mind let us understand this problem and its deeper significance. We accept it first of all through environmental influences and are conditioned by it. Also this nationalistic spirit feeds our vanity. The assertion that we are of this or that race or country feeds our petty, small, poor egos, puffs them out like sails, and we are ready to defend, to kill or be maimed for our country, race, and ideology. In identifying ourselves with what we consider to be the greater, we hope to become greater. But we still remain poor, it is only the label that looms large and powerful. This nationalistic spirit is used for economic purposes and is used, also, through hatred and fear to unite one people against another. Thus when we become aware of this problem and its implications, we perceive its effects: war, misery, starvation, confusion. In worshipping the part, which is idolatrous, we deny the whole. This denial of human unity breeds endless wars and brutalities, economic and social division and tyranny.

We understand all this intellectually, with that thin layer which we call the conscious mind, but we are still caught up in tradition, opinion, convenience, fear, and so on. Until the deep layers are exposed and understood, we are not free from the disease of nationalism, patriotism.

Thus in examining this problem, we have cleared the superficial layer of the conscious into which the deeper layers can flow. This flow is made stronger through constant awareness—by watching every response, every stimulation of nationalism or of any other hindrance. Each response, however small, must be thought out, felt out, widely and deeply. Thus you will soon perceive that the problem is dissolved and the nationalistic spirit has withered away. All conflicts and miseries can be understood and dissolved in this manner—to clear the thin layer of the conscious by thinking out and feeling out the problem as comprehensively as possible; into this clarity, into this comparative quietness, the deeper motives, intentions, fears, and so on can project themselves; as they appear examine them, study them and so understand them. Thus the hindrance, the conflict, the sorrow is deeply and wholly understood and dissolved.

Question: Please elucidate the "surety in negation" idea. You spoke of negative and positive thought. Do you mean when we are positive, we make statements that are valueless because they are hidebound and smug; while when we are negative, we are open to thought because we are bankrupt of traditions and able to inquire into the new? Or do you mean we must be positive in that there is no choice between the true and the false, and that negation means becoming part of compromise?

KRISHNAMURTI: I said that in negation there is surety. Let us expand this idea. When we become aware of ourselves, we find that we are in a state of self-contradiction, of wanting and not wanting, of loving and hating, and so on. Thoughts and actions born of this self-contradiction are considered to be positive, but is it positive when thought contradicts itself? Because of our religious training we are certain that we must not kill, but we find ourselves supporting or finding reasons for killing when the state demands; one thought denies the other, and so there is no thinking at all. In a state of self-contradiction thought ceases and there is only ignorance. So let us discover if we think at all or exist in a state of self-contradiction in which thinking ceases to be.

If we look into ourselves, we realize that we live in a state of contradiction, and how can such a state be positive? For that which contradicts itself ceases to be. Not knowing ourselves profoundly, how can there be agreement or disagreement, assertion or denial? In this self-contradictory state how can there be surety? How can we in this state assume that we are right or wrong? We cannot assume anything, can we? But our morality, our positive action is based on this self-contradiction, and so we are incessantly active, craving for peace and yet creating war, longing for happiness and yet causing sorrow, loving and yet hating. If our thinking is self-contradictory, and therefore nonexistent, there is only one possible approach for understanding, which is the state of nonbecoming, a state which may seem to be negation, but in which there is the highest possibility.

Humility is born of negation, and without humility there is no understanding. In negative comprehension we begin to perceive the possibility of surety of agreement and so of greater relationship and of highest thinking. When the mind is creatively empty—not when it is positively directing—there is reality. All great discoveries are born in this creative emptiness, and there can only be creative emptiness when self-contradiction ceases. As long as craving exists there will be self-contradiction. Therefore instead of approaching life positively, as most of us do, giving rise to the many miseries, brutalities, conflicts of which we know so well, why not approach it negatively, which is not really negation?

When I use the terms positive and negative, I am not using them in opposition to each other. When we begin to understand what we call the positive, which is the outcome of ignorance, then we shall find that from this there comes a surety in negation. In trying to understand the ever-contradictory nature of the self, of the "me" and the "mine", with its positive craving and denial, pursuit and death, there comes into being the still, creative emptiness. It is not the result of positive or negative action, but a state of nonduality. When the mind-heart is still, creatively empty, then only is there reality.

Question: You said a man who meets anger with anger becomes anger. Do you mean that when we fight cruelty with the weapons of cruelty, we too become the enemy?—yet if we do not protect ourselves the bandit fells us.

KRISHNAMURTI: Surely that thing which you fight you become. (Must we explain this too? All right.) If I am angry and you meet me with anger, what is the result—more anger. You have become that which I am. If I am evil and you fight me with evil means, then you also become evil, however righteous you may feel. If I am brutal and you use brutal methods to overcome me, then you

become brutal like me. And this we have done thousands of years. Surely there is a different approach than to meet hate by hate. If I use violent methods to quell anger in myself, then I am using wrong means for a right end, and thereby the right end ceases to be. In this there is no understanding; there is no transcending anger. Anger is to be studied tolerantly and understood; it is not to be overcome through violent means. Anger may be the result of many causes, and without comprehending them there is no escape from anger.

We have created the enemy, the bandit, and through becoming ourselves the enemy— this in no way brings about an end to enmity. We have to understand the cause of enmity and cease to feed it by our thought, feeling and action. This is an arduous task demanding constant self-awareness and intelligent pliability, for what we are the society, the state is. The enemy and the friend are the outcome of our thought and action. We are responsible for creating enmity, and so it is more important to be aware of our thought and action than to be concerned with the foe and the friend, for right thinking puts an end to division. Love transcends the friend and the enemy.

May 21, 1944

Third Talk in The Oak Grove

In my first talk I tried to explain that right thinking can come only with self-knowledge. Without right thinking you cannot know what is true. Without knowing yourself, your relationship, your action, your everyday existence has no true basis. Our existence is a state of opposition and contradiction, and any thought and action that spring from them can never be true. And before we can understand the world, our conduct and relationship with another, we must know ourselves. When the individual puts himself in opposition to the mass, he is acting in ignorance, in fear, for he is the result of the mass, he is the result of the past. We cannot separate ourselves or put ourselves in opposition to anything if we wish to understand it.

In the second talk we somewhat touched upon thought putting itself in opposition, thereby creating duality. We should understand this before we begin to be concerned with our everyday thought and activity. If we do not understand what it is that brings about this dualism, this instinctive opposition as yours and mine, we shall not understand the meaning of our conflict. We are aware in our life of dualism and its constant conflict— wanting and not wanting, heaven and hell, the state and the citizen, light and darkness. Does not dualism arise from craving? In the will to become, to be, is there not also the will of not becoming? In positive craving there is also negation, and so thought-feeling is caught up in the conflict of opposites. Through the opposites there is no escape from conflict, from sorrow.

The desire to become, without understanding duality, is a vain struggle; the conflict of the opposites ceases if we can grapple with the problem of craving. Craving is the root of all ignorance and sorrow, and there is no freedom from ignorance and sorrow save in the abandonment of craving. It is not to be set aside through mere will, for will is part of craving; it is not to be set aside through denial, for such denial is the outcome of opposites. Craving can be dissolved only through becoming aware of its many ways and expressions; through tolerant observation and understanding it is transcended. In the flame of understanding craving is consumed.

Let us examine the desire to become virtuous. Is there virtue when there is consciousness of vice? Do you become virtuous by putting yourself in opposition to vice or is virtue a state which is not anchored in the opposites? Virtue comes into being when there is freedom from opposites. Is generosity, kindliness, love opposite to greed, envy, hate, or is love something that is beyond and above all contradictions? By putting ourselves in opposition to violence, will there be peace? Or is peace something that is beyond, transcending both the opposites? Is not true virtue a negation of becoming? Virtue is the freedom from craving.

We must become aware of this complex problem of duality through constant watchfulness, not to correct but to understand; for if we do not understand how to cultivate right thinking, from which comes right endeavor, then we shall be continually developing opposites with their endless conflicts.

Does right thinking come through the conflict of opposites, or does it come into being when the cause of opposites, craving, is thought out, felt out and so understood? Freedom from the opposites is only possible when thought-feeling is able to observe without acceptance, denial, or comparison its actions and responses; out of this awareness comes a new feeling, a new understanding which is not anchored in the opposites. Thought-feeling that is caught in duality is not capable of understanding the timeless. So, from the very beginning of our thinking, we must lay the right foundation for true endeavor, for right means lead to right ends and wrong means will produce wrong ends. Wrong means will not at any time take us to right ends, only in right means lie right ends.

Question: I find it extremely difficult to understand myself. How am I to begin?

KRISHNAMURTI: Is it not very important that one must understand oneself above everything else? For if we do not understand ourselves, we shall not understand anything else, for the root of understanding lies in ourselves. In understanding myself, I shall understand my relationship with another, with the world; for in me, as in each one, is the whole; I am the result of the whole, of the past. This concern to understand oneself may appear superficially to be egocentric, selfish; but if you consider it, you will see that what each one of us is, the world, the state, society is; and to bring a vital change in the environment, which is essential, each one must begin with himself. In understanding himself and so transforming himself, he will inevitably bring about the necessary and vital change in the state, in the environment. The recognition and understanding of this fact will bring a revolution in our thinking-feeling. The world is a projection of yourself, your problem is the world's problem. Without you, the world is not. What you are, the world is; if you are envious, greedy, inimical, competitive, brutal, exclusive, so is society, so is the state.

The study of yourself is extremely difficult for you are very complex. You must have immense patience, not lethargic acceptance, but alert, passive capacity for observation and study. To objectify and study that which you are subjectively, inwardly, is very difficult. Most of us are in a whirl of activity, inwardly confused and wandering, torn by many conflicting desires, denying and asserting. How can this enormously complex machine be studied and understood? A machine which is moving very rapidly, revolving at a tremendous speed, cannot be studied in detail. It is only when it can be slowed down that you can begin to study it. If you can slow down your thinking-feeling, then you can observe it, just as in a slow motion picture you can study the movement of a horse as it runs or jumps a hurdle. If you stop the machine you cannot understand it, then it becomes merely a dead matter, if it goes too fast you cannot follow it; but to examine it in detail, to understand it thoroughly, it must go slowly, revolve gently. Just so

must the mind work to follow each movement of thought-feeling. To observe itself without friction it must slow down. To merely control thought-feeling, to apply a brake to it, is to waste the necessary energy required to understand it; then thought -feeling is more concerned in controlling, dominating, than in thinking out, feeling out, understanding each thought-feeling.

Have you ever tried to think out, feel out each thought-feeling? How extremely difficult it is! For the mind wanders all over the place, one thought is never finished, one feeling never concluded. It flutters from one subject to another, a slave driven hither and thither. If the mind cannot slow itself down, the implication, the inward significance of its thoughts-feelings cannot be discovered. To control its wanderings is to make it narrow and petty, and then thought-feeling is expended in checking, restraining, rather than in studying, examining, and understanding. The mind has to slow itself down, and how is this to be done? If it forces itself to be slow, then opposition is brought into being which creates further conflict, further complication. Compulsion of any kind will nullify its effort. To be aware of each thought-feeling is extremely arduous and difficult; to recognize that which is trivial and to let go, to be aware of that which is significant and to follow it, penetratingly and deeply, is strenuous, requiring extensional concentration.

I would like to suggest a way, but don't make of it into a hard and fast system, a tyrannical technique or the only way, a boring routine or duty. We know how to keep a diary, writing down all the events of the day in the evening. I do not suggest that we should keep a retrospective diary, but try to write down every thought-feeling whenever you have a little time. If you try it, you will see how extremely difficult even this is. When you do write, you can only put down one or two thoughts because your thinking is too rapid, disconnected, and wandering. And as you cannot write down everything, because you have other things to do, you will find after a while that another layer of your consciousness is taking note. When again you have leisure to write, all those thoughts-feelings to which you have not given conscious attention will be "remembered." So at the end of the day you will have written down as much of your thoughts and feelings as possible. Of course only those who are earnest will do this. At the end of the day look at what you have written down during the day. This study is an art, for out of it comes understanding. What is important is how you study what you have written, rather than the mere writing down.

If you put yourself in opposition to what you have written, you will not understand it. That is, if you accept or deny, judge or compare, you will not grasp the significance of all that is written, for identification prevents the flowering of thought-feeling. But if you examine it, suspending judgment, it will reveal its inward contents. To examine with choiceless awareness, without fear or favor, is extremely difficult. Thus you learn to slow down your thoughts and feelings but also, which is enormously important, to observe with tolerant dispassion every thought-feeling, free from judgment and perverted criticism. Out of this comes deep understanding which is cultivated not only during the waking hours but during sleep. From this you will find there comes candor, honesty.

But then you will be able to follow each movement of thought-feeling. For in this is involved not only the comprehension of the superficial layer but also of the many hidden layers of consciousness. Thus through constant self-awareness there is deeper and wider self-knowledge. It is a book of many volumes; in its beginning is its ending. You cannot skip a paragraph, a page, in order to reach the end quickly and greedily. For wisdom is not bought by the coin of greed or impatience. It comes as the volume of self-knowledge is read diligently—that which you are from moment to moment, not at a particular, given moment. Surely this means incessant work, an alertness which is not only passive but of constant inquiry, without the greed for an end. This passivity is in itself active. With stillness comes highest wisdom and bliss.

Question: I am very depressed, and how am I to get over it?

KRISHNAMURTI: It is natural, it is not, to be depressed at this present time when there is so much killing, confusion, and sorrow? Now, do we learn when we are up or down, at the heights or in the shadows, in the valleys? Our lives are lived in undulation, up and down, in great heights and in great depths. When we are at the heights, we are so exhilarated, so consumed with happiness or joy, with that sense of completeness, that the depths, the shadows are forgotten. Joy is not a problem, happiness does not seek a solution, in that state of completeness there is no striving after understanding. It is. But it does not last and we grope after it, remembering, grasping, comparing. Only when we are in the depths, in the valley, conflict, confusion, sorrow arise. From this we want to run away, craving to reach the heights once again. But we will not attain through want, for joy comes uninvited. Happiness is not an end in itself; it is an incident in wider and deeper understanding.

But if we try to comprehend conflict and sorrow, we shall begin to understand ourselves in relation to that conflict and sorrow—how we meet it or evade it, how we condemn it or justify it, how we rationalize it or compare it. In this process we get to know ourselves, our deceits, escapes, excuses; you may escape from depression, but it will catch you up again and again. But if we try to understand it, and to understand we must observe all the reactions in relation to it—how we try to escape from it, to find substitutions for it—we will find that the very desire to get over it indicates the lack of its comprehension. Through becoming aware of the causes and significance of depression, wider and deeper understanding comes into being, in which there is no place for depression, for self-pity, for fear.

Question: You talked about the state. Will you please explain more about it.

KRISHNAMURTI: What you are, that your state will be. If you are envious and passionate, seeking power and wealth, then you will create the state, the government that will represent you. If you are seeking power and dominance as most are in the family, in the town, or in the group, you will create a government of oppression and ruthlessness. If you are competitive, worldly, you bring about a society that is organized for violence, whose values are sensate, which will give rise ultimately to wars, to disasters, to tyrannies. Having helped to create a society, a state, according to your cravings, it runs away with you; it becomes an independent entity, dominating, commanding. But it is we, you and I, who have produced it through our ill will, greed, and worldliness. What you are, the state is.

Organized religion, to exist at all, must and does become a partner of the state and thereby loses its true function—to guide, to teach, to uphold at all times what is true. In this partnership religion becomes another means of oppression and division. If you who are responsible for the creation of the state do not understand yourself, how can you bring about the necessary change in the machinery of the state? You cannot effect a deep, radical change in the state unless you

understand yourself, and thereby free yourself from sensuality, from worldliness and the craving for fame. Unless you become religious in the fundamental sense of the word, not of any particular organized religion, your state will be irreligious and therefore responsible for war and economic disaster, for starvation and oppression. If you are nationalistic, separative, racially prejudiced, then you will produce a state that will be the cause of antagonism, oppression and misery. Such a state can never be religious; it becomes evil the larger and more powerful it becomes. I am using the word *religious* not in any specialized sense, not according to any doctrine, creed, or belief but living the life of nonsensuality, nonworldliness, not seeking personal fame or immortality.

Do not let us be clouded by words, names, or labels which only bring confusion as Hindus, Buddhists, Christians, and Mohammedans, or as Americans, Germans, English, Chinese. Religion is above all names, creeds, doctrines. It is the way of the realization of the supreme, and virtue is not of any country, race, or of any specialized religion. We must free ourselves from names and labels, from their confusion and antagonism, and try to seek through highest morality that which is. Thus you will become truly religious and so will your state. Then only will there be peace and light in the world. If each one of us can understand that there can be unity only in right thinking, not in mere superficial, economic devices—when we become religious, transcending craving for personal immortality and power, for worldliness and sensuality—only then shall we realize the deep inward wisdom of peace and love.

Question: Are you merely teaching a more subtle form of psychology?

KRISHNAMURTI: What do we mean by psychology? Do we not mean the study of the human mind, of oneself? If we do not understand our own make up, our own psyche, our own thought-feeling, then how can we understand anything else? How can you know what you think is true if you have no knowledge of yourself? If you do not know yourself, you will not know reality. Psychology is not an end in itself. It is but a beginning. In the study of oneself, right foundation is laid for the structure of reality. You must have the foundation, but it is not an end in itself, it is not the structure. If you have not laid the right foundation, ignorance, illusion, superstition will come into being, as they exist in the world today. You must lay the right foundation with right means. You cannot have the right with wrong means. The study of oneself is an extremely difficult task, and without self-knowledge and right thinking, ultimate reality is not comprehensible. If you are not aware of and so do not understand the self-contradiction, the confusion, and the different layers of consciousness, then on what are you to build? Without self-knowledge that which you build, your formulations, beliefs, hopes will have little significance.

To understand oneself requires a great deal of detachment and subtlety, perseverance and penetration, not dogmatism, not assertion, not denial, not comparison which leads to dualism and confusion. You must be your own psychologist, you must be aware of yourself, for out of yourself is all knowledge and wisdom. Nobody can be an expert about you. You have to discover for yourself and so liberate yourself; not another can help you in freeing yourself from ignorance and sorrow. You create your own sorrow, and there is no savior but yourself.

Question: Do I understand you to say that through the constant practice of instantaneously discerning the cause of every thought that enters the mind, the true self will begin to be revealed?

KRISHNAMURTI: If we assume that there is a true and a false self, then we shall not understand what is true. Don't you see it is like this: We are out on a voyage of discovery. To discover, thought-feeling must not be clogged by any hypothesis or belief; they hinder. To discover there must be freedom, there must be alert passivity. The knowledge of others is of little value in the discovery of truth. It must be found by yourself, not another can give it to you, not another can bring you wisdom. Truth is not a reward, it is not the result of a practice nor is it to be assumed nor formulated. If you formulate it you will miss it, your hypothesis will only cloud it. Through constant awareness you will discover what is true of the self. It is this discovery that matters, for it will liberate thought from ignorance and sorrow; what you discover on this journey—that will liberate, not your assertions and denials of the true and the false. To discover how one's thought-feeling is entrenched in creed, in belief, to discover the significance of the conflict of the opposites, to become aware of lust, of worldliness, of craving for self-continuity, is to be liberated from ignorance and sorrow. Through self-awareness comes self-knowledge and right thinking. There is no right thinking without self-knowledge.

Question: Do you mean that right thinking is a continual process of awareness while right thought is merely static? Why is right thought not right thinking?

KRISHNAMURTI: Right *thinking* is a continual process born of self-discovery, of self-awareness. There is no beginning and no end to this process, so right thinking is eternal. Right thinking is timeless; it is not bound by the past, by memory, not limited by formulation. It is born of freedom from fear and hope. Without the living quality of self-knowledge, right thinking is not possible.

Right thinking is creative, for it is a constant process of self-discovery. Right *thought* is thought conditioned; it is a result, it is made up, is put together; it is the outcome of a pattern, of memory, of habit, of practice. It is imitative, accumulative, traditional. It shapes itself through fear and hope, through greed and becoming, through authority and copy. Right thinking-feeling goes above and beyond the opposites, whereas right or conditioned thought is oppressed by the opposites. The conflict of the opposites is static.

Right thinking is the outcome of how to think, not what to think. But most of us have been trained or are training ourselves what to think, which is to think in terms of conditioning. Our civilization is based on what to think, which is given to us through organized religions, through political parties and their ideologies and so on. Propaganda is not conducive to right thinking; it tells you what to think.

Through self-awareness the pattern, the copy, the habit, the conditioned thought is discovered; this perception begins to free thought-feeling from bondage, from ignorance; through constant awareness and self-knowledge, which bring about right thinking, there is that creative stillness of reality. The craving for security brings about conditioned thought; to seek certainty is to find it, but it is not the real. Highest wisdom comes with that creative stillness of the mind-heart.

May 28, 1944

Fourth Talk in The Oak Grove

In the last three talks I have been trying to explain that right thinking, which comes from self-knowledge, is not to be acquired through another, however great, nor through any book, but rather through the experience of self-discovery, through that discovery which is creative and liberating. I tried to explain that as our life is a series of struggles and conflicts, unless we understand right endeavor, we will be creating not clarity and peace but more conflict and more pain; that without self-knowledge, to make a choice between the opposites must inevitably lead to further ignorance and sorrow.

I do not know how clearly I explained this problem of conflict between the opposites; for until we deeply understand its cause and effect, our endeavor, however earnest and strenuous, will not liberate us from our confusion and misery. However much we may formulate or try to understand that which we call God or truth, we cannot comprehend the unknown until the mind itself becomes as vast, as immeasurable as the thing it is trying to feel, to experience. To experience the immeasurable, the unknowable, mind must go beyond and above itself.

Thought-feeling is limited through its own cause, the craving to become, which is time binding. Craving, through identifying memory, creates the self, the 'me' and the 'mine'. It is the actor taking different rôles to suit different occasions but inwardly ever the same. Until this craving, the cause of our ignorance and sorrow, is understood and dissolved, the conflict of duality will continue and effort to disentangle from it will only plunge us more into it. This craving expresses itself through sensuality, through worldliness, through personal immortality, through authority, mystery, miracle. Just as long as the mind is the instrument of the self, of craving, so long will there be duality and conflict. Such a mind cannot comprehend the immeasurable.

The self, the consciousness of the 'me' and the 'mine', is built up through craving, by a series of thoughts and feelings not only in the past but by the influence of that past in the present. We are the result of the past; our being is founded in it. The many interrelated layers of our consciousness are the outcome of the past. This past is to be studied and understood through the living present; through the data of the present, the past is uncovered. In studying the self and its cause, craving, we shall begin to understand the way of ignorance and sorrow. To merely deny craving, to merely oppose its many expressions is not to transcend it but to continue in it. To deny worldliness is still to be worldly; but if you understand the ways of craving, then the tyranny of the opposites, possession and non-possession, merit and demerit, ceases. If we deeply inquire into craving, meditating upon it, becoming aware of its deeper and wider significance and so begin to transcend it, we shall awaken to a new, different faculty which is not begotten of craving nor of the conflict of the opposites. Through constant self-awareness there comes unidentifying observation, the study of the self without judgment. Through this awareness the many layers of self-consciousness are discovered and understood. Self-knowledge brings right thinking which alone will free thought-feeling from craving and its many conflicting sorrows.

Question: Does the understanding of oneself lead to a change of the problem and idea? One can understand how nationalism comes into being: education, persecution, vanity et cetera, but the nationalist remains still a nationalist. The will to change, to understand the problem, does not bring the real dissipation of that problem. So what is the next step after knowing the causes in this thought process?

KRISHNAMURTI: To identify oneself with a particular race, with a particular country, or with certain ideologies yields security, satisfaction, and flattering self-importance. This worship of the part, instead of the whole, cultivates antagonism, conflict, and confusion. If you think this out, feel this out clearly and intelligently, not examining the mere ideas but your response to them, then in comprehending the full implication of nationalism, order and clarity will come into that thin layer of consciousness with which we function every day. It is important to do this to become conscious of the full significance of nationalism—how it divides humanity which is one, how it breeds antagonism and oppression, how it encourages the ownership of property and of family, how it conditions thought-feeling through organizations, how it cultivates economic barriers and poverty, wars, miseries and so on.

In deeply understanding the implication of nationalism, order and clarity are brought into the conscious mind and into this clarity the hidden, the stored-up responses project themselves. Through studying these projections diligently and intelligently, the whole consciousness is freed from the disease of nationalism. Then you do not become an internationalist, which still maintains separatism and the worship of the part; but there is an awareness of unity and non-nationality, a freedom from labels and names, from racial and class prejudice.

The same process can be applied to all our problems—to think-feel over the problem as widely and freely as possible, thus bringing order and clarity to the conscious mind which then can respond with understanding to the projections of the hidden, inner impulses and injunctions—thus wholly resolving the problem. Until the many layers of memory are searched out, exposed and their responses fully understood, the problem will continue; but this search, this inquiry, is not possible if the conscious mind has not cleared itself of the problem. Not to be completely identified with the problem is our difficulty, for identification prevents the flow of thought-feeling; identification implies acceptance or denial, judgment or comparison, which distort our understanding. Thought-feeling to free itself from any problem, from any hindrance, is not the work of a moment. Freedom demands outer and inner awareness, the outer ready to receive the inner responses; this constant awareness brings deeper and wider self-knowledge. In self-knowledge there is the freedom of right thinking and only in self-knowledge are problems, bondages, understood and dissolved.

Question: I am a very active person physically. A time is coming when I shall not be. How shall I then occupy my time?

KRISHNAMURTI: Most of us are caught up in sensate values, and the world around us is organized to increase and maintain them. We become more and more involved in them and unthinkingly grow old, worn out by outward activity but inwardly inactive and poor. Soon the outward, noisy activity comes to an inevitable end, and then we become aware of loneliness, poverty of being. In order not to face this pain and fear, some continue ceaselessly to be active socially, in organized religion, politically, and in the business world, giving justifications for their activity and noisy bustle. For those who cannot continue outward activity, the question of what to do in old age arises. They cannot become suddenly inwardly active, they do not know what it means, their whole life has been against it. How are they to become inwardly aware?

It would be wise if after a certain age, perhaps let us say forty or forty-five, or younger still, you retired from the world, before you are too old. What would happen if you did retire not merely to enjoy the fruit of sensate gatherings but retired in order to find yourself, in order to think-feel profoundly, to meditate, to discover reality? Perhaps you may save mankind from the sensate, worldly path it is following, with all its brutality, deception, and sorrow. Thus there may be a

group of people, being disassociated from worldliness, from its identifications and demands, able to guide it, to teach it. Being free from worldliness, they will have no authority, no importance, and so will not be drawn into its stupidities and calamities. For a man who is not free from authority, from position, is not able to guide, to teach another. A man who is in authority is identified with his position, with his importance, with his work and so is in bondage. To understand the freedom of truth there must be freedom to experience. If such a group came into being, then they could produce a new world, a new culture.

It is sad for him who, with old age approaching, begins to question his empty life; at least he has begun to wake up. A couple came to see me the other day. They were working in a factory earning large sums. They were old. In the course of conversation a suggestion naturally arose that they withdraw, considering their age, to think, to live anew. They looked surprised and said, "What about?"

You may laugh but I am afraid most of us are in the same position. For most of us thinking, searching, is along a clear cut groove of a particular dogma or belief, and to follow that groove is considered religious, intelligent. Right thinking begins only with self-knowledge and not in the knowledge of ideas and facts which is only an extension of ignorance. But if you, whether you are old or young, begin to understand yourself, you will discover great and imperishable treasures. But to discover demands persistent awareness, adjustment and application—awareness of every thought-feeling—and out of this the treasure of life is discovered.

Question: How can we truly understand ourselves, our infinite riches, without developing a whole complete perception first?—otherwise with our comparative perception of thought, we get only a partial understanding of that infinite flow of cause in whose order we move and have our true conscious being.

KRISHNAMURTI: How can you understand the whole when you are worshipping the part! Being petty, partial, limited, how can you understand that which is boundless, infinite? The small cannot grasp the great, but the small can cease to be. In understanding what makes for limitation, for partiality, and transcending it, you will then be able to comprehend the whole, the limitless. From the known the unknown is realized, but to speculate about the unknowable is merely to deny the limited, the trivial; and so all speculation becomes a hindrance for the understanding of reality.

Begin to understand yourself and in that there will be discovered immeasurable riches. Begin with the known, with the trivial, the limited, the confused, the small that is bound by fear, by belief, by lust, by ill will. It is petty, partial, because it is the product of ignorance. How can such a mind understand the whole? It cannot. If thought-feeling frees itself from craving and so from ignorance and sorrow, then only is there a possibility of understanding the whole. How can there be understanding of the causeless when our thought-feeling is a result, when it is bound to time? This seems so obvious that it does not require much explanation, but yet so many are caught up in the illusion that we must first have the vision, the perception of the whole, a working hypothesis of it as a beginning, before there is understanding of the part. To have a perception of that completeness, the realization of that infinite reality, the singularistic, the limited mind must break down the barriers that confine it. From a small, narrow opening the wide heavens are not to be perceived. We try to perceive the whole through the small aperture of our thought-feeling, and what we see must inevitably be small, partial, incomplete. We say we want to understand the whole, yet we cling to the petty, to the 'me' and the 'mine'. Through self-awareness, which brings self-knowledge, right thinking is nurtured, which alone will free us from our triviality and sorrow. When the mind ceases to chatter, when it is not playing any part, when it is not grasping or becoming, when it is utterly still, in that creative emptiness is the whole, the uncreated.

Question: Do you believe there is evil in the world?

KRISHNAMURTI: Why do you ask me that question? Are you not aware of it? Are not its actions obvious, its sorrow crushing? Who has created it but each one of us? Who is responsible for it but each one of us? As we have created good, however little, so we have created evil, however vast. Good and evil are part of us and are also independent of us. When we think-feel narrowly, enviously, with greed and hate, we are adding to the evil which turns and rends us. This problem of good and evil, this conflicting problem, is always with us as we are creating it. It has become part of us, this wanting and not wanting, loving and hating, craving and renouncing. We are continually creating this duality in which thought-feeling is caught up. Thought-feeling can go beyond and above good and its opposite only when it understands its cause—craving. In understanding merit and demerit there is freedom from both. Opposites cannot be fused and they are to be transcended through the dissolution of craving. Each opposite must be thought out, felt out, as extensively and deeply as possible, through all the layers of consciousness; through this thinking out, feeling out, a new comprehension is awakened which is not the product of craving or of time.

There is evil in the world to which we are contributing as we contribute to the good. Man seems to unite more in hate than in good. A wise man realizes the cause of evil and good, and through understanding frees thought-feeling from it.

Question: Last Sunday I understood from what you said that we do not take time from our jobs, family, activities, to study ourselves. This seems a contradiction of your former statement that one can be aware in everything one does.

KRISHNAMURTI: Surely you begin by being aware in everything that you do. But what happens when you are so aware? If you pursue this awareness more and more, you come to be alone but not isolated. No object is ever in isolation; to be is to be related, whether alone or with many. But when you begin to be aware in everything you do, you are beginning to study yourself, you are beginning to be more and more aware of your inward private thoughts-feelings, motives, fears, and so on. The more there is self-awareness, the more self-recollected you become; you become more silent, more purely aware. We are too much occupied with family, job, friends, social affairs and we are little aware; old age and death creep upon us and our life is empty. If you are aware in your daily relationship and activity, you will begin to disentangle thought-feeling from the cause of ignorance and sorrow. Through becoming aware of the inward as well as the superficial actions and responses, distractions will naturally cease, and a simple life will inevitably follow.

Question: Do you think you will ever come back to the Masters?

KRISHNAMURTI: The questioner, believing and hoping in the Masters, wishes to bring me back to his fold; perhaps he thinks that having once accepted his belief, I will return to it.

Let us examine this belief in the Masters intelligently, without identifying ourselves with it. For some it will be difficult as they are greatly taken up with it, but let us try to think-feel as openly and freely as possible concerning it. Why do you need Masters? Those supposed living beings with whom you are not directly in contact? You will say probably that they act as signposts to reality. If they are signposts, why do you stop and worship them? Why do you accept the signposts, the mediators, the messengers, the in-between authorities? Then why do you form organizations, groups, round about them? If you are seeking truth, why all this bother about them, why the exclusive organizations and secret conclaves? Is it not because it is easier and pleasanter to linger, to worship at a wayside shrine, taking comfort in it, rather than to go on the long journey of search and discovery? No one can lead you to truth, neither the Masters nor the gods nor their messengers. You alone have to toil, search out, and discover.

A teacher with whom you are directly in contact is one thing, though it has its own dangers; but to be supposedly in contact with those whom you are not directly in touch with, or in touch with through their supposed representatives or messengers, is to invite superstition, oppression and other grave hindrances. The worship of authority is the very denial of truth. Authority blinds and the flowering of intelligence is destroyed; arrogance and stupidity increase, intolerance and division grow and multiply.

Fundamentally what can the Masters tell you? To know yourself, to cease to hate, to be compassionate, to seek reality. Any other teaching would be of little importance. None can give you a technique, a set formula to know yourself. If you had one and you followed it, you would not know yourself; you would know the result of a formula but not yourself. To know, you will have to search and discover within yourself. The result of a technique, of a practice, of a habit is uncreative, mechanical. Not another can help you to understand yourself and without understanding yourself there is no comprehension of reality. This search for the Masters is the prompting of worldliness. A super sensate value is still of this world and so the cause of ignorance and sorrow.

Then one might ask, "What are you doing, are you not a signpost?" If I am and you gather round it to put flowers, to build a shrine and all the stupidities that go with it, then it is utterly foolish and unworthy of grown-up people. What we are trying to do is to learn how to cultivate right thinking—which comes only through self-knowledge. On the foundation of right thinking is the highest. This knowledge none can give you, but you yourself have to become aware of all your thoughts-feelings. For in yourself is the beginning and the end, the whole of life. The highest is to be discovered, not formulated.

To read the pages of the past, you must know yourself as in the present, for through the present the past is revealed. With you is the key that opens the door to reality; none can offer it for it is yours. Through your own awareness you can open the door; through your own self-awareness only can you read the rich volume of self-knowledge, for in it are the hints and the openings, the hindrances and the blockages that prevent and yet lead to the timeless, to the eternal.

June 4, 1944

Fifth Talk in the Oak Grove

Till we understand the problems involved in craving, as I was explaining last Sunday, the conflict and sorrow of our daily life cannot be dissolved. There are three principal forms craving takes: sensuality, worldliness, and personal immortality—the gratification of the senses, the desire for prosperity, personal power and fame. In analyzing the craving for the gratification of the senses, we realize its insatiability, its torments, its everincreasing demands; its end is misery and conflict. When we examine worldliness, it too reveals incessant strife, confusion, and sorrow. The craving for personal immortality is born of illusion, for the self is a result, is made up, and that which is put together, a result, can never comprehend that which is causeless, that which is immortal.

The way of craving is very complex and difficult to dissolve; it is the cause of our misery, of our confusion and conflict. Without putting an end to it there is no peace; without its complete extinction, thought-feeling is in torment and life becomes an ugly struggle. It is the root of all selfishness and of all ignorance. It is the cause of frustration and hopelessness. Without transcending it there is no happiness, no creative peace.

Craving for sensuality indicates inward poverty; the desire to accumulate creates a competitive, brutal world; sensate values and craving for personal immortality or personal power must bring about authority, mystery, miracle, which prevent the discovery of the real. Violence and wars are the outcome of worldly desires, and there can be peace only when craving, in all its different forms, is understood and transcended.

If we do not understand this primary motive but merely develop virtue, we are only strengthening the self, the cause of ignorance and sorrow, the self which takes different roles and cultivates different virtues to gratify itself. We have to understand this changeable quality of craving, its cunning adaptability and its self-gratifying protective ways. The development of virtue becomes the stronghold of the self, but to free thought-feeling from craving is true virtue. This freedom from craving, which is virtue, is as a ladder; it is not an end in itself. Without virtue, the freedom from craving, there can be no understanding, no peace. To develop virtue as an opposite is still to give strength to the self. For all craving, all desire is singularistic, limited; being singularistic, however much you may try to make it noble, virtuous, it will always remain limited, small, and therefore the cause of conflict, antagonism and sorrow. It will ever know death.

So, as long as the seed of craving remains in any form there will be torment, poverty, death. If we develop virtue without understanding craving we are not bringing about that creative stillness of the mind-heart in which alone there is the real. Without understanding the subtleties of craving, merely to adjust ourselves to our environment, to bring peace in our relationship with the family, with the neighbor, with the world, will be in vain; for the self, the instrument of craving, is still the chief actor. How is it possible to free thought-feeling from craving? By becoming aware; by studying and understanding the self and its actions is there freedom from craving. To understand, all denial or acceptance, judgment or comparison must be set aside. In becoming aware we shall discover what is honesty, what is love, what is fear, what is simple life, and the complex problem of memory.

A mind that is uncertain, self-contradictory, cannot know what is candor, honesty. Honesty demands humility, and there can be humility only when you are aware of your own state of self-contradiction, of your own uncertainty. Self-contradiction and uncertainly will ever exist if there is craving, uncertainty of value, of action, of relationship. He who is certain is obstinate, thoughtless. He who knows does not know. In becoming aware of this uncertainty, surely you are cultivating detachment, dispassion. The beginning of humility is detachment. And surely this is the first step of the ladder. This step of the ladder must be worn away for you have trodden on it so often. A man who is conscious of detachment ceases to be detached; but he who has concerned himself with craving and its ways is becoming virtuous without striving after virtue; he is dispassionate without seeking it. Without candid awareness, understanding and peace are not possible.

Question: Besides wasting so much paper, do you seriously intend that we shall put down every thought and feeling?

KRISHNAMURTI: I suggested the other day that in order to understand ourselves we must become aware, and to study ourselves thought-feeling must slow itself down. If you become aware of your own thinking-feeling, you will perceive how rapid it is—one disconnected thought-feeling following another, wandering and distracted—and it is impossible to observe, examine such confusion. To bring order and so clarity, I suggested that every thought-feeling be written down. This whirling machinery must slow itself down to be observed, so writing every thought-feeling may be of help. As in a slow motion picture, you are able to see every movement, so in slowing down the rapidity of the mind, you are then able to observe every thought, trivial and important. The trivial leads to the important, and do not brush it aside as being petty. Since it is there it is an indication of the pettiness of the mind, and to brush it aside does not make the mind any the less trivial, stupid. To brush it aside helps to keep the mind small, narrow, but to be aware of it, to understand it leads to great riches.

If any of you have tried to write as I suggested a couple of weeks ago, you will know how difficult it is to put down every thought and feeling. You will not only use a lot of paper but you will not be able to write down all your thoughts-feelings, for your mind is too rapid in its distractions. But if you have the intention of putting down every thought-feeling, however trivial and stupid, the shameful and the pleasant, however little you may succeed at first, you will soon discover a peculiar thing happening. As you have not the time to write every thought-feeling, for you have to give your attention to other matters, you will find that one of the layers of consciousness is recording every thought-feeling. Though you do not give your attention directly to write down, nevertheless you are inwardly aware and when you have time to write again, you will find that the recordings of inward awareness will come to the surface. If you will look over what you have written, you will find yourself either condemning or approving, justifying or comparing. This approbation or denial prevents the flowering of thought-feeling and so stops understanding. If you do not condemn, justify, or compare but ponder over, try to understand, then you will discover that these thoughts-feelings are indications of something much deeper. So you are beginning to develop that mirror which reflects your thoughts-feelings without any distortion. And by observing them you are comprehending your actions and responses, and so self-knowledge becomes wider and deeper. You not only comprehend the present momentary action and reaction but also the past that has produced the present. And for this you must have quiet and solitude. But society does not allow you to have them. You must be with people, outwardly active at all costs. If you are alone you are considered antisocial or peculiar, or you are afraid of your own loneliness. But in this process of self-aware-

ness, you will discover many things about yourself and so of the world.

Do not treat this writing down as a new method, a new technique. Try it. But what is important is to become aware of every thought-feeling, from which arises self-knowledge. You must start out on the journey of self-discovery; what you find does not depend on any technique—technique prevents discovery—and it is the discovery that is liberating and creative. What is important is not your determination, conclusion, choice, but what you discover, for that will bring understanding.

If you do not wish to write down, then become aware of every thought-feeling, which is much more difficult. Become aware, for example, of your resentment if you have any. To be aware of it is to be aware of what caused it, why and how it has been stored up, how it is shaping your actions and responses and how it is your constant companion. Surely to be aware of resentment, antagonism, involves all this and more, and it is very difficult to be aware of it so completely, comprehensively as in a flash; but if you are, you will find that it soon transforms itself. If you cannot be so aware, put down your thoughts-feelings, learn to study them with tolerant dispassion and little by little the whole content of your thoughts-feelings is discovered. It is this discovery, this understanding, that is the liberating and transforming factor.

Question: Did you seriously mean what you said when you suggested last week that one should retire from the world when one is around forty-five or so?

KRISHNAMURTI: I suggested this seriously. Almost all of us, until death overtakes us, are so caught up in worldliness that we have no time to search out deeply, to discover the real. To retire from the world necessitates a complete change in educational and economic systems, does it not? If you did retire, you would be unprepared, you would be lost, you would be lonely, you would not know what to do with yourself. You would not know how to think. You would probably form new groups, new organizations with new beliefs, badges and labels, and once again be active outwardly, doing reforms which will need further reform. But this is not what I mean. To retire from the world you must be prepared by the right kind of occupation, by creating the right kind of environment, by setting up the right state, by right education and so on. If you have been so prepared, then to withdraw from worldliness at any age is the natural, not abnormal, sequence; you withdraw to flow into deep and pure awareness, you withdraw not into isolation but to find the real, to help to transform the ever-congealing, conflicting society and state. All this would involve a wholly different kind of education, an upheaval in our social and economic order. Such a group of people would be completely disassociated from authority, from politics, from all those causes which produce war and antagonism between man and man. A stone may direct the course of a river; so a small number may direct the course of a culture. Surely any great thing is done in this manner.

You will probably say most of us cannot retire however much we may want to. Naturally all cannot but some of you can. To live alone or in a small group requires great intelligence. But if you really thought it worthwhile, then you would set about it, not as a wonderful act of renunciation, but as a natural and intelligent thing for a thoughtful man to do. How extraordinarily important it is that there should be at least some who do not belong to any particular group or race or to any specialized religion or society! They will create the true brotherhood of man for they will be seeking truth. To be free from outward riches there must be the awareness of inward poverty, which brings untold riches. The stream of culture may change its course through a few awakened people. These are not strangers but you and me.

Question: Are there not times when issues are so important that they need to be approached from without as well as through individual comprehension? For instance, the pouring of deadly narcotics into China by Japan? This is only one of the many forms of exploitation for which we are really responsible. Is there any way without violence in which we can contribute towards the stopping of this awful procedure, or must we wait for individual awareness to take its course?

KRISHNAMURTI: Periodically one group exploits another group, and the exploitation brings on a violent crisis. This has been happening throughout the ages—one race dominating, exploiting, murdering another race and in turn being oppressed, cheated, poverty-stricken. How is this to be solved? Is it to be adjusted only through outward legislation, outward organization, outward education, or by understanding the inner conflicting causes that have produced the outer chaos and misery? You cannot grasp the inner without understanding the outer. If you merely try to put down one race exploiting or oppressing another, then you will become the exploiter, the oppressor. If you adopt evil methods for a righteous end, the end is transformed by the means. So until we grasp this deeply, lastingly, mere reformation of evil by evil methods is productive of further evil; thus reform ever needs further reform. We think we see its obviousness, and yet we allow ourselves to be persuaded to the contrary through fear, propaganda, and so on, which means really that we do not grasp its truth.

As the individual, so the nation, so the state; you may not be able to transform another, but you can be certain of your own transformation. You may stop one country exploiting another by violent methods, by economic sanctions and so on, but what guarantee is there that the very nation that is putting an end to the ruthlessness of another is not going to be also oppressive, ruthless? There is no guarantee, no guarantee whatsoever. On the contrary, in fighting evil by evil means, the nation, the individual becomes that which he is fighting. You may build an outer, superficial structure of excellent legislation to control, to check, but if there is no goodwill and brotherly love, the inward conflict and poverty explode and produce chaos. Mere legislation does not prevent the West from exploiting the East or perhaps the East from exploiting the West in its turn, but just as long as we, individually or in groups, identify ourselves with this or that race, nation, or religion, so long will there be wars and exploitation, oppression and starvation. Just as long as you admit to yourself division, the long list of absurd divisions as an American, Englishman, German, Hindu, and so on, just as long as you are not aware of human unity and relationship, so long will there be mass murder and sorrow. A people that is guided, checked by mere legislation is as an artificial flower, beautiful to look upon but empty within.

You will probably say that the world will not wait for individual awakening or for the awakening of a few to alter its course. Yes, it will go on its blind, set course. But it will awaken through each individual who can throw off his bondage to division, to worldliness, to personal ambition and power; through his understanding, through his compassion can brutality and ignorance be brought to an end. In his awakening only is there hope.

Question: I want to help people, serve them. What is the best way?

KRISHNAMURTI: The best way is to begin to understand yourself and change yourself. In this desire to help another, to serve another, there is hidden pride, conceit. If you love you serve. The clamor to help is born of vanity.

If you want to help another, you must know yourself for you are the other. Outwardly we may be different—yellow, black, brown, or white—but we are all driven by craving, by fear, by greed, or by ambition; inwardly we are very much alike. Without self-knowledge, how can you have knowledge of another's needs? Without understanding yourself, you cannot understand another, serve another. Without self-knowledge you are acting in ignorance, and so creating sorrow.

Let us consider this. Industrialization is spreading rapidly throughout the world, urged on by greed and war. Industrialization may give employment, feed more people, but what is the larger result? What happens to a people highly developed in technique? They will be richer, there will be more cars, more airplanes, more gadgets, more cinema shows, bigger and better houses; but what happens to them as human beings? They become more and more ruthless, more and more mechanical, less and less creative. Violence must spread and government then is the organization of violence. Industrialization may bring about better economic conditions, but with what appalling results!—slums, antagonism of the worker against the non-worker, the boss and the slave, capitalism and communism, the whole chaotic business that is spreading in different parts of the world. Happily we say that it will raise the standard of living, poverty will be stamped out, there will be work, there will be freedom, dignity, and so on. The division of the rich and the poor, the man of power and the seeker after power—this endless division and conflict will go on. What is the end of it? What has happened in the West? Wars, revolutions, continual threat of destruction, utter despair. Who is bringing help to whom and who is serving whom? When everything is being destroyed about you, the thoughtful must inquire as to the deeper causes, which so few seem to do. A man who is blasted out of his house by a bomb must envy the primitive man. You certainly are bringing civilization to the so-called backward people, but at what price! You may be serving but consider what comes in its wake. But few realize the deeper causes of disaster. You cannot destroy industry, you cannot do away with the airplane, but you can eradicate utterly the causes that produce its misuse. The causes of its appalling use lie in you. You can eradicate them, which is a difficult task; since you will not face that task, you try to legalize war; you have covenants, leagues, international security, and so on, but greed, ambition overrule them and war and catastrophe inevitably follow.

To help another, you must know yourself; like you, he is the result of the past. We are all interrelated. If you are inwardly diseased by ignorance, ill will, and passion, you will inevitably spread disease and darkness. If you are inwardly healthy and integrated, you spread light and peace; otherwise you help to produce greater chaos, greater misery. To understand oneself requires patience, tolerant awareness; the self is a book of many volumes which you cannot read in a day, but when once you begin to read, you must read every word, every sentence, every paragraph for in them are the intimations of the whole. The beginning of it is the ending of it. If you know how to read, supreme wisdom is to be found.

Question: Is awareness only possible during waking hours?

KRISHNAMURTI: The more you are conscious of your thoughts-emotions, the more you are aware of your whole being. Then the sleeping hours become an intensification of the waking hours. Consciousness functions even in so-called sleep, of which we are well aware. You think over a problem pretty thoroughly and yet you cannot solve it; you sleep over it, which phrase we often use. In the morning we find its issues are clearer, and we seem to know what to do; or we perceive a new aspect of it which helps to clear up the problem. How does this happen? We can attribute a lot of mystery and nonsense to it, but what does take place? In that so-called sleep the conscious mind, that thin layer is quiet, perhaps receptive; it has worried over the problem and now, being weary, is still, the tension removed. Then the promptings of the deeper layers of consciousness are discernible and when you wake up, the problem seems to have become clearer and easier to solve. So the more you are aware of your thoughts-feelings during the day, not for a few seconds or during a set period, the mind becomes quieter, alertly passive and so capable of responding and comprehending the deeper intimations. But it is difficult to be so aware; the conscious mind is not used to such intensity. The more aware the conscious mind is, the more the inner mind cooperates with it, and so there is deeper and wider understanding.

The more you are aware during the waking hours, the less dreams there are. Dreams are indications of thoughts-feelings, actions not completed, not understood, that need fresh interpretation, or frustrated thought-hope that needs to be fully comprehended. Some dreams are of no importance. Those that have significance have to be interpreted, and that interpretation depends on your capacity of nonidentification, of keen intelligence. If you are deeply aware, interpretation is not necessary, but you are too lazy and so, if you can afford it, you go to a dream specialist; he interprets your dreams according to his understanding. You gradually become dependent upon him; he becomes the new priest, and so you have another problem added to you. But if you are aware even for a brief period, you will see that the short, sharp awareness, however fleeting it be, begins to awaken a new feeling which is not the result of craving, but a faculty which is free from all personal limitations and tendencies. This faculty, this feeling, will gather momentum as you become more deeply and widely aware, so that you are aware even in spite of your attention being given to other matters. Though you are occupied with necessary duties and give your attention to daily existence, inward awareness continues; it is as a sensitive photographic plate on which every impression, every thought-feeling is being imprinted to be studied, assimilated, and understood. This faculty, this new feeling, is of the utmost importance, for it will reveal that which is eternal.

June 11, 1944

Sixth Talk in The Oak Grove

I have been saying in my talks that self-knowledge is the beginning of right thinking, and without self-knowledge true thinking is not possible. With self-knowledge comes understanding, in it is the root of all understanding. Without self-knowledge there is no comprehension of the world about us. To bring about this understanding there must be right endeavor, for without it, as I explained, thought-feeling will ever be in the conflict of duality, of merit and demerit, the 'me' and the 'mine' as opposed to the not 'me' and the

not 'mine', which causes deep anguish and sorrow. This conflict of the opposites will ever exist if craving is not observed and understood and so transcended; craving for worldliness and for personal immortality is the cause of sorrow. Craving for these in different forms creates ignorance, antagonism, and sorrow. The desire for personal immortality is not only the continuation of the self in the hereafter, but also in the present which expresses itself in the pride of family, of name, of position, in the desire for possessions, for fame, authority, mystery, and miracle. The craving for these is the beginning of sorrow, and in yielding to them there is no end to sorrow.

So freeing thought-feeling from craving is the beginning of virtue. Virtue is a negation of the self rather than the positive becoming of the self, for negative understanding is the highest form of thinking-feeling. The socalled positive becoming or the qualities of the self are self-enclosing, self-binding and so there is never freedom from conflict and sorrow. The desire to become, however noble and virtuous, is still within the narrow sphere of the self, and so such a desire is the means of producing conflict and confusion. This process of constant becoming, supposedly positive, brings death with its fears and hopes. Freeing thought from craving, though it may appear as negation, is the essence of virtue, for it is not building up the process of the self, the 'me' and the 'mine'.

As I said in my previous talks, in freeing thought-feeling from craving, in becoming aware of its ways, we begin to perceive the significance of candor, love, fear, simple life, and so on. It is not that one must become candid, honest, but in thinking-feeling about it, in becoming extensively aware of it, its deeper implications are perceived rather than the self becoming honest. Virtue is not a structure upon which the self can build, for in it there is no becoming. The self can never become candid, open, clear, for its very nature is dark, enclosing, confusing, contradicting.

To become aware of ignorance is the beginning of candor, of honesty. To be unaware of ignorance breeds obstinacy and credulity. Without being aware of ignorance, to try to become honest only leads to further confusion. Without self-knowledge mere sincerity is narrowness and gullibility. If one begins to be self-aware and observes what is candor, then confusion yields to clarity. It is the lack of clarity that leads to dishonesty, to pretension. To be aware of escapes, distortions, hindrances, brings order and clarity. Ignorance, which is the lack of self-knowledge, leads to confusion, to dishonesty. Without understanding the contradictory nature of the self, to be candid is to be hard and to produce more and more confusion. Through self-awareness and self-knowledge there is order, clarity, and right thinking.

The highest form of thinking is negative comprehension. To think-feel positively, without understanding craving, is to raise values that are separative, disruptive, and uncreative.

Now, love is sorrowful; we are aware that there is in love sorrow, bitterness, disillusionment; the pain of love is a torment; in it we know fear and resentment. There is no escape from love, but yet in it there is torture. The foolish blame love, without understanding the cause of pain; without knowing its conflict there is no transcending anguish. Without becoming aware of the source of conflict, craving, love brings pain. It is craving, not love, that creates dependence and all the sorrowful issues that arise out of it. It is craving in relationship that gives rise to uncertainty, not love; and this uncertainty breeds possessiveness, jealousy, fear. In this possessiveness, in this dependence, there is a false sense of unity which sustains and nourishes the temporary feeling of well-being; but it is not love, for in it there is inward fear and suspicion. This outward stimulation of seeming oneness is parasitical, the living of the one on the other; it is not love, for inwardly there is emptiness, loneliness, and the need for dependence. Dependence breeds fear, not love. Without understanding craving is there not domination, oppression, taking the form of love? In relationship with the one or with the many, such love of power and dominance, with its submissiveness and acceptance, brings conflict, antagonism, and sorrow. Having the seed of violence within oneself, how can there be love? Having the seed of contradiction and uncertainty within oneself, how can there be love? Love is beyond and above all these; it transcends sensuousness. Love is in itself eternal, not dependent, not a result. In it there is mercy and generosity, forgiveness and compassion. With love, humility and gentleness come into being; without love they have no existence.

Question: I am already an introvert and it seems to me that from what you have been saying, is there not a danger of my becoming more and more self-centered, more of an introvert?

KRISHNAMURTI: If you are an introvert in opposition to an extrovert, then there is a danger of self-centeredness. If you put yourself in opposition, then there is no understanding; then your thoughts, feelings, and actions are self-enclosing, isolating. In intelligently comprehending the outer you will come inevitably to the inner, and thereby the division of the outer and inner ceases. If you oppose the outer and cling to the inner, or if you deny the inner and assert the outer, then there is the conflict of the opposites, in which there is no understanding. To understand the outer, the world, you must begin with yourself, for you, your thoughts-feelings and actions, are the result of both the outer and the inner. You are the center of all objective and subjective existence, and to comprehend it, where are you to begin, save with yourself? This does not encourage unbalance, on the contrary it will bring creative understanding, inward peace.

But if you deny the outer, the world, if you try to escape from it, if you distort it, shaping it to your fancies, then your inner world is an illusion, isolating and hindering. Then it is a state of delusion which brings misery. To be is to be related, but you can block, distort, this relationship, thus becoming more and more isolated and self-centered which leads to mental disorder. The root of understanding is within yourself, in self-knowledge.

Question: You, like so many Orientals, seem to be against industrialization. Why are you?

KRISHNAMURTI: I do not know if many Orientals are against industrialization, and if they are I do not know what reasons they would give, but I thought I explained why I consider that mere industrialization is not a solution for our human problem with its conflicts and sorrows. Mere industrialization encourages sensate value, bigger and better bathrooms, bigger and better cars, distractions, amusements, and all the rest of it. External and temporal values take precedence over eternal value. Happiness, peace is sought in possessions, made by the hand or by the mind, in addiction to things or to mere knowledge. Walk down any principal street and you will see shop after shop selling the same thing in different colors, shapes—innumerable magazines and thousands of books. We want to be distracted, amused, taken away from ourselves, for we are so wretched and poor, empty and sorrowful. And so where there is demand, there is

production and the tyranny of the machine. And we think by mere industrialization we shall solve the economic and social problem. Does it? You may temporarily, but with it come wars, revolutions, oppression, exploitation, bringing so-called civilization—industrialization with all its implications—to the uncivilized.

Industrialization and the machine are here, you cannot do away with them; they take their right place only when man is not dependent for his happiness on things, only when he cultivates inner riches, the imperishable treasures of reality. Without these mere industrialization brings untold horrors; with inner treasures industrialization has a meaning. This problem is not of any country or race; it is a human issue. Without the balancing power of compassion and unworldliness, you will have, through the mere increase of the production of things, of facts, and of technique, bigger and better wars, economic oppression and frontiers of power, more subtle ways of deception, disunity, and tyranny.

A stone may change the course of a river, so a few who understand may perhaps divert this terrible course of man. But it is difficult to withstand the constant pressure of modern civilization unless one is constantly aware and so is discovering the treasures that are imperishable.

Question: Do you think that group meditation is helpful?

KRISHNAMURTI: What is the purpose of meditation? Is not right thinking the foundation for the discovery of the supreme? With right thinking the unknowable, the immeasurable, comes into being. You must discover it, and to discover, your mind must be utterly uninfluenced. Your mind must be completely silent, still, and creatively empty. The mind must free itself from the past, from conditioning influences, cease creating value.

You are the one and the many, the group and the single; you are the result of the past. There is no understanding of this whole process save through the result; you must study and examine the result which is yourself. To observe you must be detached, uninfluenced, cease to be a slave to propaganda, the subtle and the gross. The influence of environment shapes thought-feeling, and from this too there must be freedom to discover the real which alone liberates. How easily we are persuaded to believe or not to believe, to act or not to act; magazines, newspapers, cinemas, radios daily shape our thought-feeling, and how few can escape from their limiting influence!

One religious group believes this and another that; their thoughts-feelings are imitative, influenced, fashioned. In this imitative confusion and assertion, what hope is there of finding the real! To understand this mad confusion, thought-feeling must extricate itself from it and so become clear, unbiased, and simple. To discover the real, mind-heart must free itself from the tyranny of the past; it must become purely alone. How easily the collective, the congregation, is used, persuaded, and drugged! The discovery of the real is not to be organized; it must be sought out by each one, uncoerced, not urged by reward or punishment. When the mind ceases to create, there is creation.

Question: Is not belief in God necessary in this terrible and ruthless world?

KRISHNAMURTI: We have had belief in God for centuries upon centuries, but yet we have created a terrible world. The savage and the highly civilized priest believe in God. The primitive kills with bows and arrows and dances wildly; the civilized priest blesses the warships and the bombers and rationalizes. I am not saying this in any cynical, sneering spirit, so please do not smile. It is a grave matter. Both of them believe, and also there is the other who is a nonbeliever, but he also resorts to liquidating those who stand in his way. Clinging to a belief or to an ideology does not do away with killing, with oppression and exploitation. On the contrary, there have been and continue to be terrible, ruthless wars and destruction and persecution in the name of peace, in the name of God. If we can put aside these contending beliefs and ideologies and bring about a deep change in our daily life, there will be a chance for a better world. It is our everyday life that has brought this and previous catastrophes, horrors; our thoughtlessness, our exclusive national and economic privileges and barriers, our lack of good will and compassion have brought these wars and other disasters. Worldliness will constantly erupt in chaos and in sorrow.

We are the result of the past and without understanding it, to build upon it is to invite disaster. The mind which is a result, which is put together, cannot hope to understand that which is not made up, that which is causeless, timeless. To comprehend the uncreated, the mind must cease to create. A belief is ever of the past, of the created, and such a belief becomes a hindrance to the experiencing of the real. When thought-feeling is anchored, made dependent, understanding of the real is not possible. There must be open, still freedom from the past, a spontaneous overflow of silence in which alone the real can flower. When you see a sunset, in that moment of beauty there is a spontaneous, creative joy. When you wish to repeat that experience again, there is no joy in the sunset; you try to receive that same creative happiness, but it is not there. Your mind, not expecting, not wanting, was capable of receiving, but having received, it is greedy for more, and it is this greed that blinds. Greed is accumulative and burdens the mind-heart; it is ever gathering, storing up. Thought-feeling is corrupted by greed, by the corroding waves of memory. Only through deep awareness is this engulfing process of the past brought to an end. Greed, like pleasure, is ever singularistic, limiting, and how can thought born of greed comprehend that which is immeasurable!

Instead of strengthening beliefs and ideologies, become aware of your thoughts-feelings, for out of them spring the issues of life. What you are the world is; if you are cruel, lustful, ignorant, greedy, so is the world. Your belief or your disbelief in God is of little significance, for by your thoughts-feelings-actions, you make the world terrible and ruthless, peaceful and compassionate, barbarous or wise.

Question: What is the source of desire?

KRISHNAMURTI: Perception, contact, sensation, want, and identification cause desire. The source of desire is sensation in its lowest and highest forms. And the more you demand to be satisfied sensually, the more of worldliness which seeks continuity in the hereafter. Since existence is sensation we can but understand it, not become slaves to it, and so free thought to transcend into pure awareness. The desire to be satisfied must produce the means for satisfaction, at whatever cost. Such demand, such craving can be observed, studied, intelligently understood, and transcended. To be enslaved to craving is to be ignorant, and sorrow is its end.

Question: Don't you think that there is in man a principle of destruction, independent of his will to destroy and of his desire at the same time for life? Life in itself seems to be a process of destruction.

KRISHNAMURTI: In all of us there is the dormant will to destroy—like anger, ill will,

which extended leads to world catastrophes—and also within us there is the desire to be thoughtful and compassionate. So there is at work within us this dual process, a seemingly endless conflict. The questioner wants to know if life itself does not seem to be a destructive process. Yes, it is, if we understand it to mean that in negation is the highest comprehension. This negation is the destruction of those values that are based on the positive, on the 'me' and the 'mine'. As long as life is self-becoming, enclosed by the thought-feeling of 'me' and 'mine', it becomes a destructive process, cruel and uncreative. The positive, assertive becoming is ultimately death dealing, which is so obviously manifest in the world at the present time. Life pursued positively as the 'me' and the 'mine' is conflicting and destructive. When this positive, aggressive wanting or not wanting is put an end to, there is the awareness of fear, of death, of nothingness. But if thought can go above and beyond this fear, then there is ultimate reality.

June, 18, 1944

Seventh Talk in The Oak Grove

I have been trying to explain in my last few talks how to cultivate right thinking; how right thinking comes with self-knowledge. The more you are aware of your thoughts-feelings, the more you are detached, and the less you identify, the greater the self-knowledge; and it is this self-knowledge that dissolves ignorance and sorrow. In understanding the self, right thinking comes into being.

Virtue, as I explained, lies in freeing thought-feeling from craving; also to liberate thought there must be candor. Dependence destroys love. Craving must ever create attachment, possessiveness, from which arise jealousy, envy and those conflicts with which we are all too familiar. Where there is dependence and attachment, there love is not.

In understanding relationship we will find that the cause of disturbance and pain lies in depending on another for our inward sustenance and happiness. Relationship then becomes merely a means for self-gratification which breeds attachment and fear. Relationship is a process of self-revelation; relationship is as a mirror in which you begin to discover yourself, your tendencies, pretensions, selfish and limited motives, fears and so on. In relationship, if you are aware, you will find that you are being exposed, which causes conflict and pain. The thoughtful man welcomes this self-exposure to bring about order and clarity, to free his thought-feeling from isolating, self-enclosing tendencies. But most of us try to seek comfort and gratification in relationship; we do not desire to be revealed to ourselves; we do not wish to study ourselves as we are, so relationship becomes wearisome and we seek to escape. We seek peace in relationship, and if we do not find it then we bring about gratifying changes until we find what we seek—dull comfort or some distraction to cover up our hollow emptiness and aching fears. But relationship will ever be painful, a constant struggle, until out of it comes deep and extensional self-knowledge. With deep self-knowledge there is inexhaustible love.

If we understand relationship and the cause of dependence, we do not bring about enmity, and this is of primary importance. The cause of enmity in all relationship cannot be discovered if relationship is not a self-revealing process. If there is no cause for enmity, then there is neither the friend nor the enemy, the forgiver nor the forgiven. We cause enmity through pride of position, knowledge, family, capacity and so awaken in another ill will and envy.

The craving to become causes fears; to be, to achieve, and so to depend engenders fear. The state of the nonfear is not negation, it is not the opposite of fear nor is it courage. In understanding the cause of fear, there is its cessation, not the becoming courageous, for in all becoming there is the seed of fear. Dependence on things, on people, or on ideas breeds fear; dependence arises from ignorance, from the lack of self-knowledge, from inward poverty; fear causes uncertainty of mind-heart, preventing communication and understanding. Through self-awareness we begin to discover and so comprehend the cause of fear, not only the superficial but the deep causal and accumulative fears. Fear is both inborn and acquired; it is related to the past, and to free thought-feeling from it, the past must be comprehended through the present. The past is ever awaiting to give birth to the present which becomes the identifying memory of the 'me' and the 'mine', the 'I'. The self is the root of all fear.

To inhibit or suppress fear is not to transcend it; its cause must be self-discovered and so understood and dissolved. In becoming aware of craving and its dependence, in observing with kindly detachment its ways and actions, fear yields to understanding. There are, surely, three states of awareness of every problem: first to become aware of it; then to be deeply aware of its cause and effect and of its dual process; and to transcend it the thinker and his thought must be experienced as one. Most of us are unconscious, let us say, of fear and if we are conscious of it, we become apprehensive, we run away from it, suppress or cover it up. If we do none of these things, then through constant awareness the cause and its processes begin to unfold themselves; if we are not impatient, if we are not greedy for a result, then this flame of awareness, which brings understanding, dissolves the cause and its ever-developing processes. There is only one cause but its ways and expressions are many.

Inhibiting, prohibiting, fear does not eradicate the cause of fear but only produces further factors of disturbance and suffering. Through tolerant observation of fear, through being aware of every happening of fear, it is allowed to unfold itself; by following it through without identification, with kindly detachment, there comes creative understanding which alone dissolves the cause of fear without developing its opposite which is another form of fear.

Question: Why don't you face the economic and social evils instead of escaping into some dark, mystical affair?

KRISHNAMURTI: I have been trying to point out that only by giving importance to those things that are primary can the secondary issues be understood and solved. Economic and social evils are not to be adjusted without understanding what causes them. To understand them and so bring about a fundamental change, we have first to comprehend ourselves who are the cause of these evils. We have, individually and so as a group, created social and economic strife and confusion. We alone are responsible for them and thus we, individually and so perhaps collectively, can bring order and clarity. To act collectively we must begin individually; to act as a group each one must understand and change radically those causes within himself which produce the outer conflict and misery. Through legislation you may gain certain beneficial results, but without altering the inner, fundamental causes of conflict and antagonism they will be overturned and confusion will rise again; outer reforms will ever need further reform and this way leads to oppression and violence. Lasting outer order and creative peace can come about only if each one brings order and peace within himself.

Each one of us, whatever his position, is seeking power, is greedy, lustful, or violent; without putting an end to these in himself by himself, mere outward reform may produce superficial results, but these will be destroyed by those who are ever seeking position, fame, and so on. To bring about the necessary and fundamental change in the outer world with its wars, competition, and tyrannies, surely you must begin with yourself and deeply transform yourself. You will say, no doubt, that in this way it will take a very long time to reform the world. What of it? Will a short, drastic, superficial revolution change the inward fact? Through the sacrifice of the present will a happy future be created? Through wrong means will the right ends come into being? We have not been shown this, and yet we pursue blindly, not thinking, with the result that there is utter destruction and misery. You can have peace, order, only through peaceful and orderly means. What is the purpose of outward economic and social revolutions? To liberate man, to help him think-feel fully, to live completely? But those who want immediate and quick change in the economic and social order—do they not also create the pattern of behavior and thought; not how to think but what to think? So it cheats its own purpose, and man is again a plaything of the environment.

I have been trying to explain in these talks that ignorance, ill will, and lust cause sorrow, and without self-purification of these hindrances we must inevitably produce outer conflict, confusion, and misery. Ignorance, the lack of self-knowledge, is the greatest "evil." Ignorance prevents right thinking and gives primary emphasis to things that are secondary, and so life is made empty, dull, and a mechanical routine from which we seek various escapes: explosion into dogma, speculation and delusion and so on, which is not mysticism. In trying to comprehend the outer world, one comes to the inner, and that inner, when properly pursued and rightly understood, leads to the supreme. This realization is not the fruit of escape. This realization alone will bring peace and order to the world.

The world is in a chaos because we have pursued wrong values. We have given importance to sensuality, to worldliness, to personal fame or immortality which produce conflict and sorrow. True value is found in right thinking; there is no right thinking without self-knowledge and self-knowledge comes with self-awareness.

Question: Don't you think there are peace-loving nations and aggressive nations?

KRISHNAMURTI: No. The term *nation* is separative, exclusive and so the cause of contention and wars. There is no peaceloving nation; all are aggressive, dominant, tyrannical. As long as it remains a separate unit, apart from others, taking pride in segregation, in patriotism, in the race, it breeds untold misery for itself and for others. You may not have peace and yet be exclusive. You may not have economic and social, national and racial frontiers without inviting enmity and jealousy, fear and suspicion. You may not have plenty while others starve, without inviting violence. We are not separate, we are human beings in common relationship. Your sorrow is the sorrow of another—by killing another you are destroying yourself, by hating another you suffer, for you are the other. Goodwill and brotherliness are not achieved through separate and exclusive nationalities and frontiers; they must be set aside to bring peace and hope for man.

And besides, why do you identify yourself with any nation, with any group, or with any ideology? Is it not to protect your small self, to feed your petty and death-dealing vanities, sustain your own glory? What pride is there is in the self which brings wars and misery, conflict and confusion? A nation is the glorification of the self and so the breeder of strife and sorrow.

Question: I am greatly attracted and yet afraid of sex. It has become a torturing problem and how is one to solve it?

KRISHNAMURTI: It has become a consuming problem because we have ceased to be creative. Intellectually and morally we have become merely imitative machines; religiously we merely copy, accept authority, and are drugged. Our education narrows us; our society, being competitive, wastes us; the cinemas, radios, newspapers are continually telling us what to think, sensually and falsely stimulating us. We seek and are fed by incessant noise. So we find a release in sex which becomes a torturing problem.

Through self-awareness the repetitive habit of thought which we consider as thinking is brought into the light of understanding; by observing it, examining it with kindly detachment, suspending judgment, we shall begin to awaken creative understanding. This is the process of disengaging thought-feeling from all hindrances, limitations; when once we become aware of this process, all our problems, trivial and complex, can be exposed to it and creative understanding extracted from it. So this is essential to grasp. Denial or acceptance, judgment or comparison, which mean identification, prevent the full flowering of thought-feeling. If you do not identify, then as thought-feeling flows, follow it through, think it out, feel it out as extensively and deeply as possible and so become aware of its wide and profound implications. Thus the narrow, small, self-enclosed mind breaks through its self-imposed limitations and blockages. In this process of clarification there is inward, creative joy.

In this manner solve the problem of lust. And as I said, mere inhibition or suppression does not solve the problem but only acts as a further factor of excitation, disturbance, only strengthening the self-enclosing process of the 'me' and the 'mine'. Become aware of the problem as extensively and deeply as possible and thereby discover its cause. Do not identify with the cause by judging or comparing it, condemning or accepting it, but watch that cause expressing itself in many ways; follow it through, think it out, feel it out intelligently, with tolerant detachment. In this extensional awareness the problem is resolved and transcended.

There is a difference between conquering sensuality and the state of nonsensuality. In nonsensuality thought-feeling is no longer a slave to the senses, and merely to conquer is to be conquered again. Awareness, which brings creative understanding, frees thought-feeling from lust, but to find substitutions for lust is still to be lustful. There is no escape from conflict and sorrow save in right thinking. Without self-knowledge there is no right thinking. Through awareness the ways of the self are discovered, and it is this discovery that liberates, that is creative. Love is chaste, but a mind that plots to be is not.

Question: Don't you think that there is a principle of destruction in life, a blind will quite independent of man, always dormant, ready to spring into action, which can never be transcended?

KRISHNAMURTI: Surely we know that within us there are these two opposing capacities—to destroy and to create, to be good and to be harmful. Now, are they independent of each other? Is the will to destroy separate from the will to live, or is the will to live, to become, in itself a process of destruction? What makes us destroy? What makes us angry, ignorant, brutal; what urges us to kill, to seek vengeance, to deceive? Is it a blind will, a thing over which we have no control whatever—let us call it the devil—an independent force of evil, or an uncontrollable ignorance? Is the urge to destroy inane or is it the response to a deeper demand to live, to be, to become? Is this reaction never to be transcended, or can it slow down to be examined or understood? To slow down a response is possible. Or is there a blind spot which can never be examined, a result of heredity, an inborn result which has so conditioned our thinking that we are incapable of looking into it? And so we think that there is a power of destruction, of evil, which cannot be transcended.

Surely anything that has been created, that has been made up, can be understood by those who have created it. This dual process of good and evil is in us to create and to destroy. We have created it and so we can understand it; but to understand it we must have the faculty of dispassionate observation of ourselves which requires great alertness and pliable awareness. Or we can say that in all of us potentially there is a dormant evil, a power that is in itself destructive. Though we may be loving, generous, merciful, this power—like an earthquake—completely impersonal, seeks an occasional outburst. And as over an earthquake, over acts of nature we have no control, so over this power we have no influence whatever.

Now is this so? Can we not, in understanding ourselves, understand the causes that exist in us to destroy and to create? If first we can clear the confusion that exists in the superficial layer of our conscious mind, then into it, because it is open, clear, the deeper layers of consciousness, with their contents, can project themselves. This clarification of the superficial layer comes when thought-feeling is not identifying but detached and so capable of observing without comparison and judgment. Then only can it, the conscious mind, discover what is true. Thus you can test for yourself whether there is in you an element which is absolutely beyond your control, an element which is destructive. Then you can find out whether it is the result of conditioning or whether it is ignorance or whether it is a blind spot or an independent, uncontrollable evil force. Only then can you discover whether or not you are cápable of transcending it.

The more you comprehend yourself and so bring about right thinking, the less you will find that there is any tendency, any ignorance, any force within you that cannot be transcended. And out of this you will discover an ecstasy that comes with understanding, with wisdom. It is not the faith and the hope of the foolish. In understanding ourselves completely and thus creating the faculty to delve deeply within, we will find there is nothing that cannot be examined or understood. Out of this self-knowledge comes creative understanding; but because we do not understand ourselves, there is ignorance. What thought has created, thought can transcend.

Question: Why are there so many insane, unbalanced people in the world?

KRISHNAMURTI: What is this civilization that we have built up? A civilization which is the result of craving, the dominant factor of sensory gratification. And having produced a world in which sensate value dominates, naturally the creative sensibilities are either destroyed or warped or blocked. Through the value of the senses, there is no release, and so individuals resort to the fabrication of delusion, consciously or unconsciously, which eventually isolates them. Unless sensate value yields to eternal value, we will have delusions and strife, confusion and war. To bring a fundamental change in value, you must become thoughtful and discard those values of the self, of craving, through constant awareness and self-knowledge.

Question: I am intensely lonely. I cannot seem to go beyond this misery. What am I to do?

KRISHNAMURTI: This is not an individual problem only; the whole human thought feels lonely. If we could think this out, feel this out deeply, we would be able to transcend it. As I explained, we create through craving a dual process in ourselves, and thus there arises the 'I', the 'me', the self, and the not-self, my work, my achievement and so on. Having created through craving this conflicting process of the 'I' and not 'I', its natural outcome is isolation, utter loneliness. In relationship, in action, if there is any self-enclosing thought-feeling, it is bound to build up isolating walls which cause intense loneliness.

Craving engenders fear, fear nourishes dependence, dependence on things, people or ideas. The greater the dependence, the greater the inward poverty. Becoming aware of this poverty, loneliness, you try to enrich it, try to fill it with knowledge or activity, with amusement or mystery. The more you try to fill it, to cover it up, the more deeply does the real cause of loneliness get buried. The self is insatiable and there is no satisfying it. It is as a broken vessel, a bottomless pit which can never be filled.

By becoming aware of thought-feeling creating its own bondage and dependence and thus bringing about isolation; by becoming aware of the cultivation of sensate values which must inevitably bring inward poverty; out of this very awareness, out of this extensional, meditative understanding, there is discovered the imperishable treasure. Through this constant awareness, if rightly unfolded, ever deeper and wider, there comes into being the serenity and joy of highest wisdom.

June 25, 1944

Eighth Talk in The Oak Grove

In the last few talks we have been discussing how to develop the faculty with which to discover what is true, in which alone is serenity and creative peace. This faculty is to be developed, as I explained, through right thinking—right thinking which is different from right, conditioned thought. In becoming aware we come upon the conflict of duality which, if we do not deeply comprehend, will lead to wrong kinds of effort. Right effort consists in thought-feeling freeing itself from this conflict of merit and demerit, the becoming and the not-becoming. To develop the perception of truth there must be candor, integrity of understanding, which can come only with humility. As I explained, virtue does not lie in developing qualities, which is to cultivate the opposites and so engender wrong effort; but in freeing thought-feeling from craving, virtue comes into being.

And we somewhat discussed relationship, dependence, fear, and love—how to set about freeing thought-feeling from dependence and fear which corrupt love.

I said that this morning we would try to understand what makes for simple life. Simple life is freedom from acquisitiveness, freedom from addiction, and freedom from distraction. Freedom from acquisitiveness surely lies in understanding the cause that breeds in us the conflict of greed and envy. The more we acquire, the greater the demand for possessions, and to deny, to say, "I will not acquire," in no way solves the problem of greed and envy. But in watching it, in becoming aware of the process of acquisition and envy on all the different levels of our consciousness, we begin to understand their deeper significance, with all the economic, social, and inward implications. This state of acquisitive conflict, competitive possessiveness is not conducive to simple life which is essential to understand the real. So if you become aware of acquisitiveness with its

problems—not putting yourself in opposition to it and therefore developing the quality of nonacquisitiveness, which is only another form of greed—you will begin to be aware of its deeper and wider implications.

Then you will begin to understand that a mind caught up in greed and envy cannot experience the bliss of truth. A mind which is competitive, held in the conflict of becoming, thinking in terms of comparison, is not capable of discovering the real. Thought-feeling which is intensely aware is in the process of constant self-discovery—which discovery, being true, is liberating and creative. Such self-discovery brings about freedom from acquisitiveness and from the complex life of the intellect. It is this complex life of the intellect that finds gratification in addictions: destructive curiosity, speculation, mere knowledge, capacity, gossip, and so on; and these hindrances prevent simplicity of life. An addiction, a specialization, gives sharpness to the mind, a means of focusing thought, but it is not the flowering of thought-feeling into reality.

The freedom from distraction is more difficult as we do not fully understand the process of thinking-feeling which in itself has become the means of distraction. Being ever incomplete, capable of speculative curiosity and formulation, it has the power to create its own hindrances, illusions, which prevent the awareness of the real. So it becomes its own distraction, its own enemy. As the mind is capable of creating illusion, this power must be understood before it can be wholly free from its own self-created distractions. Mind must be utterly still, silent, for all thought becomes a distraction. Craving is the distorting factor, and how can the mind that is capable of delusion know the simple, the real? Until craving in its multiple forms is understood and transcended, there is no joy of the inward, simple, full life. If you begin to be aware of the outward distractions and so trace them to the cause which is inner, then thought-feeling, which in itself has become the means of its own escape, its own cause of ignorance, will disentangle itself from the jungle of distractions. Through becoming aware of the outward distractions—possessions, relationships, amusements, pleasures, addictions—and by thinking-feeling them out, the inner distractions—escapes, knowledge, speculations, self-protective beliefs, memories, and so on—are discovered. When there is an awareness of the outer and inner distractions, there comes deep understanding, and only then is there a natural and easy withdrawal from them. For thought-feeling to discipline itself not to be distracted prevents the understanding of the nature and cause of distraction, and so discipline itself becomes an escape, a means of distraction.

Simple life does not consist in the mere possession of a few things but in the freedom from possession and nonpossession, in the indifference to things that comes with deep understanding. Merely to renounce things in order to reach greater happiness, greater joy that is promised, is to seek reward which limits thought and prevents it from flowering and discovering reality. To control thought-feeling for a greater reward, for a greater result, is to make it petty, ignorant, and sorrowful. Simplicity of life comes with inner richness, with inward freedom from craving, with freedom from acquisitiveness, from addiction, from distraction.

From this simple life there comes that necessary one-pointedness which is not the outcome of self-enclosing concentration but of extensional awareness and meditative understanding. Simple life is not the result of outward circumstances; contentment with little comes with the riches of inward understanding. If you depend on circumstances to make you satisfied with life, then you will create misery and chaos, for then you are a plaything of environment, and it is only when circumstances are transcended through understanding that there is order and clarity. To be constantly aware of the process of acquisitiveness, of addiction, of distraction brings freedom from them, and so there is a true and simple life.

Question: My son was killed in this war. I have another son twelve years old and I do not want to lose him too in another war. How is another war to be prevented?

KRISHNAMURTI: I am sure this same question must be put by every mother and father throughout the world. It is a universal problem. And I wonder what price the parents are willing to pay to prevent another war, to prevent their sons from being killed, to prevent this appalling human slaughter; how much they really mean when they say that they love their children, that war must be prevented, that they must have brotherhood, that a way must be found to stop all wars.

To create a new way of life, you must have a new revolutionary way of thinkingfeeling. You will have another war, you are bound to have another war, if you are thinking in terms of nationalities, of racial prejudices, of economic and social frontiers. If each one really considers in his heart how to prevent another war, he must put aside his nationality, his particular specialized religion, his greed and ambition. If you do not you will have another war, for these prejudices and the adherence to specialized religions are merely the outward expressions of your selfishness, ignorance, ill will, lust.

But you will answer that it will take a very long time for each one of us to change and so to convince others of this point of view; society is not prepared to receive this idea; politicians are not interested in it; the leaders are incapable of this conception of one universal government or state without separate sovereignties. You might say that it is an evolutionary process which will gradually bring about this necessary change. If you replied in this manner to the parent whose son is going to be killed in another war and if he really loved his son, do you think he would find hope in this gradual evolutionary process? He wants to save his son, and he wants to know what is the surest way to stop all wars. He will not be satisfied with your gradual evolutionary theory. Is this evolutionary theory of gradual peace true or invented by us to rationalize our lazy and egotistic thought-feeling? Is it not incomplete and so not true? We think that we must go through the various states, the family, the group, the nation, and the inter-nation and then only will we have peace. It is but a justification of our egotism and narrowness, bigotry and prejudice; instead of sweeping away these dangers we invent a theory of progressive growth and sacrifice to it the happiness of others and ourselves. If we apply our mind and heart to the disease of ignorance and selfishness, then we shall create a sane and happy world.

We must not think and feel horizontally but vertically. That is, instead of following the course of lazy, selfish, ignorant thought-feeling of gradualism, of slow enlightenment through the process of time, of following this stream of continual conflict and misery, of constant mass murder and a period of rest from it—called peace—and an eventual paradise on earth; instead of thinking-feeling along these horizontal lines, can we not think-feel vertically? Is it not possible to pull ourselves out of the horizontal continuance of confusion and strife and to think-feel away from it, anew, without the sense of time, vertically? Without thinking in terms of evolution which helps to rationalize our laziness and postponement, can we not think-feel directly, simply? The love of the mother thinks-feels directly and simply, but her egotism, her national pride, and so on help

her to think-feel in terms of gradualism, horizontally.

The present is the eternal, neither the past nor the future can reveal it; through the present only the timeless is realized. If you really desire to save your son and so mankind from another war, then you must pay the price for it: not to be greedy, not to have ill will, and not to be worldly; for lust, ill will, and ignorance breed conflict, confusion, and antagonism; they breed nationalism, pride, and the tyranny of the machine. If you are willing to free yourself from lust, ill will, and ignorance, then only will you save your son from another war. To bring happiness to the world, to put an end to this mass murder, there must be complete inward revolution of thought-feeling which brings about new morality, a morality not of the sensate but based on freedom from sensuality, worldliness, and the craving for personal immorality.

Question: You talk of meditative awareness but you never talk of prayer. Are you opposed to prayer?

KRISHNAMURTI: In opposition there is no understanding. Most of us indulge in petitionary prayer, and this form of prayer cultivates, strengthens duality, the observer and the observed, which are a joint phenomenon. Only when this duality ceases is there the whole. However much you may petition, your answer will be according to your demand, but it will not be of the real. The answer to a desire is in the desire itself. When the mind-heart is utterly still, utterly silent, then only is there the whole, the eternal.

Some time ago I saw a person who said he had been praying to God, and one of his petitions was for a refrigerator. Please do not laugh. And he had acquired not only a refrigerator but also a house, so his prayers were answered, and God was a reality, he asserted.

When you ask you will receive, but you will have to pay for it; according to your demands you are answered, but there is a price for it. Greed replies to greed. When you ask out of greed, out of fear, out of want, you will have an answer, but you must pay for it, and you pay for it through wars, strife, and misery. The centuries of greed, cruelty, ill will, ignorance manifest themselves when you call upon them. So to indulge in prayer without self-knowledge, without understanding, is disastrous. The meditative awareness of which I have been speaking is the outcome of self-knowledge in which alone there is right thinking, and it is this that frees the mind-heart from the dual process of the observer and the observed, for they are a joint phenomenon, a joint occurrence. The observer is ever conditioning the observed and it is extremely difficult to go beyond the observer and the observed, to go beyond and above the created. The thinker and his thought must cease for the eternal to be.

I have been trying to explain in my talks how to clarify the confusion that exists between the observer and the observed, the thinker and his thought, through self-knowledge and right thinking. For without self-clarification, the observer is ever conditioning the observed and so cannot go beyond himself and becomes imprisoned. He is caught in his own delusion. For the realization of that which is not created, not made up, thought-feeling must transcend the created, the result, the self; thought-feeling must cease to demand, cease to acquire, cease to be distracted by any form of ritualism and memory. If you will experiment, you will discover how extremely difficult it is for thought to be wholly free from its own chattering and creation. Only when it is so free, only when the observer and the observed have ceased, is there the immeasurable.

Question: I have been writing down as you suggested. I find that I cannot get beyond the trivial thoughts. Is it because the conscious mind refuses to acknowledge the subconscious cravings and demands and so escapes into an empty blockade?

KRISHNAMURTI: I suggested that to slow down the mind in order to examine the thought-feeling process, you should write down every thought-feeling. If one wishes to understand, for example, a machine of high revolution, one has to slow it down, not stop it, for then it becomes merely a dead matter; but make it turn gently, slowly, to study its structure, its movement. Likewise if we wish to understand our mind, we must slow down our thinking—not put a stop to it—slow it down in order to study it, to follow it to its fullest extent. And to do this I suggested that you should write down every thought-feeling. It is not possible to write down every thought and feeling, for there are too many of them, but if you attempted to write a little every day, you would soon begin to know yourself; you would begin to be aware of the many layers of your consciousness, of their interrelation and interresponse. This awareness is difficult, but if you would go far you must begin near.

Now, the questioner finds his thoughts are trivial and that he cannot get beyond them. He wants to know if this triviality is the result of an escape from the deeper cravings and demands. Partly it is and also our thoughts and feelings are in themselves petty, trivial, small. The root of understanding lies through the small, the trivial. Without understanding the small, thought-feeling cannot go beyond itself. You must become aware of your trivialities, your narrowness, your prejudices to understand them, and you can understand only when there is humility, when there is neither judgment nor comparison, acceptance nor denial. Thus there is the beginning of wisdom. Most of our thought-feeling is trivial. Why not recognize and understand its cause: the self, the result of vast and petty ignorance. Just as in following a thin vein you may come upon riches, so if you follow, think-out, feel-out the trivial, you will discover deep treasures. The small may hide the deep, but you must follow it. The trivial, if you study it, gives promise of something beyond. Do not brush it aside, but become aware of every thought-feeling, for it has a significance.

The blockages may occur either because the conscious mind does not want to respond to deeper demands, which may necessitate a different course of action and so bring about trouble and pain, or it is incapable of wider and deeper thought-feeling. If it is the lack of capacity, you can create it only through persistent and constant awareness, through searching, observing, studying.

I only suggested writing down every thought-feeling as a means of cultivating this comprehensive, extensional awareness which is not the concentration of exclusion, not the concentration of self-enclosing isolation. This extensional awareness comes through understanding, not through mere judgment or comparison, denial or acceptance.

Question: What guarantee have I that the new faculty of which you speak will come into being?

KRISHNAMURTI: I am afraid none whatever! This is not an investment, surely. If you are seeking surety then you will meet death, but if you are uncertain, therefore adventuring, seeking, the real will be discovered. We want to be guaranteed, we want to be sure of the result before we even try, for we are lazy and thoughtless and do not wish to set out on the long journey of self-discovery. We do not apply ourselves; we want enlightenment to be given to us in exchange for our effort which indicates possessive security. In security there is no discovery of the real; this search for security is self-protectiveness and in the self there is ignorance and sorrow. To understand, to discover the real, there must be the abandonment of the self; there must be negative comprehension for that which lies beyond all the cunning schemes of the self. What is discovered in the search of self-knowledge is true, and it is this truth that is liberating and creative—not my guarantee that you will be liberated, which would be utter folly. We are in conflict, in confusion, in sorrow and it is this suffering, not any promise of reward, that must be the compelling force to seek, to search out and to discover the real. This search must be made by each one of us and self-knowledge is to be cultivated through constant self-awareness; right thinking comes with self-knowledge which alone brings peace and understanding. The end is made distant through greed.

Question: Is it wrong to have a Master, a spiritual teacher on another plane of existence?

KRISHNAMURTI: I have tried to answer the same question put in different ways at different times, but apparently few wish to understand. Superstition is difficult to throw off, for the mind creates it and becomes its prisoner.

How difficult it is to find what is true in what one reads, in one's daily relationship and thought! Prejudice, tendency, conditioning dictate our choice; to discover what is true these must be set aside; mind must discard its own self-restricting, narrow thoughts-feelings. To discover what is true in our thoughts, feelings, and actions is extremely difficult and how much more difficult it is to discern the true in a supposedly spiritual world! If we want a teacher, a guru, it is sufficiently difficult to find a physical one, and how much more complex, deceptive, confusing it must be to search out a teacher in a so-called spiritual world, in another plane of existence. Even if a supposedly spiritual teacher chooses you, you are really the chooser—not the supposed teacher. If you do not understand yourself in this world of action and interaction, of lust, ill will, and ignorance, how can you trust your judgment, your capacity to discern, in a supposedly spiritual world? If you do not know yourself, how can you discern what is true? How do you know that your own mind which has the power to create illusion has not created the Master, the teacher? Is it not vanity that persuades you to seek the Master and be chosen?

There is a story of a pupil going to a teacher and requesting him to lead him to the Master; the teacher said that he would only if he, the pupil, did exactly as he was told. The pupil was delighted. For seven years he was told he must live in the nearby cave and there follow the teacher's instruction. He was told that first he must sit quietly, peacefully, in concentrated thought; then in the second year he was to invite the Master into the cave; the third he was to make the Master sit with him; in the fourth he was to talk with him; in the fifth year he was to make the Master move about in the cave; in the sixth to make him leave the cave. After the sixth year the teacher asked the pupil to come out and said to him, "Now you know who the Master is."

The mind has the power to create ignorance or to discern what is true. In this search for the Master, there is always in it the desire to gain, and so there arises fear, and a mind that is seeking a reward and so inviting fear cannot understand what is true. It is the height of ignorance to think in terms of reward and punishment, of the superior and the inferior. Besides can anyone help you to discover what is true in your own thoughts-feelings? Others may point out but you, yourself, have to search out and discover what is true.

If you look to another to be saved from suffering and ignorance, from this chaotic and barbarous world, you will only create further confusion and ill will, further ignorance and sorrow. You are responsible for your own thoughts-feelings-actions; you alone can bring clarity and order; you alone can save yourself from yourself; by your understanding alone can you transcend greed, ill will, and ignorance.

Each one of us, here, I hope, is trying to seek the real, the imperishable, and is not to be distracted by the beauty of wayside shrines, by the trimmings of the sign post, by ritualism. There is no authority that can lead you to the ultimate reality, and that reality lies in the beginning as in the end. Do not stop at the sign posts nor be caught up in the pettiness of groups, nor become enamored of the chanting, or the incense, of the ritual. The reliance on another for self-knowledge adds more ignorance, for the other is yourself. The root of understanding is hidden in yourself. The perception of the true lies in right thinking, in humility, in compassion, in simple life, not in the authority of another. The authority of another, however great, leads to further ignorance and sorrow.

July 2, 1944

Ninth Talk in The Oak Grove

It is important at all times and especially in times of much suffering and confusion to find for ourselves that inward, creative joy and understanding. We have to discover it for ourselves, but sensuousness, prosperity and personal power, in all their different forms, prevent creative peace and happiness. If we use our energies for the gratification of the senses, we will inevitably create values which will bring prosperity, worldliness, but with these come war, confusion, and sorrow. If we seek personal immortality, we will nourish the greed for power which expresses itself in many ways: national, racial, economic, and so on, from which flow great disasters with which we are all familiar.

We have been discussing during the last eight talks these matters. It is necessary to understand ourselves, for in understanding ourselves we will begin to think rightly, and in the process of right thinking, we will discover what it means to live deeply and creatively and to realize that which is beyond all measure. To live fully and creatively there must be self-knowledge; and to know, there must be candor and humility, love and thought freed from fear. Virtue lies in the freedom from craving, and craving brings multiplicity and repetition and makes life complex, tormenting, and sorrowful.

A simple life, as I explained, does not merely consist in the possession of few things, but in right livelihood and in the freedom from distractions, addictions, and possessiveness. Freedom from acquisitiveness will create the means of right livelihood, but there are certain obvious wrong means. Greed, tradition, and the desire for power will bring about the wrong means of livelihood. Even in these times when everybody is harnessed to a particular kind of work, it is possible to find right occupation. Each one must become aware of the issues of wrong occupation with its disasters and miseries, weary routine and death dealing ways. Is it not necessary for each one to know for himself what is the right means of livelihood? If we are avaricious, envious, seeking power, then our means of livelihood will correspond to our inward demands and so produce a world of competition, ruthlessness, oppression, ultimately ending in war.

So surely it is imperative that each one should think over his problem; perhaps you will not be able to do anything immediately, but at least you can think-feel seriously about it, which will bring its own action. Talent and capacity have their own dangers, and if we are not aware we become slaves to them. This slavery produces antisocial action, bringing misery and destruction to man. Without right understanding, talent and capacity become an end in themselves, and so disaster follows for him who has it and for his fellow man.

Without the discovery and the understanding of the real, there is no creative joy, no peace; our life will be a constant struggle and pain; our actions and relationships will have no significance; outward legislation and compulsion will never produce inward riches, treasures that are imperishable. To understand the real, we must become aware of the process of our thinking, of the way of our memory and of the interrelated layers of our consciousness. Our thought is the result of the past. Our being is founded on the past. Organically and in thought we are copies. Organically we can understand the copies that we are, and we can, by understanding them, comprehend their reactions, imitative actions, and responses. But if our thought-feeling is merely imitative, the result of mere tradition and environment, there is little hope of going beyond itself. But if we recognize and understand the limits of environmental influences and are capable of going beyond their imitative restrictions, then we shall find that there is a freedom from copy in which is the real.

A copy, a thing that is put together, the self, can never understand that which is not made up, the uncreated. It is only when the copy, the self, the 'me' and the 'mine' ceases that there is the ecstasy of the imperishable. The self thinks-feels in terms of gathering, accumulating, experiencing; it thinks-feels in terms of the past, of the future, or of continuing the present. This accumulative process of memory strengthens the self which is the cause of ignorance and sorrow. Without understanding the ways of the self, those of us who are politically and socially inclined are apt to sacrifice the present with the hope of creating a better world in the future; or there are some who wish to continue the present; or there are those who look to the past. Without understanding the self and transcending it, all such actions must end in calamity. In becoming aware of the process of the self with its accumulative memory, we shall begin to understand its time-binding quality, the craving for continued identification. Until we understand the nature of the self and transcend its time-binding quality, there can be no peace, no happiness. As the self is, so is the environment, political and social.

It is the time-binding quality of the self with its identifying memory that must be studied, understood, and so transcended. Desire, especially pleasurable desire, is singularistic; and it is memory that gives identified continuity to the 'me' and the 'mine'. Thought-feeling which is ever in movement, ever in flux, when it identifies itself with the 'me' and the 'mine', becomes time-binding, giving identified continuity to memory, to the self. It is this memory which is ever increasing and multiplying that must be abandoned. It is this memory that is the cause of copy, of the movement of thought from the known to the known, thus preventing the realization of truth, the uncreated. Memory must become as a shell without a living organism in it. To discover the unknowable reality, we have to transcend the time-binding quality of the self,

the identifying memory. This is an arduous task. Through meditative awareness the binding process of memory is to be understood; through constant awareness of every thought-feeling, craving for identity is observed and understood. Thus through alert and passive awareness, thought-feeling frees itself from the time-binding quality of memory of the 'me' and the 'mine'. It is only when the self ceases to create that there is the uncreated.

Question: In the Bhagavad-Gita, Krishna urges Arjuna to enter into battle. You say right means to right ends. Are you opposed to the teachings of Krishna?

KRISHNAMURTI: Perhaps some of you have not heard of this book; it is the sacred book of the Hindus in which Krishna, supposed to be the manifestation of God, urges Arjuna, the warrior, to enter into battle. Now, the questioner wants to know if I am opposed to this teaching which urges Arjuna to fight. This teaching can be interpreted in many ways, each interpretation creating contention. We can think of many interpretations, but I do not want to indulge in speculation which would be futile. Let us think-feel without the crippling burden of spiritual authority. This is of primary importance to understand the real.

To accept authority, especially in matters that concern right thinking, is utterly foolish. To accept authority is binding, hindering, and the worship of authority is self-worship. It is a form of laziness, thoughtlessness, leading to ignorance and sorrow.

Most of us desire to have a world in which there is peace and brotherhood, in which ruthlessness and war have no place, in which there is kindliness and tolerance. How are we to achieve it? To bring about right ends surely right means must be employed. If you would have tolerance, you must be tolerant, you must put away intolerance from you. If you would have peace, you must use right means for it, not wrong methods, brutality and violence. This is obvious, is it not? If you would be friends with another, you must show courtesy and kindliness; there must be no anger, no cause for enmity. So you must use right means to create right ends, for in the very means is the end. They are not separate; they do not lie distant. So if you would have peace in this world, you must use peaceful methods. You may have right ends, but wrong means will not achieve them. Surely this is an obvious fact, but unfortunately we are carried away by repetitive authority, by propaganda, by ignorance. The thing in itself is simple and clear. If you would have a brotherly, unified world, then you must put away the causes of disruption: enmity, jealousy, acquisitiveness, nationality, racial difference, pride, and so on. But very few of us are willing to put aside our craving for power, our specialized religion, our ill will and so on; we are unwilling to abandon these and yet we want peace, a noncompetitive and sane world!

You cannot have peace in the world except through peaceful means. You must eradicate in yourself the causes of enmity by right and intelligent means, by right thinking. Self-knowledge cultivates right thinking. But as most of us are ignorant of ourselves, and as our thinking-feeling is self-contradictory, our thought is nonexistent. So we are led, driven, and made to accept. Through constant awareness of every thought-feeling, the ways of the self are known, and out of self-knowledge comes right thinking. Right thinking will create the right means for a sane and peaceful world.

Question: How am I to get rid of hate?

KRISHNAMURTI: There are similar questions with regard to ignorance, anger, jealousy. In answering this particular question, I hope to answer the others also.

A problem cannot be solved on its own plane, on its own level. It must be understood and so dissolved from a different and deeper level of abstraction. If we wish merely to get rid of hate by suppressing it or treating it as a tiresome and interfering thing, then we shall not dissolve it; it will reoccur again and again in different forms, for we are dealing with it on its own limited, petty level. But if we begin to understand its inner causes and its outer effects, and so make our thought-feeling wider and deeper, sharper and clearer, then hate will disappear naturally, for we are concerned with deeper and more important levels of thoughts-feelings.

If we are angry and if we are able to suppress it, or so control ourselves that it does not rise up again, our mind is still as small and insensitive as before. What has been gained by this effort not to be angry if our thought-feeling is still envious and fearful, narrow and enclosed? We may get rid of hate or anger, but if the mind-heart is still stupid and petty, it will create again other problems and other antagonisms, and so there is no end to conflict. But if we begin to be aware and so understand the causes of anger and their effects, then surely we are widening and freeing thought-feeling from ignorance and conflict. In becoming aware we shall begin to discover the causes of anger or of hate which are self-protective fears in different forms. Through awareness we discover we are angry, perhaps, because our particular belief is being attacked; on examining it further we question if belief, creed are necessary at all. We become more aware of its wider significance; we perceive how dogmas, ideologies divide people, giving cause to antagonism, to various forms of cruel and stupid absurdities. So through this extensional awareness, through comprehension of its inward significance, anger soon fades away; through this process of self-awareness the mind has become deeper, quieter, wiser, and so the causes of hate and anger have no place in it. In freeing thought-feeling from anger and hate, from greed and ill will, there comes a gentleness, the only cure. This gentleness, compassion, is not the result of suppression or substitution but is the outcome of self-knowledge and right thinking.

Question: Though you have talked about it, I find concentration extremely difficult. Would you kindly go into it again.

KRISHNAMURTI: Is not interested attention necessary if we would understand? Especially is it necessary if we would understand ourselves, for our thoughts and feelings are so vagrant, quick, and apparently disconnected. To understand ourselves an extensional awareness is essential, not an exclusive mind with its rejections and judgments, not a narrowing concentration. From extensional awareness comes one-pointedness, true concentration.

Now why is it that we find concentration so difficult? Is it not because most of our thinking is a distraction, a dissipation? Either through habit, laziness, or through interests, or because our thought-feeling has not completed itself, thought wanders or is repetitive. If it wanders because of interest, merely to suppress or control thought is of little use, for such suppression and control is another additional factor for further disturbance. Thought will revert to that interest, however trivial, over and over again until all its value ceases. So if thought wanders because of interest, why not think it through instead of resisting it? Go with it, become aware of all its implications, study it disinterestedly until that particular thought, however stupid and petty, is understood and so dissolved. Thus you will discover through this process of extensional awareness that repetitive thoughts of trivial interest cease; and they cease only when you consciously think-feel them out, not suppress them. If thought wanders because of habit, it is indicative, and to become aware of it is important. If thought-feeling is caught in habit, it is merely mechanical repetition and copy, and so is not thinking at all. If you examine such habit of thought, you will perceive that it might be caused by education, through fear of opinion, through religious upbringing, through environmental influence, and so on. So your thought follows a groove, a pattern which reveals your own state of being. It might be through laziness that thought wanders. Again this is also very indicative, is it not? To be aware of laziness is to become alert, but to be unaware of it is to be truly lazy. We allow ourselves to become lazy through wrong diet, not paying sufficient attention to health, or through circumstances or relationships that put us to sleep, and so on. Thus when we become aware of the causes of our laziness, we may produce inward disturbances which have outward effect, and so we may prefer to be lazy. Or thought is repetitive because it is never allowed to complete itself. Just as an unfinished letter becomes a source of irritation, so unfinished thought-feeling becomes repetitive.

Through constant awareness you will begin to find out for yourself why your thought-feeling wanders or is repetitive, whether because of interest or habit or laziness, or because it is not completed. If you pursue your thoughts-feelings diligently, alertly, with passive disinterested watchfulness, there comes an extensional concentration which is essential for the understanding of the real. A mind that is formulating, creating, cannot understand creation, the uncreated. How can a chattering, noisy mind comprehend the immeasurable? Of what value is a beautiful piece of art to a child? It will play with it and is soon tired of it. So it is with most of us. We believe or disbelieve; we have other people's experiences and knowledge. Our minds are petty, cruel, ignorant. Our minds are broken up, there is no integration and stillness. How can such a mind understand that which is beyond all measure, beyond all formulation! To be truly concentrated all valuation must cease. Awareness flows into deep and quiet pools of meditation.

Question: Do I not owe something to my race, to my nation, to my group?

KRISHNAMURTI: What is your nation, your race? Each people says, "Its nation, its group, its race." Out of this thoughtless assertion there is confusion and conflict, untold sorrow and degradation. You and I are one; there is neither the East nor the West. We are human beings, not labels. We have artificially created nations, races, groups in opposition to other nations, races, and groups. We have created them, you and I, in our search for power and fame; in our desire to be exclusive; in our delight in those singularistic, self-enclosing cravings; through greed, ill will, and ignorance, we have created national, racial, and economic barriers. We have artificially separated ourselves from our fellow men. Does a thoughtful man owe something to that which is the outcome of ill will and ignorance? If you are still part of the nation, the group, the race, the result of fear and greed, then being of it you are responsible for sorrow and cruelty. Then what you are—your race, your nation, your group is. Then how can you owe something to that of which you are a part? Only when you put yourself in opposition to the mass, then in your individualistic, exclusive response, debt is incurred. But surely such a reaction is false, for you are the group, the nation, the race; out of you it has come into being; without you it is not.

So the question is not whether you are indebted to it but how to transcend it; how to go beyond the causes that have produced this separative, exclusive existence. By asking yourself what is your duty, your karma, your relationship with the mass, with the nation, you are putting to yourself a wrong question which will have only a wrong answer.

You have created the nation in your desire for self-worship, for self-glory, and any answer to that will still be conditioned by your craving. An answer to a desire is in the desire itself. So the question is how to transcend the responses of individuality, of the mass, or of the nation. You can go above and beyond them only through self-awareness in which the self, the cause of conflict, antagonism and ignorance, is observed disinterestedly and so understood and dissolved. Right thinking is its own reward.

Question: Are there different paths to reality?

KRISHNAMURTI: Would you not put the question differently? Each one of us has several tendencies, each tendency creating its own difficulties. In each one of us there is a dominant tendency, intellectual, emotional, or sensuous—a tendency towards knowledge, devotion, or action. Each has its own complexity and trial. If you pursue one exclusively, rejecting the others, you will not discover completeness, reality; but by becoming aware of the difficulties of each tendency, thus understanding them, the whole is realized. When we ask if there are not different paths to reality, do we not mean the difficulties and hindrances which each tendency meets with and how they are transcended so as to discover the real? To transcend them you have to become aware of each tendency and watch it with disinterested, passive alertness; and through understanding its conflicts and trials, go beyond and above it. Through constant meditative awareness these various tendencies with their hindrances and joys are understood and made whole.

July 9, 1944

Tenth Talk in the Oak Grove

I have been saying that to lay emphasis on the immediate does not solve the very complex human problem. I mean by the immediate, the urgent consideration of the senses and their gratification. That is, to lay emphasis on the economic and social values instead of on the primary and eternal, leads to distorted and terrible actions. The immediate becomes the future when sensate values and their gratifications are promised by sacrificing the present; when the present is sacrificed in the hope of a future happiness or of a future economic well-being, then is the beginning of cruel thoughtlessness and disaster. Such emphasis must inevitably lead to further chaos, for in giving importance to that which is secondary, we miss the whole, the real, and so bring about confusion and misery. Each one must become aware, must think out and feel out for himself what is involved in giving primary importance to the gratification of sensory desires. To yield to the values of the senses is to ultimately bring about war, economic and social catastrophes. To seek enrichment in things, made by hand or by mind, is to create inward poverty which brings untold misery. Accumulation and its importance deprives thought-feeling of the realization of the real which alone will bring order, clarity, and happiness.

If one seeks first to cultivate the inner, the real, then the secondary, the economic and social order, will come wisely into being; otherwise there will be constant economic and social upheavals, wars and confusion. In seeking the eternal we will be able to bring order and clarity. The part is never the whole, and the cultivation of the part brings ceaseless confusion, conflict, and antagonism.

To comprehend the whole we must first understand ourselves. The root of understanding lies in oneself, and without the understanding of oneself, there is no comprehension of the world; for the world is oneself. The other—the friend, the relation, the enemy, the neighbor, near or far—is yourself.

Self-knowledge is the beginning of right thinking, and in the process of self-knowledge, the infinite is discovered. The book of self-knowledge has no beginning and no end. It is a constant process of discovery, and what is discovered is true and truth is liberating, creative. If in that process of self-understanding, we seek a result, such a result is binding, enclosing, and hindering, and so the immeasurable, the timeless is not discovered. To seek a result is to search out value, which is to cultivate craving and so to engender ignorance, conflict, and sorrow. If we are seeking to understand, to read this complex rich book, then we will discover its infinite riches. To read this book of self-knowledge is to become aware. Through self-awareness each thought-feeling is examined without judgment and thus allowed to flower, which brings understanding; for in following each thought-feeling fully, we will find that in it all thinking is contained. We can think-feel completely only when we are not seeking a result, an end.

In this process of self-knowledge, right thinking comes into being; and right thinking frees the mind from craving. The freedom from craving is virtue. Mind must free itself from craving, the cause of ignorance and sorrow. For the mind to be virtuous, to be free from craving, complete candor, honesty, which comes with humility, is essential. And such integrity is not a virtue, not an end in itself but is a byproduct of thought freeing itself from the process of craving, which principally expresses itself in sensuality, in prosperity or worldliness, in personal immortality or fame. Thought, in freeing itself from craving, will comprehend the nature of fear, and so in transcending it there will be love which is in itself eternal. Simple life does not consist merely with the contentment of a few things but rather in the freedom from acquisitiveness, dependence, and distraction—inner and outer. Through constant awareness the time-binder, the identifying process of memory which builds up the self is thus dissolved. Only then can the ultimate reality come into being.

To understand oneself, this complex entity, is most difficult. A mind that is burdened with value and prejudice, judgment and comparison, cannot comprehend itself. Self-knowledge comes with choiceless awareness, and when craving no longer distorts thought-feeling, then in that fullness when the mind is utterly still, creatively empty, the highest is.

Question: I had a son who was killed in this war. He did not want to die. He wanted to live and prevent this horror being repeated. Was it my fault that he was killed?

KRISHNAMURTI: It is the fault of every one of us that this present horror is going on. It is the outward result of our everyday inner life of greed, ill will, and lust, of competition, acquisitiveness, and specialized religion. It is the fault of everyone who, indulging in these, has created this terrible calamity. Because we are nationalistic, singularistic, passionate, each one of us is contributing to this mass murder. You have been taught how to kill and how to die, but not how to live. If you wholeheartedly abhorred killing and violence in any form, then you would find ways and means to live peacefully and creatively. If that were your chief and primary in-

terest, then you would search out every cause, every instinct that makes for violence, for hatred, for mass murder. Are you so wholeheartedly interested in stopping war? If you are then you must eradicate in yourself the causes of violence and killing for any reason whatsoever. If you wish to stop wars, then there must take place a deep, inner revolution of tolerance and compassion; then thought-feeling must free itself from patriotism, from its identification with any group, from greed and those causes that breed enmity.

A mother told me that to give up these things would not only be extremely difficult but also would mean great loneliness and utter isolation which she could not face. So was she not responsible for untold misery? You might agree with her, and so by your laziness, thoughtlessness, add fuel to the ever-increasing flames of war. If, on the contrary, you attempted seriously to eradicate the causes of enmity and violence in yourself, there would be peace and joy in your heart which would have immediate effect about you.

We must reeducate ourselves not to murder, not to liquidate each other for any cause, however righteous it may appear to be for the future happiness of mankind—for an ideology, however promising, not merely be educated technically, which inevitably makes for ruthlessness—but to be content with little, to be compassionate and to seek the supreme.

The prevention of this ever-increasing destruction and horror depends on each one of us, not on any organization or planning, not on any ideology, not on the inventions of greater instruments of destruction, not on any leader but on each one of us. Do not think that wars cannot be stopped by so humble and lowly a beginning—a stone may alter the course of a river—to go far you must begin near. To understand the world chaos and misery, you must comprehend your own confusion and sorrow, for out of these come the magnified issues of the world. To understand yourself there must be constant meditative awareness which will bring to the surface the causes of violence and hate, greed and ambition, and by studying them without identification, thought will transcend them. For none can lead you to peace save yourself; there is no leader, no system that can bring war, exploitation, oppression to an end save yourself. Only by your thoughtfulness, by your compassion, by your awakened understanding, can there be established goodwill and peace.

Question: Though you explained last week how to get rid of hate, would you mind going into it again as I feel that what you said was of great importance.

KRISHNAMURTI: Hate is the result of a petty mind, of a small mind. A narrow mind is intolerant. A mind that is in bondage is capable of resentment. Now, a little mind saying to itself that it must not hate still remains little. An ignorant mind is the cause of enmity and of conflict.

So the problem then is not how to get rid of hate but rather how to destroy ignorance, the self, that causes narrow thought-feeling. If you merely overcome hate without understanding the ways of ignorance, then that ignorance will produce other forms of antagonism, and so thought-feeling will be violent and ever in conflict. How then are you to free the mind from ignorance, from stupidity? Through constant awareness—by becoming aware that your thought-feeling is small, petty, and narrow and not being ashamed of it, by understanding the causes that have made it little and self-enclosed. In understanding the deep and extensional causes, intelligence, disinterested generosity, and kindliness come in to being and hate yields to compassion. Through constant awareness the cause of ignorance, the process

of the self, with its burden of the 'me' and the 'mine', my achievement, my country, my possessions, my god, is being discovered, understood and dissolved. To understand there must be no judgment or comparison, no acceptance or denial, for all identification prevents that passive awareness in which alone the discovery of what is true is made. And it is this discovery that is creative and liberating. If the mind is aware negatively, passively, then being open it is able to discover the bondage, the limiting influence or idea, and so free itself from them.

So no problem can be solved on its own level; it is to be solved on a different level of abstraction. Thinking is a process of expansion, of inclusive inquiry, not a concentrated denial or assertion. In trying to understand hate and its causes, in trying to free thought-feeling from hindrances, from delusions, mind becomes deeper and more extensive. In the greater the lesser ceases to be.

Question: Is there anything after death or is it the end? Some say there is continuation, others annihilation. What do you say?

KRISHNAMURTI: In this question many things are involved; and as it is complex we will have to go into it, if you wish, deeply and openly. First of all, what do we mean by individuality? For we are not considering death abstractly but the death of an individual, of the particular. Will the individual self with name and form continue, or will he cease to exist? Will he take birth again? Before we can answer this question, we must find what makes up individuality. A wrong question has no right answer; only a right question may have an answer. And all questions concerning the deep problems of life have no categorical answer, for each one must discover what is true for himself. Truth alone gives freedom.

Is not individuality, though it may have a different form and name, the result of a series of accumulated responses and memories from the past, from yesterday? Each one of us is the result of the past and the past contains the you and the many, the you and the other. You are the result of your father and mother, of all the fathers and mothers; you are the father, the maker of the past, the father of the future. Thus through identifying memory the self is created, the 'me' and the 'mine'; so the self becomes the time-binder. From this arises the question of whether the self continues or is annihilated after death. Only when the self, the becomer and the nonbecomer, the creator of the past, the present and the future, the time-binder, is transcended, then only is there that which is deathless, timeless.

In this there is also the question of cause and effect. Are cause and effect separate or is effect within the cause? They flow together, they exist together and they are a joint phenomenon, not to be separated. Though effect may take "time" to come into being, the seed of effect is in the cause, it coexists with the cause. It is no longer cause and effect but a much more subtle, delicate problem to be thought out, to be experienced. Cause-effect becomes the means of restricting, conditioning consciousness, and these restrictions produce conflict and sorrow. These restrictions, subtle and inward, must be self-discovered and understood, which will ultimately free thought from ignorance and pain.

In this question of birth and death, of continuity and annihilation, is there not implied progress, gradualism? Do not some of us think that gradually, through repeated birth and death, through time, the self, becoming more and more perfect, will ultimately realize supreme bliss? Is the self a permanent entity, a spiritual essence? Is the self not made up, put together and so impermanent? Is not

the self a result and so, in itself, not a spiritual essence? Has not the self a continuity through identifying memory, subject to time, and therefore impermanent and transitory? That which is in itself impermanent, put together, a result—how can it reach the causeless, the eternal? That which is the cause of ignorance and sorrow—how can it attain supreme bliss? That which is the product of time—how can it know the timeless?

Realizing the impermanency of the self, there are those who say the permanent is to be found by throwing off the many layers of the self, which requires time, and so to reincarnate is necessary. The self, the result of craving, the cause of ignorance and sorrow, continues, as we observe; but to understand it and to transcend it, we must not think in terms of time. Through time the timeless is not realized. Is not this approach to reality through gradualism, through slow evolutionary process, through birth and death, erroneous? Is it not the rationalization of conditioned thought, of postponement, of laziness and ignorance? This idea of gradualism exists, does it not, because we do not think-feel directly and simply. We choose a satisfactory explanation, a rationalization of our confused and lazy effort. Through conditioned thinking, through postponement, can the real be discovered? The self, the cause of ignorance and sorrow—can it gradually through time become perfect? Or through time can the self dissolve itself? That which is in its very nature the cause of ignorance—can it become enlightened? Must it not cease to be before there can be light? Is its cessation a matter of time, a horizontal process, or is enlightenment only possible when thought-feeling abandons this horizontal process of time and so can think-feel vertically, directly? Along this horizontal path of time, of postponement, of ignorance, truth is not; it is to be found vertically at any point along the horizontal process if thought-feeling can step out of it, freeing itself from craving and time. This freedom is not dependent on time but on the intensity of awareness and the fullness of self-knowledge.

Must thought go through the stages of the family, the group, the nation, the inter-nation to come to the realization of human unity? Is it not possible to think-feel directly the human unity, without going through these stages? We are prevented, are we not, by our conditioning. If we rationalize our conditioning and so accept it, then we shall never realize human unity and so shall have ceaseless wars and terrible disasters. We rationalize our conditioning because it is easier to accept *what is,* to be lazy, to be thoughtless, than vigorously to examine it, to discover what is true. We are afraid to examine, for it might reveal hidden fears, bring greater conflicts and suffering, force us to pursue actions that might bring uncertainty, insecurity, isolation, and so on. So we accept our conditioning, inventing a theory of gradual growth towards ultimate human unity, and force all thought-feelingaction to conform to our gratifying theory.

Similarly do we not gratifyingly accept this theory of gradualism, of evolutionary growth toward perfection? Do we not accept it because it soothes our anxious fear of death, of insecurity, of the unknown? In accepting it conditioning takes place, and we become slaves to wrong ideas, to false hopes. We must break through these conditionings not in time, not in the future, but in the ever present. In the present is the eternal.

Only right thinking can free our thought-feeling from ignorance and sorrow; right thinking is not the result of time but of becoming intensely aware in the present of all conditioning which prevents clarity and understanding.

The realization of that which is immortal, deathless, does not lie along the path of self-continuity, nor is it in its opposite. In the opposites there is conflict but not truth. Through self-awareness and in the clarity of self-knowledge, there comes right thinking. The capacity to realize truth is with us. In cultivating right thinking which comes with self-knowledge, thought-feeling unfolds into the real, into the timeless.

I shall be told that I have not answered the question, that I have evaded it, gone round about it. What would you have me say—that there is or that there is not? Is it not more important to know how to discover for yourself what is true than to be told *what is?* The one will be merely verbal and so of little significance while the other will bring true experience and so is of great importance. But if I assert merely that there is continuity or that there is not, such a statement will only strengthen belief, and that is the very thing that stands in the way of the real. What is necessary is to go beyond our narrow beliefs and formulations, our cravings and hopes to experience that which is deathless and timeless.

Question: Will not the scientists save the world?

KRISHNAMURTI: What do we mean by the scientists? Those who work in the laboratories and outside of them are human beings like us, with national and racial prejudices, greedy, ambitious, cruel. Will they save? Are they saving the world? Are they not using their technical knowledge to destroy more than to heal? In their laboratories they may be seeking knowledge and understanding, but are they not driven by the self, by competitive spirit, by passions like other human beings?

One has to be on guard, alertly watchful of an organized group; the more you are organized, controlled, shaped the more you are incapable of thinking wholly, completely.

You are thinking then in part, which brings calamity and misery. One has to be watchful of the professionals; they have their vested interests, their narrow demands. One has to be on guard with the specialists along any line. Through the specialization of the part, the whole is not understood. The more you rely on them and leave the deliverance of the world from misery and chaos to them, the more confusion and catastrophes there will be. For who is to save you except yourself? For the leader, the party, the system is created in your being and what you are, they are; if you are ignorant and violent, competitive and acquisitive, they will represent what you are.

The scientists and the laymen are ourselves; we think in part, rejecting the whole; thoughtlessly we allow ourselves to be fashioned by lust, by ill will, and ignorance. Through fear and dependence we allow ourselves to be regimented, oppressed. What can save us except our own capacity to free ourselves from those bondages which bring about conflict and misery? None can reeducate us save ourselves, and this reeducation is an arduous task.

In ourselves is the whole, the beginning and the end. We find the book of self-knowledge difficult to read, and being impatient and greedy for results, we turn to the scientists, to the organized groups, to the professionals, to the leaders. So we are never saved, none can deliver us, for deliverance from ignorance and sorrow comes through our own understanding. To reeducate ourselves is a strenuous task demanding constant awareness and great pliability, not opinion and dogma, but understanding. To understand the world each one must understand himself, for he is the world; out of self-knowledge comes right thinking. It is right thinking alone that will bring order, clarity, and creative peace. To think-feel anew of the pain of existence, each one must become aware so as to think out, feel out each thought-feeling, and this is prevented if there is identification or judgment.

Question: I am not particularly interested in nationality nor in virtue. But I am greatly impressed by what you say about the uncreated. Will you please go into it a little more, though it is difficult.

KRISHNAMURTI: You cannot pick and choose; for nationality, virtue and the uncreated are interrelated. You may not accept what pleases and reject what is unpleasant; the pleasant and the unpleasant, ritualism and sorrow, virtue and evil are interrelated; to choose the one and reject the other is to be caught in the net of ignorance.

To think about the uncreated without the mind truly freeing itself from craving is to indulge in superstition and speculation. To experience the uncreated, the immeasurable, mind must cease to create. It must cease to be acquisitive, must free itself from ill will, from copy. Mind must cease to be the storehouse of accumulated memories. That which we worship is our creation, and so it is not the real. The thinker and his thought must come to an end for the uncreated to be.

The uncreated can only be when the mind is capable of utter stillness. A mind that is riven, burning with craving, is never tranquil. There is no virtue if thought is not free from craving. When thought begins to free itself from craving, there is right thinking. It is right thinking that will ultimately bring about clarity of perception. Surely there is a difference between that which is thinkable and that which is experienceable. Out of formulation, out of imagination, out of the known we experience, but few are capable of experiencing without symbols, without imagination, without formulations. Negative understanding frees the mind from copy, from the created. Our minds are filled with memories, with knowledge, with action and response to relationship and things. There is no inward, rich stillness without pretension and desire, and so there is no creative emptiness. A mind rich in activity, rich in possession, rich in memory is not aware of its own poverty. Such a mind is incapable of negative comprehension; such a mind is incapable of experiencing the uncreated. Supreme wisdom is denied to it.

Question: Is not the practice of a regular discipline necessary?

KRISHNAMURTI: A dancer or a violinist practices many hours a day so as to keep his fingers supple, his muscles flexible. Now, do you keep your mind pliable, thoughtful, compassionate, by practicing any particular system of discipline? Or do you keep it alert, keen by constant awareness of thought-feeling? To think, to feel is not to belong to any system. We cease to think if we think in terms of systems, and because we think within systems, our thought needs strengthening. A system will only produce a specialized form of thought, but it is not thinking, is it? Mere practice of a discipline to gain a result only strengthens thought to function in a groove and thereby limits it; but if we become aware and realize that we are thinking in terms of systems, formulas, and patterns, then thought-feeling, in freeing itself from them, is beginning to become pliable, alert, and keen. If we can think every thought through, go with it as far as we can, then we shall be capable of understanding and experiencing widely and deeply. This expansive and deep awareness brings its own discipline—a discipline not imposed outwardly or inwardly according to any system or pattern but the outcome of self-knowledge and therefore of right thinking and understanding. Such discipline is creative without forming habit and encouraging laziness.

If you become aware of every thought-feeling, however trivial, and think it out, feel it out as deeply and extensively as possible, thought then breaks down the limitations it has imposed upon itself. Thus there comes an understanding adjustment, a discipline far more effective and pliable than the imposed discipline of any pattern. Without awakening the highest intelligence through awareness, practice of a discipline merely creates habit, thoughtlessness. Awareness itself through self-knowledge and right thinking brings its own discipline. Habit, thoughtlessness, as a means to an end, makes the end into ignorance. Right means create right ends, for the end exists in the means.

Question: How am I to still the mind in which it may be possible to realize something which will affect daily problems? How am I also to retain the still mind?

KRISHNAMURTI: Just as a lake is calm when the breezes stop, so when the mind has understood and thus transcended the conflicting problems it has created, great stillness comes into being. This tranquillity is not to be induced by will, by desire; it is the outcome of the freedom from craving.

Most of our so-called meditation consists of stilling the mind by various methods which only further strengthens self-enclosing, exclusive concentration; such narrowing concentration brings its own result, but it is not extensional understanding—not the highest intelligence and wisdom which bring naturally, without compulsion, tranquillity. This understanding is to be awakened, cultivated, through constant awareness of every thought-feeling-action, of every disturbance whether small or great. In understanding and so dissolving the conflicts and the disturbances which are in the conscious mind, in the external layer, and thus bringing clarity, it is able then to be passive and so understand the

deeper, the interrelated layers of consciousness with their accumulations, impressions,
memories. Thus through constant awareness,
the deep process of craving, the cause of self
and so of conflict and pain, is observed and
understood. Without self-knowledge and right
thinking there is no meditation, and without
meditative awareness there is no self-
knowledge.

July 16, 1944

Questions

Ojai, 1936

New York City, 1936

Eddington, 1936

Ommen, 1936

7. I have lost all enthusiasm, all urge in life, which at one time I remember I had.   69
    Now, life to me is colorless, a hopeless void, a burden that somehow I must bear.
    Could you indicate the possible causes which might have brought about this condi-
    tion, and explain how I might break through this hard shell in which I seem to be?

8. It may sound impertinent to say it, but it is easy for you to advise others to experi-   70
    ment with intelligent action; you will never lack bread. Of what use is your advice
    to the vast numbers of men and women in the world for whom intelligent action
    will only mean more hunger?

9. My sorrows have brought it home to me that I must no longer seek comfort of any   70
    kind. I feel convinced that another cannot heal the ache which is in me. And yet,
    since my sorrow continues, is there something wrong in the way I have taken my
    suffering?

10. It is said that occult initiations, such as those described by Theosophy and other   71
    ancient rites and mysteries, form the various stages of life's spiritual journey. Is this
    so? Do you remember any sudden change in consciousness in yourself?

11. Is fear a fundamental part of life, so that the understanding of it merely enables us   72
    the better to accept it; or is it something that can be transmuted into something
    else; or again, something that can be wholly eliminated? One often seems able to
    trace the cause of a particular fear, and yet in other forms fear continues. Why
    should it be so?

12. I am beginning to think that material possessions tend to foster vanity and in addi-   72
    tion are a burden; and now I have decided to limit my own material requirements.
    However, I find it difficult to come to a decision as regards leaving inheritance to
    my children. Must I, as their parent, take a decision in the matter? I know that I
    would not consciously pass on a contagious disease if I could possibly avoid it.
    Would I be right in taking a similar view regarding inheritance and so depriving my
    children of it?

13. You have talked about the vital urge, the ceaseless awakened state, which, if I un-   73
    derstand rightly, would be possible only after one had been through utter loneliness.
    Do you think it is possible for one to have that great urge and yet be married? To
    me it seems that however free the husband and wife may be, there will always be
    invisible threads between the two which must inevitably prevent each from being
    wholly responsible to himself or herself. Will not the awakened state, therefore,
    lead to utter and complete detachment from each and all?

14. If I understand you rightly, awareness alone and by itself is sufficient to dissolve   73
    both the conflict and the source of it. I am perfectly aware, and have been for a
    long time, that I am "snobbish." What prevents my getting rid of snobbishness?

15. Will you kindly explain the difference between change in will and change of will?   74

16. Is the renewal of the individual sufficient for the solution of the problems of the   74
    world? Does intelligence comprise action for the liberation of all?

17. How can I awaken intelligence?   76

18. I realize that the liberation of the individual is essential, but how can lasting social   76
    order be established without mass effort?

Madras, 1936

Ommen, 1937

Ommen, 1938

Ojai, 1940

Ojai, 1944

Index